Glass Throughout Time

History and Technique of Glassmaking from the Ancient World to the Present

Glass Throughout Time

History and Technique of Glassmaking from the Ancient World to the Present

Edited by
Rosa Barovier Mentasti,
Rosanna Mollo, Patrizia Framarin,
Maurizio Sciaccaluga, Anna Geotti

Project and Coordination
Giuliana Cunéaz

SKIRA

Art Director
Marcello Francone

Graphic design
Stefano Tosi

Editing
Giorgio Bigatti
Monica Maroni

Layout
Serena Parini

Cover
Kantharos, second half of 1st century AD
"Ice" goblet, Murano, late 16th - early 17th century AD
Giò Pomodoro, *Bubbles*, 1982

Back cover
Edging of ice glass

The first edition of this book has been published for the exhibition "Glassway. Le stanze del vetro", held in Aosta (Italy), Museo Archeologico Regionale, from June 15 to October 27, 2002.

First published in Italy in 2003 by
Skira Editore S.p.A.
Palazzo Casati Stampa
via Torino 61 - 20123 Milan - Italy

Printed and bound in Italy.
First edition

ISBN 88-8491-345-4

Distributed in North America and Latin America by Rizzoli International Publications, Inc. through St. Martin's Press, 175 Fifth Avenue, New York, NY 10010.
Distributed elsewhere in the world by Thames and Hudson Ltd., 181a High Holborn, London WC1V 7QX, United Kingdom.

Editorial Coordination
Antonella Crippa

Critical and Scientific Entries
Ancient Glass Section
Gabriele Baldelli (G.B.)
Paolo Bellintani (P.B.)
Dominique Benazeth (D.B.)
Alessandro Betori (A.B.)
Margherita Bolla (M.B.)
Simonetta Bonomi (S.B.)
Teresa Carreras Rossell (T.C.R.)
Francesco Ceselin (F.C.)
Roberto Conti (R.C.)
Ernesto De Carolis (E.D.C.)
Marcella de Paoli (M.D.P.)
Ivo Fadić (I.F.)
Lorenzo Fergola (L.F.)
Patrizia Framarin (P.F.)
Heike Gregarek (H.G.)
Daria Jorioz (D.J.)
Beniamino Lavarone (B.L.)
Peter Lazarus (P.L.)
Domenica Lissia (D.L.)
Marinella Marchesi (M.M.)
Carla Martini (C.M.)
Gioia Meconcelli Notarianni (G.M.N.)
Rosanna Mollo (R.M.)
Iacopo Ortalli (I.O.)
Laura Pizzi (L.P.)
Olga Puklina (P.O.A.)
Elisabetta Roffia (E.R.)
Margherita Tirelli (M.T.)
Carlo Tronchetti (C.T.)
Maria Cristina Vallicelli (M.C.V.)
Daniela Vicquéry (D.V.)
Maria da Villa Urbani (M.d.V.U.)
Franca Zanchi Roppo (F.Z.)
Emanuela Zanda (E.Z.)
Alla Zeltikova (A.Z.)
Carmen Ziviello (C.Z.)

Creators of Glass Section
Rosa Barovier Mentasti
Puccio Migliaccio (P.M.)

Contemporary Art Section
Maurizio Sciaccaluga

Biographies of the artists
Antonella Crippa
Silvana Gubetta

Translations in English
Language Consulting, Milan

Credits
Markku Alatalo
Francesco Barasciutti
Mario Brogiolo
Mario Carrieri
Pietro Diotti
Virgilio Fidanza
Finotti
A. Granholm
Norbert Heyl
Frédéric Jaulmes
Walter Klein
Landesbildstelle Rheinland
Per Larsson
Christoph Lehmann
Photo Maniscalco
Richard Marquis
Mascheroni-Lorenzi
Alma Morceddù
Andrea Morucchio
Joe Oppedisano
Goran Ortegren
G. Poncet
Quattrone
Foto Studio Rapuzzi
Photo Robin
Foto Saporetti
Paolo Terzi
Umberto Tomba
Luca Trascinelli
Paolo Vandrash
Anna C. Wagner
Jaroslan Zahradnik
Alessandro Zambianchi, studio Comunica s.n.c.
S. E. Zanelli
Ron Zijlstra
Fabio Zonta
and the other photographers,

Acknowledgements

Accademia di Sant'Anselmo, Aosta
Antiquarium, Rome
Civiche Raccolte d'Arte Applicata - Castello Sforzesco, Milan
Civici Musei d'Arte e Storia, Brescia
Ente Cattedrale, Aosta
Ente Chiesa Parrocchiale, Avise
Ente Parrocchia Exceney, Arpuilles
Fondazione Il Vittoriale degli Italiani, Gardone Riviera
Fondazione Cassa di Risparmio di Venezia, Venice
Galleria Nazionale di Arte Antica, Rome
Diageo Glass Collection, Santa Maria Vittoria d'Alba
Iittala and Nuutajarvi Glass Museum, Iittala
Istituto per lo Studio del Vetro e dell'Arte vetraria, Altare
Musée du Louvre, Paris
Museo Ala Ponzone, Cremona
Museo Archeologico, Acqui Terme
Museo Archeologico Il Teatro Romano, Verona
Museo Archeologico, Cagliari
Museo Archeologico Nazionale delle Marche, Ancona
Museo Archeologico Nazionale, Adria
Museo Archeologico Nazionale, Altino
Museo Archeologico Nazionale, Ferrara
Museo Archeologico Nazionale, Naples
Museo Civico Archeologico, Padua
Museo Civico Archeologico, Milan
Museo Civico Archeologico, Bologne
Museo Civico, Treviso
Museo dei Grandi Fiumi, Rovigo
Museo del Duomo, Monza
Museo Vetrario, Murano
Museo di Antichità, Turin
Arheološki Muzej, Split
Museo di Storia della Fisica - University of Padua, Padua
Museo Nazionale G. Sanna, Sassari
Museo Nazionale del Bargello, Florence
Arheološki Muzej, Zadar
National Museum of History of Ukraine, Kiev
Arheološki Muzej, Zagreb
Museu d'Arqueologia de Catalunya, Barcelona
Museum of Decorative Arts, Prague
Procuratoria del Tesoro di San Marco, Venice
National Park of History and Culture, Kerč

Römisch Germanisches Museum der Stadt, Cologne
Smalands Museum, Vaxjo
Sovrintendenza Archeologica of Cagliari and Oristano
Sovrintendenza Archeologica of Naples and Caserta
Sovrintendenza Archeologica of Sassari and Nuoro
Sovrintendenza Archeologica of Piedmont
Sovrintendenza Archeologica of Veneto
Sovrintendenza Archeologica of Emilia Romagna
Sovrintendenza Archeologica of Marche
Sovrintendenza Archeologica of Pompei
Sovrintendenza Beni Culturali, Aosta
Stazione Sperimentale del Vetro, Venice
Stiftung Museum Kunst Palast, Düsseldorf
The Finnish Glass Museum, Riihimaki

B&B Arte Galleria d'Arte, Mantua
B&D Art Promotion, Milan
Galeria Espai Vidre, Barcelona
Galerie Place des Arts, Montpellier
Galleria Astuni, Fano and Pietrasanta
Galleria Continua, San Gimignano
Galleria d'Arte e di Vetro, Bergamo
Galleria d'Arte Emilio Mazzoli, Modena
Galleria d'Arte Scaletta di Vetro, Milan
Galleria Flora Bigai, Venice
Galleria Fumagalli, Bergamo
Galleria Rossella Junck, Venice
J. & L. Lobmeyr, Vienna
Karsten Greve Gallery, Cologne
Galleria Alberto Peola, Turin
Spirale Arte, Milan
Tornabuoni Arte, Florence

Barberini S.p.a., Silvi
CGDB S.r.l., Livraga
Co Co Shop, Milan
Isoclima S.p.a., Este
Kosta Boda Afors Glassfactory, Eriksmala
Lalique Italia S.r.l., Milan
Ercole Moretti, Murano
Nason & Moretti, Venice
Orrefors Kosta Boda AB, Orrefors
Angelo Orsoni, Venice
Pilkington, Porto Marghera
Pirelli Cavi e Sistemi, Milan
Salir S.n.c., Venice
Vetreria Anfora, Venice
Vetrerie Venete, Ormello
Vetrital, Favaro Veneto

Emmanuel Babled
Philip Baldwin
Ruth Baljohr
Alfredo Barbini
Pierangela Barile
Maurizio Bertinetti
Corrado Bonomi
Lucio Bubacco
Michele Burato
Erwin Walter Burger
Maurizio Camerani
Elena Camerone
Roberto Casamonti
Piero Cicutto
Luciano Colantonio
Piergiorgio Colombara
Lucrezia De Domizio Durini
Laura de Santillana
Maurizio Eltri
Guido Farinati
Volker Feierabend
Gerard and William Figliola
Peter Fischer
Luciano Gemin
Florence and Daniel Guerlain
Monica Guggisberg
Laura Intilia
Silvia Levenson
Massimo Micheluzzi
Ritsue Mishima
Eva Moosbrugger
Carlo Moretti
Yoichi Ohira
Danna Olgiati
Jaume Plensa
Peter Pelzel
Antonio Riello
Rosanna Rossi
Silvano Rubino
Markku Salo
Timo Sarpaneva
Marina and Susanna Sent
Mauro Staccioli
Marialuisa Tadei
Lino Tagliapietra
Caterina Tognon
Manoli Traxler
Antonio Trotta
Mònika Uz
Anna Venini
Giorgio Vigna

and who preferred to remain anonymous

We also thank

Ministero Beni e Attività Culturali
Direzione Generale Beni Archeologici, Servizio II, Rome
Soprintendenze ai Beni Artistici Storici ed Archeologici
Musée du Verre, Liège
Musées d'Amiens Métropole
Musées de Charleville-Mézières
Museo Civico, Bellinzona
Museo Civico, Locarno
Hermitage, Saint Petersburg
Ufficio Cantonale Monumenti Storici, Bellinzona
Museo Civico, Alba
Museo Archeologico, Fiesole
Museo Civico "G. Rossi", Ventimiglia
Museo Civico, Biella
Museo Olivieri, Pesaro
Stazione Sperimentale del Vetro
Sovrintendenza Archeologica, Trieste
Ufficio Beni Archeologici, Province of Trento
Comitato Trieste Contemporanea, Trieste
Vetreria Anfora, Murano
Vetreria Artistica FW Glass, Gressan

Special thanks to all the people who have contributed to the realization of this book:

Ermanno Arslan
Enrico Astuni
Marina Ballocco
Alfredo Barbini
Oceania Barbini
Andrea Bellini
Aldo Bellini
Louise Berndt
Flora Bigai
Omar Borettaz
Erwin Walter Burger
Maria Rosaria Borriello
Luisa Brecciaroli Taborelli
Oreste Brondi
Lucio Bubacco
Maria Cristina Cappellazzo
Alberto Careggio
Teresa Carreras Rossel
Cecilia Chung
Serghej Michajlovic Cjaikovskkij
Paolo Consigli
Malio D'Alpaos
Antonio D'Ambrosio
Stefano De Caro
Giuliano De Marinis
Adriana Del Bue
Davide Di Maggio
Maria Grazia Diani
Attilia Dorigato
Marinella Dotto
Maurizio Eltri
Guido Farinati
Salvatore Ferlito
Sabrina Fogliani
Daniela Gandolfi
Paolo Gasparotto
Ilaria Gianoli
Giuliana Godio
Chiara Guarnieri
Piero Guzzo
Hansgerd Hellenkemper
Tunnel Holmér
Ivana Iotta
Piotr Ivanovic Ivanenko
Rosella Junck
Miro Juric
Barbro & Borge Kamras
Mario Kezic
Kaisa Koivisto
Marinella Lista
Bruno Locardi
Roberta Magliano
Marc Maier Olivé
Maria Grazia Maioli
Luigi Malnati
Eugenio Manzato
Emilio Marin
Mirella Marini Calvani
Mario Marubbi
Marisa Mastroroberti
Teresa Medici
Antonio Meneguolo
Cathérine Metzger
Francesco Molè
Miquel Molist
Laura Morandotti
Ercole Moretti
Nicola Moretti
Cristina Morigi Govi
Anna Mura Sommella
Alessandra Nart
Francesco Nicosia
Gilda Odorisio
Angelo Orsoni
Beatrice Paolozzi Strozzi
Raffaele Peretto
Piero Ragazzi
Gianluca Ranzi
Andreas Rath
Harald Rath
Giovanna Luisa Ravagnan
Ante Rendic Miocevic
Helmut Ricke
Claudio Salsi
Vincenzo Santoni
Gianbenito Segato
Mara Silvestrini
Gabriel Soucheyre
Grete Stefani
Sofia Talas
Tiina Tervaniemi
Cristina Tonini
Franco Torterolo
Gigi Toso
Antonio Tucci
Anna Venini de Santillana
Gianni Vetrini
Marina Volonté
Marisa Zaccagnini
Girolamo Zampieri
Sabrina Zannier
Andrea Zilio

Contents

Introduction

Giuliana Cunéaz

Glass: the generic name for an amorphous substance, perfectly homogeneous and compact, and in general transparent, having a vitreous aggregation, that is, structurally similar to a liquid but with a solid consistency.
La Nuova Enciclopedia delle Scienze, *Garzanti, Milan*

Glass is very difficult to define because of its physical and symbolic properties; it makes us think of the threshold of materiality, of an element on the borderline between the visible and invisible, between fantasy and reality. It is a fascinating material and is known chiefly for its transparency, lustre and lightness. It has surprising metamorphic qualities, and can have an opaque, silky, iridescent, watermarked or polychrome surface, depending on how it is produced.

During its production glass undergoes extraordinary transformations ranging from an incandescent and fluid state during melting to a hard and compact state as it cools. Captivating and charged with infinite expressive potential, glass has inspired poets for its transparency, purity and value. Throughout the centuries it has undergone wide-ranging industrial and technological experimentation, but it has never lost its identity. Today it continues to be produced in furnaces in the traditional way, creating works of great art and artisanship.

This book is designed as a thorough philological and scientific study that aims to deepen an understanding of the aesthetic qualities of glass. It is also an evocative journey into a mysterious universe that has not yet been totally discovered.

This vast survey gathers together great and rare works of glass art from the ancient to the modern that are held in major Italian and international museums and private collections. It is the result of a collective effort by a team of specialists comprising Rosanna Mollo and Patrizia Framarin for archaeology, Rosa Barovier Mentasti for glass production from the 16th to the 20th century and Maurizio Sciaccaluga for contemporary art.

The research goes beyond traditional chronological divisions and gives life to a single great event in which glass is the guiding element in an itinerary that crosses time and space and that enables the reader to come into contact with the diverse cultures that have used and interpreted glass throughout history.

The project developed around the important collection of Roman glass found in excavations of the necropolises in Aosta Valley and held in the Museo Archeologico Regionale of Aosta. Three exquisite historiated stained-glass windows, recently restored and from the Aosta cathedral and the Avise church, are also reproduced in the volume. In order to bring glass to the attention of the wider public, the history of this splendid material is told in an innovative way and through masterpieces by great master glassmakers and by unknown artists that equally merit attention.

The more than 400 published works interact with each other through an itinerary comprising 10 thematic rooms highlighting the main issues and ideas that have inspired the art of glass.

The rooms include the Room of Water, the Room of Nature and the Room of the Body; the Room of the Orient and the Room of the Fantastic; the Room of Play and the Room of Geometry; the Room of the Fragment, the Room of the Sacred and the Room of the Everyday. The visitor is immersed in a constantly changing atmos-

Edward Hald, bowl, 1920 [Room II.14]

Two-handled globular bottle, first half of 4th century AD [Room IX.13]

phere where there are surprising and unusual juxtapositions between objects. These combinations are never casual but are part of an underlying theme that unites all the considered objects.

In my opinion, moving through the images of glass creations throughout the world means realizing that there is an imagination common to all eras and all places.

The rooms are intended not only as physical places but also as immaterial entities or a succession of musical chords that together form an order in which man, myth, symbol, technology and artistry are not rigid categories but poetic and evocative reflections echoing within the glass and crystalline forms on show to the readers.

Often in my artistic work I come face to face with the specific qualities and characteristics of materials and the influence these have in the creation of shapes and objects. I believe it is impossible to ignore the inherent language of a particular material type, as this is one of the first sources of inspiration for shapes and volumes.

Alongside the extensive panorama of the different artistic trends in glass, the Techniques and Materials Section curated by Anna Geotti gives the finishing touch

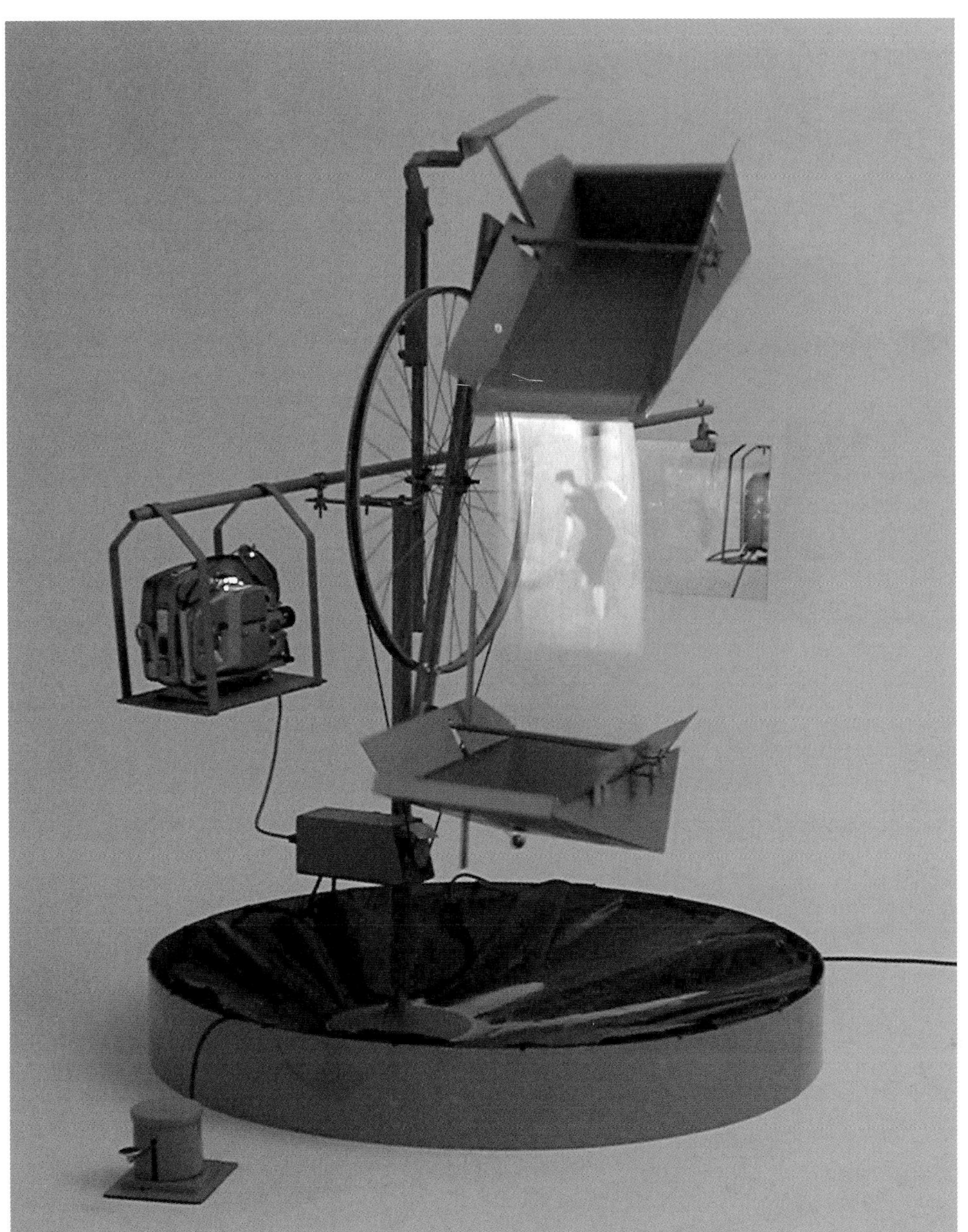

Peter Fischer,
Repellus, *1998*
[Room VI.7]

to the book. This section traces the various phases of glass making from the raw materials used to recent products in glass technology and examines the relationship between glass and ecology. In addition to the natural and artificial glass that is part of our everyday life, there are, in this technical and technological universe, innovative products that are the result of recent research and sophisticated technology and which are also used in the communications and medicine fields.

As an artist I am always fascinated by the ambiguous and manifold aspects of glass, this strongly experimental material able to sustain complex metamorphic processes. I was inspired to take on this project alongside a specialized team because of my desire to uncover the secrets of glass. And I undertook the project with the same passion and desire for knowledge that guides me in the creation of a video installation or a photographic work.

Glass and Areas of Production in the Ancient World

Rosanna Mollo
Patrizia Framarin

The exhibition project is structured around ten themes, covering a very long timespan. On each occasion the theme has represented the sphere of selection of glass products, which in this section range from the final Bronze Age to the Middle Ages. The transversal reading that results evaluates the finds from the territory of Aosta Valley, presented in the exhibition, but also required an addition. To meet this need, it was decided to complete the development of the proposed subjects by resorting to glass finds from gradually more extensive spheres, broadening the field of research from Italy to the Mediterranean basin, without ruling out particular areas of Europe, such as the Pontic area to the East and the Rhenish one in the opposite direction. As well as the aspects of daily life, body care and entertainment, the selected spheres attempt to isolate unusual lines of interpretation not normally considered in archaeological studies. The formal interpretation could respond to the treatment of the geometrical theme or to suggestions from the marine world, and even of the natural world as a whole.

The genesis of glass can be grasped in the glass production from the Orient, the true propagating centre for technological innovations and the source of irradiation of Classical culture. The religious theme associates aspects of the pagan and Christian ritual, ranging from mythology to works of religious art, with Christian representations.

The Glass of Aosta

The geographical location of Aosta, the Roman *Augusta Praetoria*, at the north-western extremity of the Po Valley, in a logistical position on the road that reaches the transalpine passes of the *Alpis Graia* and *Poenina*, favoured the influx and coexistence of glass material coming from East and West. The collection of the Museo Archeologico of Aosta is not of ancient formation, but is essentially due to the systematic excavations of the necropolises starting from the 1970s[1]. In parallel, also the stratigraphic excavations from the urban sphere reveal a consistent presence of glass, both common and precious, fragmentary of course. The material in good condition for the purposes of interpretation comes from the urban necropolises and from those of the Praedial type[2], sometimes particularly rich in glass furnishings.

Despite the good quantities of glass, widely used in the residential *insulae* and tomb contents, currently lacking are the indicators of processing to attest to the presence of manufacturing in the territory. The stimulus for the hypothesis of a local production[3] is suggested by the identification of morphological differences shown by specimens that cannot be easily associated with known productions.

Pre-Roman Glass

The oldest evidence of the working of glass in the exhibition is represented by objects of ornamentation, coming from the settlement and necropolis of Frattesina, in the Polesano territory. Elements of necklaces with spiral and eye-shaped decorations, prevalently belonging to women's jewellery sets, are evidence at the end of the 2nd millennium BC, during the final Bronze Age, of the imitation in loco of models deriving from the Mycenean world. Ornaments from jewellery sets typical of Celtic culture[4] (La Tène C2), originate from the hill of Aosta: a bracelet made of blue glass

Decorative panel with fishes, second quarter of 3rd century AD [Room II.3]

Pyxis in mosaic glass, from Adria, early 1st century AD

paste and a two spiralled armilla, held in place by two pearls with eye motif, from the ancient Mediterranean tradition.

An *alabastron* and an *amphoriskos* document the core-formed technique, the first enabling the glass paste to be modelled, obtaining minuscule closed forms, mostly ointment or perfumes holders. The forms, in miniaturistic version, are mediated by the Greek ceramic repertoire of the Classical period and widespread in the necropolises of Magna Grecia and Etruria.

Hellenistic Glass and its Tradition

Following the affirmation of the pressing technique, starting from the 3rd-2nd century BC[5], western cups and polychrome and monochrome plates, for use by a small Italiote élite, became established on the market. The presence of these Hellenistic materials along the coasts of the Adriatic, and particularly the cups of the Canosa group in the Daunia, is explained as the result of commercial exchanges with the Middle Eastern area, in need of grain products. Inserted into this context are the most ancient polychrome bowls, *reticello* (lace-mosaic glass), mosaic with spiral motifs from Ancona. Belonging to the same cultural horizon is a version of a green monochrome cup that comes from Adria.

At the end of the 1st century BC, glassmaking workshops were established in Rome and in southern Italy, on the initiative of Alexandrian artisans, who initially devoted themselves to the production of molded manufactured articles. The cups from Adria were probably produced from manufactured items from the central southern area. In the wake of the Hellenistic tradition of mosaic glass, polychrome cane working[6] became established, especially in Italy, as is proven by the cup of Adria and the most refined gold band production, with exemplars of luxury *pyxides* and toilet bottles. It is difficult to identify the area of production[7] and the particular techniques of execution.

The banded small "plate" of Aosta, similar to other discoveries in northern Italy, belongs to the series of products of the height of the Roman Age, for the production of which the Aquileia centre has been hypothesized, but so has the Piedmontese area[8].

With the mosaic glass technique, complex themes of a figurative type have also been dealt with, as in the surviving fragments of a decorative panel from Aosta, with a floral motif, in conformity with models from the late Hellenistic tradition. The survival of this technique and the figurative repertoire with naturalistic subjects is still visible in the composition of a noteworthy panel from Rimini, from the late Imperial Age.

The Advent of Blowing and the Roman World

The introduction of the blowing technique has allowed the widespread diffusion of glass objects, due to the speed of execution and the possibility of creating a wide variety of forms. The innovation occurs in the Middle Eastern environment and may be located in the second half of the 1st century BC[9]. From a product reserved for a social élite, glass entered the everyday life of all classes, along with ceramic and metal pots and pans, the forms of which it often imitated. Only during the 1st century AD, however, did the comprehensive diffusion of blown glass occur, to the point of its predominating. The expansion of the range of forms is the expression of the productive potential of the technique.

Soon afterwards, the additional use of blowing within a mould, a technique that also came about in the Syro-Palestinian environment, was to facilitate the execution of complex forms, decorated in relief[10].

Unguentaria of small dimensions and with strong blue, yellow, green and purple colours first became widespread in the Romanized world, in the Augustan-Tiberian Age, produced in the North of the peninsula by the workshops of Aquileia. For the needs of the table and the pantry, glass containers of various styles and dimensions, bottles, jars, plates, cups, beakers, were favourably welcomed on account of their functionality and impermeability. The western production in common glass, generally blue, relates back to parallelepiped amphoriskos (Isings 62), similar to our jars, and the ovoid or exceptionally cylindrical ones, of various capacities, with or without lids, characterized by plastic handles: they are forms suited to conserving food[11].

A particular quality of wine could be contained in glass amphoriskos produced in Campania, imitating the clay ones, but the containers by far the most frequently used between the table and the pantry were conical, cylindrical and prismatic bottles. Those with cubic and parallelepiped bodies were preferred during transportation, due to their easy storage capabilities. They were recurrent in western productions (Isings 50, 51, 55), mostly from the Po Valley and north-eastern Italy, but were also frequent in the East.

The table glassware drew inspiration from contemporary ceramic services. The apodal forms of plates, similar to the *paterae* of the *Terra sigillata*, were frequent in the 1st century, made in common blue and green glass. They were accompanied by *acetabula* with semi-spherical shapes and of various formats[12].

A close dependence upon clay forms can be seen in the cup with Isings form 69. The type of Isings cup 12, widespread in its variations, is dependent on the glass cups modelled using a mould. A type of beaker, much more widespread during the 1st century AD, has an elongated ovoid body, with a disc foot, and lasted a long time with slight variations. There is no lack of unusual forms of *pocula,* such as the sample from Adria with a double cone trunk[13].

In the uniform panorama of glassware for everyday use, there are

Bottles with cylindrical and prismatic bodies, from Saint-Martin-de-Corléans necropolis, Aosta

two services from the first half of the 1st century AD that stand out, particularly on account of the type of glass used. A first group made of black glass, in imitation of obsidian, consists of a dish and two cups; the second, opaque blue glass, is a set with two plates and a small *amphora* that seems characteristic of the eastern Po Valley area.

A particular taste for stained decoration seems to characterize the production of northern Italy during the 1st century. The speckles of colour that appear on small *amphorae* and ewers (Isings 15 and 13), on bottles with conical bodies and jars (Isings 55 and 67), have been interpreted as the desire to imitate the most expensive polychrome mosaic glasses[14]. During the 2nd century, there occurred a change in taste, which led to a preference for colourless, thin and transparent glass. This preference involved the most contemporary glass productions, from toilet bottles to containers for domestic use and was not exclusive to the western world.

Toilet Bottles

A particular field of application of the new blowing technique was the class of *unguentaria*[15], which were very widespread in the provinces of the empire during the 1st century.

In Italy the first attestations of blown glass were precisely the toilet bottles produced in Aquileia, of small dimensions and made of coloured glass, pyriform, globular and discoid (Isings 6, De Tommaso 7). In the Canton Ticino and in the areas West of the Verbano, characteristic containers for ointments were produced in the shape of doves and with spherical bodies, made of multi-coloured glass; a simple but exceptional vial form made of colourless glass has been recovered in Aosta. Dependent upon the formal clay repertoire, apart from the dimensions, are the small two-handled amphora from Oplontis, the one with pointed termination from Aosta and the oil-holding jar, *aryballos*, for the gymnasium, fitted with chains for suspension and accompanied by the strigil, a glass model from Cologne, a faithful representation of the equipment for cleansing sweat, normally made of bronze.

Typical products of Campania's factories are the toilet bottle with feet and the cluster-shaped one. The cocada-shaped balm-bottle, which, like the fly-shaped amulet, was carved in rock crystal, is probably of Alexandrian production and Egyptian-style taste.

Pestles and mortars were used for grinding aromatic substances; these were also of reduced dimensions, and the funnels for decanting liquids could also be made of glass. Rods of twisted glass, sometimes adorned with bird-shaped terminations, were used for mixing and drawing substances. Also among the group of containers used for women's cosmetics were *pyxides* and small ovoid or sack-*ollae*, made of common glass.

During the century and even more in the following one, the production of common *unguentaria* with truncated conical bodies took on new morphological characteristics. The body was flattened to the advantage of the neck, which was elongated for the evaporation of the content. As well as the bulbiform-bodied toilet bottles (Isings 82 and variants, De Tommaso 30 and 31), and candlestick type (De Tommaso 49), there are particular models, characterized by bodies indented and lenticular forms (De Tommaso 64 and 69) of Gallic-Rhineland production. Evidence of the control of the production of balms and ointments by the imperial house are the moulded stamps that ap-

Bottom of a bottle, from insula *32, Aosta, 2nd century AD*

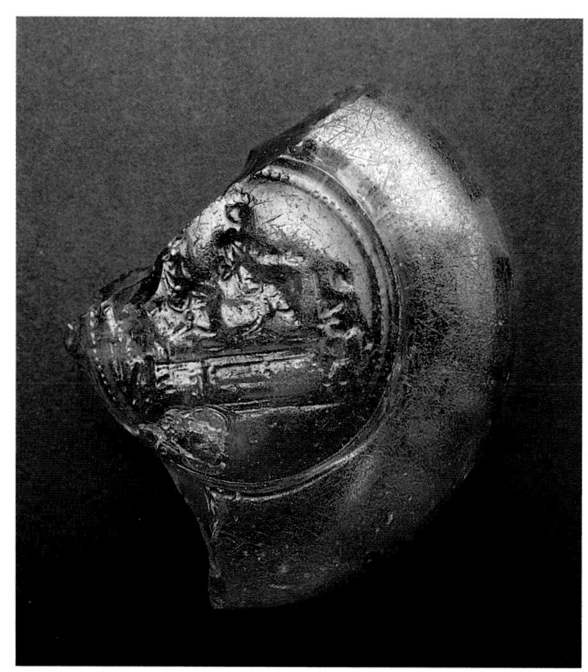

pear on the bottoms of some types of containers[16]. Belonging to a specific series of stamps made from minting dies is a sample from Aosta[17]. Specifically for pharmacological use, Mercury bottles (Isings 84), often with marks, were widespread in the West and particularly in the Gallo-Rhine area[18]. Cubic bottles (Isings 50) were also used to contain medicines, as can be seen from the context of the find of a specimen from Murecine (Pompeii)[19].

The 4th and 5th centuries were the period of the double- and multiple-bodied toilet bottles of Syro-Palestinian origin[20], among the last "inventions" in this particular production sector for cosmetic purposes. In the late Classical Age in fact, with the advent of the Christian religion, the final forms of spindle-shaped "*unguentaria*", according to a widespread opinion, characterize the burials of clergymen[21] or else can be connected with the celebration of the new rites (Isings 105). Linked to the practice of pilgrimages, some objects, on account of their content or origin, became devotional articles, such as the *ampullae* of the Treasure of Teodolinda and the bottle with the representation of Saint Simeon Stylites.

Glasses of Toreutic Inspiration

In the creation of table glassware most functional for pouring and consuming drinks, there was often recourse to imitation of metal forms. Produced in northern Italy, coloured glass ewers, with ovoid bodies and wide necks, are variants of form Isings 58. The Late Hellenistic tradition is the basis for cups whose model was borrowed from silverware. The *skyphos* from Pompeii and the *kantharos* from Altino are elegant forms, from Classical memory, the first directly imitated from the silver service found in the house of the Menander.

The *askòs* also has a glass replica, with gadroon and finishing touches engraved on the handle. The colourless glass *modioli*, single-handled cups typical of Pompeii, were inspired by a metal version; a fine specimen of blue glass from Verona is produced in the East and belongs to a later time, between the 1st and the 2nd century AD. A *patera* from Aosta also falls within this taste for derivations from metal objects: it is in fact reminiscent of a type of bowl with "omega-shaped"[22] handles belonging to metal production from Capua.

We may attribute to Oriental production the plates and cups with Isings 43 form, made of colourless transparent glass, with more or less developed festoon han-

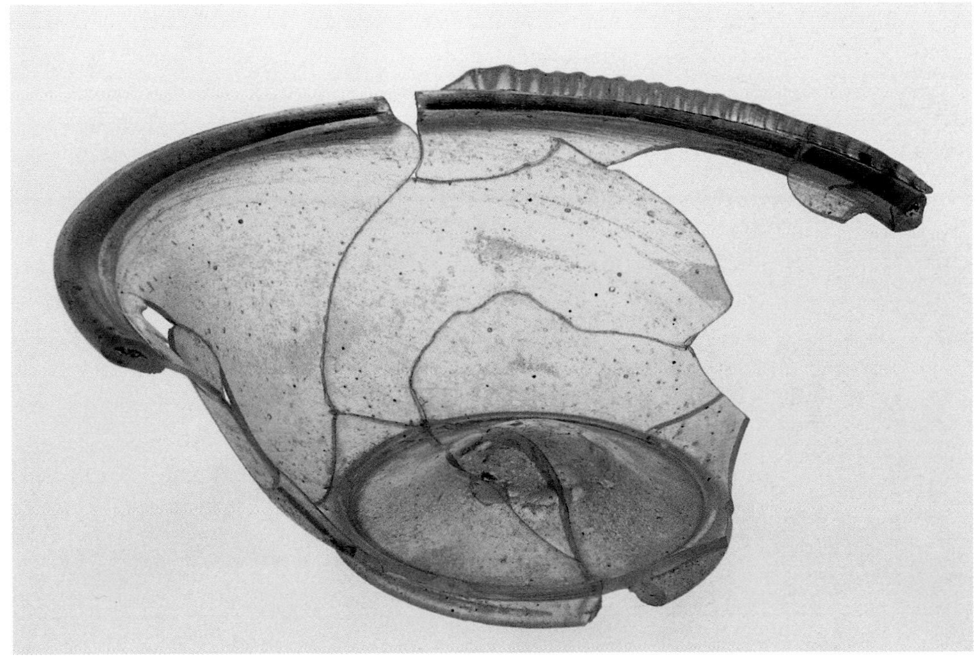

Small cup with festoon-shaped handles, from Saint-Martin-de-Corléans necropolis, Aosta

dles, a motif taken from silverware. These products circulated along the routes of the Mediterranean[23] and their production, also taken up in the West, perhaps thanks to the activities of travelling *vitrarii*, involved the Po Valley up to its north-western extremity, reaching Aosta.

The unusual shape of a drinking vessel, mostly used for ritual, the shape of which dates back to Oriental metal prototypes, is represented by a horn with a zoomorphic head from Adria (Isings 73a). The continuity of the form is confirmed in the High Middle Ages by the naturalistic horn termination, with trails applied, coming from Cagliari[24].

The Sydonian Artists and Production in Moulds

It is thanks to the activities of Ennione that we have the most refined production of cups using the technique of the blowing inside a mould, with epigraphic attestation dated the second quarter of the 1st century AD. His school is responsible for a bottle[25] with gadroon and vegetable motifs from the Ennionian repertoire, which also appear on the so-called "sydonian flasks" of Barcelona and Murano. Besides the figure of the great *vitrarius,* the Oriental sphere is characterized by the presence of many glassmaking schools of a noteworthy technical level, which disseminated throughout the West mould-decorated products with stylized phytomorphic motifs, such as the bottle with ovoidal body and narrowing from Verona. This production is linked with a series of vessels with an augural-commemorative significance, such as the cup fragments from Barcelona with circus scenes and the beaker from Cagliari. One beaker belonging to the series has representations of mythological figures inside temple structures; symbols recalling the myth of Hercules, together with a procession of faces, appear on the "almond" beaker from Zara.

Using the same technique with matrices, containers with geometrical decorations were produced. The same current of taste accounts for a rare example of a bottle with helicoidal ribs from Aosta.

Produced in the Orient, between the 2nd and the 3rd centuries, were head-shaped bottles with single or double faces, with representations of Dionysus or Medusa[26]. Also made from moulds are flasks from the 3rd century with schematic decorations of vaguely vegetal inspiration.

There is a very unusual toilet bottle from Acqui Terme, which used a silver mesh as a "mould": similar techniques can be found with a beaker from Brindisi[27], blown inside a cage of the same material.

The creativity of the Oriental world is associated with the production of painted glass. In this area of production, which has not benefited from many finds, due to the precariousness of conservation of the enamel used for the decoration, there have been two finds of exceptional significance, both produced by Oriental workshops. A glass with indentations from Aosta, with representation of a figure in limited attire and headgear, probably an athlete-juggler, on the basis of the burial context of the find, dates back to the end of the 1st century AD. The specimen could constitute a connecting link between the semi-spherical cups with naturalistic subjects produced in northern Italy[28] and the later beakers from Bégram[29], attesting to the commercial importance of the Aostan centre, positioned on a traffic route of European importance. The Sardinian cup on stem, with a scene of a naturalistic genre, expresses the predominance of precious products of Oriental manufacture, circulating between the 2nd and 3rd centuries, in the continuity of the relationships of exchange.

The Tradition of Molded Glass

Particularly in the western regions of the Empire, as well as vessels of everyday use, obtained using the blowing technique, there remained productions of particular forms, mostly open, which were still made using the old pressing method. Form Isings 3, the

Ribbed bowl in brownish-yellow glass, from Altino, first half of 1st century AD

ribbed cup characteristic of this production from the first half of the 1st century, was produced in the monochrome coloured glass and in the common green-blue glass versions. In the latter form, thanks also to the work of various workshops in northern Italy, continued for most of the 1st and 2nd centuries AD, with good evidence in all the areas of settlement, including Aosta. Belonging to the group of "pillar-moulded" items is the marble-effect mosaic glass cup[30] from Zara. These significant productions were frequently found in Cisalpine Italy[31], from where they were extensively exported to the north-western provinces (Locarno, Vindonissa, Treviri). A tangible sign of other currents of traffic, still active in the first half of the 1st century, is the *skyphos* from Adria, made of translucent blue glass, imported from the East. Included among the objects of refined manufacture, obtained through successive phases of engraving and grinding from an initial cast product, are the object-holder boats, coming from

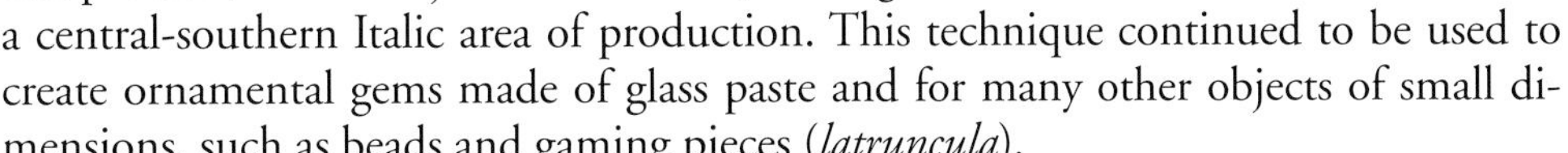

a central-southern Italic area of production. This technique continued to be used to create ornamental gems made of glass paste and for many other objects of small dimensions, such as beads and gaming pieces (*latruncula*).

More precisely the result of the application of different techniques, blowing, moulding and blowing again, the production of the *zarte Rippenschale*[32] involved the activity of the two poles that were traditionally the venues for glass manufacture, to the East Aquileia and Croatia, to the West Locarno and Turin. The same technique was to be used, surprisingly, between the 12th and 13th centuries in a cup of central eastern production, of Paduan origin.

Also cameo type glass, perhaps the most prized product of the ancient glassmaker's art, was obtained by exploiting different technical procedures, including a preliminary casing. The few known pieces, primarily of Pompeian origin, belong to a limited production[33], destined for a high-class clientele, the chronological scope of which does not go beyond the mid-1st century AD.

Cut and Engraved Glass

Beginning from the middle of the 1st century AD, the cutting technique became widespread; it was applied both on manufactured objects obtained from founding in moulds, and on those blown freely or in a matrix, and was to last a long time, until it became almost the only one to characterize the precious products of the mid- and late Imperial Age[34].

A particular mention is merited for the beaker from the second half of the 1st century (Isings 21), decorated with plant shoots, using the openwork technique, with reference to prototypes in precious materials. Also in a small beaker from Aosta, despite the simplicity of the profile, we can observe the taste for refined detail, obtained by alternating engraved motifs with fine mouldings.

The sumptuary nature of engraved glass is represented by the products decorated with embossed facets. These are products of Oriental origin, characterized by the use of a colourless glass. The "honeycomb" motif is reproduced on trays (Isings 97c), rarely on trilobate ewers (Isings 56), whereas it is very frequently found on beakers with a truncated conical shape (Isings 21). The extreme simplification of the engraved motif appears on a brimmed plate from Aosta, found in association with other tomb contents from the late 2nd century. Resolved in a design key is the geometric motif engraved on the bottom of a plate from Split, from the 3rd century, openly inspired by that plastic one of the "honeycomb". Simple bundles of engraved lines adorn the body of a single-handled cylindrical bottle from Aosta; concentric circles engrave the spherical surfaces of an Isings 103 bottle from Sassari.

The contemporary flask from Turin has windmill-like incisions on the upper part of the biconical body with an unusual shape. The late figured production and the taste for the still-life inspired the engraved decoration on the plate from Zagreb and the cup from Corte Cavanella, from the late 3rd century, belonging to Egyptian production[35].

A production characteristic of late antiquity is that of the precious *vasa diatreta*, also known as cage cups, destined for a very select élite. The small fragment deriving from a more complex scene, similar to those present on the beakers from Bégram, belongs to a vase attributable to a Roman workshop and can be placed in the early production of 3rd century.

On the bottom of a cup from Cagliari is the representation of the haloed figure of Christ, created with an essential engraving and edged by elements of exotic landscape.

The survival of the formal language of the embossed technique survived in the East in the 10th-11th centuries, applied to a religious object on which the decorative apparatus was also entirely entrusted to the mimetic virtues of the paste and blown glass.

Late Productions and Rhine Glassmaking

During the 3rd century, the diffusion of glass products fell significantly, due to changing economic conditions and changes in contemporary taste. Preference was given to a restricted number of forms, associated with pouring functions, particularly bottles, flasks and beakers with essential lines, corresponding to types Isings 103, 104 and 106. Appearing, however, on the markets of the West and the Po Valley were products of more complex conception, enriched by plastic decoration and trails. These were manufactured articles from the glassworks of the Rhine, soon the object of imitation. Indeed, in the provincial environment production activities had arisen, already beginning from the 1st century AD, which in the course of the 2nd century developed autonomous characteristics of fantasy and technical ability, becoming stimuli for production on the markets of the West[36]. The coloniate inspiration was applied particularly to traditional forms of *unguentaria* and bottles, remodelling their proportions and decorations. Spiral trails adorn toilet bottles inspired by the shapes of barrels or embroider the surfaces of transparent glass ewers with ivy leaves; there was highly effective use of snake-threads on bottles with essential profiles.

A series of shaped bottles was inspired by the natural world, giving an original interpretation to standard phytomorphic or zoomorphic themes. A decorative motif, re-elaborated in the Rhine setting, became particularly accepted in the Po Valley and elsewhere. Applications of coloured blobs, generally blue in colour, made their appearance on the austere glasses of the late epoch: isolated stamps or groups of them punctuate the forms of ewers, beakers and cups on stem. In the 4th-5th centuries, the large ewers, inspired by metalworking technique, that are still produced in the East, take up the Rhine taste for applied plastic decorations.

After the Hellenistic experience[37], only at the end of the 3rd century and during the 4th did production of gilded glasses resume in Rome and the Rhineland. These products were distinctive of a high social class and, because of the subjects represented, from the Dionysiac repertoire, are associated with the convivial themes of the banquet.

The Roman production from the urban sphere[38] gave preference to religious themes linked to funeral uses. Belonging to the group of *fondi d'oro* ("gold bottoms") is the specimen from Florence, which combines the portrait of the married couple in a central position, a procession of Saints and Apostles, represented between columns supporting *tabulae ansatae* indicating the name. The gilded beaker from Aosta from the late 4th century also belongs to a workshop operating in Rome; it has form Isings 106, with representation of Saints and Apostles, alongside couples, rendered with a certain physiognomic fidelity and identified by inscriptions. A rare "gold bottom" and blue glass represents a rare iconographic subject, linked to aspects of circus life in its late Classical meaning. The character represented has been identified as an *ursarius*, that is a bear tamer, who performed in the circus.

[1] Barocelli, 1920, pp. 97-8, 1921, p. 76 and 1948, zone IV, no. 3b, col. 140; Finocchi, 1959, pp. 103-15; Mollo Mezzena 1981, pp. 63-138 and 1982, pp. 205-315; 1982b, pp. 319-33; 1992, pp. 273-320.

[2] Along the roads leading to the city were the areas used as necropolises. To the East, the monumental necropolis of San Rocco, to the West the necropolis of the former Hotel du Mont Blanc, of the "case Cogne" site, of the Gomiero site and even of the former Polveriera and Via Piccolo San Bernardo. In the suburban sphere were small funeral areas linked to praedial estates, such as in the region of Saint-Martin-de-Corléans (the area of the parish church of the same name in Viale Europa) and in the Consolata region. Other groups of graves have been found on the Aosta hill at Saint-Christophe.

[3] The toponym *Vitricium*, to which general references have been made, can also be linked to a Celtic root. No evidence comes from the zone of the presence of kilns, such as waste and melting cores. Glass from the late Classical Age have been found at Saint Vincent, as part of the excavation of a thermal bath plant, exposed in the subsoil of the parish church. The presence of an ancient glassworks, which exploited the quartz caves of Saint-Christophe and Valpelline, was only established in Aosta, along the course of the Buthier, beginning from the 19th century (Colliard, 1979, p. 140). First archaeometric analisys have been made on some specimens (Mirti *et al.*, 1993).

[4] Finocchi, 1959, p. 58 *et sqq.*; Mollo Mezzena, 1994, pp. 153-5.

[5] Oliver, 1967, p. 13 *et sqq.*; Harden, 1968, pp. 21-47.

[6] Grose, 1984, pp. 28-9; Harden, 1988, pp. 15-20.

[7] Grose, 1983, pp. 43-4.

[8] Roffia, 1993, pp. 51-2; Negro Ponzi, 1988, pp. 70 onwards. Fragments of mosaic glass from the first half of the 1st century AD, in the urban area of Aosta (Giardino dei Ragazzi site, *Insula* 51), would seem to be evidence of a certain diffusion of the type.

[9] In Harden, 1988, pp. 88 onwards, the first attempts are described in the field of the blowing, on the base of the scrap from workmanship found in a set of tanks from the old city of Jerusalem.

[10] Harden, 1988, p. 151; Price, 1991, p. 71, on the other hand, considers that this technique came about in the West.

[11] However, they were extensively used as cinerary urns, especially in the eastern areas of northern Italy. See, for example, the data sheets on the finds from Altino, Room VII, 2 and 5.

[12] Green glassware from the necropolis of Saint-Martin-de-Corléans: plates Isings 46 (*ustrinum* 17 and T.6), cups Isings 42 (T.1 and *ustrinum* 16, where combined with plates).

[13] There are similar forms that are mold-blown (Bonomi, 1996, no. 288).

[14] Grose, 1983, p. 45; on the production and chronology, cf. Biaggio Simona, 1991, pp. 235-40.

[15] The containers for various types of essences and balms, which could be straw-covered and labelled, were closed with tops made of perishable material, probably cork.

[16] Taborelli, 1982, pp. 322 *et sqq.* and 1999, pp. 267-98; De Tommaso, 1990, pp. 109-11.

[17] Taborelli, 1982 and 1992. The Aostan exemplar represents Pius Antoninus and Marcus Aurelius (Cohen 763).

[18] Taborelli, 1983, pp. 50-2; De Tommaso, 1990, pp. 27-8; Facchini, 1995.

[19] Sensi, 1992, p. 184, pl. 285-6. A wooden cosmetic casket is similar to the container for Pompeian bottles.

[20] Hayes, 1975, p. 88.

[21] De Tommaso, 1990, p. 27.

[22] Maccabruni, 1983, p. 40, note 22; Tassinari, 1993.

[23] Roffia, 2000, pp. 37-41, with letter of distribution. In the Po Valley they have been found in Modena, Verona, Brescia, Milan and Alba.

[24] Hellenkemper, 1988, p. 117.

[25] Harden, 1944-45, p. 86.

[26] Roffia, 2000, pp. 15-6; Stern, 1995, pp. 201-15.

[27] *Vetri dei Cesari*, 1988, no. 78, p. 156.

[28] Painter, 1988, pp. 259-62.

[29] Coarelli, 1963, pp. 72 *et sqq.*

[30] Painter, 1988, no. 27, p. 51.

[31] In the levels of destruction of the first phase of installation of *Augusta Praetoria* (*insula* 51), numerous fragments of mosaic glass ribbed cups in various polychrome combinations have been found.

[32] Haevernick-Pfeffer, 1958, pp. 79-81 with distribution map; also Biaggio Simona, 1991, pp. 71-4 for technical data on the manufacture and for the manufacturing centres.

[33] Harden, 1988, pp. 53-7; Painter, Whitehouse, 1990, pp. 138-65.

[34] Paolucci, 1997, pp. 63 *et sqq.*

[35] Paolucci, 1997, pp. 134-5.

[36] Morin, 1922-23, pp. 159 *et sqq.*; Fremersdorf, 1959, 1960, 1961 and 1962.

[37] Stern-Schlick, Nolte, 1994, pp. 97 *et sqq.*, with bibliography.

[38] Painter, 1988, pp. 262-9; Morey, 1959; Zanchi Roppo, 1969, no. 34, pp. 44-5.

Glass and Glassmakers from the Renaissance to the Present Day

Rosa Barovier Mentasti

Writing about glass does not mean writing about a single reality but a set of varied realities in which functional needs, scientific research, technological progress and artistic aspiration interact.

Ancient Roman glass which derives from the several provinces of the Empire is relatively uniform in terms of technological aspects and aesthetics, so much so that it is sometimes difficult to ascribe a piece to a particular area, with the exception of certain typologies connected to specific production centres. This changed in the Middle Ages. First in the Islamic and Byzantine Empire and then in a Europe experiencing a rebirth in the arts, glass gradually began to have distinctive stylistic and technical characteristics relative to each area.

Without a doubt, the supremacy of Venetian glass in the Renaissance and the spread of *façon de Venise* glass delayed this process, creating considerable productive uniformity in glass art, with the exception of certain regional peripheries that escaped Venetian influence. However very soon, as early as the 17th century in certain countries such as Bohemia and England, new and unique glass traditions were developing, from glass composition and the adoption of techniques that made the most of the material to the evolution of types and forms unique to the place. With the passing of time, but above all in the 20th century, national "schools" became more and more widespread, each one having specific technology and a very individual sensibility in relation to glass. An exhibition or a publication that gathers works conceived and created in different countries heightens their beauty and at the same time draws out their individual characteristics. For this to be meaningful and enriching, the viewer, or in this case the exhibition visitor, must approach the material with an open mind. He or she must reject *a priori* the temptation to establish a ranking, or enquire into which of the different glass traditions is the most valid, because each one should be valued according to an individual reading: a visitor should not try to find the lightness of Venetian glass in Bohemian glass or the essential sculptural quality of glass from the North in Venetian glass; he or she should not reproach the Finnish for excessive chromatic simplicity.

Variety in glass was further enhanced with the industrial revolution, though this occurred later than other production sectors. As early as the ancient Roman era, the invention of glass blowing had developed alongside extremely sophisticated glass production for the élite – the invention enabled low cost production within the reach of most people. Nonetheless, production areas and methods remained the same in the two different sectors. On the other hand, the industrial revolution caused a sharp separation between the two areas of glass production and there was no longer any interaction between the two. The glassmaker with his or her astounding manual skills now stood supreme on the one side, and on the other side were the engineer and the chemist with their equipment. Because of this our daily lives are now enriched with glass objects that are conceived with a specific use in mind and created utilizing suitable materials, for example, Pyrex, security glazing, and dicroic glass.

Industrialization of glassmaking did not bring an end to glass art. On the contrary, almost as a reaction to it, it was stimulated in new ways. Glass art unashamedly asserted itself in the 1970s, although it looked back to the 1950s or even to the end of the 19th century to find its origins. The glass art movement of that decade estab-

Emile Gallé, vase painted in enamel, 1880 [Room IV.14]

Reticello *goblet, Murano, first decade of the 18th century [Room I.20]*

lished glass as a legitimate expressive medium and one that had great potential for an artist as a channel for very personal sensations, especially in the creation of one-off pieces.

Glass therefore continues to surround us and has not been replaced by recently invented materials, as some may have thought in the past. This is because glass is able to constantly take on new forms and respond to new demands. It is fundamental though, to know how to distinguish the various types of glass – the typical practical object, the handcrafted item, and an artist's piece – keeping in mind that there are no clear borders between the various sectors because creativity, fantasy and experimentation know no bounds.

An historical reconstruction of the development of glass art and glass making, though brief, may assist in clarifying how and why glass has come to have such extraordinary success from medieval times to the present day.

Following the fall of the Roman Empire glass art in Europe, like other more sophisticated craft arts, experienced a long period of decline both in terms of quality and quantity of production, though it never disappeared all together. During the Roman era, after the invention of glass blowing in the 1st century BC, all social classes had access to glass, whilst in the early Middle Ages more modest materials, such as terracotta, were generally the preferred materials. However, in certain areas there were periods in which glass products were created with quite unique forms and technical characteristics. Examples of glass items have been found in Longobard sites in northern Italy; though not very sophisticated they have quite original shapes and decoration. At that time and up to the 15th century, Islamic glass art distinguished itself for the variety and sophistication of its techniques. In the 1400s it suddenly declined and the baton passed to Venice.

In the late Middle Ages, glass production spread widely in Europe; coarse items of greenish glass with bubbles and impurities came chiefly from the "glass forests" North of the Alps. However, as early as the 13th century, Venice was producing decoloured glass in a notable variety of shapes, and in a well-known group of glasses, decorated using multi-coloured enamels. Venetian glass had close technical affinities with Oriental glass, where its roots lay, if not completely, at least in the tendency to produce glass for the élite. The soda glass of Venice and other Mediterranean centres that was tied to the Roman and Islamic traditions, contrasted with the potash glass of the North. Soda was produced by burning marine plants while potash was ash derived from burning plants from forest undergrowth, such as ferns. This technical difference, which was partly due to geography, later had a decisive influence on the aesthetic choices made by the various northern and southern glass centres.

In the mid 1400s the quality of Venetian glass production (indeed Murano glass production, as glassworks had been concentrated in Murano for more than two centuries) increased notably due to the invention of *cristallo* by Angelo Barovier. This *cristallo* was a transparent, colourless glass resembling rock crystal, white opaline and variegated chalcedony. In a short time master glass makers, stimulated by this beautiful glass and other varieties of coloured glass, perfected their manual skills and created shapes that were an expression of the refined elegance of the Renaissance. At the same time decorators, renewing a technique that had been abandoned for more than a century, embellished these shapes with jewel-like gold and enamel designs. Immediately Murano glass became an art that was highly coveted by nobles and the privileged classes all over Europe.

The fame of Venetian glass reached its apex in the 16th century, between 1520 and 1540, when a new glass style developed characterized by curved shapes on elegant stems, delicacy, and transparent pieces devoid of enamel decoration. In addition, extraordinary new techniques were invented: twisted filigree in 1527, netted filigree in the mid 1500s, diamond point engraving, applied to blown glass in 1549, and frosted glass just prior to 1569. This style of glass making, though in step with the times, lasted until the 18th century.

Sometimes the Venetians produced their *cristallo* in shapes that were fashionable in the importing countries; at other times they emigrated overseas to produce Venetian models *in situ* using Venetian techniques and raw materials. Glassmaking works *à la façon de Venise* opened everywhere in Europe: Flanders, Spain, France, the Netherlands, England, Sweden, Germany, and Austria. This indirectly influenced Bohemian glass works. In these European countries collaborators and apprentices came into possession of Venetian "secrets" relating to the correct choice and refining of raw materials, fusion management, and production processes recently invented in Murano. This gave rise to a glass art tradition that differed from, and competed with, the Venetian one.

In the 17th century new colours and unusual varieties of glass were invented: aventurine and the girasol. The Baroque introduced the fashion for naturalistic decoration with animal and vegetable motifs and a technical virtuosity that reached its apex at the beginning of the 18th century.

The emigration of Venetian glassmakers was illegal and severely punished by the laws of the Republic. On the other hand, no restrictions limited the glassmakers of Altare (Savona), who made the most of their professionalism in the difficult role of emigrants to France. There are no known early works of Altare glassmakers, but it can be assumed that their art did not differ greatly from Venetian work, though it may have been less sophisticated. It was certainly an Altare man, Bernardo Perrotto who moved to Orléans and devised the revolutionary system of pouring molten glass on a flat surface to produce large sheets of mirror. He was granted a patent for this method in 1688, which was later unfairly revoked.

Vase, Klostermühle, Bohemia, 1900 [Room I.24]

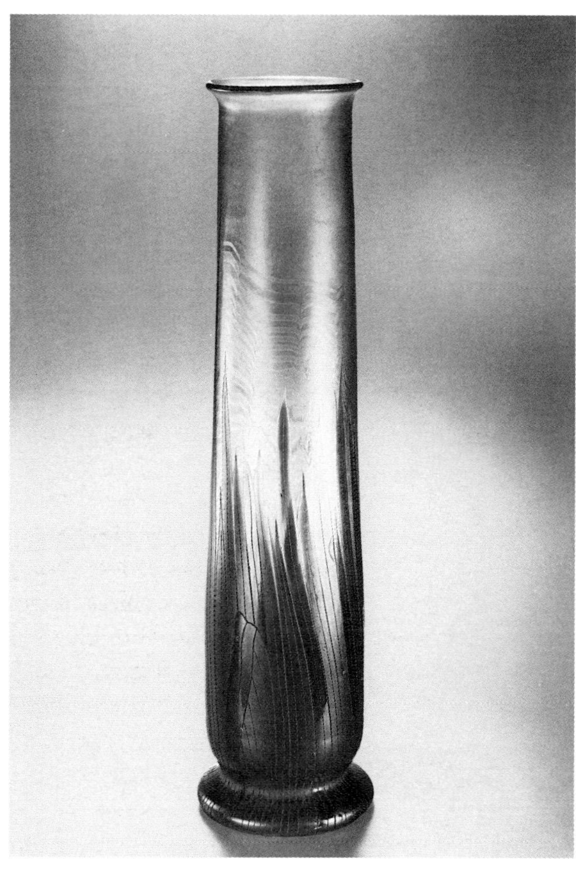

Whilst in German countries the fashion for coarse greenish glass and production *à la façon de Venise* continued, a new glass tradition was developing in Bohemia: thick, engraved crystal glass. The first known glass wheel-engraver was Caspar Lehman who signed and dated an engraved drinking glass in 1605. He worked for Rudolf II of Hapsburg, who established his home in Prague, and was in reality a hardstone wheel-engraver. After the Thirty Years War and the peace of Westphalia, hardstone and glass engraving flourished once more. Engraving was initially applied to Venetian type soda crystal but before the end of the century a potash crystal was perfected which was very bright and particularly suited to shaping thickly and to intaglio and engraving. This technique, which was quite simple when it was introduced, quickly became more sophisticated around 1700 when it was used to create deep sculptural engraving and complex decorative motifs.

Venetian glass was light, created exclusively in a furnace and coloured, and when it emerged from the furnace was clearly blown and hot formed. Bohemian glass on the other hand, was different. Its beauty was commeasurable to that of hard stone, and like it, was engraved with greater definition.

Cut and engraved potash crystal also flourished in Silesia, which belonged to the Kingdom of Bohemia until 1942. It developed an individual style in the second quarter of the 18th century and specialized in relief engraving. Potash crystal engraving reached sophisticated levels in Germany (Potsdam, Berlin, Nuremberg, and Kassel). The glassmakers and engravers of Bohemia, Silesia and Germany spread their style and engraving technique to Scandinavia, Russia, Holland, Spain and America too, revealing their unique sensitivity to glass. Venice did not escape Bohemian influence either. The Netherlands, which had always been tied to the Venetian glass style, also yielded to Bohemian engraving, even after developing a unique diamond point graffito. It imported Bohemian products and set up laboratories for German and Bohemian engravers.

At this time a new glass tradition had established itself in Great Britain. From the mid 1500s Great Britain had welcomed glassworks *à la façon de Venise*; in the 1600s these glassworks had experimented coal as a fuel. One of these glassworks was managed by George Ravenscroft, who in 1774 applied for a patent for "*a perticuler sort of Christaline Glasse resembling Rock Cristall*" [*sic*]. This flint or lead glass, which was suitable for glass blowing and extremely bright, was enormously successful the moment it was perfected. As it was impossible to blow thinly and decorate with glass threads in the Venetian manner, it was created in simple shapes, often through mould blowing. In this way a new and simple style was born, based on solid forms that suited the taste of the time, which continued to depart from Venetian styles. Very soon English lead crystal, like Bohemian crystal, was successful in the rest of Europe and the demand grew there for suitably skilled engravers. It was imitated in the Netherlands, Belgium, France, and Norway. Engraving was practised in England only in the 18th century, when the House of Hanover ascended the throne.

Goblet with lid, 1740-50 [Room II.13]

The profound crisis that affected the glassworks in Murano on the one hand led them to imitate the composition and style of crystal from the North and on the other hand stimulated greater appreciation of their own typically Venetian products, such as polychrome glass, white opaline embellished with enamel, and mirrors. After the fall of the Republic of Venice in 1797, the Venetian glass tradition appeared to have finally come to an end. During the neoclassical and Empire periods English crystal triumphed, and the new, deeply cut and engraved coloured glass and crystal of Bohemia dominated the Biedermeier market.

Nonetheless, after 1860 Venetian glass came back to life and became irresistibly fashionable, as glassmakers recovered lost techniques, even techniques that had not been practised since ancient Roman times, such as murrina. Their products

Jug with dragons, second half of the 16th century [Room VII.54]

– light, greatly coloured and decorated and freely interpreting styles from the past – invaded markets and were widely imitated. This success so reassured Murano glassmakers that when Art Nouveau began to take root after the Revival period, they were caught unprepared.

Art Nouveau was born in the 1880s through a break with the styles of the past. It was inspired directly from nature. In reality it too looked to historical styles, but to the more unusual ones, such as those of the distant Orient, which offered a sophisticated range of stylized motifs from nature. The large French glassmakers also observed Eastern techniques, in particular cameo glass, which they interpreted in an entirely new way. Gallé, the Nancy school's great leader, did not aim for a sharp colour contrast in relief engraving as in Chinese works, but rather hazy chromatic variations, alongside tireless experimentation in technique. His most beautiful works, one-off pieces, were a channel for ideas and emotions, as a critic observed at the time and as the works themselves were received. The splendid works by French creators – at times scabrous like stone, at other times seemingly soft as wax – were imitated widely throughout Europe. Another great leader of a school was the American Louis Comfort Tiffany, who developed extremely beautiful and sophisticated glass with an iridescent surface. He too was widely imitated. Venice finally freed itself from the Revival style, but quite late, and shifted to Art Nouveau when the style was already outmoded.

Goblet with the coat of arms of Princess Anne, 1740 [Room VII.59]

At the very moment when artisan glass was at its strongest, the industrial revolution shook the production of daily-use glass. This was due mainly to mechanization in the production of containers and large-sized sheets, which was adopted gradually between 1882 and the First World War. After the war these innovations would stimulate architects and designers to design in altogether new ways.

The softness of Art Nouveau forms gave way to clean-cut, geometric decoration based on colour contrasts and monochromes in the sphere of the Wiener Werkstätte, founded in 1903. The designer entered the glassworks and with a design defined the aesthetic quality of both a mass produced product and a one-off piece. The designs of Josef Hoffmann for Lobmeyr, for example, were extraordinary. This occurred on a more notable scale after the First World War in the most important glass centres of Europe. In the 1920s the designers Simon Gate and Edward Hald in a short time laid the foundations for Swedish glassmaking, which up to that time had no well-defined style. The Swedish style began to be known for its cut crystal that was classical and yet strongly modern, and for the techniques of Graal and later of Fish Graal and Ravenna, all based on evocative colour effects. In Holland, the Leerdam glassworks on the one hand promoted avant-garde design for industrially produced objects, and on the other preferred the Leerdam Unica art series. Murano had, as leader of its revival, Venini, who proposed modernizing artisan glass on the basis of a reinterpretation of Renaissance glass. In France, Lalique created masterpieces by making the most of the industrial technique of mould blowing using compressed air.

Stanislav Libenský and Jaroslava Brychtová, Head T, *1996-97 [Room IX.24]*

Throughout the 1930s, experimentation continued on two parallel tracks: industrial design and sophisticated artisan work, in which a sculptural approach prevailed in step with the art of the times. In that decade the Finnish glassmaking industry began to assert its originality. The pure, organic crystal of Gunnel Nyman was the prelude to the exquisite works of the post war period designed by Tapio Wirkkala, Timo Sarpaneva, and Kaj Franck, inspired by the raw beauty of Nordic ice landscape and more concretely, by the Helsinki school of architecture and design.

Today, artists travel, participate in international collaborations and teach in the schools of distant continents. Yet the glass art of a particular country is marked by its recent and past history. Officially born in the 1960s, the Studio Glass Movement defends the work of glass created in studios, where artisans explore glass as an artistic medium and the work produced has a strong personal stamp, though the technical and cultural heritage of the past is clearly visible. Libenský and Brychtová are the heirs of Bohemian engravers and sculptors of the Baroque, and for the sculptural size of their works, Tagliapietra can only be from Murano and Valien the son of Hald who invented Graal glass.

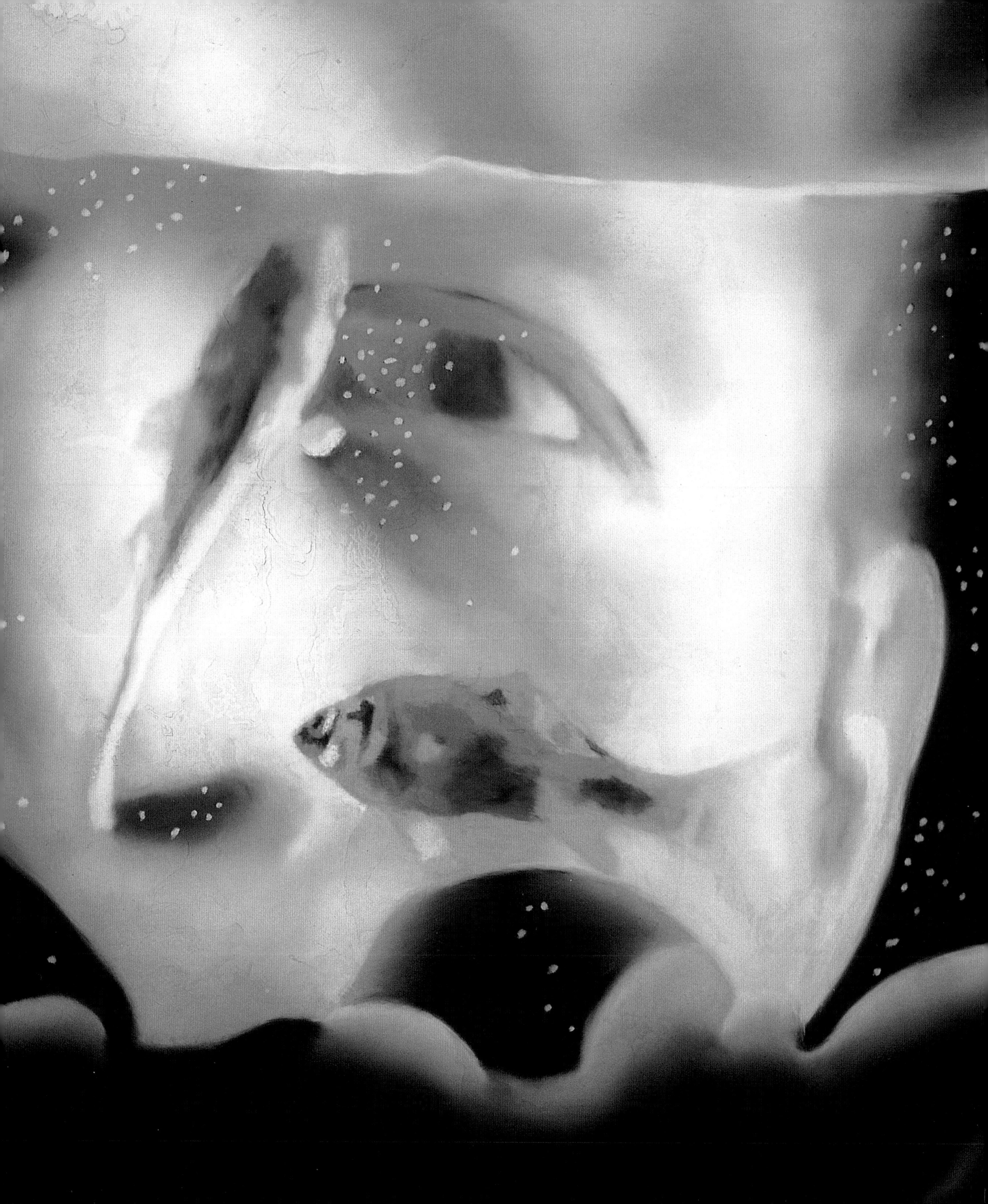

City of Glass (Reusing is Better than Realizing)

Maurizio Sciaccaluga

Two artists, two masterpieces, two provocative and revolutionary intuitions. And, consequently, a clear demarcation line between before and after. An impassable watershed, interrupting and fracturing the historical continuity of art. With *Fountain*, in 1917, and with *Colonne sans fin*, from more or less the same period, Marcel Duchamp and Constantin Brancusi changed the rules, changed habits, sparked a Copernican revolution around the way art was produced. If, prior to that crucial couple of decades, technical realization performed a leading role in the aesthetic value of the work, and therefore the artist's ability in treating the material could determine or deny the success and expressive strength of a work, following the construction of the very famous toilet sculpture and the infinite stele – but also of many other masterpieces that, together with these, went towards making up the core and the soul of the avant-garde – the hand crafting qualities of creators were brutally annihilated. And they were granted the possibility both of demanding from others the task of giving concrete and material form to the project, and, in extreme but common cases, of taking absolutely no interest in the making and quality of the techniques. In practice, the spectator at an exhibition risks no longer being confronted with a work, a sculpture, but with the artists themselves, with their ideas, their intentions and their desire to provoke. And, fatally, with the body of the work no longer being at the centre of the scene but instead the intention that motivated it, the material used for the construction, together with the technique, fades into the background.

Glass is no exception to this rule. From the avant-garde onwards, its destiny was decisively separated from that of bronze and marble. The latter two, not being materials of everyday use, could not be recovered from everyday reality and transported, directly, physically, into the world of art, therefore remaining confined in the sphere of purely technical workmanship and treatment. Glass, on the other hand, suffers a fate determined by the success of the ready-made product. This practice enables artists to no longer have to specially design the materials for their works, but to use their typical forms of industrial production, or low-level craftsmanship, conceived for everyday life.

The artist can address glass for its transparency or brightness, but, from the triumph of ready-made goods onwards, the duty was no longer felt to make them specially, but to make use of what everybody knows, which society already offers in large quantities. Paradoxically, it could be said that, though with all of its characteristics and its wealth of expressiveness, decidedly antithetical to that of poor materials, such as wax and plastic, glass was very much compared, from the mid-20th century onwards, to cement and metal, those anti-artistic elements par excellence. And it is no coincidence that these materials are associated with the development of urban industrial societies and certainly not that of art.

If the use or not of a given material is never casual, but motivated by its most evident physical characteristics, as regards glass, it is clear that the artist's attention is very often concentrated on its qualities of transparency, brightness, fragility. As on the other hand, in the case of cement, it is its inexpressiveness, heaviness, inertness and toughness that are addressed. It does not aim to elaborate new peculiarities, to develop more or less particular variants, but to recover elements that already exist,

Thorsten Kirchhoff,
Life Size, *1999*
[Room X.16]

bringing out their characteristics or inverting them in an ironic way. Even the most important and famous known glass work, Duchamp's *Large Glass*, was not a project born and developed for that material, but the fruit of perhaps a paradoxical use of it. This, disproportionately magnified, became the support for a cycle of notes for realizing a visionary and utopian instrument. And the transparent surface of glass, by definition unsuited to conserving notes, makes the work even more surreal. When faced with *Large Glass*, the question of how it was realized does not arise. The only concern is whether the material selected for the creation is perfectly functional to the original idea, and its origin is of little importance. The question of whether it is a plate specially built or an industrial product re-used for the occasion is certainly not of vital importance for judging the value of the work. Contemporary art has a new watchword to replace the term realize: re-use.

Even those, such as Costas Varotsos, Tony Cragg, Jan Vercruysse, Vittorio Corsini and Oki Izumi, just to give a few names, who devote themselves frequently, if not exclusively, to glass, usually do not possess any artisan quality to treat it and must avail themselves of the help of third parties. Furthermore, only rarely are processes encouraged other than the most common industrial ones, and almost never privileging special effects. And although the material lends itself to more complex technical elaborations, in the world of art it often ends up only appearing in its most elementary forms.

As art is not subject to laws, unless it is for the sake of breaking them, the above is obviously not the rule. However, wishing to evaluate the proposals of the most significant international artistic events, ignoring those specifically devoted to glass and the crafters of its multiform and multi-coloured evolutions, it is nevertheless the most widespread way of treating this material, the most used and common approach with the medium. Contemporary art stormed into the history of glass creations above all with the military role of the sapper. His task is to break down the (guide) lines (and not only with regard to glass). Indeed, he ends up interrupting most formal developments, scorning techniques, flattening schemes, denying the very ideas of manner and composition. With the second part of the 20th century, with the lesson of the avant-garde digested, chewed over and assimilated in the DNA, contemporary research commits itself to placing in crisis and concealing the qualities and configurations of the material, even the recent history of its use. If for clarifying examples, we think of *Bulborundum*, *750 ml* and all the other (recent) works of the same cycle realized by Tuscan Luca Pancrazzi – covering commonly used elements such as bottles, light bulbs, chairs and cars, with a dense network of sharp glass fragments, similar to those that the owners of houses and land place broken up on the walls surrounding their estates, to prevent those with suspicious intentions from climbing over them easily – we discover that the very conformations of the objects are concealed and denied by the artist; they seem to explode, they prove difficult to identify, almost as though the molecules no longer find it possible to stay together in that given way, almost as though the inertia of the material could be overcome by the desire for defence and survival. One of the characteristics of glass – that of becoming an offensive weapon, due to its capacity to cut – replaces the form of the element and its intended use, as though the object, feeling threatened, were capable of raising its spines like a porcupine and hiding its tender flesh and vulnerability behind a blanket of pointed blades.

In *Glassway* contemporary art, often provocative and ironic, tending to make a clean sweep, antithetical to the lightness of historical pieces and to the technical attention of works of high craftsmanship, interprets a subversive and bothersome role. It wishes to remove the gaze from the beauty of the transparencies, colours, reflections, veins, it intends to rout and render derisory the gratification of craftsmen, praised and respected, who protect with circumspection and jealousy the secret of the

Umberto Mariani, Mirror no. 169, *1989-91*

various processes of which they find themselves the mentors, as though they were the multi million dollar recipe for Coca Cola. Contemporary art – which must cast its gaze a few years forward, which ends up anticipating times, does not respect codes, surprises and discourages the uninitiated, as in the very famous "Le vacanze intelligenti" episode, filmed by Alberto Sordi as part of the film "Dove vai in vacanza?" – reads the themes of rooms in a paradoxical way, it encumbers spaces, it short circuits the refinement of ancient crystal glass, setting it against common bottles, shattered plate glass, pyramids and parallelepipeds of glass of no value.

In *Glassway* the most up-to-date research, close to experimentation, breaks ranks, embodies the role of the adversary, proposes and does what the public would not expect. And if Joseph Beuys, the mentor of the relationship between art and nature, the shaman of the dialogue between creator and spectator, the guru of the art-

Giuliano Giuman,
Oven, *2001*

life-environment equation, uses glass in its most accepted form (such as the bottle, and without even denying its intended use), Omar Galliani associates the virginal purity of crystal glass with phallic symbology, rereading and revisiting the iconography of the *Lady with Unicorn* by Raphael, with sacred respect for the master's design but disrespectful as regards the theme and the subject. In the Room of the Everyday, between Roman glassware and lamps from the 17th century, amid soffuse lights and polite display cases, Argentine Silvia Levenson hangs from the ceiling dozens of sharp glass knives, which threaten to fall on spectators, and instead of showing the refinement of the lines and transparency of the worked object, she calls to mind the violence of which married life is full. In an exhibition running the risk of self-satisfaction, amid a plethora of works of impalpable perfection, in an overcrowding of purely technical themes, contemporary art draws the attention back to pragmatic and concrete questions posed by everyday reality, forces creators' imaginations to come to grips with popular imaginings. It reflects and idealizes, averts the spectator's concentration from the pyrotechnic exhibitions of artisan ability, to project it onto the relations between material and life, between what the form of an element can evoke and the endless ways according to which these evocations can be exploited and varied.

In the Room of Play – which presents a Roman cup with engravings devoted to Olympic disciplines, ancient chess pieces, the vexating goblets from the Baroque period, which, in a naïve *divertissement*, would inevitably upset wine onto the inattentive drinker – contemporary research breaks out with the irreverent and caustic, wicked violence of Conrad Bonomi and Wim Delvoye. Without paying attention to the refinement of the lines and treatments, to the purity of the reflections, they propose an unusable, absurd Meccano of crystal that mocks the much-extolled delicacy of the material, or a ridiculous tennis racket with mosaic in place of strings. In the Room of Water, among the many testimonies to the efforts made by the glassworkers of the past to conquer the absolute transparency and purity, between lines similar to waves shaped by the masters of Liberty and the skilled artisans of Murano, contemporary art resorts to the fake goblets of young Milanese artist Carlo Benvenuto – solid geometrical and full, similar to glasses of water filled to almost overflowing – and to the visionary and futuristic work of Maurizio Camerani, for which, to the confusion of appearance between glass and water sought by the processing techniques, he prefers the more common glass-aquarium association. And, into a great tank with crystal glass walls, as a bottom he inserts the screen of a monitor, flowing on which are the images of the Atlantic and the Pacific, while a sad and solitary goldfish goes round, frightened and attracted by the great sea.

Contemporary artists, obviously, do no limit themselves to that provocative approach of which Man Ray, Duchamp, Arman, Delvoye, Nam June Paik, Bertinetti, De Paris, Riello and Mondino, just to cite a few, are the masters. The Egyptian Medhat Shafik reconstructs on canvas the panoramas, atmospheres and mirages typical of his desert, the great sea of the Sahara, using pieces of worn glass found on the beach and imagining that the materials smoothed by the water and sand can conserve something of that world that has moulded and modified them. The *Entr'acte* cycle, a series of intimate and discreet works by Chiara Dynys, devotes great attention to the techniques of realization inherited from high quality craftsmanship, but concentrating on silence and the sense of loss evoked by fleeting memories, embodied here by the ashes of the artist's old diaries contained in transparent urns. *Crystal landscape of inner body*, by the Chinese Chen Zhen, is a melancholy confirmation of man's fragility, when, on a glass table, it proposes a stomach, kidneys, a bowel and a heart, all of crystal, ready to break at the slightest contact or act of carelessness.

Arman, Gianfranco Baruchello, Carlo Benvenuto, Maurizio Bertinetti, Joseph Beuys, Corrado Bonomi, Louise Bourgeois, Maurizio Camerani, Chen Zhen, Piergiorgio Colombara, Wim Delvoye, Enrico Tommaso De Paris, Chiara Dynys, Marcel Duchamp, Peter Fischer, Lucio Fontana, Omar Galliani, Ale Guzzetti, Thorsten Kirchhoff, Silvia Levenson, Giuseppe Maraniello, Igor Mitoraj, Aldo Mondino, Nam June Paik, Luigi Ontani, Luca Pancrazzi, Jaume Plensa, Giò Pomodoro, Man Ray, Antonio Riello, Rosanna Rossi, Silvano Rubino, Medhat Shafik, Sandy Skoglund, Daniel Spoerri, Mauro Staccioli, Maria Luisa Tadei, Antonio Trotta and Gilberto Zorio are not artists of glass. They use it. And that is enough, for a section that wishes to be the devil's advocate, intending to be relegated to the inconvenient role of the sapper.

The Rooms of Glass

I.

Room of Nature

ANCIENT GLASS

Nature has undoubtedly been a rich source of inspiration for the ancient craft of glass. Like the wall paintings at Pompeii, a fragmentary plaque from Aosta offers a glimpse of a garden filled with lush vegetation and inhabited by a colourful fauna. Vessels made out of mosaic glass draw on the same decorative repertory, but use it in more abstract form: multicoloured stylized flowers appear on verdant grounds that recreate the atmosphere of the *viridaria*.
The reference to flowers and fruit is also a mark of Oriental glassware, whether produced for religious purposes or to meet everyday needs. Plastic forms in full relief reproducing figs, bunches of grapes and dates are the product of a common taste that characterizes the glass of East and West. At times, the shape and decoration of the bodies of some containers is a reminiscence of this repertory.
The animal world also attracted the interest of the glassworkers in antiquity. An example of this is the naturalistic perfume bottle in the shape of a dove in the Adria Museo Archelogico: intended for women, it represents an animal sacred to Venus. The imagination of the Rhenish glassworkers found expression in the field of *unguentaria*, which were given fantastic and monstrous shapes, like the animal in the Cologne Museum (2nd-3rd century AD). Small reproductions of flies and cicadas in rock crystal (Museums of Naples and Altino) may have been used to ward off evil. The decoration engraved on a cup from Corte Cavanella, probably derived from metal prototypes, consists of a genre scene, a sort of still life with a fish, a basket of fruit and several bunches of grapes.

CREATORS OF GLASS

The most elementary way in which inspiration is drawn from nature is through the representation of natural organisms on the surface of blown glass with decorative techniques. Diamond-point engraving, applied to blown glass, was invented in the furnaces of Murano in 1549, but was used for conventional and repetitive decorations. It was in the Baroque period that nature gained the upper hand, so that the colourless surface of Venetian blown glass was embellished with graffiti reproducing flowers, leaves, birds, butterflies. Even richer were the naturalistic decorations created by the hot molding of polychrome glass, used to adorn the stems of goblets and the handles of lids with flowers. The first half of the 18th century saw the invention on Murano of the glass chandelier decorated with a profusion of hot-molded leaves and polychrome flowers, called a *ciocca*, or "bunch." The Venetian neo-Baroque of the second half of the 19th century proposed even more sumptuous triumphs of naturalistic motifs, which provided the opportunity for a virtuoso display of skill.
It was in French Art Nouveau glassware, however, that nature really came to the fore, culminating in the great international exhibition of Paris in 1900. "Our roots are in the ground of the woods, the banks of springs, the mosses", wrote Emile Gallé above the door of one of his studios. While the French had looked first to Japanese art as a perfect model of the stylization of natural organisms, their style became more intellectual and "abstract" in the 1920s, especially in the sublime creations of René Lalique, who brought the finest period of French glassworking to a close.
A new genre emerged in the 1930s: that of the plastic work in glass, of the glass sculpture. This took the form of reproductions of animals and plants in blown or solid glass, hot-molded in the furnace, which obliged the glassworkers of Murano to invent new methods and processes, pioneered by Napoleone Martinuzzi.

CONTEMPORARY ART

Joseph Beuys left an indelible mark on the history of art in the second half of the 20th century. He transformed political actions into performances and works of art into conservationist slogans, uniting art and nature in an indissoluble symbiosis. His work brought themes like the protection of the environment into artistic research and, thanks to him, great international exhibitions became the theatre of gigantic happenings. After his symbolic operation *Defense of Nature*, conceived in 1984, Beuys fused art and nature with *Paradise Plantation*. The artist required the workers on the Durini estate at Bolognano to cultivate the fields according to the rules of organic farming. No exception was permitted. The final work of art, still being produced today sixteen years after Beuys's death, consists of the bottles of oil and wine labeled with the symbol of the Free International University.
If on the one hand art won attention and respect for nature with Beuys, on the other it has always betrayed a great longing to change it, to alter its distinctive traits. Among contemporary artists there are many who seem to have concentrated on a single visionary theme and its numerous facets: redesigning the earth and its inhabitants. From Giulio Paolini to Yves Klein, from Wim Delvoye to Riccardo Gusmaroli and from Corrado Bonomi to Alexis Rockman and Dario Ghibaudo, artists have placed the world under vacuum in a glass jar, have shrunk it down and exhibited in a Plexiglas showcase, have transfixed it with a great screw. Reassessed and redesigned in their works, humans, animals and plants are no longer what they were. They are no longer creatures of reality. What natural selection, evolution and pollution have not been able to bring about, artists instead have, presenting to dumbfounded spectators (even if only on canvas, or in sculpture, or in photographs retouched on the computer) creatures of the strangest kind, worthy of science-fiction movies.

1

2
Beaker with plant decoration

second half of 1st century AD
Colourless glass with a greenish hue, cast, wheel-cut, ground and polished, h. 6.9 cm, ∅ of mouth 8.3 cm, ∅ of foot 4.7 cm, thickness of wall *c.* 0.2 cm
From the Esquiline (zone I; block 19th), Rome, 1882
Antiquarium Comunale, Rome, inv. 279
State of conservation: broken into four pieces and reassembled; the missing parts of the rim, wall and foot have been reintegrated with plastic

Beaker in the shape of a truncated cone with a slightly oblique rim underlined externally by a thin rib with a semicylindrical section. Convex bottom with a ring-shaped foot. Wall with plant decoration carved in high relief consisting of two continuous shoots: one of ivy with four leaves (two of which are still complete) and one of uncertain identity, with leaves with serrated edges and a spherical berry with a small notch, probably a sprig of bay or strawberry tree. The veins of all the leaves are represented by deeply incised grooves. The edges of the ivy leaves are sharp, while the berry is softer and rounded. The edges of the other type of leaf are rendered by small incisions.
The form of the drinking glass, Isings 21, although with some notable differences in the proportions and in the design of the foot, is that of glasses in the shape of a truncated cone with a faceted, painted, engraved and applied decoration, which are believed to have been produced (late 1st century - early 2nd century AD) in Alexandria. The plant decoration, represented in such high relief that it can be considered to belong a phase only slightly precedent to the technique of the *vasa diatreta*, is similar to the style found on vases made of silver and of semiprecious stone. In fact the type of intaglio is an obvious imitation of the latter, as is evident from its resemblance to two rock-crystal beakers from Naples and Begram. The dating is confirmed by comparison with specimens showing a similar type of decoration and executed by the same technique, such as a glass fragment found at Fishbourne, in a layer datable to between 75 and 100 AD, and a drinking glass, found together with materials from the 1st century AD and now in the Slovak National Museum, which is decorated with a spray of petals.

1
Floral plaque

late 1st century BC - early 1st century AD
Mosaic glass, h. 4.7 × 2.3 cm; h. 4.1 × 3.3 cm; thickness 0.5 cm
From Couronne excavation, stratum Ia (from the reworked levels) to the North of the temple building, Aosta
Deposito della Sovrintendenza, Aosta Valley Autonomous Region, Aosta, cod. lab. 03-222 / 03-223
State of conservation: highly corroded, flaked and devitrified fragments

Two fragments of a plaque in glass paste with a dark blue-greenish ground. On the first we can still see a vertical greenish-yellow twig with small leaves and a roundish yellow fruit with a small central cross at the top; at the bottom, just to the left of the twig, a small flower with six blue petals.
On the second fragment we see some yellow-green foliage at the base and a little flower with six pale blue petals and another yellow fruit with a small central cross above. On the edge, more flowers and leaves, incomplete. Some details are emphasized by translucent blue or gold edgings.
The fragments were part of a larger composition of elegant vegetable motifs – plants, flowers and fruit – made up of a large variety of combinations and a wealth of details.
The pursuit of detail is clear from the naturalistic representation of the plant species: colour is provided by the floral motifs, composed out of a mosaic of glass of different hues and tones.
The production of glass plaques representing naturalistic subjects can generally be traced back to late-Hellenistic glassworks in Ptolemaic Egypt. Floral panels from Egypt, and in particular from Chatby (Alexandria), Karanis and Alexandria (Toledo Museum), are of Alexandrine make and very similar from the viewpoint of both style and the formal exuberance of the composition to the ones found in Aosta, datable to between the 1st century BC and the 1st century AD.
Bibliography: Kisa, 1908, p. 368; Harden, 1936, p. 299; Davidson Weinberg, 1973, pp. 46-51, figs. 5-7; Goldstein, 1979, pp. 254-7, no. 769 a; *Vetri dei Cesari*, 1988, pp. 32-3, no. 10; Grose, 1989, p. 355.
(R.M.)

2

Comparable objects from the same period come from Begram. The same type of decoration is again found on a beaker in the shape of an upside-down truncated cone blown into a quadrangular mold that was discovered in a 3rd-century AD tomb at Trier.
Bibliography: Hackin, 1954, p. 264, no. 121, fig. 270; Isings, 1957, pp. 37-8; Harden, Price, 1971, pp. 333-6, no. 30, fig. 138, pl. XXVI; Goethert-Polaschek, 1977, p. 47, no. 144, pl. 15, no. 177a.; Gasparri, 1979, p. 5, fig. 3; Kraskovská, 1981, p. 12, fig. 1; Oliver, 1984; Pirzio Biroli Stefanelli, 1988, p. 190, no. 100 with previous bibl.
(C.M.)

3
Hexagonal bottle decorated with fruits
second quarter of 1st century AD
Free-blown neck, mold-blown body,
h. 8.6 cm, ∅ 4.5 cm
Phoenician (perhaps from Salamia)
Museu d'Arqueologia de Catalunya, Barcelona, N.I.G. 7987
State of conservation: good

Small bottle with a hexagonal body, cylindrical neck and lip with a triangular section, sloping on the outside and inside. Circular-convex shoulder and bottom framing the body. Flat base. The body, blown into a triple mold, made of three vertical sections, has a vertical rib in the joins that ends at the centre of the base. Made from a semitransparent paste of an opaque white colour. The shoulders are decorated with a somewhat vague relief of floral motifs in reverse (pomegranate, lotus and roundish leaf). On the body there are six rectangular panels separated vertically by slender ribs: each panel is decorated with pomegranates, bunches of grapes and cedar flowers, alternating in accentuated relief, while the lower part has a narrow border of small hemispherical motifs. On the base the decoration is completed by a ring of six triangular leaves, each set in the middle under the respective panel, alternating with small oval petals.
These pieces come from the Middle East, and more precisely from Phoenicia, modern Syria or Palestine. They have a decoration characterized by fruit typical of the zone, with a proven symbolic value: in fact their disposition, among architectural structures, columns and niches, suggests a possible ritual or religious use.
Typological comparisons: Israeli, no. 158; Kunina, nos. 132-3; Maccabruni, no. 8; Saldern, no. 406; Stern, Fruit type, series A, nos. 36-9.
Bibliography: Saldern *et al.*, 1974, pp. 143-4; Maccabruni, 1983, pp. 31-2, no. 8, pl. 2; Stern, 1995, pp. 113-34; Kunina, 1997, nos. 132-3; Israeli *et al.*, 2001, pp. 134, 106, fig. 158.
(T.C.R.)

4
Toilet bottle in the shape of a fruit
1st century AD
Mold-blown glass,
h. 8.6 cm; ∅ 4.3 cm
From Pompeii (I, 11, 5)
Archeological Deposit, Pompeii, inv. no. 12848a
State of conservation: missing part of the neck and rim

Toilet bottle with long cylindrical neck and everted rim. The body is ovoid and shaped like a bunch of grapes or a pinecone. The bottom is rounded. The peculiar shape of the body probably derives from the Oriental world. The *unguentaria* were containers used for cosmetics.
Typological comparisons: De Tommaso, 1990, type 78.
Bibliography: *Homo Faber*, 1999, p. 214, no. 285.
(E.D.C.)

3

4

5

6

5
Toilet bottle in the shape of a date
middle of 2nd century AD
Mold-blown glass,
h. 7.6 cm; max. width 3.4 cm, ∅ of rim 1.7 cm
From western necropolis, former Hotel du Mont Blanc, T. 94, Aosta
Deposito della Sovrintendenza, Aosta Valley Autonomous Region, Aosta, cod. lab. 03-475
State of conservation: reassembled with a few small gaps

Small amber-yellow glass container in the shape of a date. Funnel-shaped mouth, cut and rounded lip. It is thought to be of Oriental production owing to the distribution of the finds, concentrated largely in the ports of the Adriatic. It is believed to have spread into the Po Valley region and then across the Alps from Aquileia. The more stylized version, with colourings that diverge from the typical ones of the fruit, circulated in Oriental areas.
Typological comparisons: Isings, 78; Trier, 68; De Tommaso, 77.
Bibliography: Isings, 1957, pp. 93-4; Calvi, 1968, pp. 102-3, pl. 17.3; Goethert-Polaschek, 1977, p. 96; De Tommaso, 1990, p. 87; Fadić, 1998, no. 43 and p. 82.
(P.F.)

6
Toilet bottle in the shape of a fig
3rd century AD
Blown glass,
h. 4.5 cm
From a Roman tomb in the Luxemburger Strasse, Cologne
Römisch-Germanisches Museum, Cologne, inv. no. N 316
State of conservation: intact

This fig made of pale green opaque glass was certainly a decorative object – just as fruit are imitated today in glass, porcelain, terracotta, stone or precious metals. It also has a tiny opening that would have made it possible to fill it with perfume. Glass figs were probably very rare, whereas receptacles in the shape of grapes or dates were very popular in various glassworks of the Mediterranean world.
Bibliography: *Niessen*, 1911, no. 316, pl. 47; Fremersdorf, 1958, p. 51, pl. 108; Fremersdorf, 1961, p. 28, pl. 24 on the right.
(H.G.)

7
Pendant
Imperial Roman era
Blue glass cast in mold,
h. 4.4 cm
Museo Civico Archeologico, Bologna
State of conservation: slightly chipped along the edge

Part of a necklace in the shape of an acorn, with a vertical hole through the tip and a flat lower part; the cup of the fruit is represented by rows of tiny hemispheres. So far no precise equivalents of this type of pendant have been found, although the acorn shape is known in Roman glassware from a few small bottles made of mold-blown glass, generically dated to the 1st-2nd century AD and coming from the Syrio-Palestinian area.
Typological comparisons: Lucerne, 1981, p. 85, no. 292; Stern 1995, pp. 182-3, no. 113 (acorn-shaped bottles).
Bibliography: Meconcelli Notarianni, 1979, p. 158, no. 220.
(M.M.)

7

8
Bottle
1st century AD
In part free blown,
in part (belly) blown into two-piece mold; applied handle,
h. 14 cm, Ø of base 2.7 cm, max. Ø 6 cm
Provenance unknown (perhaps from the Verona area)
Museo Archeologico al Teatro Romano, Verona, inv. no. 20288
State of conservation: whole

Medium-sized bottle in blue glass, with body divided into two parts by a waist under the shoulder; the lower, ovoid part is decorated with seven superimposed rows of triangles in relief. Double-ribbed ribbon handle, attached to neck and shoulder.
The form and decoration of the lower part of the belly are reminiscent of bottles in the shape of fruit; Oriental production.
Bibliography: Mandruzzato, 1997, p. 85, no. 12.1, with previous bibl.; Facchini, 1999, p. 167, no. 384.
(M.B.)

9
Dropper in the shape of a pomegranate
end of 3rd - first half of 4th century AD
Blown glass,
h. 10.9 cm, Ø 6.6 cm
Museu d'Arqueologia de Catalunya, Barcelona, N.I.G. 7347
State of conservation: good

Globular body with a small hole in the upper part, base formed out of six small appendages in the shape of pomegranate flowers. Cylindrical neck with very wide bell-shaped mouth, fire-polished rim. The underside of the lip is decorated with a ring in relief formed out of a thread of the same colour as the piece, applied to the object when hot. On the body are set five vertical ribs in relief with two pressure points on each. Made out of an amber-coloured paste, it shows a certain amount of wear on the surface. Objects of this type were made in two pieces: the body and the neck. Subsequently they were heated and joined together, with a sort of diaphragm with a small opening set in the junction of the body and the neck so that the liquid it contained would only emerge in drops.
These toilet bottles come from countries of the eastern Mediterranean and were produced over a fairly long period of time.
Typological comparisons: Israeli, no. 336; Platz-Horster, nos. 174-5; Saldern, no. 110; Stern, nos. 135-6.
Bibliography: Platz-Horster, 1976; Israeli *et al.*, 2001, p. 241; Stern, 2001, pp. 249-50.
(T.C.R.)

8

9

10
Container in the shape of a dove
first half of 1st century AD
Free-blown glass,
l. 21 cm, max. Ø 8.9 cm
From Salvadego-Molin fund, Cavarzere (Venice)
Museo Archeologico Nazionale, Adria,
IG AD 9098
State of conservation: whole apart from the deliberately broken-off tail

A dove-shaped vial with a small spheroidal head and long beak; long neck; ovoid body squashed at the bottom; elongated tail, broken off at the end. The object is an elegant perfume vial, whose contents could only be extracted after breaking off the tail. It is thought to have been made by a glassworks in the Ticino Canton.
Typological comparisons: Isings, 11; De Tommaso, 80.
Bibliography: Bonomi, 1996, p. 146, no. 331.
(S.B.)

11
Rod ending in the shape of a bird
second half of 1st - first half of 2nd century AD
Threadlike canes laid parallel and twisted; the figure of the bird is cast and pressed,
h. 7 cm
Kerch State Historico-Cultural Reserve, Kerch,
inv. KMAC - 1002,
KGIKZ funds
State of conservation: incomplete rod. The bird's tail is missing, and there are parts of the surface where weatherings of the glass are visible

Surface with spiral ornamentation and the figure of a bird at the top. Transparent, colourless glass.
This type of object was found in the Pricernomor'ja region and the eastern Mediterranean in the 1st century AD
Bibliography: Kunina, 1997, pp. 263-4, cat. nos. 79, 80.
(A.Z.)

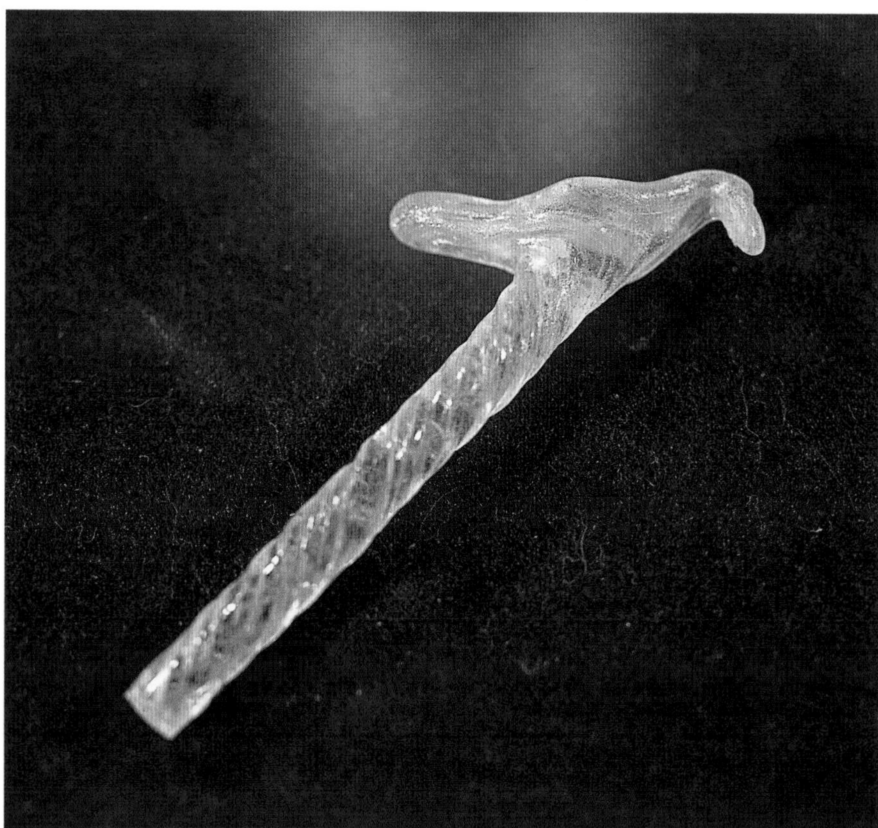

11

10

12
Toilet bottle in the shape of a cicada
1st century AD
Intaglio,
5.5 × 3.2 cm
From the southwest necropolis of Via Annia, isolated find in the vicinity of the Mausoleum of the Decurion, 1952 excavations, Altino
Museo Archeologico Nazionale, Altino, inv. no. AL.1377
State of conservation: the cicada is fragmented at one eye and at the tips of the wings

Unguentarium in colourless and very clear rock crystal, in the shape of a cicada. The insect has an oval body with a biconvex section. The head, underlined by two grooves converging in a V, has protruding eyes, separated by two more converging grooves framed by parallel lines. The lower part of the body is also decorated with incisions converging in a V at the head and by rows of parallel lines. The cicada is one of the most common subjects of rock crystal carvings, found both in the form of an amulet, like the numerous examples from Pompeii (Pannuti, 1983, nos. 301-6, 371-2), and with the function of a toilet bottle, as documented by other specimens of diverse origin (Gasparri, 1975; Arezzo, 1988, cat. nos. 128-9). The series of rock-crystal containers in the shape of cicadas has been attributed by Bühler to Alexandrine workshops (Bühler, 1973), but it is likely that such objects were also made in other parts of the empire (Maioli, 1994, p. 368). The type, almost unknown in northern Italy, finds a close parallel in a piece from Aquileia (Brusin, 1929, p. 160, fig. 26), and, in the Veneto region, in an object with a different function, a pendant-amulet, whose provenance is unfortunately not known with precision but may be the Padua area (Maioli, 1994, p. 366, figs. 1, 4).
Typological comparisons: Bühler, 1973; Gasparri, 1975; Arezzo, 1988; Maioli, 1994.
Bibliography: Bologna, 1964, p. 374, no. 542, pl. CXXXXIX, 288 (with previous bibl.); Scarfì, Tombolani, 1985, p. 95, fig. 74.
(M.T.)

14

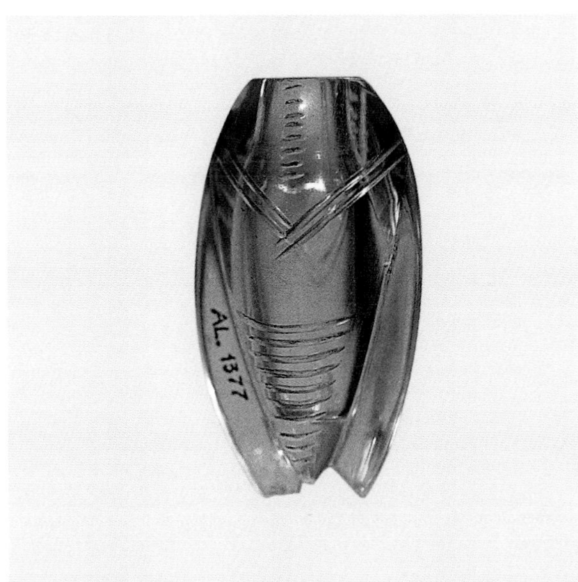

12

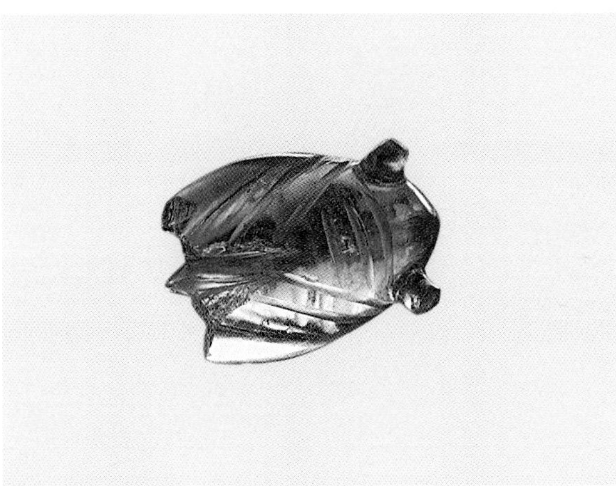
13

13
Amulet in the shape of a fly
1st century AD
Engraved and polished rock crystal,
width 2.8 cm
From Pompeii
Deposito Museo Archeologico Nazionale, Naples, inv. no. 158836
State of conservation: incomplete. Body of elongated oval shape, eyes represented by irregular, modeled protuberances; three parallel, horizontal incisions on the back, other transverse ones on the sides that emphasize the profile of the closed wings

This object may have been used as a pendant for a necklace or been part of a small collection of precious rock crystals, or it may have had some quite different purpose, difficult to demonstrate given the present state of conservation. However, its evidently apotropaic character takes its inspiration from the *ofef*, Egyptian faience amulets believed to protect against flies (cf. no. 129488 from Pompeii) and is typical of the taste for things Egyptian widespread in Pompeii and Campania in general in the 1st century AD
Bibliography: *Collezioni Napoli*, 1986, pp. 228-9, no. 3.
(E.D.C.)

14
Unguentarium in the shape of a dog (?)
early 4th century AD
Blown glass,
l. 12.2 cm
From Roman necropolis in the Jakobstrasse, Cologne, found in a tomb along with coins of Claudius II and Constantine
Römisch-Germanisches Museum, Cologne, inv. no. 29.1051
State of conservation: intact

Unguentarium of colourless glass with a greenish cast in the shape of an animal with hornlike ears and open jaws. Small drops of glass are applied to form the eyes. The tip of the tail is turned upward and ends in a threadlike opening. It is possible that the receptacle was the work of an "apprentice," perhaps intended to be a dog with a collar, that did not turn out quite right. This interpretation is certainly more plausible than the previous one of a "legendary animal."
Bibliography: Fremersdorf, 1939, fig. 29; Fremersdorf, 1961, 23, pl. 13; Doppelfeld, 1966, 52, fig. 103; Borger, 1977, 58, fig. 203.
(H.G.)

15
Rhyton in the shape of an animal's head
1st century AD
Free-blown glass; tooled, h. 22.2 cm, Ø of mouth 8 cm
From Cavarzere, loc. Cuora (Venice) - Raule Collection
Museo Archeologico Nazionale, Adria, IG AD 9027
State of conservation: reassembled and with piece missing from rim

The horn of dark yellow, translucent glass has a simply cut rim, a body with fifteen slender ribs and a tip in the shape of an animal's head, with an elongated muzzle and long, thin ears terminating in little balls. The execution of the piece, in which hot working with tools played a preponderant part, required consummate skill on the part of the craftsman. The form is a rare one, but the decoration of slender ribbing is reminiscent of objects normally attributed to glassworks in northeastern Italy.
Typological comparisons: Isings, 73a.
Bibliography: Bonomi, 1996, p. 199, no. 449.
(S.B.)

15

16
Drinking horn
6th-7th century AD
Blown blue glass with applied threads,
h. 18 cm, ∅ of rim 7.7 cm
From Domusnovas, Cagliari, unknown context
Deposito Museo Archeologico Nazionale, Cagliari, inv. 17291
State of conservation: whole

The horn has a slightly flared rim with a thickened edge. The conical and somewhat convex body tapers markedly to end in a rounded and curling tip. The rim is marked by two slender horizontal cordons while the upper part of the convex section is underlined by three more horizontal cordons in relief, all of a green colour. The part underneath is decorated with festoons made from applied threads. The terminal section is wrapped in a spiral formed out of a similar thread.
The horn has no exact parallels among pieces of this kind, well known in the early medieval production of glass. The variations with respect to specimens from other parts of the Italian peninsula suggest it was made locally.
Typological comparisons: Evison, 1983, pp. 7-21, p. 12, fig. 3b.
Bibliography: Stiaffini-Borghetti, 1994, pp. 83-4, 145, no. 460, pl. 121.
(C.T.)

17
Engraved cup
end of 3rd century AD
Free-blown glass; wheel engraved and scratched with a point,
h. 9.8 cm, ∅ of rim 15.3 cm
From Corte Cavanella, Loreo (Rovigo)
Museo Archeologico Nazionale, Adria, IG AD 38176
State of conservation: reassembled from various fragments with small gaps

Decolourized, translucent glass cup, greenish where broken, with slightly everted rim, cut and emphasized by engraved lines, hemispherical body, slightly flattened bottom. The decoration engraved on the outside consists of a figured band on the body, comprising a large fish, a basket filled with fruit and leaves and two symmetrically reversed bunches of grapes. On the bottom a circular medallion encloses a man's wreathed head in profile and facing left. The iconography of the band, a sort of still life, could be interpreted as a representation of *xenia*, or gifts of hospitality made to guests at a banquet.
In this case the head would be that of Dionysius, god of wine, certainly an auspicious presence at a symposium.
The style of the decoration is reminiscent of Rhenish and Alexandrine examples from the decades spanning the 3rd and 4th centuries AD.
Typological comparisons: Isings, 96b1.
Bibliography: *Antico Polesine*, 1986, p. 247, no. 42; Bonomi, 1986, cc. 440-50.
(S.B.)

16

17

18

18
Goblet with applied flowers
Murano, early 18th century
Blown glass, applied flowers, h. 22 cm
Galleria Nazionale di Arte Antica, Palazzo Barberini, Rome
State of conservation: good

Crystal goblet with spikes at the base of the bowl, emphasized by an undulating thread. Crystal stem with intermediate zone made of a twisted cane to which flowers with aquamarine and opaline petals and yellow and green leaves are applied. Base in crystal.
The slender form of the goblet and the very broad base are typical of the end of the 17th century and the beginning of the 18th. The two-colour flowers are characteristic of the early 18th century. Similar articles are reproduced in still lives from the early 1700s, especially in the works of Cristoforo Munari.
Typological comparisons: Barovier Mentasti, 1982, figs. 113, 114; Lanmon, Whitehouse, 1993, no. 81.
Bibliography: *Colori e trasparenze*, 2001, p. 33.

19
Engraved fruitstand
Murano, early 18th century
Blown glass engraved with a diamond-point and with application,
h. 6.5 cm
Civiche Raccolte d'Arte Applicata, Castello Sforzesco, Milan
State of conservation: excellent

Fruitstand in blown crystal with applied foot in the shape of a truncated cone. The outer part of the dish is decorated with foliage and birds, engraved with a diamond-point. Inside the decoration two threads of crystal are applied in circles, and inside these two pinched threads of aquamarine glass form a cable pattern.
This model is very common among works conserved in museums in Italy and abroad. The most interesting is the one in Rosenborg Palace in Copenhagen, as it used to belong to a collection donated to the king of Denmark by the Republic of Venice in the winter of 1708-09 and is therefore of known provenance and date.
Typological comparisons: Boesen, 1960, nos. 97-98; Mariacher, 1963, p. 92; Causa Picone, 1967, pp. 71, 72; *Poldi Pezzoli Ceramiche-Vetri*, 1983, no. 110, pl. 109.
Bibliography: Alberici, 1976, p. 73, fig. 70; Mori, 1996, p. 34.

19

20

20
"Reticello" goblet
Murano, first decade of 18th century
Blown glass with a *reticello* pattern, applied flowers, h. 38 cm
Galleria Nazionale di Arte Antica, Palazzo Barberini, Rome
State of conservation: good

Tall goblet with bowl, foot and lower part of the stem in *filigrana a reticello*, a network of threads of crystal and the milky glass known as *lattimo*. The lower part of the stem has two small handles decorated with *morise*, a thread worked into a serpentine pattern. The upper part has a cluster of leaves with flowers of *lattimo* and aquamarine and yellow glass. Executed with exceptional skill, this goblet belongs to a particularly creative period in the history of Venetian glass, preceding the crisis of the 18th century. Examples very similar to this goblet can be seen at the Rosenborg Palace in Copenhagen, where they form part of a collection donated by the Venetian Republic to King Frederick IV of Denmark during his stay in Venice in the winter of 1708-09.
The same model but with a lid is reproduced in Gabriele Salci's *Still Life with Parrot*, signed and dated 1716, now in the art collection of the princes of Liechtenstein on display at the Fürst Liechtensteinische Gemäldegalerie in Vaduz.
Typological comparisons: Boesen, 1960, no. 15; Barovier Mentasti, 1982, figs. 130, 131.
Bibliography: *Colori e trasparenze*, 2001, p. 35.

21
Small turquoise bottle with flowers
Salviati & C. (The Venice and Murano Glass and Mosaic Company), Murano, *c.* 1870
Blown glass, cased with applications,
h. 13.9 cm
Rossella Junck Collection
State of conservation: excellent

Small turquoise bottle in white enamel cased in aquamarine with, applied on each face, a plant volute with green leaves and a flower in white enamel cased in ruby with an applied yellow button. On the sides: nipped *morise* in a *"gelosia"* pattern (nipper with lattice mold). Pinnacle stopper in white enamel cased in aquamarine with a cordon of crystal applied in a spiral and sprocket-shaped crystal foot with nipped *"gelosia"* border.
The type and the technique of turquoise casing in neo-Rococo style with flowers suggest the object dates from before 1877, that is prior to Salviati's separation from his British partners. The low catalogue number implies a model that remained in production at the Compagnia di Venezia e Murano after the breakup. There is a tureen in the Museo Vetrario in Murano that presents the same stylistic and technical characteristics as the bottle.
Typological comparisons: *Catalogo Compagnia di Venezia e Murano*, n.d., no. 449; Barovier Mentasti, 1978, p. 14, no. 135.
(P.M.)

22
Shell-shaped goblet with flowers
Fratelli Toso, Murano, *c.* 1885
Blown and molded glass coloured with powder,
h. 22.1 cm
Rossella Junck Collection
State of conservation: excellent

Bowl in gold-leaf crystal with irregular ruby-red colouring obtained with glass powder, in the shape of a shell. The stem is formed from two flowers with petals in gold-leaf crystal and their crystal stems in opposed spirals. The foot is also in crystal, with irregular ruby-red colouring made with glass powder.
This model is a late 19th-century interpretation of a Venetian baroque model in *façon de Venise*: the pilgrim's flask with a body in the shape of a shell. It was produced in numerous variants at all the Murano factories over the last two decades of the 19th century. The attribution to the Fratelli Tosi glassworks is based on the resemblance of some details to pieces that were definitely produced by that factory.
(P.M.)

21

22

23
Fruitstand with dolphins
The Venice and Murano Glass and Mosaic Company, Murano, *c.* 1880
Blown glass with combed threads and applications, h. 16.1 cm
Rossella Junck Collection
State of conservation: partially damaged

Fruitstand with yellow glass bowl decorated with plumes in opaque white glass (threads wrapped around wall and combed to make festoons). The cup is decorated in *morise* and with three applied lion's heads. It is supported by three blown-crystal dolphins, spotted with turquoise glass powder and with eyes made of yellow-black murrines. The dolphins are fused with the foot of the fruitstand, in yellow glass decorated with plumes like the bowl.
The dolphin had traditionally been represented in Murano glassware since the 18th century and was very common in the 19th as well. The attribution to the Venice and Murano Company is based on the resemblance of details to pieces undoubtedly made by the factory.
(P.M.)

24
Vase
Loetz Witwe, Klostermühle, Bohemia, 1900
Iridescent blown glass, h. 42.8 cm
Kunstmuseum, Düsseldorf
State of conservation: excellent

Slender vase, blown and modeled freehand, in highly iridescent glass. Variously coloured and decorated with glass threads with a brightly coloured surface.
The suggestive material from which it is modeled was rendered iridescent by a process for which the company had obtained a patent, making it similar to the glassware produced by Louis Comfort Tiffany.

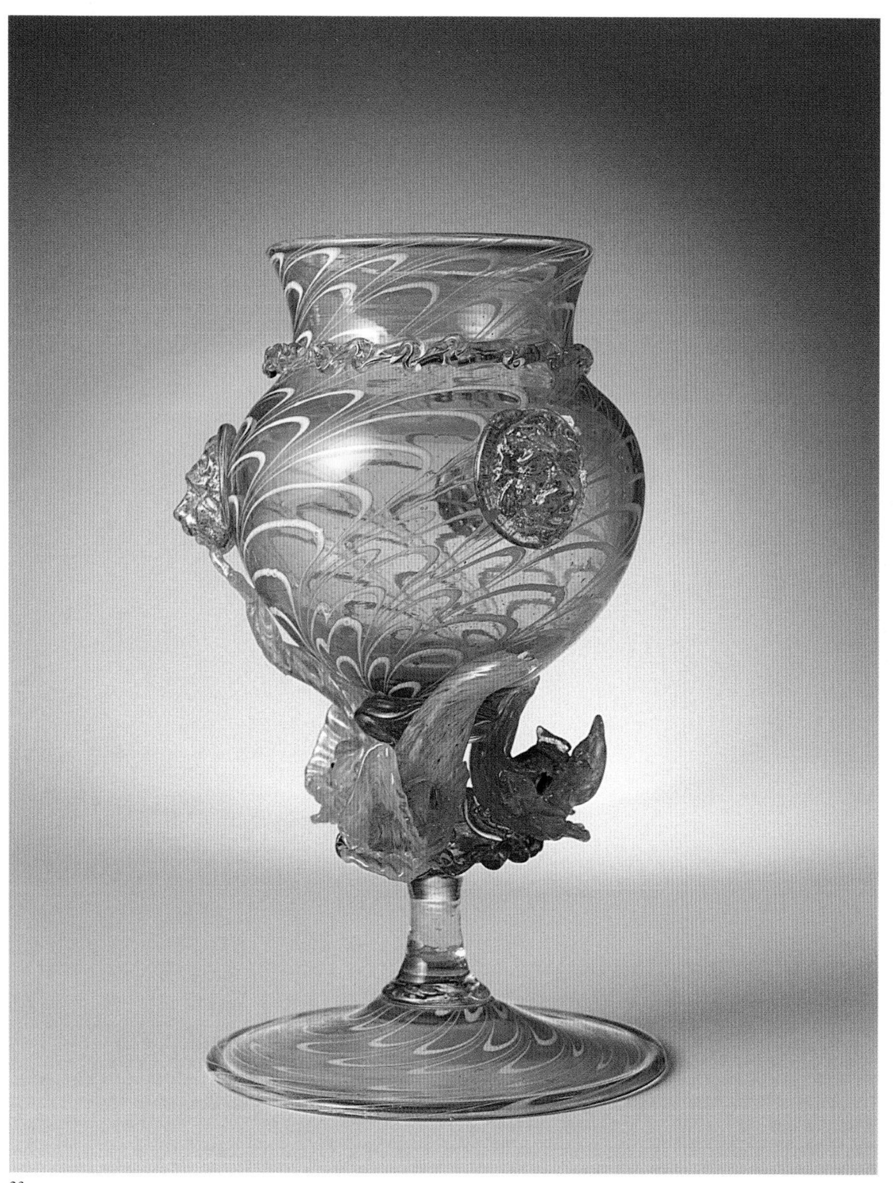
23

24

25
Legras
Pair of vases
1900
Vase in quadruple glass imitating semiprecious stone, decorated with leaves and seaweeds etched with acid and painted in enamel, 35 × 20 cm each
Private collection, Turin
Signature or mark: Legras.

26
Emile Gallé
Hemerocallis vase
Gallé, Nancy, 1900
Blown and modeled freehand, cased and decorated with engravings and *marqueterie*, h. 32.8 cm
Kunstmuseum, Düsseldorf

Vase blown and modeled freehand with a colourless inner layer, cased in white and brown. The technique of *marqueterie de verre*, or "glass marquetry," was used to decorate it with a dark red day lily with a green stalk and leaves. The lower part has an additional, trilobate casing of colourless glass. The decoration also includes incisions and reliefs. The surface is partly mat and partly polished. The word "Hemerocallis" is engraved in Greek letters on one side. Grand Genre vase. The decoration is created by a range of techniques, triple casing, engraving and *marqueterie*. The latter was developed by Emile Gallé himself and inspired by marquetry in wood. Decorative motifs produced separately were pressed into glass of contrasting colour while still hot so that the surface remained flat. The whole could be finished with engraving, as in this example.
Signature or mark: Gallé.
Typological comparisons: Arwas, 1987, p. 125.
Bibliography: Hilschenz-Mlynek, Ricke, 1985, no. 268.

25

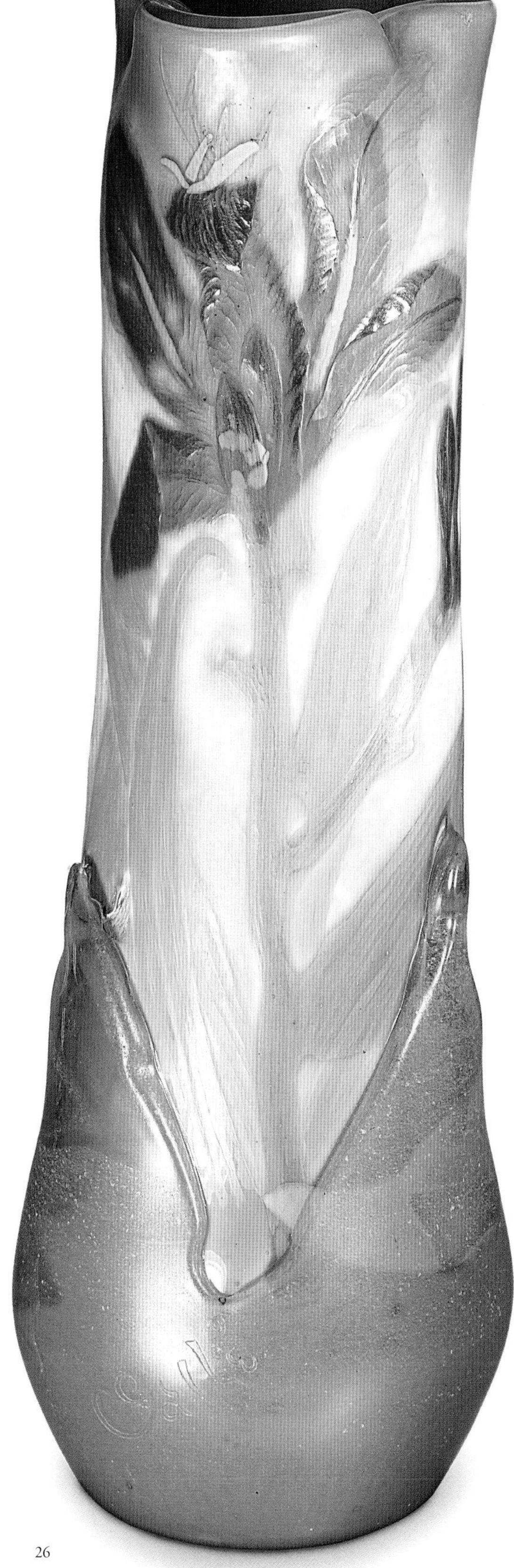

26

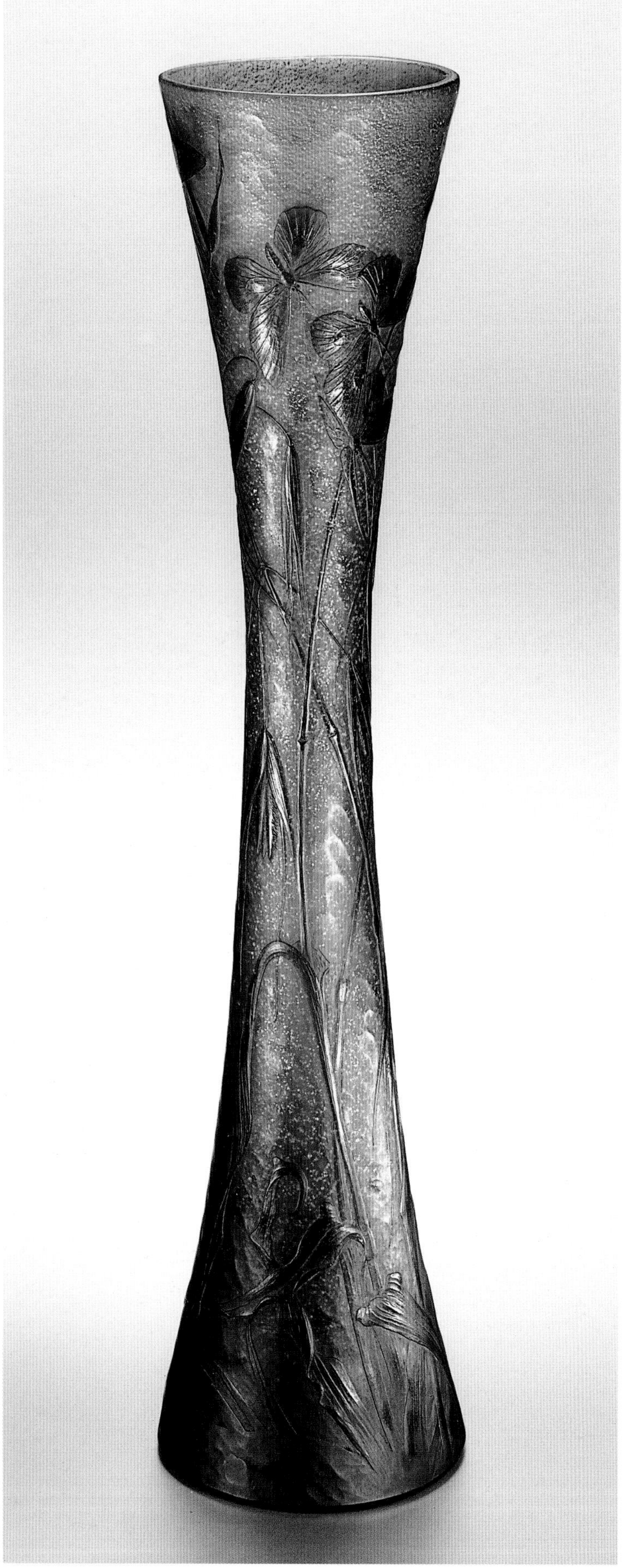

27

28

27
Emile Gallé
Engraved vase
Gallé, Nancy, 1900
Cased, etched and engraved vase,
h. 50.3 cm
Kunstmuseum, Düsseldorf
State of conservation: slightly damaged

Mold-blown vase of silvered colourless glass with greenish-yellow and violet casing. The etched and engraved decoration consists of ears of oats and butterflies. The ground is partly engraved to create a "beaten" effect.
It is a Grand Genre piece and probably belonged to a series produced for the 1900 International Exhibition in Paris.
After centuries of sparkling crystal, French glassworkers turned to hazy and semi-opaque materials, closer to the world of nature. Decorations were for the most part obtained by engraving vases made of layers of different coloured glass so as to bring out the layer underneath and leave the decorative motifs in relief, which were then carefully finished. This technique derived from traditional cameo glass but the boundaries between the various layers are blurred and soft, creating more picturesque effects.
Bibliography: Ricke, 1995, no. 239.

28
Vase with chestnut leaves
Daum Frères, Nancy, 1907-10
Cased, mold-blown vase, with glass powders,
h. 42 cm
Kunstmuseum, Düsseldorf
State of conservation: excellent

Vase cased in several colours, with glass powders, mold-blown and etched. The decoration consists of leaves in relief and chestnuts. With a layer of brownish-yellow powder.
The use of powders, on the inside of the wall or the outside, was one of the techniques characteristic of the Daum glassworks. In this example the opaque brown powders create an extraordinary autumnal effect.
Signature or mark: Daum, Nancy, Cross of Lorraine.
Bibliography: Hilschenz-Mlynek, Ricke, 1985, no. 84; Ricke, 1995, no. 253.

29
Vase
Biandrate Glassworks, 1920
Vase in blue glass with decoration of inlaid silver flowers,
h. 30 cm
Private collection, Turin

29

30
René Lalique
Plume vase
Lalique, Combs-la-Ville, 1921-25
Mold-blown glass with compressed air, etched and polished,
h. 21.5 cm
Kunstmuseum, Düsseldorf
State of conservation: excellent

Vase in opaline glass with transparent casing, blown into a mold with compressed air. The relief decoration of feathers is created by the mold. The etched surface has been left mat on the ground and polished on the parts in relief.
The beauty of Lalique's works stemmed from the refinement of their design and while many specimens could be produced by the mold, their finishing was always very accurate. Works like this were decidedly ahead of their time, in their rejection of polychromy, in their highly stylized decorations in relief and in the modern processes of manufacture.
Signature or mark: R. Lalique, France N° 944
Typological comparisons: *Lalique Glass*, 1981, 944; Bayer, Waller, 1988, fig. 233; Marcilhac, 1989, p. 427.
Bibliography: Hilschenz, 1973, no. 261; Hilschenz-Mlynek, Ricke, 1985, no. 389.

31
René Lalique
Formose vase
Lalique, Combs-la-Ville, 1921-25
Mold-blown glass with compressed air,
h. 17 cm
Kunstmuseum, Düsseldorf
State of conservation: excellent

Spherical vase of opaline glass cased in red, blown with compressed air into a mold to create a relief decoration with fish.
The elements in relief are polished, the recessed parts mat.
It was one of Lalique's most popular pieces, produced in large numbers and several colours up until after 1937. The presence of two signatures, one molded and one engraved, as in this example, indicates an early data.
Signature or mark:
R. Lalique, France.
R. LALIQUE.
Typological comparisons: *Lalique Glass*, 1981, 934; Bayer, Waller, 1988, no. 262; Marcilhac, 1989, p. 425.
Bibliography: Hilschenz, 1973, no. 260; Hilschenz-Mlynek, Ricke, 1985, no. 393; *Silice e fuoco*, 1992, no. 258.

32
Napoleone Martinuzzi
Elephant
Venini & C., Murano, 1930
Blown glass,
h. 25.5 cm
Il Vittoriale degli Italiani, Gardone Riviera
State of conservation: whole

Animal blown in blue glass with gold leaf and applied paws. One of Napoleone Martinuzzi's favorite animals.
Typological comparisons: *Gli artisti di Venini*, 1996, no. 30; *Napoleone Martinuzzi*, 1992, nos. 102, 103, p. 22.
Bibliography: Venini Diaz de Santillana, 2000, p. 23.

30

31

32

33
Altare glassworkers
Flower vase with engraved reptile
first quarter of 20th century
Blown glass modeled by hand and engraved,
h. 28 cm
Istituto per lo Studio del Vetro e dell'Arte Vetraria, Altare, inv. no. 47

34
Napoleone Martinuzzi
Cactus
Venini & C., Murano, 1930
Hot-modeled glass,
h. 20 cm
Il Vittoriale degli Italiani, Gardone Riviera
State of conservation: restored

Vase in iridescent, opaque black glass, bordered at the top with opaque red glass; inside is set a cactus in coral-red glass and gold leaf. It is one of a pair that D'Annunzio placed in two large vases from which only the branches protruded, in the Stanza della Leda of the Priory at the Vittoriale degli Italiani. The Priory, a monument to D'Annunzio's personality created by the poet himself, is filled with works of decorative art from every age and every country. They include many objects in glass, of which D'Annunzio was particularly fond, and above all articles designed by Martinuzzi for Venini.
Typological comparisons: *Murano oggi*, 1981, no. 57, no. 29; *Murano alle Biennali*, 1995, p. 31.
Bibliography: *Catalogo Blu*, n.d., no. 2490; *Napoleone Martinuzzi*, 1992, p. 20; *Gli artisti di Venini*, 1996, no. 46; Venini Diaz de Santillana, 2000, fig. 41.

33

34

35

35
Napoleone Martinuzzi
Fruitstand
Venini & C., Murano, 1928-30
Blown glass,
h. 16 cm
Il Vittoriale degli Italiani,
Gardone Riviera
State of conservation: whole

Fruitstand in transparent amethyst glass with molded radial ribbing and tall applied foot. The fruitstand was used by D'Annunzio himself to hold glass fruit.
Bibliography: *Napoleone Martinuzzi*, 1992, p. 16; *Gli artisti di Venini*, 1996, no. 26; Venini Diaz de Santillana, 2000, no. 19.

36
Napoleone Martinuzzi
Eggplant
Venini & C., Murano, 1930
Blown glass,
h. 11 cm
Il Vittoriale degli Italiani,
Gardone Riviera
State of conservation: whole

Iridescent violet glass with iridescent opaque green stalk.
Typological comparisons: *Napoleone Martinuzzi*, 1992, p. 45.
Bibliography: *Gli artisti di Venini*, 1996, no. 26.

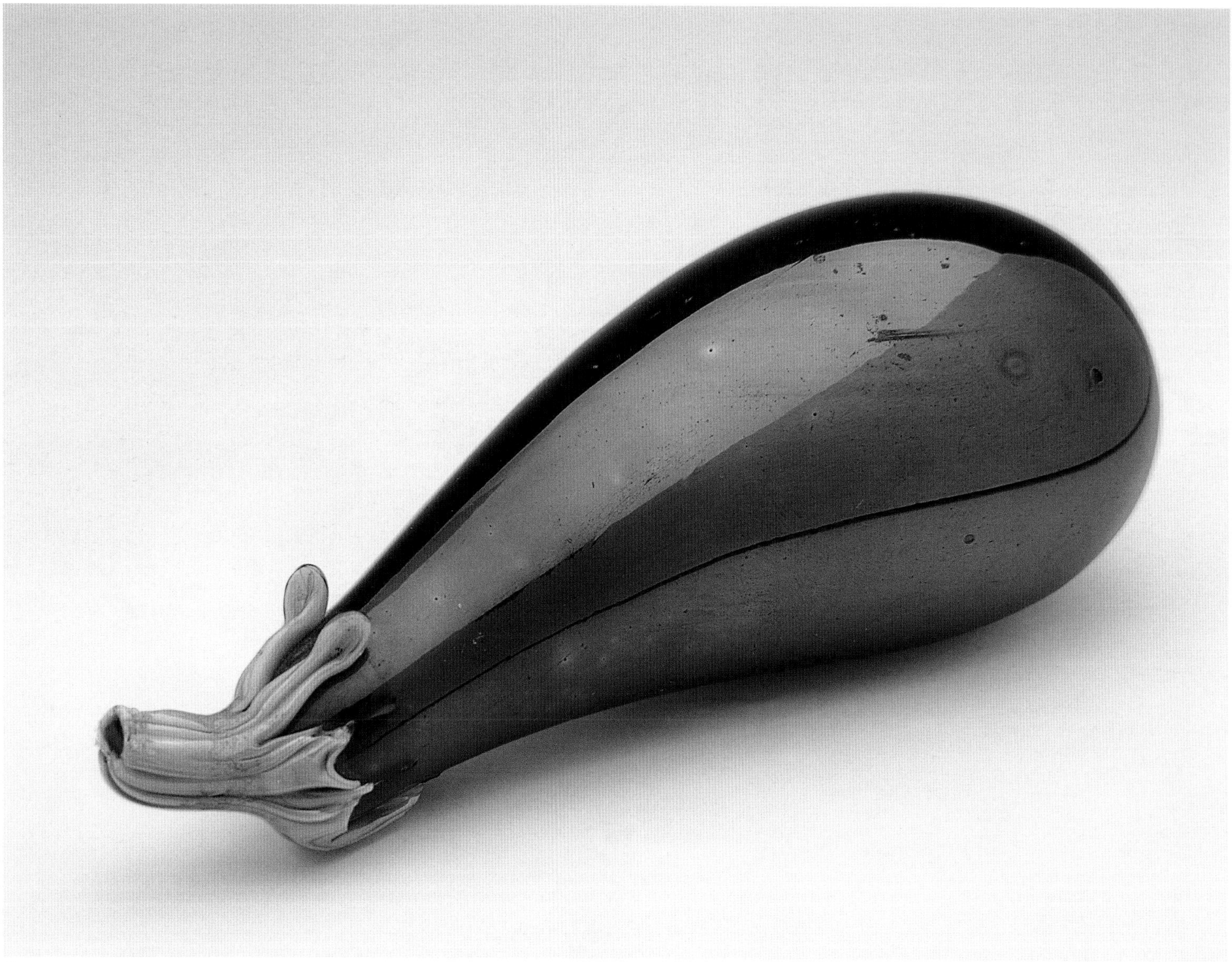

36

37
Tapio Wirkkala
Chanterelle
1946
Blown and wheel-engraved glass
Tehtaan Museo (Glassmuseum), Iittala
State of conservation: whole

Crystal vase blown and modeled in the shape of a chanterelle mushroom, finished with vertical wheel engravings. It is one of the most famous models in the history of glass, a symbol of Finnish design based on natural forms. It was the first in a long series of articles designed by Tapio Wirkkala for the Iittala glassworks, inspired by his love for the far North and in keeping with the course taken by design and architecture after the war, which moved from the geometric forms of rationalism toward more organic ones. It was shown at the Milan Triennale of 1951, where Finnish glass was represented by Tapio Wirkkala alone, with three collections, including Chanterelles (*Kantarelli*). First series of production 1948-60, numbered series from 1981.
Bibliography: *La Verrerie Européenne des années 50*, 1988, p. 63; *Silice e fuoco*, 1992, p. 316, no. 429; *Autriche, Suède et Finlande*, 1995, p. 102; *Finnish post-war Glass*, 1996, pl. 9; *Tapio Wirkkala, eye…*, 2000, p. 295; Fiell, 2001, p. 179.

38
Tapio Wirkkala
Lichens
Iittala, 1950
Mold-blown and etched glass,
max. h. 20.5 cm
Suomen Lasimuseo (Finlands Glassmuseum), Riihimäki

Vases in mold-blown and etched colourless glass. In this work, as in many others, Wirkkala continued with his investigation of the theme of organic forms, suggested to him by the nature of Lapland where he spent the summer months, which for him were a time of reflection and creativity.
Bibliography: *Tapio Wirkkala, eye…*, 2000, p. 299.

37

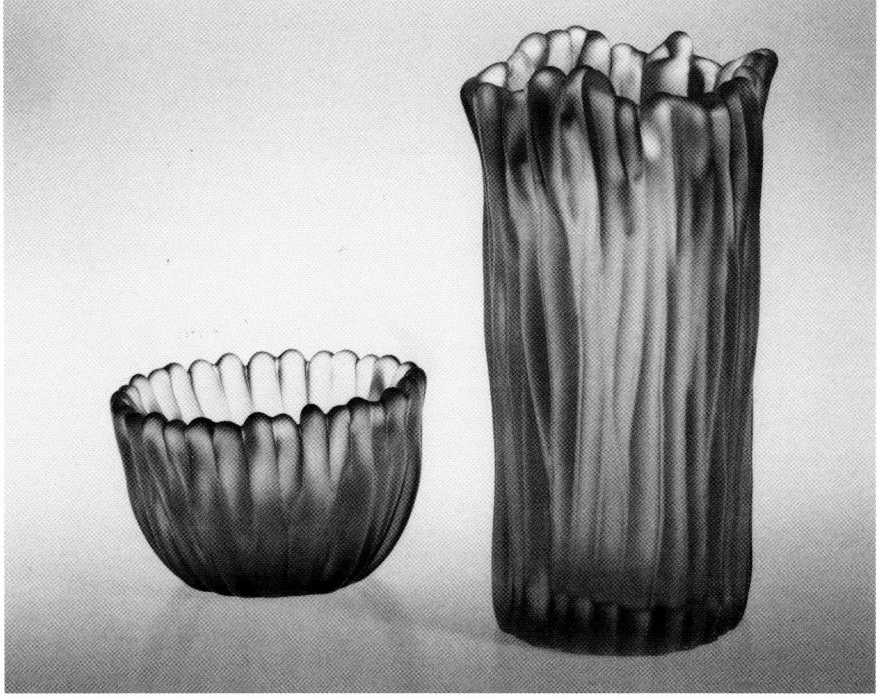
38

39
Eva Moosbrugger
Three Black Stones
Murano, 2002
Blown sunk glass,
h. 15 cm; h. 10.5 cm;
h. 18.5 cm
Collection of the artist

Installation made up of three sculptural forms in blown sunk glass: inner layer black, outer layer blue. Surface cold polished by hand and scratched to create rough streaks, apparently white in colour. The soft and highly tactile forms are inspired by river pebbles rounded by the water. Yet they reveal the essence of glass and the colour of their outer layer in the light.
Moosbrugger has long been fascinated by the natural forms of stones, which she used to reproduce in polychrome and richly decorated glass. Today, however, she has arrived at a new essentiality and seeks to create a fundamentally tactile effect. She has created installations characterized by spaces animated by paintings and glass sculptures.
Typological comparisons: *Eva Moosbrugger*, 1999, pp. 22, 23; *New Glass Review*, Corning Museum of Glass, 2002.

40
Antonio Riello
Pteria
1993
Glass, fabric and metal,
180 × 47 cm
Private collection, Verbania

Irreverent and caustic, Antonio Riello is an artist of paradox and provocation. His work always sets out to be “politically incorrect”: he challenges common sense, denigrates good taste and is intolerant of those who always want to look on the bright side of things. In addition, he espouses lies and mystification. The artist from Marostica always seems to be on the side of the villains, and – even if his choice of evil and injustice serves to reveal the perverse logic that governs the world today – does not appear to be troubled by them. The sculpture *Pteria* – in mixed media, but with glass playing the most significant part in the work, the immense presumed black pearl found in an evidently gigantic oyster – is part of a cycle of works that constitute a genuine museum of deception, a monument to the fake. A falsification that is openly declared by the absurdly ostentatious claims of these supposedly historical or naturalistic exhibits, including an enormous *Tyrannosaurus rex* egg and Adolf Hitler’s coffee cup (discovered in his last bunker). If it were real, *Pteria* would be the main attraction in any museum of natural history, yet another demonstration of the grandeur of creation, and in fact is presented here in the Room of Nature. The dark, blurred glass, deep and heavy in its hue, is used to disguise the object, to reproduce – on a huge and impossible scale – the refined perfection of a pearl the colour of anthracite.

39

40

41
Sandy Skoglund
Breathing Glass
2000
Cibachrome,
99 × 133 cm
B&D Art Promotion, Milan

Like the world that Alice entered through the looking glass, the environments constructed and photographed by Sandy Skoglund are illogical and paradoxical. They are also irritating, because the people living in them, the figures we see in them, do not appear to be aware of the absurdity of the situation they are in. Instead, seeing a group of Barbie dolls sunbathing on a beach of French fries (*At the Shore*, 1994) ought to be as disorienting as an unbirthday party. And using eggs to floor a lavatory (*Walking on Eggshells*) ought to seem as eccentric as dancing a quadrille with lobsters. And yet the people chatting amiably in *The Cocktail Party* (1992), the boy getting out of bed in *Revenge of the Goldfish* (1981) and the busy office staff of *A Breeze at Work* (1987) are not at all bothered by the unnatural strangeness of the setting. They do not appear to notice the fish swimming through the air in the bedroom, the forest of blue leaves in the workplace and the cheese snacks that have invaded the drawing room. This uncertain and inconsistent relationship between normality and absurdity, between naturalness and irrationality, is of fundamental importance in many of the American artist's works. Skoglund inserts a disturbing effect into a banal situation, where monotony ought to hold sway, and thereby demonstrates how the border between normality and madness, especially in the light of recent environmental and genetic disasters brought about by humanity, is absolutely unstable and blurred. To create the photograph of the work *Breathing Glass* the artist constructed a blue setting, completely covered with small glass dragonflies that are always in movement (because they are all attached to springs), and placed in it manikins dressed in crystal and flesh-and-blood figures. In this case a further element of confusion is introduced by turning the image upside down, undermining not just the laws of logic but also those of physics and gravity. This work, included in the Room of Nature as an example of the environment violated and turned on its head, represents the artist's first, and highly effective, encounter with the material of glass.

41

42
Joseph Beuys
Wine F.I.U. and Oil F.I.U. - Defense of Nature
1983-84
Glass bottles containing wine in carton of 12 bottles and 30 bottles of oil with label and case,
130 × 75 cm
Lucrezia De Domizio Durini Collection, Milan

With a felt hat permanently jammed onto his head and the air of a shaman, Joseph Beuys left an indelible mark on the history of the art of the second half of the 20th century. He defied traditions, broke down the barriers between disciplines and ignored dominant ideologies. He turned political actions into performances and works into environmentalist slogans, uniting art and nature, creativity and social commitment in an indissoluble symbiosis. For the first time his work brought themes like the protection of the environment and freedom in teaching into artistic research. Thanks to him, great international exhibitions became theaters of gigantic happenings, capable of attracting thousands of young people. Beuys created many of his best works in Italy, including the famous *Olivestone*, exhibited at the Venice Biennale of 2001, and the *Paradise Plantation*, set up at Bolognano with the help of Buby and Lucrezia De Domizio Durini. The work, conceived in the middle of the 1980s, fuses artistic creativity with that of nature. The German artist obliged the workers of the Durini estate to cultivate the fields according to the rules of organic farming. No exception was permitted. The final work of art, still being produced today sixteen years after Beuys's death, consists of the bottles of oil and wine labeled with the symbol of the Free International University.

42

43
Giò Pomodoro
Bubbles
1982
Blown Prussian-blue glass, variable dimensions
Private collection, Milan

Bronze and marble on the one hand, glass and crystal on the other. In sculpture some materials can have an absolute value that even transcends the characteristics of the individual works. And if metal and stone, for their specific weight, represent the earth, strength, power, stability and authority, glass, for its transparence and for the impalpability of its surfaces, symbolizes air, lightness, freedom. In *Glassway*, Giò Pomodoro, an artist known for the expressive force and ponderous stability of his works, tackles forms that have to convey an idea of lightness, that have to aspire to ascent, to flight. The *Bubbles* reach for the sky in the way that many of the artist's other works cling to the earth, and the material is used to suggest an idea of nature in the figure of the work and to re-create the magical lightness of a soap bubble.

43

43

II.

Room of Water

ANCIENT GLASS

With its colour and transparency, the material of glass immediately evokes the mutability of water. The bubbles to be found in ancient glass recall frothy streams of liquid, springs, waterfalls and sprays. Real transparency has only been achieved in the attempt to imitate rock crystal, the exclusive material used for a limited number of forms, often of diminutive size.

The marine environment, moreover, has provided the inspiration for a figurative current linked to aquatic themes and even seafaring activities. A disparate range of objects of functional character but a high level of quality, dating from the 3rd-4th century AD, are decorated with representations of fish, mollusks and crustaceans: whether painted, as in the fine drinking glass of Sassari, or engraved, as on the bottom of a plate from Zagreb, they may imply a specific use of this glassware. The unusual form of the vessels in the Cologne Römisch-Germanisches Museum, shaped like a fish and a shell, is probably connected with a precise gastronomic use. An exceptional panel produced by a mixed technique, mosaic glass and inlay, from the *triclinium* of a *domus* at Rimini and dating from the first half of the 3rd century AD, offers an extraordinarily realistic representation of the marine world, depicting several species of fish in their natural environment. The small boat of Treviso, a model of a shallop probably used to hold objects, is linked to the theme of water with implications of a symbolic-funerary character. In a close connection between material and representation, the naval vessel carved in the diaphanous glass of a *vasum diatretum* evokes images of shipwrecks in the vast expanses of the sea.

CREATORS OF GLASS

Visiting a furnace in operation and looking at the molten glass, we get the impression of an incandescent liquid. One of the most recent theories on the structure of glass defines it as a "supercooled liquid," a description consistent with the appearance it assumes once modeled into an artistic form. Many of the most evocative creations in glass are suggestive of water, almost as if it had taken on solid form while maintaining unaltered its transparency and the mobility of its molecules.

Glassmakers put much of their efforts into the production of a pure, colourless and glossy material. An exception to this is provided by techniques like that of ice glass, developed in Venice in the 16th century, which gives the surface a crackled appearance, achieved by dipping the incandescent glass into a bucket of water. It was the goal of Bohemian and English glassworkers to rival the purity achieved by the Venetian glassworkers of the Renaissance. Only at the end of the 19th century, when the technology of pure lead crystal was well established, was there a change in direction. First in the brightly coloured blown glass of Venice and then in the Art Nouveau works of the French: more daring in their innovation, the latter proposed vaguely coloured, turbid glassware, clouded with highly suggestive effects, similar to the murky depths of the sea. With sunk, bubble and *Graal* glass, this research continued in the 1930s and after the war, as reflected in the works of Edward Hald and Alfredo Barabini, and in the more recent ones of Laura Diaz de Santillana, Massimo Micheluzzi and Richard Neumann.

References to the sea can also be found in some Bohemian or English glassware and in objects in the form of fish, shells, boats, from the sunk glass of Flavio Poli to the crystals of Tapio Wirkkala and the installations of Bertil Vallien and Lino Tagliapietra.

CONTEMPORARY ART

As the subject of paintings or as a cardinal element of creation, water has frequently attracted the attention of great artists. It suffices to think, on the one hand, of the pictures of Joseph Mallord William Turner and, on the other, of Pino Pascali's installation *The Sea*. For its capacity to evoke the transparency and consistency of the precious liquid, or simply because it has always been used for the manufacture of watertight containers, in modern times glass has often been associated with water, especially in installations. Carlo Benvenuto exploits the appearance of solid glass to simulate the surface of a liquid, while in his video sculpture *Ocean*, which has a structure similar to that of an aquarium, although revised and amended, Maurizio Camerani uses the material in the same way as in the majority of contemporary works. That is to say, he makes the same use of it as do industry and the crafts, adding that touch of paradoxical lunacy that can render a work of art visionary.

1
Flask in the shape of a fish
3rd century AD
Blown glass with glass paste applications, l. 15.5 cm
From a tomb in the Roman necropolis in the Luxemburger Straße, Cologne
Römisch-Germanisches Museum, Cologne, inv. no. N 307
State of conservation: made up of different pieces

Transparent, colourless, container for perfume in the shape of a dolphin swimming with its jaws open. The undulating modeling on the back and the decoration on the belly were made with a flat nipper. To make it easier to pour in the perfume, the tail fin has been given the shape of a funnel. The eyes are made out of black glass paste, with an opaque turquoise blue thread forming the "eyebrow." These small and curious containers were evidently turned out continuously by the glassblowers of the workshops, as there was a market for such "kitsch" forms.
Typological comparisons: Froehner, 1903, pl. 249 top left; Sunkowski, 1956, pl. 25.
Bibliography: *Niessen*, 1911, pl. 5, no. 307; Merten, 1935, pl. 26, no. 260; Fremersdorf, 1961, p. 19. no. N37 (printing error = N 307), pl. 3; Doppelfeld, 1966, p. 52, fig. 101; Wirges, 1969, pp. 22 *et sqq*., fig. 23 on left; Borger, 1977, p. 58, fig. 201.
(H.G.)

2
Flask in the shape of a fish
first half of 3rd century AD
Mold-blown glass with glass paste applications, l. of conserved part 17 cm (with completion 19.8 cm)
From Cologne
Römisch-Germanisches Museum, Cologne, Glass inv. no. 234
State of conservation: assembled from several fragments; the end of the tail has been completed

Flask of colourless glass in the shape of a swimming fish. Eyes and gills made of brilliant glass, olive-green in colour. Vessels in the shape of fish were common throughout the Roman empire. On the basis of numerous finds made in tombs at Cologne, the animal-shaped flasks have been dated to the late 2nd century AD or the beginning of the 3rd century. Many similar containers in the shape of fish have been found among the Roman exports (from Egypt or Palestine?) to Begram, Afghanistan. Given that the modelling of the fins out of flat pieces of glass is clearly different from that of the fins made from threads in the specimens from Cologne, we have to assume they were made by separate workshops, but probably at times that were not very far apart. Residues of perfumed oils have been found in vessels at Begram.
Typological comparisons: Froehner, 1903, pl. 203.2; Hackin, 1939, pl. 10.19; Fremersdorf, 1961, p. 20, pl. 4; Menninger, 1996, pp. 73 *et sqq*., pl. 24.
Bibliography: Fremersdorf, 1939, fig. 28; Isings, 1957, p. 112, form 95; Fremersdorf, 1961, p. 20, pl. 5; Doppelfeld, 1966, p. 52, fig. 102; Borger, 1977, p. 58, fig. 204.
(H.G.)

1

2

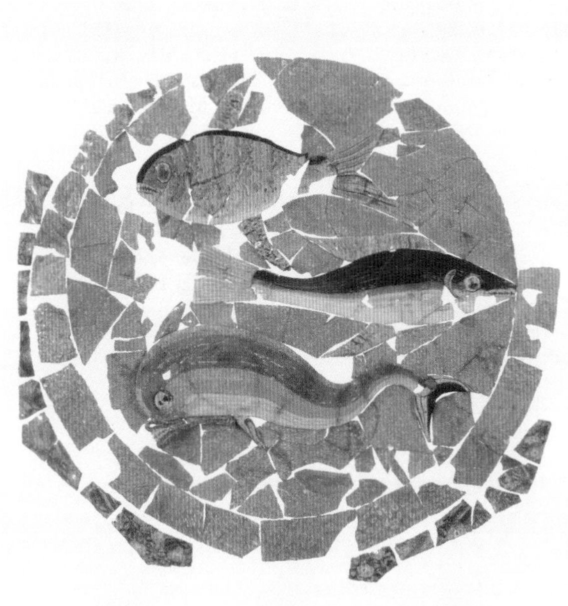

3

4
Cup with stem
second half 2nd-3rd century AD
Blown glass, cold-painted
h. 20.7 cm, ∅ of rim 8.3 cm, ∅ of foot 8.4 cm
Museo Nazionale G.A. Sanna, Sassari, inv. no. 3753
State of conservation: reassembled from numerous fragments; patchy and abraded painted decoration; iridescent surfaces

Clear colourless glass with thin walls. Tall cylindrical body with rounded, slightly thickened rim; foot in the form of a slightly bell-shaped disc; drop-shaped stem squashed at the poles. Decoration made up of an applied glass thread, wrapped in a spiral under the rim; immediately underneath there is a band with a plant motif, cut by wheel; a second thread of glass is applied on the foot. Only a very small part of the pictorial decoration on the surface of the goblet has been preserved: all that can be seen of the original representation, perhaps a marine scene, is the shape of a fish, outlined in a dark colour on a pale-blue ground. Some dark lines underneath probably belonged to the figure of another fish.
It can be hypothesized that the goblet in the Sassari Museum, an example of high-quality imported glassware, comes from the Oriental area where the decorative technique of painting on cold glass had developed and spread from the late 2nd century to mid-3rd century AD onward (*Vetri dei Cesari*, 1988, pp. 259-62).
The form is drawn from the ceramic repertory and in particular finds analogies in a cup on stem goblet of the 3rd century AD produced in African "c" *terra sigillata* (*Atlante*, 1981, Forma Salomonson XVII, Atlante I, p. 150). A close parallel can be found in a glass goblet with applications of decorative medallions, from the second half of the 2nd century AD, recently found during the excavation of the *circus* in Arles (Taborelli, 1999, no. 8, p. 43).
Bibliography: Lissia, 2000, no. cat. 65, pp. 62, 67, 78.
(D.L.)

3
Decorative panel with fishes
second quarter of 3rd century AD
Polychrome *opus sectile* with inserts in mosaic glass, max. width 32 cm, ∅ of central disc 27 cm, thickness 0.15-0.20 cm
From the *domus* "of the Surgeon," Piazza Ferrari, Rimini
Deposito Soprintendenza per i Beni Archeologici dell'Emilia Romagna, Bologna
State of conservation: incomplete, reassembled from several fragments; some alterations of colour and deformations caused by heat

The square panel, originally fixed to a wooden support and hung on the wall in the *triclinium* of the *domus*, which was destroyed by fire around 258 AD, has a geometric-figurative composition depicting a marine subject. At the centre is set a disc with a turquoise blue ground on which three fish swim in alternating directions. They are characterized by a fluid and lively representation, with varied tones of colour and meticulous attention to detail, but in a more naturalistic than realistic manner, so that it is only the one at the bottom that can be clearly identified as a dolphin. All around runs a circular green band bordered by an octagonal purplish-blue frame, closed at the corners by white and yellow sections.
Sheets of glass with polychrome mosaic inserts representing naturalistic subjects, often fish, are products of great value and rarity, and at the same time with a long history. They are customarily attributed to Alexandrine workshops linked to the traditions of late Ptolemaic Hellenism (Davidson Weinberg, 1962, p. 36; Grose, 1989, pp. 355-6). In reality, for the late imperial age, the most significant comparisons are with Greece, and Corinth in particular, such as the well-known slabs from the port of Kenchrai (Ibrahim, Scranton, Brill, 1976, pp. 57, 62-3) of the mid-4th century AD, and above all the panel with four fish found in the vicinity of the theatre, in a building destroyed in the late 3rd century AD (Williams, 1982, pp. 133-4; Oliver, 2001), which shows close parallels with the example from Rimini and was evidently produced by the same workshop.
Bibliography: Ortalli, 2000, pp. 519-20, no. 183.
(I.O.)

4

5

6
Shell-shaped mold
2nd century AD
Blown glass,
h. 4 cm, Ø 5 cm
From Roman necropolis in the Neusser Strasse, Cologne
Römisch-Germanisches Museum, Cologne, inv. no. N 312
State of conservation: whole

Small mold, produced in Cologne, blown in a single concave piece in the shape of a scallop. The border is chipped and cut subsequently. The model was a very popular one, and was already present among glass objects dating from the beginning of the 1st century AD found in Pompeii. This type of mold spread from Italy to the most remote provinces of the Roman empire.
Typological comparisons: Maiuri, 1932, pl. 62; Fremersdorf, 1961, p. 73, pls. 154-6, p. 74, pl. 158.
Bibliography: *Niessen*, 1911, no. 312, pl. 38; Fremersdorf, 1961, p. 73, pl. 157.
(H.G.)

6

5
Rounded plate
3rd-4th century AD
Milky glass, mold-made and engraved, cut lip,
h. 4.6 cm, Ø of rim 18.7 cm
From Bakar
Arheološki Muzej, Zagreb, inv. no. 11086
State of conservation: cracked, glued

The bottom and body of the dish are rounded, the lip slightly everted and cut. Representation of marine animals, probably a dolphin and jellyfish, engraved on the bottom inside two concentric circles filled with short engraved lines. Two fish, a shrimp and a crab are engraved around the shoulder.
Typological comparisons: Isings, 1957, form 116; Doppelfeld, 1966, group 3.8, figs. 156-8, 160; Baume, 1978, form 2; Barkóczi, 1988, pp. 46-52; Harden, 1988, pp. 226-9, nos. 126-8; Kocsis, 1991, pp. 29-31; Berti, 1993, 171-4; Ceselin, 1996, nos. 201-2.
Bibliography: Damevski, 1976, p. 86, pl. 14.1.
(I.F.)

7

7
Shell-shaped flask
3rd century AD
Blown glass,
h. 19 cm
Cologne, Roman necropolis in the Luxemburger Strasse
Römisch-Germanisches Museum, Cologne, inv. no. N 308
State of conservation: assembled from many fragments; opaque glass

Shell-shaped flask with no handles, a long hollow neck and standing on a foot with a stem. Blown in a concave two-part mold. The colourless and transparent glass in the lower half is slightly greenish and now partly opaque. The shell is clearly a scallop, a favorite model drawn from nature. The form was immediately adopted for both glass and metal containers. It is still not clear whether the various "shell-shaped vessels," produced in large quantities, were a reminiscence of the typical symbol of Venus.
Typological comparisons: Isings, 1957, form 91c; Fremersdorf, 1961, p. 74, pls. 160-1.
Bibliography: Kisa, 1908, p. 773, fig. 313; *Niessen*, 1911, no. 308, pl. 17; Fremersdorf, 1961, p. 74, no. 308, pl. 159.
(H.G.)

8
Small boat
Cast in mold, cut,
h. 4.1 cm, l. 20 cm, width 5.7 cm, thickness 0.3 cm
From Santa Elena di Melma, Silea (Treviso)
Museo Civico, Treviso, inv. no. MCTV 908
State of conservation: part of prow missing, not perishable

Small boat in dark violet, opaque glass with hull of elongated oval form to which four small feet have been applied. Broken-off prow and curved stern with the two flattened sides very prominent with respect to the planking. On the outside, a groove underlines the washboard about half a centimetre from the edge, while two more narrow grooves run along the keel. The boat is smooth on the inside.
Typological comparisons: Painter, 1988, p. 48, no. 24.
Bibliography: Calvi, 1974-75, coll. 479-86.
(F.C.)

9

9
Fragment of *vasum diatretum* with representation of a ship
second half of 3rd century AD
Colourless, transparent, blown and cut glass;
wall: l. 3.9 cm, width 0.7 cm, thickness 0.1 cm;
ship: l. 6 cm, h. 2.6 cm;
total thickness 1.2 cm
From Via del Colosseo, Rome, 1939
Antiquarium Comunale, Rome, inv. IAC 3192
State of conservation: extremely thin fragment of wall connected, by a long and thin bridge, to a ship. The surface is almost completely covered with an iridescent whitish patina, tending to flake off especially on the inner part of the wall, and is pocked with tiny bubbles of air

The fragment is too small for the form of the vessel to be recognizable.
The ship, represented in abundant detail, appears to be of a military type: it has a bow with a ram on the left, two rows of seven oars, coffered side, highly simplified tiller-leeboard, and stern of indented form decorated with a pattern of reliefs. The quadrangular elements on the deck may be elements of protection or the shields of soldiers. The element set diagonally in the bows seems to be the broken mast of the ship. This detail might indicate a scene of shipwreck or battle.
The motif of the ship finds a direct parallel in the drinking glass from Begram with a representation of a harbour in which there are three ships, either merchant vessels or pleasure craft. This glass, datable to around 250 AD, is the earliest known example of the entire class.
In the type of working and in particular the decoration, represented with long, straight and deep incisions, as well as the quality and colour of the glass, the fragment closely resembles a cage flask found in a catacomb in Rome and now in the Biblioteca Apostolica of the Vatican. The similarity between the two objects suggests they were made by the same workshop, perhaps in Rome, providing support for the hypothesis of the existence of a local centre of production.
Typological comparisons: Hackin, 1939, pp. 42-4, figs. 37-40; Hackin, 1954, pp. 101-2, figs. 359-2; Harden, Toynbee, 1959, p. 206, A8, pl. LVIII; Pirzio Biroli Stefanelli, 1988, p. 244, no. 138.
Bibliography: Pirzio Biroli Stefanelli, 1984, pp. 35-8, figs. 1-2; Pirzio Biroli, Stefanelli, 1989, p. 38, fig. 4.
(C.M.)

8

10
"Ice" bucket
Murano, late 16th - first half of 17th century AD
Blown glass with crackled surface,
h. 15 cm
Civiche Raccolte d'Arte Applicata, Castello Sforzesco, Milan
State of conservation: excellent

Crystal bucket with ice effect in the shape of an inverted truncated pyramid on an octagonal base. A thread of aquamarine glass is applied under the mouth, profiled by a thick thread of crystal; two rings of crystal are applied vertically on opposite sides of the mouth, into which a handle made out of a twisted cordon of crystal is inserted. There is an identical example, but of smaller size, in the collection of the Museo Poldi Pezzoli.
Typological comparisons: Mottola Molfino, 1972, p. 194, fig. 380; *Poldi Pezzoli Ceramiche-Vetri*, 1983, no. 165, pl. 161.
Bibliography: Alberici, 1976, p. 74, fig. 71; Mori, 1996, p. 37.

11
"Ice" goblet
Murano, late 16th - early 17th century AD
Blown glass with crackled surface,
h. 21.5 cm
Galleria Nazionale di Arte Antica, Palazzo Barberini, Rome
State of conservation: excellent

Goblet with bowl mold-blown to form a diamond pattern and treated to create an ice effect on the lower part. The undecorated upper part grows narrower and suggests the use of a lid, now lost. The modeled stem and the foot are decorated with ribs created by mold blowing.
The proportions of the goblet are still those of the Renaissance, with a fairly thick stem and small foot. Ice glass appears in the Venetian records from around 1569 and was obtained by dipping the incandescent glass into water and then heating it again. The type and the combination of mold blowing with an additional decorative technique are typical of the late 16th century.
Typological comparisons: Tait, 1979, nos. 148, 151; Barovier Mentasti, 1982, fig. 87; *Mille anni*, 1982, no. 163.
Bibliography: *Colori e trasparenze*, 2001, p. 31.

12
Goblet with lid
Silesia or Bohemia, 1720-40
Blown, engraved and cut crystal,
h. 29.6 cm
Civiche Raccolte d'Arte Applicata, Castello Sforzesco, Milan
State of conservation: excellent

Crystal goblet on broad foot with modeled stem cut into facets. The bowl is cut into facets on the lower part, while a seascape runs all around the upper part: on one side a three-masted ship laden with merchandise at full sail, on the other a mountainous island and another ship. Above the ship is set an inscription in Dutch, which translates as: "prosperity in trade." The rounded lid is engraved with volutes of leaves and the double knob is faceted. Similar goblets were frequently used as gifts in trade, especially to the Low Countries.
Bibliography: Mori, 1996, p. 43.

13
Goblet with lid
Hirschberger Tal, Silesia, 1740-50
Mold-blown, cut and engraved crystal,
h. 25.2 cm
Kunstmuseum, Düsseldorf
State of conservation: excellent

Mold-blown crystal on broad cut foot and cut stem, with bowl cut in the lower part. Around the wall runs a wheel-engraved decoration with wagons in front of a city on one side and a harbour and two ships on the other, surmounted by the Latin inscription "Floreat Commercium." Goblets of this kind seem to have been gifts in trading circles, and an important element in exports to the Netherlands. It was not just the craftsmen of Bohemia who displayed exceptional skill in engraving but also those of other regions like Silesia.
Typological comparisons: Klesse, Saldern, 1978, no. 127.
Bibliography: Ricke, 1995, no. 161.

10

11

12

13

14
Edward Hald
Bowl
1920
Blown, wheel-engraved glass, 66 × 27 cm
Signed
Kosta Boda AB, Orrefors
Typological comparisons: *The Brilliance of Swedish Glass*, 1996, no. 34.

15
Edward Hald
Fish Graal vase
Orrefors Glasbruk, 1937
Fish Graal technique, h. 15.8 cm
Kosta Boda AB, Orrefors

Vase in crystal with rounded forms decorated with coloured fish encased in the thick wall of glass. The *Fish Graal* technique produced the extraordinary effect of fish and other decorative motifs in coloured glass that seem to be suspended within the mass of colourless crystal. This was a development of the *Graal* technique, invented by the glassworker Knut Bergkvist and the designer Simon Gate at Orrefors in 1916. They began to experiment with double layers of glass that were then cut away so as to bring out the layer underneath. As Gate did not like the sharp edges of the incisions, he tried heating the object again and later on immersing it in the crucible to cover it with a new layer of crystal. Thus the incision was encased in the wall, which was left smooth on the outside.
At the beginning of the 1930s the *Graal* technique was almost abandoned because it was considered too dense with colour, but Edward Hald stepped in to revitalize it, producing sparser decorations by removing most of the colouring of the outer layer and covering it up with several layers of crystal, creating the aforementioned effect of the decorative elements being suspended in the body of the glass. Since the first examples of the new *Graal* technique used fish as their decorative theme, it came to be known as *Fish Graal*.
Typological comparisons: *The Brilliance of Swedish Glass*, 1996, no. 124; *Svenskt Glas*, n.d., no. 45.

14

15

16

18
Flavio Poli
Valve Vase
Seguso Vetri d'Arte, Murano, 1954
Blown, hot-modeled and cut glass, h. 10 cm
Gerard and William Figliola Collection, Turin
State of conservation: excellent

Vase in blown and hot-modeled transparent violet glass, finished by cutting. It has the form of a half-closed valve, with the opening at the top. Poli was very fond of this model and he proposed it in various forms and colours at the Triennali of 1951, 1954 and 1957 and the Biennali of 1954 and 1956.
Typological comparisons: *Silice e fuoco*, 1992, no. 385; Deboni, 1996, fig. 142; *Il vetro a Milano*, 1998, no. 147.

16
Timo Sarpaneva
Kayak
Iittala Glassworks, Iittala, 1953
Cut crystal, h. 10.5 cm
Tehtaan Museo (Glassmuseum), Iittala
State of conservation: excellent

Very pure cut and polished crystal inspired by the form of the kayak but in reality an abstract work. Some have seen the influence of Constantin Brancusi in this object. It was shown at the Milan Triennale of 1954 along with others by Sarpaneva, who was awarded a Grand Prix. It is a work emblematic of the exceptional purity that characterized the Finnish glasswork of the 1950s. The same purity was to be found in the utilitarian articles that dominated the Milan Triennale of 1957.
Bibliography: *The New Look*, 1991, p. 25; *Silice e fuoco*, 1992, no. 431; *Autriche, Suède et Finlande*, 1995, no. 56; *Finnish Post-war Glass*, 1996, pl. 20; *Moderne Zeiten*, 1998, no. 37.

17
Flavio Poli
Fishes
Seguso Vetri d'Arte, Murano, 1954
Sunk solid glass, h. 11 cm
Gerard and William Figliola Collection, Turin
State of conservation: excellent

Sculpted fish of essential elongated form in blue glass sunk in violet glass. Moonfish of sunk blue, violet and amethyst glass. Shown at the Milan Triennale of 1954. They were executed by the craftsman Angelo Seguso, partner in the company. The abstraction of the forms designed by Flavio Poli reached its peak in these fish made by the same technique as the vases in the collections shown at the Biennali and Triennali of the 1950s.
Signature or mark: A. Seguso, Murano.
Typological comparisons: Barovier Mentasti, 1982, p. 306.
Bibliography: *Fotografia Archivio Triennale*, vol. 5, nos. 233, 247, 249; *Triennale*, 1954, pl. XL; *Il vetro a Milano*, 1998, no. 132.

17

18

19
Flavio Poli
Bowl
Seguso Vetri d'Arte, Murano, 1956
Blown and cut glass, h. 9 cm
Fondazione Cassa di Risparmio di Venezia, Venice
State of conservation: excellent

Bowl in pure violet glass blown and modeled freehand and finished on the cutting wheel. Inspired, like much of Flavio Poli's glassware, by the form of the shell, the piece was acquired at the 1956 Biennale.
In his quest for perfect forms Poli often resorted to retouching with the cutting wheel. In this phase, during the 1950s and 1960s, he can be considered the most "Nordic" of the Murano glassworkers and designers, as his forms and predilection for limpid glass resembled the work of the great masters of Finnish glassware, with the difference that he made constant use of colour in line with the Venetian tradition.
Bibliography: Barovier Mentasti, 1994, no. 41.

19

20
Alfredo Barbini
Sunk
Vetreria Alfredo Barbini, Murano, 1963
Sunk glass of great thickness, h. 45 cm
Alfredo Barbini Srl Collection

Abstract sculpture in sunk solid aquamarine glass of several layers with a lateral mass in gray glass and horizontal black threads dividing up the three zones of sunk glass. It belongs to a series of abstract one-off pieces, true masterpieces of the glassworker's art in which the sculptural ability of Barbini, a great master of sunk glass, and the modernity of the conception are outstanding. What can be defined as the fourth dimension of the sculptural work in glass, the internal one, is evident in the watery effect of the superimposed layers.
Typological comparisons: *The Secret of Murano*, 1997, p. 30; Barovier Mentasti, 1992, no. 13; Barovier Mentasti, 1998, p. 26.
Bibliography: *Maestri vetrai creatori*, 1995, no. 44.

20

21
Mónika Uz
Llueve
2000
Thermocasting,
128 × 42 × 32 cm
Collection of the artist,
Barcelona

21

22
Richard Neumann
Blue Night Tribal
Canberra, 2001
Layered, cast and blown
sheets of glass,
h. 31 cm; h. 43 cm
La Scaletta di Vetro, Milan

Two glass sculptures made by superimposing sheets of coloured glass, casting them and blowing them in the furnace. The glass has an irregular colouring with inclusions of ceramic material. Technically extremely interesting, both for the inclusions of different materials and for the difficult final phase of the blowing of the cast block, these works are born out of observation of the natural world, the movement of water, the strata of rocks. As the author himself declares, this source of inspiration is also revealed in the details.
Typological comparisons: *Milano meets Canberra*, 2001.

22

23

23
Bertil Vallien
Canoe on Base
Orrefors, 2001
Glass cast in sand mold,
h. 20 cm, l. 300 cm
VIDA Museum, Borgholm

Sculpture in the shape of a canoe made out of solid glass cast in a mold of sand with coloured inclusions made in advance out of hot glass. The sand of the mold gives the surface a rough appearance reminiscent of objects found in archeological excavations. The theme of the canoe, one of the artist's favorites, was inspired by a visit to Ireland and the peculiar craft he saw in that country. He made his first boats out of ceramic material for an exhibition in Stockholm in 1979, and it was not until 1983 that he experimented with making canoes by casting them in sand molds.
Apart from its archeological associations, the boat takes on many symbolic values for Vallien: the voyage, the passage, and in the last analysis, as he has said of his own works, life itself, which is a journey from its beginning to its end. In addition, the boat is a container and can hold an infinity of messages, symbolized by the inclusions in the glass.
Typological comparisons: *Bertil Vallien*, 1990, pp. 116-62; *Aperto Vetro*, 1996, p. 86; *Global Art Glass*, 1999, no p. no.

24
Laura Diaz de Santillana
Installation
Murano, 2002
Blown and cut glass, on metal support,
h. 150 cm (h. of parts in glass 50 cm)
Collection of the artist

Installation made up of three sculpted vases in blown colourless, iridescent glass of great thickness, on a metal base. The theme of the vase is a mere pretext for sculptural forms that are flattened until they lose their internal cavities and assume a watery appearance, lent consistency by the treatment of the surface. The light caresses the surfaces and contours and brings the works to life.
Typological comparisons: *Laura de Santillana*, 2001, pp. 61, 63.

25
Massimo Micheluzzi
Untitled
Murano - Venice, 2002
Blown and cut glass,
h. 55 cm
Collection of the artist

Blown and wheel-cut vase with deep incisions, in transparent and slightly gray glass. The deep horizontal incisions create an effect of waves.
Signature: Massimo Micheluzzi.
Typological comparisons: *Massimo Micheluzzi*, 2000, no p. no.; *Designer Year Book*, 2002, no p. no.

24

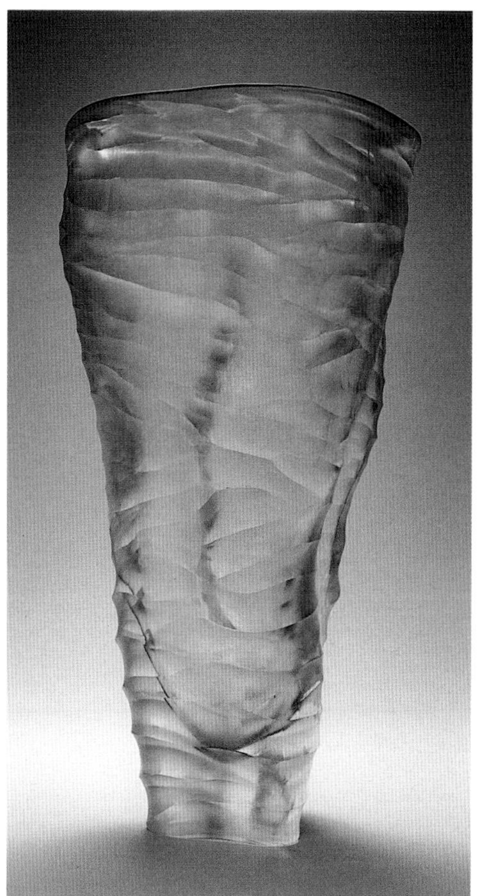
25

26
Carlo Benvenuto
Untitled
1999
Murano glass,
8 × 9.5 cm
8 × 11 cm
8 × 10 cm
Galleria d'Arte Emilio Mazzoli, Modena

In his painstaking and rarefied photographic works, which sometimes propose the theme of the still life with extreme refinement and in a hyper-contemporary key, Carlo Benvenuto often creates little contradictions, unlikely and paradoxical situations. These are inconsistencies that are difficult to notice, concealed, barely hinted at: a table poised on four fountain-pen tops, a drinking glass standing well beyond the edge of a table, vessels in which water does not obey the laws of gravity. Thus the absolute perfection of the compositions comes into conflict with their absurdity, creating a short circuit between beauty and logic. In *Glassway*, in the Room of Water, the artist presents one of his paradoxes in the form of a sculpture. Three geometric volumes are shaped exactly like drinking glasses. They seem to be filled to the brim with water, and the liquid about to overflow. In reality, they are three solid blocks of glass that only look as if they were filled with water.

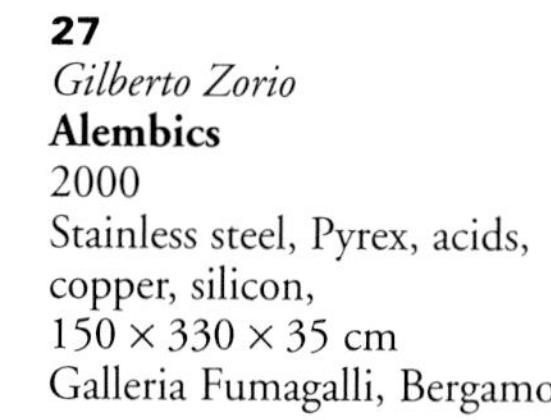

27
Gilberto Zorio
Alembics
2000
Stainless steel, Pyrex, acids, copper, silicon,
150 × 330 × 35 cm
Galleria Fumagalli, Bergamo

Oxides, copper and alembics are often to be found in the work of Gilberto Zorio. The artist has moved on from Arte Povera, a movement in which he played a leading role, to recovering and emphasizing the alchemical and esoteric values of matter. His continual effort to capture traces of the presence of static energy in the environment, his desire to turn his installations into living and pulsating presences (as in the case of

Dolphins), betrays a wish to lay bare and display the very soul of the elements, in an impulse that has as much art in it as alchemy. The work *Alembics*, placed in the Room of Water because the process of distillation is a central phase in the transformation of matter, suggests, in silence and with discretion, the presence of a moment of mutation in the exhibition.

28
Maurizio Camerani
Ocean
2002
Crystal, metal, monitor, video, water, live fish, 175 × 50 × 50 cm
Collection of the artist, Ferrara

Even before the affirmation of virtuality and the digital world, before movies like *Matrix* and *Nirvana*, Maurizio Camerani brought reality and make-believe together in his work, showing how it was possible to posit effects of entanglement, relationships of cause and effect between the two "environments." In some of his video sculptures – the artist was among the first in Italy to pursue this artistic and technological line of research with coherence and rigor – real and simulated space are mixed up, extending one into the other, reflecting one another without a break. In the sculpture *Ocean* – presented in the Room of Water because, notwithstanding appearances and the electronic instruments, it is in fact an aquarium – the universe in pixels is mixed up with that of reality, and the former ends up increasing twofold, or tenfold, the spaces of the latter. The screen of a monitor provides the base for this aquarium, in which a few fish swim, and shows the images of the sea, of waves, of an infinite and unimaginable expanse of water. The real element (the water in which the fish are swimming) merges with the one shown on the video, the submerged horizon seems to fade into the distance, while a small and enclosed place, a cage, appears to take on the grandeur and immensity of the ocean.

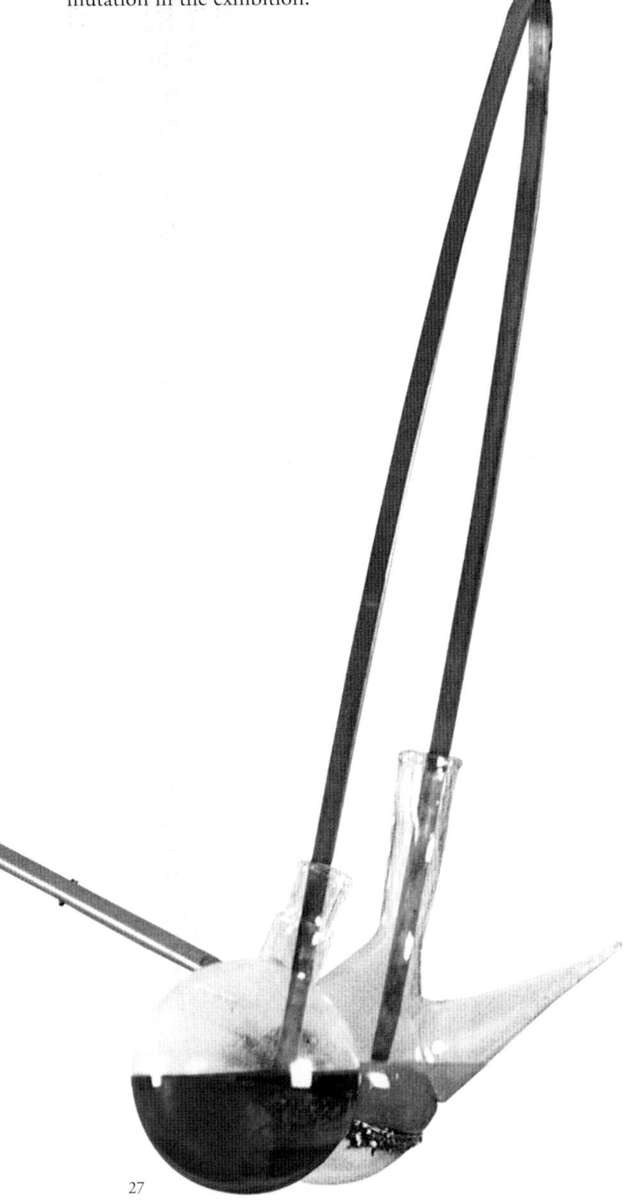
27

28

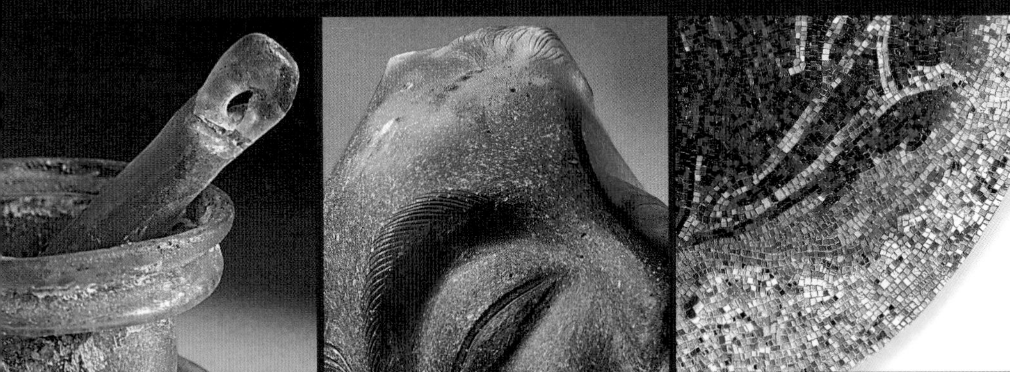

Room of the Body

ANCIENT GLASS

Since ancient times glass vessels have been used to hold medicinal substances, oils, unguents and perfumes. The latter in particular were greatly valued by the Romans, as Pliny tells us (*Naturalis Historia*, XIII, 4). In fact, perfumes were used by both sexes, in all sorts of social situations, from banquets to funerals and ritual leave-takings. The oldest types of container, such as the *alabastra* and the small multicoloured receptacles known as *amphoriskoi* (Milan and Aosta), were gradually replaced by precious products of the East, later imitated in the West, such as toilet bottles decorated with bands of gold and molded (Split). With the introduction of the technique of free blowing, these objects became very widespread: from Aosta come *unguentaria* of small dimensions, whose contents could be drawn out by means of little rods of twisted glass. Creams, powders and makeup for the eyes were contained in special jars with lids. There were numerous *pyxides*, "sack" bowls and small jars with wide mouths, also made out of mosaic glass and bands of gold. Over the course of the 3rd and 4th century AD, production diminished owing to changes in the economic situation and to the spread of Christianity, with a consequent shift in burial customs.

Visitors to the baths made use of special equipment, such as the *aryballoi* for unguents fitted with chains (Naples Museum) and the rare examples of strigils (Römisch-Germanisches Museum, Cologne), scrapers used to remove sweat, in imitation of the more common ones made out of metal.

The room also houses ornaments, the oldest of them made out of beads of glass paste, dating from the end of the 2nd millennium BC. The bracelets in monochrome glass paste from the collection of the Accademia of Sant'Anselmo and pendants and beads with characteristic "eye" decorations come from the Celtic and Celticized world.

CREATORS OF GLASS

Over the last millennium as well glass has been connected with the adornment and care of the body. Phials, for balsams, cosmetics and perfumes, triumphed in Bohemian Biedermeier glassware, which dominated the European market in the early 19th century. As far as ornaments are concerned, *veriselli*, coloured glass gems imitating precious stones, were produced in medieval Venice, and in the 15th century were joined by beads in colourless, coloured and polychrome glass, some made with the *millefiori* technique. From the 16th century onward, tiny beads, or *conterie*, and "rose" beads, made of concentric layers of glass, each with the profile of a star or rosette, were exported to the colonized countries, where they were used for barter with native peoples. The production of beads for the European market expanded in the 19th century, when flame-working reached its height. Toward the end of the same century the *conteria*, a bead made in the furnace by cutting thin and hollow canes of glass, was discovered by fashion, which used it in the embroidery of clothes. The type of *conterie* that remained popular for the longest time was the one known in the factory jargon as *pippi macà*, made from oblong black tubes with a polygonal section and as brilliant as cut gems. Dresses covered in their entirety with beads were highly fashionable in the 1920s, and then temporarily forgotten with the Great Depression. The *conteria* and the flame-worked glass bead were long the realm of tradition. Today creators of glass jewelry (Giorgio Vigna and Susanna Sent) are proposing exciting objects that sometimes go beyond the point of wearability to become works of art in their own right. Previously made out of metal, the glass mirror first appeared in the Renaissance and was manufactured chiefly in Venice, until France emerged as a worthy and formidable competitor in the 17th century. A favored item of furnishing in the 18th century, its reflections today attract the attentions of a number of designers and artists, such as Alessandro Diaz de Santillana.

CONTEMPORARY ART

"I am not afraid of ghosts. The living are frightening only because they have a body." So said Marguerite Yourcenar in *Feux*, and it is a belief shared by many contemporary artists, who in order to attract the attention of the public often choose direct and shocking images and languages, carved into the flesh or drawn onto the skin. To escape the anemic phantoms of the conceptual, these artists have for several years turned their interest, without limits nor censorship, to what is the most concrete and immediate part of the human being: the body. Returning once again, after the dazzling period of body art, to the conditionings of human physicality has been the great revolution of the research of the 1990s. If this has on the one hand looked back to the intimist lesson of some great artists of the 20th century who are now idolized, from Viola to Bourgeois, on the other it has been influenced by the innovations in genetics and the disconcerting revolutions of the virtual. *Blade Runner* and *The Fly* have been followed by *Nirvana* and *Matrix*, and Photoshop has acquired the same dignity in the world of art as oil and bronze. In recent times, the dramatic substantiality of blood, skin and guts has been supplemented by an epidermis made up of pixels, and internal organs created out of software. The human being has discovered a new dimension and new limbs, which really have very little to do with spatiotemporal coordinates and DNA. The most interesting artists have made these new frontiers their own and, returning to the body, have no longer focused on its weakness, on its potentialities and on its evident reality, but imagined instead new developments in the chain of evolution. By contrast, glass, for its apparent fragility, has been used by artists to give emphasis to the impermanence of the body, to underline the impossibility of the physical surviving in eternity, as is demonstrated by the sculptures/organs of Chen Zhen and the fragmented and broken eyes of Maria Luisa Tadei.

1

1
Alabastron
second half of 5th century BC
Core-formed,
h. 9.5 cm, ∅ of rim 2.9 cm; ∅ of belly 2.5 cm
Rivalta sul Mincio, Rodigo (Mantua)
Civiche Raccolte Archeologiche, Milan, inv. no. A.0.9.6731bis; MPA 2327
State of conservation: part of the rim is missing; small hole at the bottom along a crack. The end parts of the handles are incomplete

Opaque brown matrix, with opaque yellow thread applied on the rim; a second opaque yellow thread and an opaque turquoise-blue thread are wound in a spiral starting from the beginning of the neck, first with irregular horizontal lines, and then in zigzags to the bottom, where the two threads wind in horizontal lines to the centre of the bottom. Small handles of opaque brown glass. Lip and handles applied. Vertical grooves are visible on the body, left by the tool used to create the zigzag decoration. Broad, horizontal lip; short cylindrical neck, rounded shoulder. Cylindrical body, tapering slightly toward the top; flat bottom. Below the shoulder two handles with vertical rings and not very pronounced terminal appendices. Produced in the eastern Mediterranean (Rhodes?).
Bibliography: Caimi, 1874, p. 25; Mirabella Roberti, Tamassia, 1964, p. 18, no. 7, pl. 1; Tamassia, 1967, p. 365, fig. 2; Quattrocchi Pisano, 1977, p. 71, no. 2, pl. L, fig. 2; De Marinis, 1986, pp. 290, 296; Frontini, 1986, p. 236.
(from Roffia, 1993)

2
Amphoriskos
5th-4th century BC
Core-formed,
h. 8.4 cm, max. ∅ 5.7 cm, ∅ of rim 3 cm
From the Manetti Collection (no. 5454)
Deposito della Sovrintendenza, Aosta Valley Autonomous Region, Aosta
State of conservation: reassembled in the lower part

Amphoriskos in blue glass paste with an ovoid body, short neck and expanded funnel-shaped rim, trimmed in turquoise and yellow. Curved handles based on the shoulder and fused to the seam of the neck, small foot with button tip, striped in yellow and turquoise. On the body, decoration with a pattern of plumes, in yellow and turquoise, bounded by irregular concentric rings in the same colours.
Toilet bottles with thread decorations became very common in the Mediterranean area from the second half of the 7th century BC, with the more archaic forms of the Egyptian tradition. The specimen in the Aosta collection, of unknown provenance, is a later model that imitates the forms of Greek pottery and is undoubtedly of eastern origin.
Bibliography: Harden, 1981, pl. XI, 182-4, pl. XII, 201 and 204 (Mediterranean Group I).
(R.M.)

3
Biconical toilet bottle
mid-1st century BC - early 1st century AD
Polychrome marbled glass with gilding, mosaic technique,
h. 6 cm, width 5.8 cm, ∅ of brim 2.1 cm
From Solin, 1884
Arheološki Muzej, Split, inv. no. G 87
State of conservation: rim very slightly damaged

Small polychrome, bottle-shaped *unguentarium* with biconical body. The regular cylindrical neck rises from the marked shoulder. Slightly inclined and horizontally flattened rim. Two circles in relief on the flat bottom, in addition to those on the body and shoulder. Vertical stripes of colour: blue, yellow, green, amber-brown and gold band.
Typological comparisons: *Glass from the Ancient*, 1957, pp. 87-9, no. 145; Isings, 1957, form 7; Calvi, 1968, group B; Baume, 1978, 145, pl. 52:2; *Constable Maxwell*, 1979, p. 26; Goldstein, 1979, pp. 203-4, nos. 556-7; Meconcelli Notarianni, 1979, p. 120; Grose, 1984, p. 33; Harden, 1988, p. 41, no. 17.
Bibliography: Saldern, 1964, 42, no. 1.
(I.F.)

2

3

4
Pyxis
1st century AD
Mosaic glass,
h. 6.7 cm; ∅ of mouth 5.9 cm
From Pompeii
Deposito archeologico, Pompeii, inv. no. 10639,
State of conservation: reassembled

Pyxis in "gold-band" and polychrome glass with lid. The body is cylindrical with a flat bottom. The rim is turned inward to permit insertion of the lid with a small central knob. The object, of remarkable quality, was used to hold cosmetics, medicinal unguents and perhaps small toilet articles. This type of container, of which only six examples have been found, one of them in the Museo Archeologico of Naples and also from Pompeii, was probably made in the workshops of the important centre of Aquileia. *Pyxides* in deep blue glass, ivory and bronze have also been found in the area of Vesuvius.
Typological comparisons: Calvi, 1968, p. 95, no. 241, pl. 10, no. 1; *Collezioni Napoli*, 1986, p. 221, no. 16.
(E.D.C.)

5
Pyxis
first half of 1st century AD
Container shaped on mold; free-blown lid
Container: h. 5.8 cm, ∅ 9.3 cm; lid: h. 0.8 cm, ∅ 10 cm
Museu d'Arqueologia de Catalunya, Barcelona, inv. no. N.I.G. 7067
State of conservation: good

Hemispherical container with straight walls. The rim, an extension of the body, is vertical and polished, while the convex base has a marked central depression. A line in relief in the form of a groove is visible in the central part of the body. Made out of green and amber paste, its surface is polished and shows a certain amount of wear and iridescence. The lid has a concave surface and the rim is turned downward and inward. Made out of greenish-blue paste, it has a work surface with a marked iridescence. Lids of this type, very common, usually have painted decorations on the outer surface, although there are plenty of examples with no decoration, like this one. It comes indisputably from Cypress.
The two pieces, catalogued as a pyxis, differ in both their technique of manufacture and the paste used: they must have been associated in ancient times.
Typological comparisons: Vessberg, 1952, pl. III, no. 17; Saldern *et al.*, 1974, no. 246; Hayes, 1975, no. 42; Grose, 1989, no. 247; Kunina, 1997, no. 182, p. 291; Whitehouse, 1997, no. 356, p. 204; Israeli *et al.*, 2001, no. 498.
Bibliography: Vessberg, 1952, pp. 109-65; Saldern *et al.*, 1974, p. 94; Hayes, 1975, p. 18, fig. 1, pl. 3; Grose, 1989, p. 268; Kunina, 1997, p. 291; Whitehouse, 1997, p. 204; Israeli *et al.*, 2001, p. 338.
(T.C.R.)

4

5

6
Toilet bottle in the shape of an amphora
first half of 1st century AD
Blown glass,
h. 12 cm; max. Ø 3.1 cm,
Ø of rim 1.9 cm
From western necropolis (Cantiere Zurzolo) T.14, Aosta
Deposito della Sovrintendenza, Aosta Valley Autonomous Region, Aosta, cod. lab. 03-383
State of conservation: reassembled and integrated, rim chipped

Toilet bottle in thin amber-yellow glass, elongated body with a continuous profile ending in a solid tip; cylindrical neck, everted and cut rim. *Amphoriskos*-shaped *unguentaria* were widespread in the East and West (Biaggio Simona, p. 139), especially in the version with no handles, in various colourings. The diversity of form (Roffia, p. 101) among the examples known indicates a multiplicity of workshops producing this type of vessel, thought to have been used as a toilet bottle owing to its small dimensions, which was common in the grave goods of the 1st century AD.
Typological comparisons: Isings, 9; De Tommaso, 26.
Bibliography: Isings, 1957, p. 25; Calvi, 1968, group B, type Beta, pp. 24-6, nos. 12-3; De Tommaso, 1990, p. 55; Biaggio Simona, 1991, 8.1.6, pp. 138-9.
(P.F. - R.M.)

7
Toilet bottle
1st century AD (79 AD)
Blown glass, handles made separately and applied,
h. 9.1 cm; Ø of belly 4.8 cm; Ø of rim 2.3 cm
Room 15, Villa B, Excavations of *Oplontis*
Magazzino Archeologico, Excavations of *Oplontis*, inv. no. 73288
State of conservation: whole

Toilet bottle in blue glass with ovoid body and flat bottom. Cylindrical neck flared at the mouth, with slightly thickened and distinct rim. Slender tubular handles, set asymmetrically on the neck and shoulder. The small vessel contains residues of a substance that was presumably an unguent. The contents of this, as well as other glass *unguentaria* from Oplontis, are being studied by Professors Baraldi and Ferioli, from the departments of Chemistry and Pharmacology of the Universities of Modena and Reggio Emilia respectively. The container, similar in shape to an amphora but whose size makes it more likely to have been a toilet bottle, belongs to a type of glassware whose production commenced in the early decades of the 1st century AD and continued until the middle of the 2nd century AD. The articles produced varied in quality, as well as in the form of the belly and handles.
Typological comparisons: comparable to the Calvi type, group A, no. 2.
Bibliography: Calvi, 1968, pp. 24-5.
(L.F.)

6

7

8
Ovoid toilet bottle
end of 1st century AD
Blown glass,
h. 8.4 cm, max. ∅ 4.6 cm
From T. 9, predial necropolis of Saint-Martin-de-Corléans, Aosta
Deposito della Sovrintendenza, Aosta Valley Autonomous Region, Aosta, cod. lab. 03-1354
State of conservation: whole, incrustations

Toilet bottle in thin, pale-blue, transparent glass, with sparse bubbles. Ovoid body that extends into a small, conical, cut appendix. The production of this unusual disposable vial, as is evident from the broken-off end, is unambiguously linked with that of the dove-shaped containers, also made in versions of great elegance in their form and the coloration of the glass. While the specimen from Aosta recalls the two finds made at the necropolis of Muralto (Canton Ticino), it differs in date and type of glass. This peculiar object, almost instinctive in its conception, could be seen as concrete evidence in support of the possibility of a local production in the region.
Typological comparisons: Biaggio Simona, 1991, pp. 129-30, pl. 15, fig. 56.
(P.F.)

9
Toilet bottle
1st century AD
Blown glass,
h. 7 cm; ∅ of mouth 2.3 cm
From Pompeii (I, 16, 3)
Deposito archeologico, Pompeii, inv. no. 11903
State of conservation: whole

Toilet bottle with flat rim, short cylindrical neck, short shoulder and globular body. The bottom has three small feet turned outward. Containers of this type, known in several examples of different proportions, are thought to have been made by workshops in the Campanian area and were used to hold cosmetics.
Typological comparisons: De Tommaso, 1990, type 25.
Bibliography: *Homo Faber*, 1999, p. 213, no. 280.
(E.D.C.)

8

9

10
Bottle with handle and double body (dilekythos)
second half of 1st - 2nd century AD
Transparent blue-green, mold-blown glass, with the two parts joined while hot; handle cast separately and applied,
h. 6.9 cm, width of body 6 cm, mouth 3.5 × 2.9 cm
Museo Civico Archeologico, Bologna
State of conservation: whole; strongly iridescent; widespread rust-coloured incrustations on the inner surface

Rounded rim, bent slightly inward; very short concave neck; cubic body, with slight depressions at the centre of the four sides; small, ribbed strap handle, running from neck to shoulder; concave bottom. A vertical glass wall divides the bottle into two parts of different sizes. The bottle is an example of a particularly rare type in the Roman production of glassware, characterized by the presence of one or even two partitions inside the body of the vase, whose function remains doubtful. Bottles with double or triple bodies of different shapes can be found in the Constable-Maxwell and Löffler collections of the Römisch-Germanisches Museum in Cologne, in the museums of Strasbourg, Avignon and Reims, at the Louvre and in the Berlin Museum, with one specimen that may come from western Anatolia. However, the closest parallel for the Bolognese piece is provided by a bottle in the Museo Vetrario on Murano and found in the necropolis of Zadar, which has been attributed to a western, perhaps northern Italian workshop, probably located in Aquileia.
Typological comparisons: Calvi, 1968, pp. 75-6; Berlin, 1976, p. 71, no. 138; London, 1979, p. 125, no. 218; Lucerne, 1981, p. 98, no. 363; Arveiller-Dulong, Arveiller, 1985, pp. 54-5, no. 70; London, 1987, p. 21, no. 33; Ravagnan, 1994, p. 135, no. 255.
Bibliography: Bologna, 1959, p. 38, no. 99; Meconcelli Notarianni, 1979, p. 64, no. 56; Bologna, 1999, p. 47, no. 183.
(M.M.)

11
Aryballos with bronze chains
1st century AD
Deep-blue and very thick blown glass, bronze,
h. 10.6 cm, ∅ of rim 4.2 cm
From R. VI, I.XVI, Pompeii
Deposito Museo Archeologico Nazionale, Naples, inv. no. 133293
State of conservation: whole

Slightly flattened bottom, depressed bulbous belly, short cylindrical neck. Fairly thick horizontal lip, flattened and folded inward. Four handles in the shape of stylized dolphins are symmetrically arranged at the base of the neck. Through each passes a ring of bronze, from which hangs a bronze chain with double links. The chains are hooked to a central ring from which run two more chains with the same linkage: one terminating in a larger ring, perhaps used for hanging, the other connected to a smaller ring to which yet another chain is attached. A small bronze stopper with a vertical knob made of small globes hangs from the latter. The example is particularly interesting owing to the presence of the four symmetrical handles with bronze chains and the system for hanging up and closing the vessel. Given the object's considerable weight, due to the thickness of the glass and its fairly large size, it was probably meant to be hung from another type of support (in addition to the usual metal ring), perhaps along with strigils and *paterae* for use at the baths, like the similar "bath sets" in bronze. Thus the presence of four handles would be explained by the practical need to make the object more stable by distributing the weight more evenly.
Typological comparisons: Isings, 61; Calvi, group A; Goethert-Polaschek, 135; De Tommaso, 10.
(C.Z.)

10

11

12

12
Aryballos with one handle
second half of 1st century - 2nd century AD
Heavy green-blue blown glass,
h. 11.1 cm, Ø of body 9.4 cm
Antiquarium Comunale, Rome, inv. no. 242
State of conservation: whole

The *aryballos* has a spherical body, squashed at the top, while the mouth is very narrow and has a lip with a spout; the raised handle runs from the shoulder to the rear part of the mouth. The body can be compared with that of the Isings 61 form of *aryballoi* while the mouth appears similar to the Isings 65b form.
Typological comparisons: Isings, 1957, pp. 78-81.
Bibliography: Martini 1990, p. 132, no. 127, fig. 30.
(C.M.)

13
Two glass strigils
c. 200 AD
Blown glass,
l. 14 cm and 20.5 cm
From a Roman tomb in Cologne
Römisch-Germanisches Museum, Cologne, inv. nos. Glas 920 and N 6050.
State of conservation: specimen 920: grip broken; the glass was twisted alternatively in two directions. N 6050: intact; end part with eyes, partly broken

Two hollow scrapers with added piece of twisted, solid, transparent glass, forming the grip. Both these objects in glass are rare pieces and are models of those made out of metal. The imitation includes eyes for hanging them up. They are too fragile to have been of any practical use and must therefore have been "collector's pieces." Strigils made out of bronze were used by athletes in competitions. Wrestlers, in particular, used to grease themselves with oil before the match, to prevent their opponents from getting a good grip. The instrument was used to scrape off the mixture of oil and dust after the match.
Typological comparisons: Fremersdorf, 1939b, p. 21, note 4; Fremersdorf, Polóny Fremersdorf, 1984, p. 111, no. 249; Follmann-Schulz, 1992, p. 94, no. 55.
Bibliography: Fremersdorf, 1939b, pl. 10.1, pp. 21 *et sqq.*, pl. 10.1; Fremersdorf, 1961, p. 37, pl. 50; Doppelfeld, 1966, p. 44, pl. 42; Fremersdorf, Polóny Fremersdorf, 1984, p. 111, no. 248, p. 112, no. 250.
(H.G.)

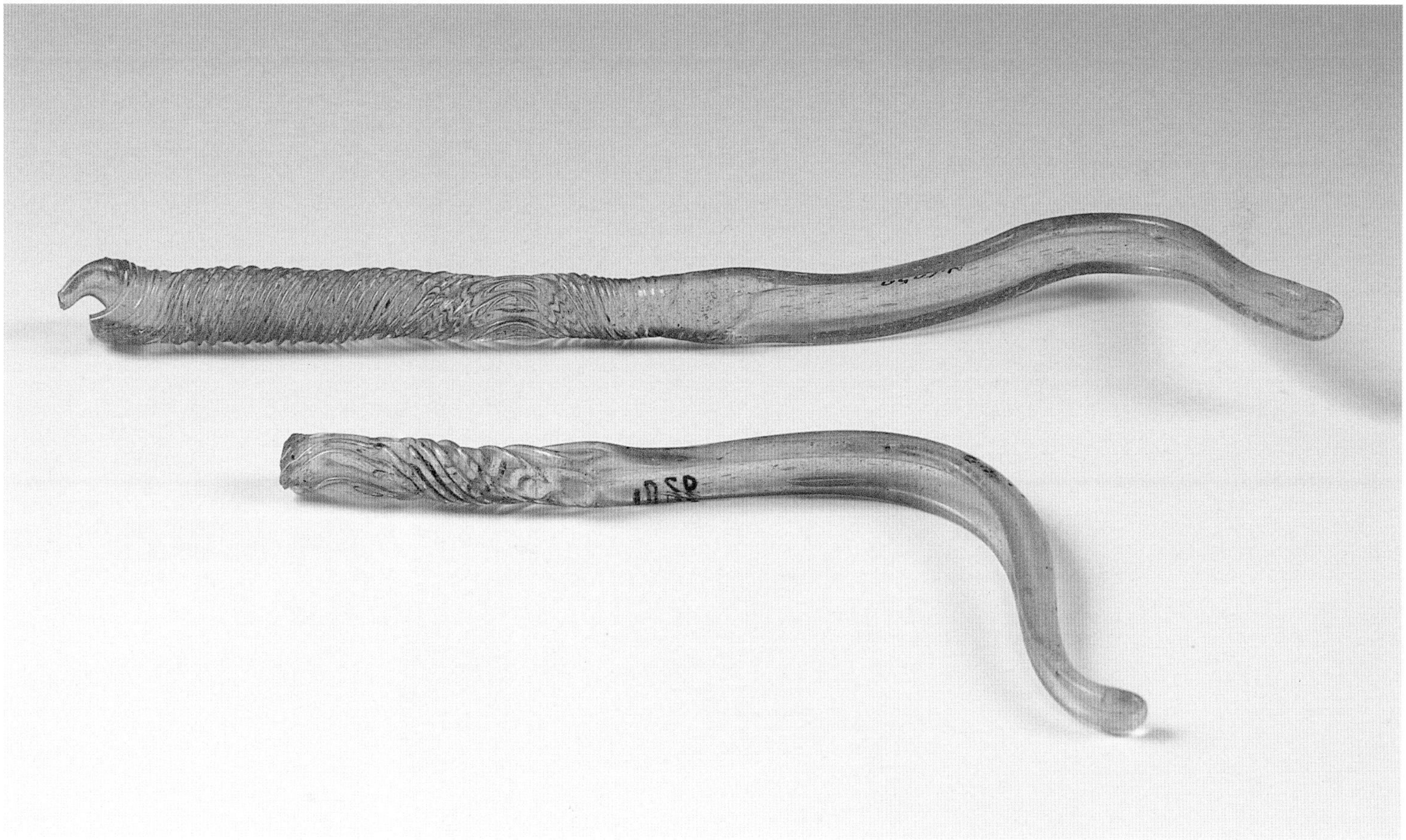

13

14

15

14
Toilet bottle
first half of 2nd century AD
Dark-green glass blown into a silver mesh,
h. cm 12.4; max. ∅ 7.5 cm
From Giarello, Strevi, 1974
Museo di Antichità, Turin, inv. no. 83245
State of conservation: incomplete

Ovoid toilet bottle blown into a silver mesh, with applied rim, collar and small foot, also made of silver. The object is exceptional for its unusual and extremely refined method of decoration, in which the semi-molten glass was enclosed in a net and then blown, as is apparent from the rather irregular meshes, in the shape of a *pelta*, which are more open at the point of maximum expansion of the body. The application of the rim, collar and foot, made out of small bars of silver, also served to cover up the points where the imperfections were most evident.
The container was found in 1974 during a limited archeological investigation following the uncovering of remains thought to be part of the paving of the Via Aemilia Scauri. It was among the grave goods deposited in the niches of a small burial chamber, which also included two iron strigils, an Isings 45 dish of whitish glass (cf. Biaggio Simona, 1991, 139.2.032), an Isings 56b glass jug (cf. Biaggio Simona, 1991, 139.1.041) and a coin from Hadrian's reign. On the basis of these data it can be dated to sometime before the middle of the 2nd century AD.
(E.Z.)

15
Small head-shaped bottle
second half of the 2nd-3rd century AD
Mold-blown green glass,
h. 9.5 cm, thickness 5 cm,
∅ of rim 3.6 cm
Solin
Arheološki Muzej, Split, inv. no. Mussale G 1044
State of conservation: whole

Small *unguentarium* with a spherical, head-shaped body and a cylindrical neck ending in a rim that is irregularly everted and folded back in a cord. On opposite sides of the pot-bellied body two figures of youthful appearance are executed in relief. The expression of the eyes, the nose and the mouth on the chubby faces is natural. A dense sequence of small circles in relief suggests a head of frizzy hair. A mark in relief is barely visible on the flat bottom, probably the letter omega.
Typological comparisons: Morin-Jean, 1922-23, form 120; Marconi, 1932, p. 41; Sunkovski, 1956, fig. 31A; *Glass from the Ancient*, 1957, pp. 140-7, nos. 279-94; Isings, 1957, form 78b; *Trois millénaires* 1958, pp. 64-5, no. 96; Doppelfeld, 1966, group 2.43, figs. 16, 17, 44, 47; Mariacher, 1966, p. 21; Calvi, 1968, pl. 16.6; Dusenbery, 1971, pp. 16-7; Yacoub, 1971-72, pp. 49-50, fig. 38; Hayes, 1975, no. 94; Auth, 1976, pp. 74-75; Petru, 1976, p. 25; Goethert-Polaschek, 1977, form 158; Foy, 1977-80, p. 212, fig. 76.4; Baume, 1978, cc. 13, 14; *Constable Maxwell*, 1979, pp. 65, 71-73; Randsborg, 1985, p. 428; Scatozza Horicht, 1986, form 33; Curina, 1993, p. 170; Roffia, 1993, p. 45; Ravagnan, 1994, p. 51, nos. 64-5; Sennequier, 1994, p. 61.
(I.F.)

16
Candlestick unguentarium
2nd century AD
Free-blown glass,
h. 12.8 cm, ∅ of rim 4.5 cm, ∅ of bottom 7.5 cm
Museo Nazionale G.A. Sanna, Sassari, inv. no. 3760
State of conservation: whole; calcareous incrustations on the surfaces

Limpid, pale-green glass of thin thickness. Conical body on which is set a cylindrical neck; small broad rim, flattened internally; slightly concave bottom. What are known as "candlestick" *unguentaria* are found over large parts of the Romanized regions from the Flavian era onward, reaching their maximum diffusion between the 2nd and 3rd century AD (Maccabruni, 1983, pp. 151-2). The form with a conical body and neck without costriction body is found throughout the Roman empire, with a particular concentration in Cyprus and in the basin of the eastern Mediterranean starting from the 2nd century AD (*Museo di Cagliari*, 1994, p. 55).
Typological comparisons: Isings 82 B2, p. 94.
Bibliography: Calvi, 1968, class C ß 2, p. 136 (pl. 22:4; pl. L:8); Goethert-Polaschek, 1977, no. 646, p. 118, pl. 53; Maccabruni, 1983, nos. 216-217, pp. 163-164; De Tommaso, 1990, type 35, p. 61; Bonomi, 1996, p. 80, no. 152 (second half of the 2nd century AD); Lissia, 2000, no. 29, pp. 33 and 44.
(D.L.)

17
Candlestick unguentarium
2nd century AD
Blown glass,
h. 18.8 cm, ∅ of base 11.3 cm, ∅ of rim 4.4 cm
From T. 387, western necropolis (former Hotel du Mont Blanc), Aosta
Deposito della Sovrintendenza, Aosta Valley Autonomous Region, Aosta, cod. lab 03-1481
State of conservation: pieces missing from the body

Example in pale-green, transparent glass, with sparse and tiny bubbles. Thin, squashed, conical body, long neck toward the top with marked constriction at the base; expanded, irregularly rounded and flattened rim; markedly concave bottom. Represents a type not very common in northern Italy. Its overall characteristics suggest it is of eastern origin, raising once again the problem of the imitation of forms coming from that area. It shows specific parallels with an example from Tipasa.
Typological comparisons: Isings, 82 A 2 var.; De Tommaso, 49.
Bibliography: Isings, 1957, pp. 97-9; Lancel, 1967, no. 137; Calvi, 1968, nos. 274, 282; Sena Chiesa, 1979, tb. 18, pp. 37-9, no. 5; De Tommaso, 1990, p. 71.
(P.F.)

16

17

18
Squashed conical unguentarium
2nd century AD
Milky-yellow, free-blown glass,
h. of surviving part 5.7 cm, thickness 5.8 cm
From Bakar
Arheološki Muzej, Zagreb, inv. no. 14625
State of conservation: upper part missing, cracked neck

Toilet bottle with a squashed conical body and cylindrical neck. The rim has not been preserved. Passage from body to neck accentuated by constriction; thickened walls. Mark PATRIMONI stamped on the bottom.
Typological comparisons: Morin-Jean, 1922-23, forms 20-5; Frova, 1971, pp. 38-44; Hayes, 1975, nos. 165-6; Paškvalin, 1976, p. 130, no. 2; Goethert-Polaschek, 1977, form 74; Fadić, 1986, form 29, no. 111; Barkóczi, 1988, p. 261; Fadić, 1988, p. 35; Fadić, 1989, pp. 36-7, no. 111; Paffgen, 1989, p. 20, fig. 2.10; Ceselin, 1996, nos. 10-15.
(I.F.)

18

19
Barrel-flask
c. 200 AD
Mold-blown glass,
l. 16.5 cm
From tomb 545, Roman necropolis on the Severinstrasse, Cologne
Römisch-Germanisches Museum, Cologne,
inv. nos. 53, 78
State of conservation: made up of fragments; originally in colourless and transparent glass, now opaque. Slight iridescences

Unguentarium of colourless glass in the shape of a barrel. The small container, resembling a double cone, rests on four small feet. The circles of the cask are suggested by threads of opaque-white glass that ring the body and start from the ends of the cask. The spout has a mouth of opaque-white glass that is flanked by two small handles in the shape of dolphins. The models for these glass objects were the very tall wooden barrels used to transport wine from the area of the Moselle to the Roman cities and the military posts along the Rhine.
Typological comparisons: Fremersdorf, 1959, 68 f. pl. 97-9; Doppelfeld, 1966, p. 116, no. 263.
Bibliography: Poppelreuter, 1906, p. 371, fig. 8d; Fremersdorf, 1955, pp. 117 *et sqq.*, pl. 29.2, p. 121, fig. 3; Fremersdorf, 1959, p. 68, pl. 96; Fremersdorf, 1961, p. 32, pl. 35; Doppelfeld, 1966, pl. 109.
(H.G.)

19

20
Flask
2nd-3rd century AD
Mold-blown glass,
h. 9.5 cm, ∅ of rim 4.8 cm,
∅ of body 6.3 cm
The National Museum of History of Ukraine, Kiev,
inv. no. 6676
State of conservation: surface covered with patina; fissures in the neck and body

Flask with a spherical body, decorated in relief with reticular ornaments. Everted, broad and flat lip. The cylindrical neck narrows slightly in the lower part, at the point where it is joined onto the body. The bottom is flat, with marks of the joints left by the mold. The glass is transparent, with bluish hues, and contains numerous bubbles.
These containers, like the *unguentaria*, were used to hold incense and aromatic substances. Similar flasks from the northern Pricernomor'ja region are to be found in the Archeological Museum of Odessa. Containers of this kind were also produced in Syria.
Typological comparisons: Sorokina, 1978, p. 273, pl. 3.19.
(P.O.A.)

21
Double toilet bottle
4th-5th century AD
Blown in air with application of threads,
h. 10.2 cm, width 5.6 cm, depth 2.5 cm
Museu d'Arqueologia de Catalunya, Barcelona,
inv. no. N.I.G. 17191
State of conservation: good

Lip flared, broad, sloping inward in the form of a double, back-to-back ring. The double tubular body narrows in the central part, the thick bottom is common to both receptacles, the base is flat and shows signs of the detachment of the blow pipe. Two broad elbow-shaped handles run from the upper part of the body to the edge of the lip and probably extended over the upper part to form a broad arch, of which only the attachment has survived. Made with paste of good quality, transparent, dense and moss-green in colour. The handles are cobalt blue with a slightly iridescent patina.
Containers of this type have been found in excavations that identify the Middle East as their zone of production, above all Syria and Palestine; their distribution, which increases over the course of time, is concentrated in the eastern Mediterranean, with only a few examples in the West. Double toilet bottle, also known as containers for kohl (powder used as a cosmetic for the eyes), were basically utilized to hold unguents and pigments, which were extracted by means of rods, or *osculatoria*, of bone, bronze or glass.
Typological comparisons: Kisa form A, 8, 9, 1; Arveiller-Dulong *et al.*, no. 96; Israeli, no. 349; Sternini, no. 409; Saldern *et al.*, no. 680; Isings, no. 16; Carreras I, 1.
Bibliography: Kisa, 1908; Isings, 1971, p. 66, no. 16, fig. 15; Saldern, 1974, pp. 231, 233; Sternini, 1990, p. 96, pl. 32, no. 194; Carreras Rossell, 1992, pp. 65-72, fig. 1; Arveiller-Dulong, 1996, p. 72; Israeli *et al.*, 2001.
(T.C.R.)

20

21

22
Mortar and pestle
1st century AD
Mortar: free-blown glass, h. 3.4 cm, ∅ 5.4 cm; pestle: double mold, l. 6.5 cm, width 1.4 cm
Museu d'Arqueologia de Catalunya, Barcelona, inv. no. N.I.G. 17205
State of conservation: good

Mortar: cylindrical body, flared mouth with a fold under the lip, whose rim is rounded and polished. The broad and flat base is ring shaped. Made from green paste with many bubbles. The slightly worn surface displays a faint iridescence. Pestle: in the shape of a truncated cone with rounded base, it has a hole in the other end. Made of greenish-yellow paste, the surface is slightly worn; faint iridescence.
These two pieces, associated as mortar and pestle, were made from different pastes and may have had independent origins. The shape of the pestle makes it suitable for pharmacological or cosmetic use, while the hole was probably used to hang it from a hook. The shape of the mortar is not the most common for this application, but any hypothesis remains uncertain given the scarcity of similar pieces.
Typological comparisons: Israeli, no. 136, for the container. There are no known comparisons for the pestle.
Bibliography: Israeli *et al.*, 2001, p. 120.
(T.C.R.)

23
Funnel
1st century AD
Mold-made glass, h. 3.3 cm, ∅ of body 2.5 cm
Northern Pricernomor'ja
From the V.P. Grin'kovskij Collection
The National Museum of History of Ukraine, Kiev, inv. no. 8402
State of conservation: surface covered with patina

Funnel with everted rim. The body is rounded and squashed, the neck narrow. Opaque glass, black in colour. These objects were used to pour liquids from one vessel to another. Funnels of transparent glass are well known in the northern Pricernomor'ja region. Found in the necropolis of Pantikapey, they were made in the craft workshops of the western provinces of the Roman Empire: they date from the second half of the 1st and the 2nd century. Objects made of opaque glass are characteristic of eastern Pricernomor'ja and are earlier in date. No other funnels of opaque glass have been found in the region of northern Pricernomor'ja.
Typological comparisons: Isings, 1957, form 74; Kunina, 1997, cat. nos. 384-5.
Bibliography: Puklina, 1997, pp. 62-5.
(P.O.A.)

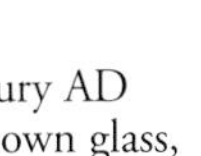

24
Bottle
1st century AD
Mold-blown glass, h. 13.4 cm, width 8.5 cm, ∅ 5 cm
From building with *triclinia*, Murecine (Pompeii)
Deposito archeologico, Pompeii, inv. no. 85200
State of conservation: whole

Bottle with flat and square bottom with four concentric circles, cubic body and flat walls. The neck is cylindrical. The handle is a strap folded to form an elbow, with a central hollow set vertically under the rim and on the shoulder. The rim is flat and everted. Bottles of this type, which belonged to table and dinner services, were used to hold and pour liquids. As they had constant dimensions, each double the size of the other, they were probably also used as measures of capacity.
Typological comparisons: Isings, 50.
Bibliography: *Homo Faber*, 1999, p. 245, nos. 302-8; *Miti, Sarni Opes*, 2000, p. 124, no. 13d.
(E.D.C.)

22

23

24

25
Mercury bottle
2nd century AD
Mold-blown glass,
h. 14.9 cm, l. of side 3.8 cm,
l. of bottom 3.4 cm,
∅ of rim 3.2 cm
From T. 89, western necropolis (former Hotel du Mont Blanc), Aosta
Deposito della Sovrintendenza, Aosta Valley Autonomous Region, Aosta, cod. lab. 03-1520
State of conservation: whole, except for missing part of rim, internal patina

Small bottle in pale-green, semitransparent glass, with bubbles and filaments. The body is prismatic and tapers slightly toward the bottom; the neck, which narrows toward the top, is embedded in the shoulder; broad rim, flattened to project inward and outward. On the bottom, four small feet at the corners and an illegible relief at the centre. Within the range for this kind of container, which seems to have been produced to hold a specific medication, the example is of medium size. The wide circulation of this type of bottle in the central and northern regions of Italy, Gaul and the Rhenish provinces, without any particular distinguishing features, makes it hard to identify areas of production. The foot with peduncles is comparable to that of an example from Cologne, but this differs in the conformation of the base of the neck and the shoulder. In Piedmont these objects have on several occasions been associated with unguentaria of Isings forms 82 and 83, which have also been found in Aosta. It has also been observed that finds of these small bottles are frequent in the vicinity of major lines of communication.
Typological comparisons: Isings 84.
Bibliography: Isings, 1957, p. 100; Taborelli, 1983 and 1999b; Fremersdorf, Polóny Fremersdorf, 1984, no. 145; Brecciaroli Taborelli, 1986, p. 54, pl. XIV, 2.2 (Susa); Filippi, 1987, p. 173, 2.2 (Cavour); Facchini, 1995b; Gabucci, 2000, p. 93, from dd. 33 and 57 (Biella).
(P.F.)

26
Mercury bottle
2nd century AD
Mold-blown glass,
h. 12.7 cm, l. of side 3 cm,
l. of bottom 2.5 cm,
∅ of rim 3 cm
From T. 72, western necropolis (former Hotel du Mont Blanc), Aosta
Deposito della Sovrintendenza, Aosta Valley Autonomous Region, Aosta, cod. lab. 03-1521
State of conservation: whole, except for missing part of rim, internal patina and evident streaks

Small bottle in colourless, semitransparent glass, with a few large bubbles. Prismatic body and long neck sunk into base; it narrows at the top, terminating in a broad rim, flattened so that it projects inward and outward, like that of the example in the previous section. In relief, on the base, four small feet at the corners and a fifth at the centre.
Typological comparisons: Isings 84.
Bibliography: see section 25.
(P.F.)

27
72 annular monochrome beads
12th-9th century BC
Probably wound around metal rod,
∅ 0.6 cm; thickness 0.3 cm
From settlement (surface find), Frattesina, Fratta Polesine
Museo dei Grandi Fiumi, Rovigo, inv. no. I.G. 272064
State of conservation: whole

Annular beads made of dark-blue glass paste. Despite their simplicity, these beads present technical and manufacturing characteristics that identify them as a specific production: translucent mixed-alkali or LMHK ("low magnesium high potassium") glass with colours obtained from copper in a pure state or associated with tin (from "aquamarine" blue to dark blue, or red); the technique of wrapping individual beads around a rod is recognizable from the thickening in the area of overlap, the short appendix left by the detachment from the thread of glass and finally the small dimensions. Thus they can be distinguished fairly easily from similar European examples made from HMG ("high magnesium glass"), typical of production in the Aegean and Near East during the 2nd millennium BC. Indications that the beads from Frattesina were locally made comes chiefly from evidence of glassworking (crucibles, probable bars of glass, cullet, etc.), also found, although in smaller quantities, at other contemporary sites in Veneto (Mariconda di Melara, Fondo Paviani, Montagnana, Caorle). The considerable number of products and cullet found in the settlement of Frattesina and the two related necropolises of Fondo Zanotto and Narde supports the hypothesis that Frattesina was, toward the end of the 2nd millennium BC, the first major centre for the production of glass in western Europe, perhaps inheriting the technological know-how (glass materials made from mixed alkalis) of the craftsmen working at least five hundred years earlier, at the beginning of the middle Bronze Age, in central and northern Italy.
Bibliography: Bietti Sestieri, 1981; Bellintani 1997; Henderson, Towle, Bellintani, Gambacurta, 2001; Angelici, 2002a and 2002b;
(P.B. - M.C.V.)

25

26

27

29

28
Bracelet in glass paste
second-third quarter of 2nd century BC
Cast glass, modeled and engraved while hot, h. 2.3 cm, max. ∅ 7.9 cm
From a tomb discovered in 1867 in the foothills to the north of the city of Aosta
Collection of the Accademia di Sant'Anselmo, Aosta
State of conservation: reassembled, slightly chipped at the rim

Bracelet in cobalt-blue glass, plano-convex in section, with five moldings on the outside. The broader median band is decorated with a continuous series of deep oblique grooves. The plastically molded bracelet, characteristic of the middle La Tène period, appears to have been uniformly spread in the Celticized zones of Central Europe, with greater concentrations in Bavaria and the territory of Switzerland. Bracelets of this type are constantly found among the grave goods of Swiss necropolises, especially in the region of Bern and the cantons of Vaud and Fribourg.
Similar examples in blue glass – a colour typical of the mid-La Tène – have been found in northern Italy, at Flero (Brescia) and Magenta.
Typological comparisons: Haevernick, group 8 C.
Bibliography: Laurent, 1868, pp. 9-14; Barocelli, 1923, pp. 93-4; Haevernick, 1960, p. 168; De Marinis, 1986b, pp. 128 *et sqq.*; Kaenel, Peyer, 1986, p. 118; Gebhard, 1989, pp. 102-4; Kaenel, 1990, pp. 246-8; Roffia, 1993, pp. 200-2, no. 405; Mollo Mezzena, 1994, pp. 150-3.
(R.M.)

28

29
Gems in glass paste
end of 1st century AD
Mold-made glass, decoration in relief, gems: h. 2 cm, width 1.5 cm (no. 1); h. 2 cm, width 1.5 cm (no. 2); h. 2.1 cm, width 1.7 cm (no. 3); plates, h. 1.9 cm, width 1 cm; h. 2 cm, width 1.5 cm; h. 2 cm, width 1.6 cm
From T. 9, predial necropolis of Saint-Martin-de-Corléans, Aosta
Deposito della Sovrintendenza, Aosta Valley Autonomous Region, Aosta, inv. nos. AO SM 34, 35; AO SM 36
State of conservation: whole

Three gems in translucent, blue-green glass paste, oval in shape, with a convex surface, representing *Venus Victrix*, and three thin plates of transparent glass, quadrangular in shape, with rounded corners.
The gems depict Venus nude from behind, standing with her right leg bent, her draped mantle covering part of the legs and falling under the arm. Her head in profile, tilted slightly forward, has the hair gathered at the nape. The outstretched right arm holds her helmet, while the left arm rests on a pillar and grips an oblique spear with the point downward. The object to the left of the pillar is probably a round shield. The iconographic theme, widespread in the Roman world, derives from a Hellenistic prototype reworked in Italy, as G. Sena Chiesa has already pointed out, and probably has the symbolic value of a political *signum*, a hypothesis supported by the frequent representation of Venus Victrix on the reverse of coins.
Originally the gems of glass paste – all reproducing the same subject – or *auro inclusae* were presumably set in the links of a necklace, mounted in bezels or inserted into a more refined gold ornament, as is suggested by the substantial traces of melted gold found among the carbonized remains of the *bustum*, or site of the funeral pyre.
The thin plates of glass must either have been used as backing for the gold mounting in order to maintain the transparency of the gems, or, as in the case of Saintes (Crew, 1988, no. 39), as jewels in their own right.
Typological comparisons: Sena Chiesa, 1966, nos. 248-62; Brandt, Krug, Gercke, Schmidt, 1972, nos. 3185-6; Maaskant-Kleibrink, 1978, nos. 529-35.
Bibliography: Mollo Mezzena, 1981; Mollo Mezzena, 1982; Crew, 1988, pp. 47-9, no. 39; Mollo Mezzena, 1997, p. 365, nos. 30-2.
(P.F. - R.M.)

30

31

30
Simon Gate
Engraved cup
1918
Blown and wheel-engraved crystal,
h. 14 cm
Kosta Boda AB, Orrefors
Orrefors Glasbruk, Orrefors
State of conservation: excellent

Cup in pure crystal engraved by wheel with nudes in classical style. It was one of the first works engraved at Orrefors to a design by Simon Gate, who often chose classical themes that were engraved in very clean and plastic lines on the walls of essential objects blown from colourless glass. These works marked the beginning of the golden age of Swedish engraving on glass.
Typological comparisons: *Svenskt Glas*, n.d., no. 29.

31
Perfume bottle
Bohemia, 1830-35
Cut Lithyalin glass,
h. 14 cm
Museum of Decorative Arts, Prague
State of conservation: excellent

Perfume vial in Lithyalin glass. Pyramid shape with cut facets, stopper in the form of a faceted pear. This is a genuine example of Lithyalin glass, created by cementing crystal cased in ruby glass onto a base of glass. Lithyalin glass, named after a semiprecious stone, was opaque with precious veins of colour. It was invented in 1828 by Friedrich Egermann, who patented it the following year. To make the first Lithyalin perfume bottles he used an opaque black, red or blue base manufactured by the Buquoy glassworks of Harrach. Later the base was also made out of coloured but transparent glass. The next stage consisted in cementing crystal onto the base under special conditions to produce a veined opaque material. The patent did not prove much use to Egermann as the glass was imitated by numerous workshops even before it ran out.

32
Evening gown
1920s-30s
Dress hand embroidered with black glass beads, h. 200 cm
Co Co Shop di Ceccolini Nicoletta Collection, Milan

33
Flavio Poli
"Modesty" Nude
IVAM, Murano, 1930-31
Solid, hot-modeled crystal
h. 28 cm
Civiche Raccolte d'Arte Applicata, Castello Sforzesco, Milan
State of conservation: excellent

Female nude in modest attitude, hot modeled from solid crystal and given an iridescent finish on base of black blown glass. It comes from the *Pudore* ("Modesty") collection made by Flavio Poli for the Milan Triennale of 1930, made up of female nudes in bashful poses. With this and earlier collections in 1929, Flavio Poli had the first nudes produced in solid glass on Murano, requiring the glassworkers to develop new techniques. The nudes of 1929 were for the most part bases of goblets or grips of the lids of urns and were not made from a single mass of glass: the limbs were modeled separately and then attached while hot to the torso. In the *Pudore* collection the figure assumed greater continuity and softness.
Typological comparisons: *Domus*, April 1930, pl. 1, no. 644; Felice, 1931, p. 320; Deboni, 1996, pp. 44-5.
Bibliography: Barovier Mentasti, 1982, fig. 273-5; Barovier Mentasti, 1992, fig. 80; Mori, 1996, p. 88; *Il vetro a Milano*, 1998, p. 174, no. 49.

32

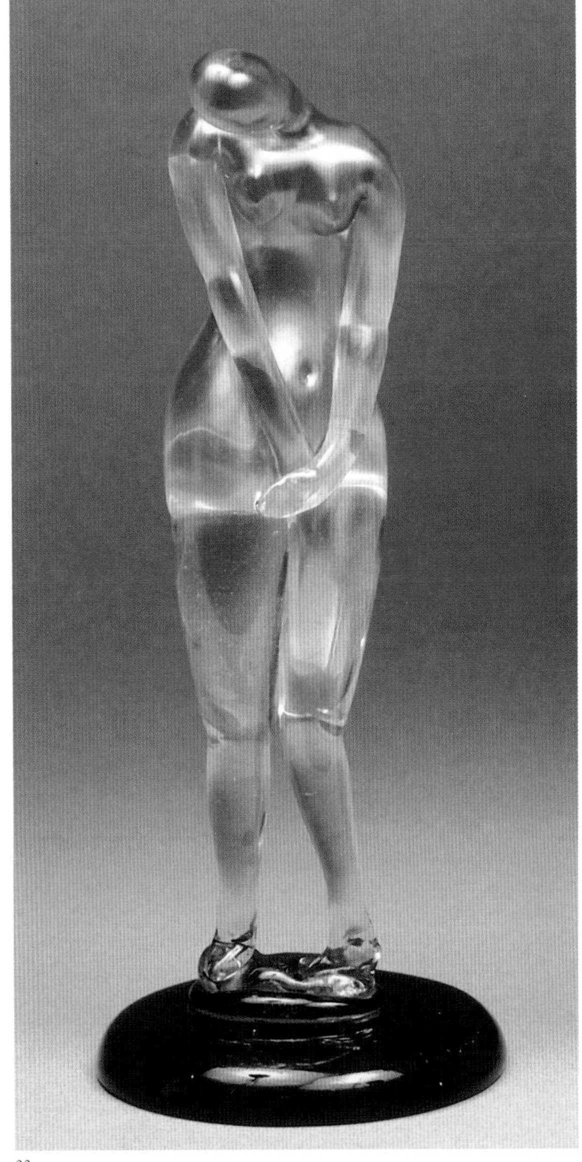

33

35
Piero Fornasetti
Mirror with a Woman
SALIR, Murano, 1940
Gilded and silvered mirror, engraved by wheel and diamond point,
h. 35 cm
SALIR Collection, Venice
State of conservation: excellent

Rectangular gilded and silvered mirror, engraved by wheel and diamond point. The decoration represents the veiled face of a woman, half concealed by two female hands with rings. One-off piece shown at the Milan Triennale of 1940.
In the same year Piero Fornasetti collaborated with the SALIR workshop on vases that were also exhibited at the Triennale and then brought into production.
Signature or mark: PIERO FORNASETTI.
Bibliography: *Fotografia Archivio Triennale*, vol. 7, no. 279; *Il vetro a Milano*, 1998, no. 87.

34

35

34
Piero Fornasetti
Vase of the Hands
SALIR, Murano, 1940
Blown glass decorated with polychrome enamels,
h. 32 cm
Gerard and William Figliola Collection, Turin
State of conservation: excellent

Vase in the shape of a truncated cone indented at the base, blown and modeled freehand in crystal and decorated around the wall with polychrome enamels. The decoration of yellow, red and black enamels consists of two hands in gloves and numerous butterflies.
Signature or mark: S.A.L.I.R.
Bibliography: Olivieri, 1940, no. 17, p. 577; *Domus* XIII, May 1940, no. 149, p. 51. Deboni, 1996, p. 54 (preparatory sketch); *Il vetro a Milano*, 1998, no. 88.

36

36
Erwin Walter Burger
Sieglinde
Erwin Walter Burger Cristalli d'Arte, 1951
Cut solid glass, h. 21.5 cm
Collection of the artist, Varese
State of conservation: excellent

Block of transparent green glass sculpted to represent the face of a sleeping woman. Some details (hair, eyebrows, eyelids, lips) are engraved. The surface is deliberately left rough to create a highly tactile effect.
Typological comparisons: *Italienisches Glas*, 1996, nos. 231-2; *Il vetro a Milano*, 1998, nos. 12-14.
Bibliography: *Il vetro a Milano*, 1998, no. 16.

37
Alfredo Barbini
Reclining Nude
Vetreria Alfredo Barbini, Murano, 1972
Solid, hot-modeled glass, width 28 cm
Collection of the artist, Murano

One-off sculpture: reclining, prone female nude, in solid, iridescent black glass.
The softness of the modeling is one of the characteristics of Barbini's work. A pupil of the Novecentista sculptor Napoleone Martinuzzi, he liked to tackle the theme of the nude in his sculpture. Even before the war he had produced nudes in crystal, and returned to the theme in the 1950s, showing a preference for dark, corroded or iridescent glass, or glass treated to create the impression it had been found in an excavation. He has gone back to the theme on many occasions up until very recent times.
Typological comparisons: Barovier Mentasti, 1992, fig. 100; *The Secret of Murano*, 1997, p. 32; Barovier Mentasti, 1998, p. 29.

37

38

39
Mats Jonasson
Magic Face
Målerås Glasbruk, 1989
Blown glass, with sand-blasted and engraved decoration,
h. 14 cm
Smålands Museum, Växjö

Crystal cup with the features of a face obtained by sand blasting and engraving. In this piece, the extraordinary Swedish art of engraving in the 20th century has been used to produce results very different from the classical Nordic tradition.
Signature or mark: Mats Jonasson Studio 1989 3/20 B. S.
Bibliography: *Svenskt Glass*, n.d., no. 93

40
Anne Nilsson
Vase
Orrefors Glasbruk, 1993
Blown glass, decorated with the Ariel technique,
h. 22.1 cm
Smålands Museum, Växjö

Black vase cased in crystal with the features of a face outlined between the two layers by the Ariel technique. This was a development of the Graal technique devised by the glassworker Gustav Berqvist in collaboration with the designers Edwin Öhrström and Vicke Linstrand in 1936. It consists in making deep cuts into blown glass of great thickness with a jet of sand and covering them quickly with another layer of transparent

38
Alfredo Barbini
Salinized Nude
Vetreria Alfredo Barbini, Murano, 1989
Solid, hot-modeled, sunk glass, salinized (excavation effect) on the surface,
h. 25 cm
Alfredo Barbini Srl, Murano

Female nude in gray sunk glass, iridescent on the inside, with a salinized outer layer of black glass. The body is cut in half vertically to reveal the glassy substance of the work and the successive layers in which it is sunk. Half the body is upright, the other half laid flat.
Typological comparisons: *The Secret of Murano*, 1997, p. 32.
Bibliography: Barovier Mentasti, 1992, fig. 176.

39

40

glass. Air is trapped where the glass has been cut away. *Signature or mark*: Orrefors 991978 Anne Nilsson EA 1-93 and the artist's signature. *Typological comparisons*: Orrefors Gallery, 1990, nos. 69-71 *Bibliography*: *Svenskt Glass*, n.d., no. 99.

41
Emmanuel Babled
Primaire XVI
Venini & C., Murano, 1999
Blown glass with applications, partially "beaten,"
h. 30 cm
Collection of the artist, Milan

Blown colourless glass with internal cavity in red glass and circular external applications of red glass with "beaten" surfaces (covered with ovoid incisions). Like other pieces in the *Primaire* collection, it is inspired by the internal organs of the body, by flesh and blood, but becomes an abstract form of absolute contemporaneity. *Bibliography*: *Primaire 9.9.99*, 1999, no. XVI.

42
Emmanuel Babled
Primaire X
Venini & C., Murano, 1999
Cased, blown and cut glass,
h. 50 cm
Collection of the artist, Milan

Red glass cased in smoked milky glass, blown and modeled into a soft and irregular form which recalls that of a human torso. Shaped with an extremely fine touch and enlivened by the internal colour, contrasting with the absolute sobriety of the surface, it is in reality an abstract form but, in the context of the collection to which it belongs, *Primaire*, is linked to the other works by the common theme of the body and its organs. But the theme is rendered aseptic and elegant in the fluidity of the profiles and the very contemporary choice of colours. The forms seem to echo the movement of incandescent glass and to embody its essence. *Bibliography*: *Primaire 9.9.99*, 1999, no. X.

41

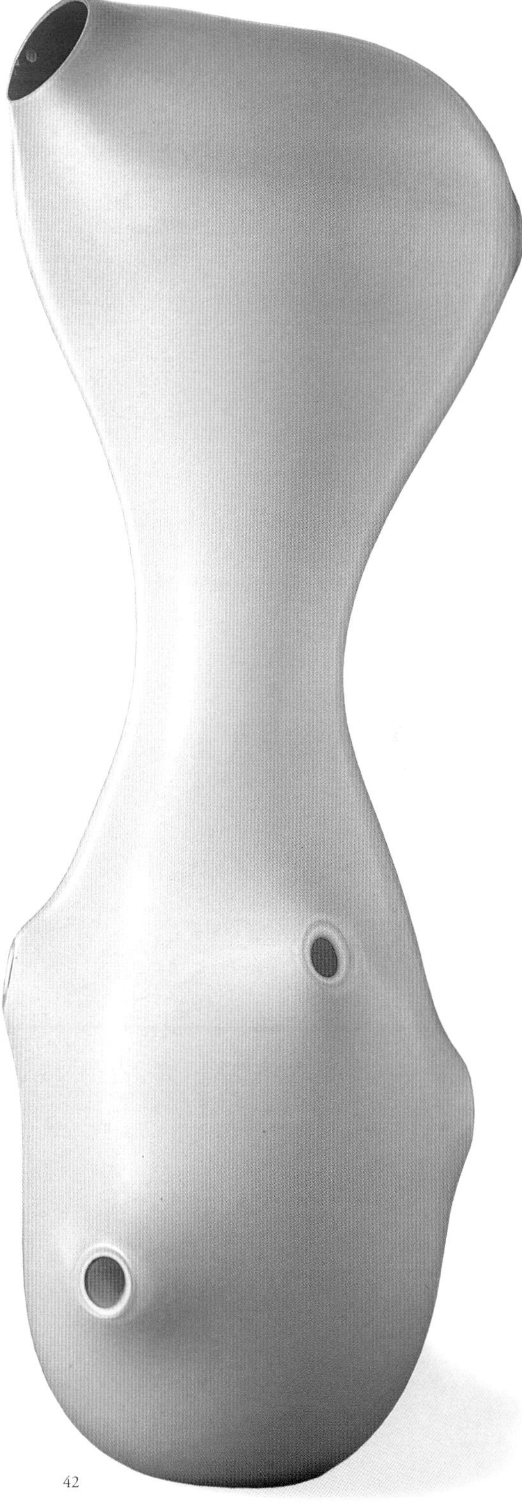

42

43
Alessandro Diaz de Santillana
Work No. 2
Venice, 2001
Flat coated glass and sheet of blown glass opened by hand with applications of gold leaf, h. 154 cm
Private collection

Wall sculpture made up of a sheet of coated glass and a sheet blown as a cylinder and opened by hand, with a gilded surface that creates a mirror effect. The artist plays with two different glass materials, one flat, the other characterized by movement and the imperfections of working by hand. The warm gilded surface reflects and transforms the light and colours of the surroundings, varying with variations in the atmosphere and interacting with the observer.
Typological comparisons: *Acciaio Arte Architettura*, 2001, no. 8

44
Marina and Susanna Sent
Soap
Sent Snc, Murano, 2002
Blown spheres of borosilicate glass
Collection of the artists

Large collar made up of blown spheres of various diameters assembled in such a way as to cover the whole of the neck. Owing to the impalpable lightness of the glass spheres, blown by mouth, and their perfect transparency, they cover the neck without concealing it and reflect the light with a highly suggestive effect. The work is a one-off piece but is accompanied by models produced in series that are equally light but less spectacular.

45
Marina and Susanna Sent
Holed
Sent Snc, Murano, 2002
Elements in cut and perforated glass, PVC thread
Collection of the artists

Elements in colourless crystal, cut and perforated by hand, linked by a thread of transparent PVC to form a bodice. Characterized by the brilliance of the glass and the irregularity of the lattice, this garment (is it wearable or not?) is the fruit of exceptionally audacious creativity. The clothes hanger is also made of cut crystal. The two artists have shown themselves to be equally innovative in other works made out of glass, such as the one shown at *Aperto Vetro* in 1998, a drape formed out of large, molded beads in autumnal colours.
Typological comparisons: *Aperto Vetro*, 1998, p. 124.

44

43

45

46
Giorgio Vigna
Gurgle
Murano, 2002
Bubbles in flame-blown glass and copper thread,
h. 34 cm
Collection of the artist

Necklace in bubbles of blown Murano glass of irregular dimensions and a transparent aquamarine colour, on copper thread. The one-off piece, which resembles foaming seawater, is an example of the boldness with which Giorgio Vigna tackles the themes on which he bases his jewelry. No deviation from the theme, no reduction to the lowest terms. It is out of experiments like this, which can be regarded as an installation on the body, that he develops his collections. The artist displays an astonishing ability to bring out the peculiarities of the materials with which he works, be they metal, glass or resin.

46

47
Giorgio Vigna
Aquaria
Murano, 2002
Hand-cut sheet of glass,
41 × 35 cm
Collection of the artist

Large bracelet-sculpture in transparent aquamarine glass, in the form of a perforated, slightly irregular disc, ground on the surface. The ethnic flavor of the work is lightened by contrast, thanks to the pale and brilliant colour and the translucent effect.

47

48
Chen Zhen
Crystal Landscape of Inner Body
2000
Crystal, iron, glass,
190 × 95 × 70 cm
Galleria Continua, San Gimignano

The last exhibition designed and staged by Chen Zhen before his death was the one-man show at the Galleria Continua in San Gimignano, over the winter of 2000 and 2001. On that occasion the artist, who died shortly afterward of a disease of the internal organs, perhaps not even diagnosed at the time, laid out a symbolic journey through the stages of existence, from birth to death, from the marriage bed of conception to the decay of the body, in the immense spaces of the gallery, formerly a cinema. Looking back, with an awareness of how the artist met his end, it is possible to identify *Crystal Landscape of Inner Body* as the pivot of that exhibition. It is a small ladder of crystal, slender and transparent, whose last rung leads to the top of a table, also made of crystal, on which are set sculptures made of the same material representing internal organs, from the stomach to the intestine to the liver. Everything speaks of the human body, of its extremely delicate equilibrium, of how very little it takes to shatter or destroy it.

49
Maria Luisa Tadei
Oculus Dei
2002
Enamel and glass mosaic,
Ø 190 cm; thickness 2 cm
Collection of the artist, Rimini

In tones of blue and azure, *Oculus Dei*, a gigantic round mosaic almost two metres in diameter, is the portrait of an eye. More precisely, the eye of its author, the young artist Maria Luisa Tadei from Romagna. In this case glass was chosen for its characteristics of refraction, brilliance and luminosity, capable of instilling in the work the sparkle and gleam that were needed to breathe life into the iris and pupil. As if in a figurative synecdoche, the part stands for the whole, and the eye reveals (or rather suggests) the presence of an enormous body concealed behind the wall from which the eyeball seems to be scrutinizing the observer. Tadei has often exploited the characteristics of materials to evoke the real or presumed physicality of parts of the body. She has used twisted pieces or lumps of metal to call to mind the weight and contorted shape of the brain, feathers to convey the grace and airy freedom of a female presence. Here glass, with its transparencies and its blurred and vibrant hues, has been entrusted with the task of simulating vision, and with vision, the movement of the world.

48

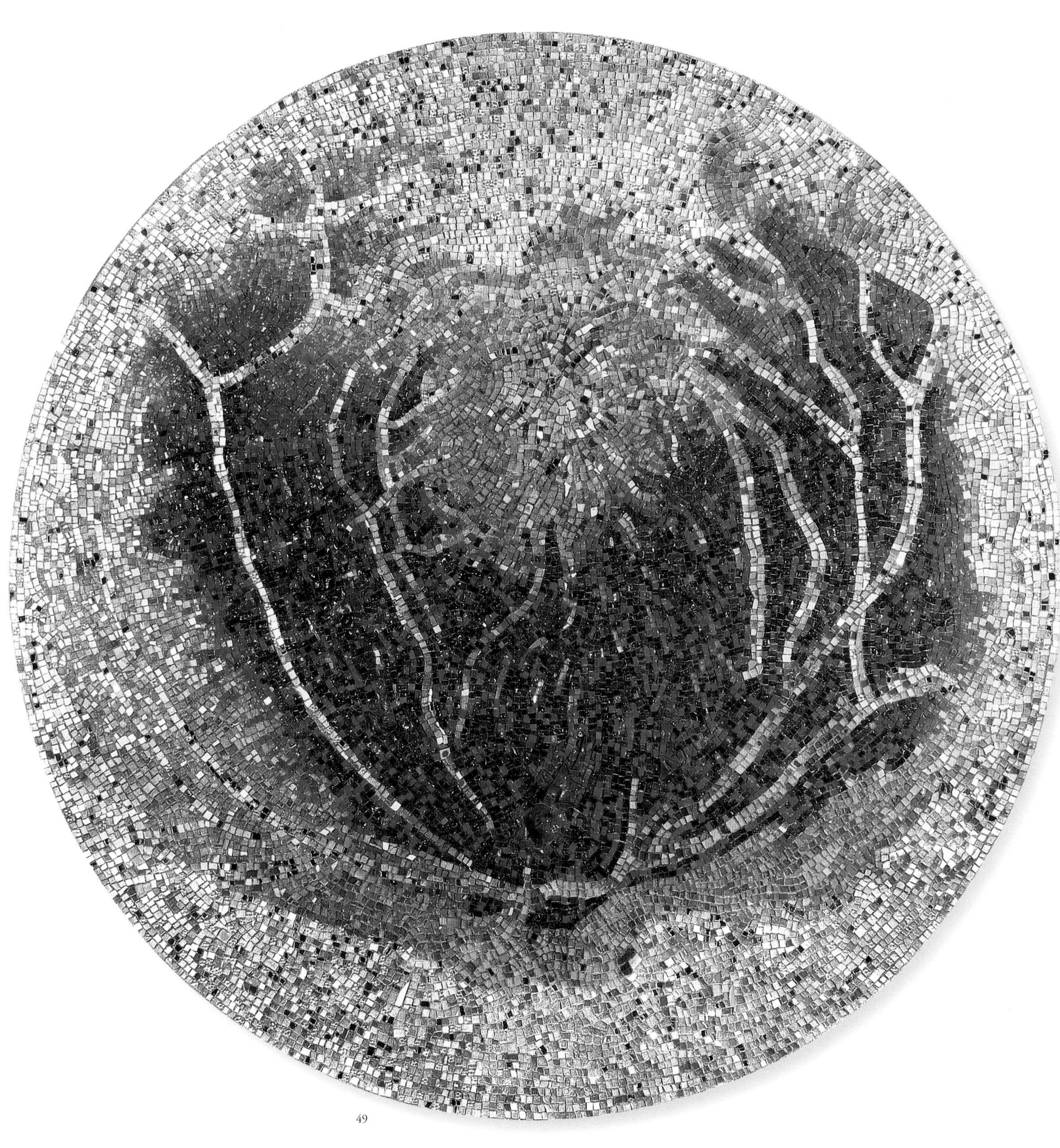

49

IV.

Room of the Orient

ANCIENT GLASS

It was in the East that glass was born and the objects made out of this material were always to retain a character of great refinement in this part of the world, associated with a constant effort to introduce new techniques and processes. This section presents a number of elegant forms, pressed in molds and finished on the grinding wheel, that were among the first to be distributed and marketed on a fairly wide scale. The new technique of mold blowing also arrived from the area of the eastern Mediterranean. Articles made by this process in northern Italy document the activity of the Syrian Ennion, a rare case of a *vitrarius* who signed his creations: not just his famous cups, but also his ewers and *amphoriskoi*, stand out for the skill and refinement of their decorations.
Over the course of the 1st century AD highly sophisticated monochrome vases were produced in imitation of metal models. These were either pressed in a mold, engraved and finished on the wheel (*skyphos* from Adria), or blown like another blue cup, the *modiolus* from Verona.
Made out of so-called cameo glass, created by a complex process in which several layers were built up and then cut away, the *patera* in the Museo Archeologico of Naples attests to the widespread appreciation of Alexandrine products and of a decorative repertoire of Hellenistic origin. Types of vessel used to meet everyday needs were also produced in the regions of the eastern Mediterranean, such as the cylindrical bottles with one handle, probably made on Cypress, from Kiev. The precious Islamic bowl in violet glass with applications of glass paste from the 12th-13th century AD, found in Padua, maintains a continuity with the oldest of Oriental traditions.

CREATORS OF GLASS

Glass may have come from the Orient, but the Far East – China and Japan – was not to discover the potential of the material until very late. The Chinese works of the 18th century, with essential forms derived from porcelain, are distinguished by their refined silky material, opaque but still clearly recognizable as glass. In the following century the objects were engraved with complex decorations in relief, although this sometimes marred the purity of the conception.
While in the Middle Ages it was Islamic culture that had the greatest influence on European glassware, over the centuries to come the European decorative arts would draw their ideas principally from the Far East. This can already be seen in the enamel decorations on glass of the 15th and 18th centuries, but is even more evident in the glassware of Japonisme, out of which Art Nouveau was born. In fact the Far East was a source of real innovation for French glassware, inducing it to make a break with the stylistic schemes of the past: simple but new and extremely harmonious forms, decorations inspired by nature but highly stylized, a perfect integration between structure and ornament.
Even later on references to the Orient continued to act as a call to return to an essentiality of structure and sobriety of colour. An example of this is provided by the Chinese vases designed for Venini in the 1930s by Carlo Scarpa, a lover of Eastern architecture and art.
Today there are a number of Japanese and Chinese artists of great interest working in glass, including Ritsue Mishima, Sunny Wang and above all Yoichi Ohira, whose extremely refined works represent at once the most demanding and the most successful synthesis of West and East.

CONTEMPORARY ART

First direction, from West to East. For the western artist, looking toward the Orient often means breaking the rules, digressing from the code, departing from a norm that everyone else respects. Aldo Mondino, for example, paints Turkish customs, Sufi mystics and Jewish rituals, but is neither an Orientalist nor a student of Sufism, nor even an observant and convinced Jew. He is not interested in transferring onto canvas something that others, be they few or many, might be thoroughly familiar with, or simply have seen on a package tour. His is always a fantastic reappraisal of places, people and events which may have attracted his attention and stirred his curiosity for just a few moments. The images that he paints are not like the frames of a documentary. Rather they are the intuitions of a creator who allows himself poetic license and dresses up in the costumes of the world in order to play a part in the great spectacle of life.
Second direction, from East to West. The globalization of culture has almost wiped out the echoes of localism that were often present in art. If you go to an international exhibition, it is increasingly difficult to guess the nationality of the artist just by looking at the work. The avant-garde art of Rumania, Japan, Argentina and the United States is disturbingly similar, and increasingly seems to adhere to codes imposed by the fashions of the moment, which are more or less the same everywhere. An exception to this is provided by the artists who moved to the West years ago from the Middle and Far East, and since then have continued to reflect on the relations between their culture of origin and their adoptive one. And while Hidetoshi Nagasawa seeks points of contact between the Zen garden and the Italian park, Medhat Shafik translates the legends and panoramas of his native land, Egypt, into western forms.

1
Hemispherical bowl
150-100 BC
Fused in mold. Colourless transparent and opaque yellow glass,
h. 7 cm, Ø of rim 13.3 cm
From tomb XLII, Ancona
Museo Archeologico Nazionale delle Marche, Ancona (depository), inv. no. 5288
State of conservation: reassembled with integrations on the rim; acquired patina in patches, with slight iridescences; traces of grinding

Hemispherical basin, with colourless bottom and polygonal inserts, the latter with yellow borders and an internal motif of the same colour in the form of a fairly irregular spiral. Rim rounded and indistinct, colourless and wrapped with two yellow threads.
Bibliography: Dall'Osso, 1915, p. 343; Mercando, 1976, p. 165, fig. 48; Colivicchi, 1999, p. 110, figs. 1 and 12 (the latter with comparisons and critical perspective).
(G.B.)

2
Ovoid bowl
late 2nd century BC
Fused in mold. Types of glass: opaque white, with small vacuoles on the surface; translucent blue, pale green and pale yellow, with small bubbles; colourless, transparent, with small bubbles; translucent violet. Gold leaf incorporated in the colourless elements,
h. 8.4 cm, Ø of rim 12.8 cm
From tomb XXXI, Ancona
Museo Archeologico Nazionale delle Marche, Ancona (depository), inv. no. 5140
State of conservation: reassembled with integrations; traces of grinding

Slightly ovoid basin with mosaic of varicoloured bands, with white threads applied in curves or spirals to the blue bands; there is no match between the internal and external colouring. Rim rounded and indistinct, formed from two canes, one white with blue windings and the other blue with white and yellow windings side by side.
Bibliography: Dall'Osso, 1915, p. 343; Mercando, 1976, p. 166, fig. 52; Colivicchi, 2000, p. 113, figs. 6 and 14 (the latter with comparisons and critical perspective).
(G.B.)

3
Hemispherical bowl
end of 2nd century BC
Mold-made,
max. h. 7.0 cm,
Ø of rim 11.7 cm
From tomb 8, necropolis of Ca' Cima, Adria
Museo Archeologico Nazionale, Adria, inv. no. IG AD 11451
State of conservation: whole

Hemispherical bowl of thick translucent green glass with cut and rounded rim, underlined by a deep incision made with the grinding wheel, and convex base with internal *omphalos*. It is a model made in Syria-Palestine, spread around the Mediterranean by Roman merchants.
Bibliography: Bonomi, 1996, p. 152, no. 334.
(S.B.)

2

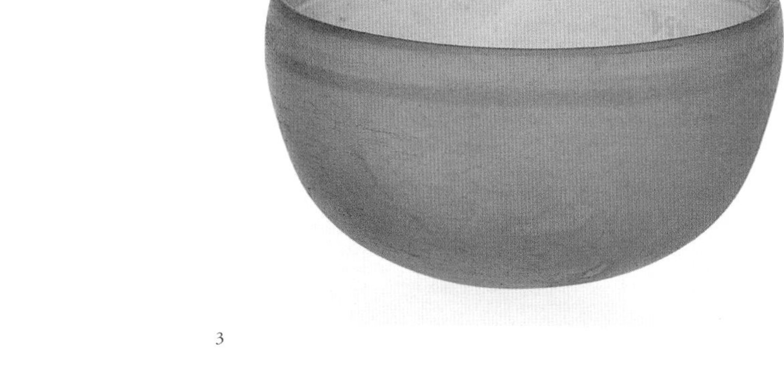

3

1

4

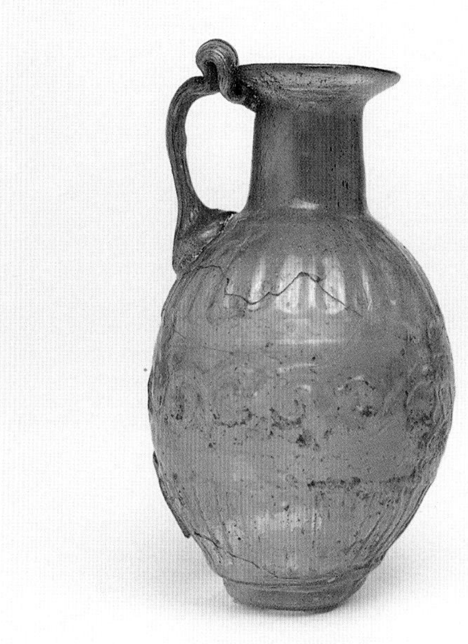
5

4
Bowl with one handle
second quarter of 1st century AD
Blown in three-piece mold, h. 10 cm, ∅ of rim 13.5 cm, ∅ of foot 6.8 cm
From Cavarzere, loc. Cuora
Museo Archeologico Nazionale, Adria, inv. no. IG AD 9100
State of conservation: whole

The large cup of transparent blue glass has a simply cut, projecting vertical rim; cylindrical body, to which the vertical circular handle is attached, terminating in a carination underlined by a molding; convex bottom with a molded ring foot. The decoration in relief is arranged in two bands. The upper one presents two rectangular, diametrically opposed scrolls, each flanked by two palmettes and two bosses, that carry two inscriptions in Greek letters: ΜΝΗΘΉΟΑΓΟΡΑΖΩΝ ("may the buyer remember," or perhaps "may the buyer be remembered [by the gods]"), and ΕΝΝΙΏΝΕΠΌΙΗΣΕΝ ("Ennion made this"), respectively. Between the two scrolls are set a stylized tree, a small Ionic column, a star, another Ionic column and another stylized tree. The lower band, like the bottom, is decorated with vertical gadrooning. The cup belongs to the well-known production of the Syrio-Palestinian glassworker Ennion, characterized by the use of the mold-blowing technique and by refined vessels decorated in relief that are clearly inspired by models in metal.
Bibliography: Bonomi, 1996, p. 158, no. 352.
(S.B.)

5
Bottle
1st century AD
Blown into two-part mold; applied handle,
h. 7 cm, max. ∅ 4 cm
Provenance unknown (perhaps from the region of Verona)
Museo Archeologico al Teatro Romano, Verona, inv. no. 30066
State of conservation: recently restored, with integration of the missing pieces

Bottle of small size, in very thin, transparent, violet glass, with an ovoid body, decorated in the central band by a series of plant volutes and in the lower band by gadrooning. Rod-shaped handle, running from rim to shoulder. Oriental production.
Bibliography: Facchini, 1999, p. 168, no. 385, with comparisons.
(M.B.)

6
Skyphos
first half of 1st century AD
Cast in mold; finished on potter's wheel and ground
h. 9 cm, ∅ of mouth 11.3 cm, ∅ of foot 8.4 cm
From tomb 34, necropolis of the Canal Bianco, Adria
Museo Archeologico Nazionale, Adria, inv. no. IG AD 430
State of conservation: reassembled, with small pieces missing from the body and from one handle

The cup of dark blue translucent glass has a cut and polished rim, underlined by an engraved line; vertical ring handles, connected to the rim by an upper plaque with concave sides with complicated lateral volutes and terminating in a long lower appendage; cylindrical body; broad base with molding. The refinement of the work suggests it was made in the eastern Mediterranean.
Typological comparisons: Isings 39.
Bibliography: Bonomi, 1996, p. 201, no. 451.
(S.B.)

6

7

7
Cup with one handle
1st-2nd century AD
Blown glass; applied handle, h. 11.6 cm, ∅ of rim 13.1 cm, ∅ of foot 6.7 cm
From the Raldon necropolis (Verona), then in the collection of Jacopo Muselli
Museo Archeologico al Teatro Romano, Verona, inv. no. 20283
State of conservation: restored with integration of the missing parts

Cup (*modiolus*) of laige size, in transparent blue glass, with broad, flat and flared lip and ovoid body tapering toward the foot. Small strap handle with two ribs.
The vase comes from a necropolis, along with materials dating from between the 1st and at least the 3rd century AD, excavated in the 18th century. The cup has been attributed by G. Facchini to the production of the eastern part of the empire.
Bibliography: Facchini, 1999, p. 177, no. 414, with previous bibl.
(M.B.)

8
Patera
1st century AD
Cameo glass, h. 5 cm, max. l. 39 cm, ∅ of rim 24.3 cm
Deposito Museo Archeologico Nazionale, Naples, inv. no. s.n. 1
State of conservation: whole but restored in several parts

Low hemispherical basin on ring foot. Circular engraving on outside of bottom, small circle in relief at the centre with raised central point. Shaped horizontal handle that ends in a ram's head in white paste.
The attachments echo the motif of a water bird's head present on silver *paterae* of smaller size (cf. no. 145518 from the house of Menander).
The inside of the basin, ringed by a circular border, is decorated with a mask of Silenus surrounded by a garland of vine leaves with sparse and irregular bunches of grapes in cameo glass.
The somewhat hybrid form appears to be inspired in part by metal *paterae* and in part by the glass pan, Isings form 75a, but the unusual dimensions of the object, the substantial restoration which it has undergone and the lack of inventory data and therefore of information about its provenance leave open many questions, which can only be answered by more thorough investigation, in the archives and elsewhere.
Typological comparisons: Isings 75a.
(C.Z.)

8

9

9
Bottle
1st-2nd century AD
Blown glass,
h. 94 cm, ∅ of rim 59 cm, ∅ of bottom 74 cm
From the ancient city of Ol'vija (Parutino village, Ochakovsky province, Nikolayevskaya region)
The National Museum of History of Ukraine, Kiev, inv. no. 5443
State of conservation: part of the lip is missing

Bottle with wide cylindrical body, narrowing toward the bottom; the everted lip is in relief, folded back and flat. The short neck is marked by a constriction at the point of contact with the body. Strap handle with three ribs that bends to form a right angle. The bottom is slightly concave. The body is decorated with seven bands of engraved lines.
Transparent glass, with a bluish nuance.
These containers were used for pouring and storing small amounts of liquid. Vessels of this kind were common in the ancient cities of northern Pricernomor'ja. They were made in the workshops of the eastern Mediterranean.
Typological comparisons: Vessberg 1952, pl. V, 21, 22; Sorokina 1978, p. 268, pl. 1.10; Kunina 1997, cat. 233.
Bibliography: Kolesnik 1996, p. 134; Var. authors 2001, p. 32, ill. 57.
(P.O.A.)

10
Ribbed bowl
Egypt or Syria,
12th-13th century
Transparent violet glass, with threads of opaque white and turquoise glass paste. Blown in mold and freehand, h. 8 cm, ∅ of rim 15.7 cm
Found in 1855 during digging work on Via Zattere in Padua
Museo Civico Archeologico, Padua, inv. no. XII-229
State of conservation: good

The object has been reassembled and about 20% of the surface in the lower part integrated.

The bowl is in the shape of a squashed hemisphere, with indented rim and flat bottom. The body is molded into vertical ribs, which run in a regular pattern from the bottom and then spread out on the sides, flattening and widening. The decoration consists of a white thread that, starting out from the central point of the bottom with a characteristic curl, runs in a spiral round the body up to the point where the circumference reaches its maximum. The same white thread reappears near the rim, above the ribbed part, while the space between the two areas decorated in this way is embellished with segments of turquoise thread. The structure is indicative of a very complicated technique of manufacture, with a phase of forming in a mold (perhaps with a first blowing), one of free blowing and then one of manipulation on the pontil to obtain the definitive form. It is likely that the bowl was blown in a mold again to incorporate the decoration of threads.
For a long time the find was thought to date from the Roman era, but more recent comparisons have placed it among the typically Islamic glassware of the Middle Ages, characterized by blue or violet colouring and the use of threads of glass paste.
The presence of a valuable object of Islamic manufacture in medieval Padua is a fact of particular interest: it may be an indication of trade links with the eastern Mediterranean, if not indirect evidence of the city's participation in expeditions to the Holy Land.
Typological comparisons: Harden, 1956b, pp. 155-6; Saldern, 1974, no. 340; Pinder-Wilson, Ezzy, 1976, no. 144.
Bibliography: Prosdocimi, 1981, p. 281, fig. 177; Zampieri, 1997, no. 6; Carboni, Whitehouse, 2001, no. 56.
(B.L.)

10

11

11
Vase
China, second half of 18th century (Ch'ing dynasty)
Mold-blown, cut glass,
h. 17.7 cm
Kunstmuseum, Düsseldorf,
inv. no. P 1971-32
State of conservation: excellent

Spherical vase of opaque yellow-green glass with cylindrical foot and neck. Cut base and mouth. For millennia China showed little interest in glass. With the Ch'ing dynasty the industry flourished. Glassworkers developed great skill in the techniques of modeling and cutting in both relief and cameo, as well as in the casting of monochrome and variegated glass. Transparent colourless glass was used rarely and most vases were made out of opaque glass in imitation of porcelain and semiprecious stone, in very refined colours. The forms were generally those of pottery.
Typological comparisons: *Cinquemila anni*, 1991, fig. 182.
Bibliography: Ricke, 1995, no. 210.

12
Philippe-Joseph Brocard
Enameled bottle
Brocard, Paris, 1869
Mold-blown glass, painted with polychrome enamel and gold,
h. 52.2 cm
Kunstmuseum, Düsseldorf,
inv. no. P 1980-2

Pale green glass, mold blown; foot blown separately and applied; painted with polychrome enamel and gold. One of Brocard's earliest known works in glass. It is a free interpretation of Indian and Islamic decorative motifs applied to a traditional form of European glassware. It was not just the Far East that stirred the interest of European decorators toward the end of the 19th century but also the worlds of Islam – the art of Syria and Persia – and of India.
Signature or mark: Signed "Brocard à Paris 1869."
Bibliography: Hilschenz-Mlynek, Ricke, 1985, no. 8; *Silice e fuoco*, 1992, no. 52; Ricke, 1995, no. 218.

12

13
Emile Gallé
Head of Japanese Monster
Gallé, Nancy, 1876
Mold-blown glass,
cut in relief and intaglio,
h. 13.1 cm
Kunstmuseum, Düsseldorf
State of conservation: excellent

Vase in mold-blown crystal, cut in relief and intaglio, in the shape of a lion's head with open jaws, which form the vase mouth, decorated with a frieze in enamel and gold. The features and fur of the lion are represented by cutting. At the base there is a decoration of leaves and blades of grass, outlined in black and gold, and an engraved grasshopper. The surface is studded with ornamental elements of Far Eastern origin. An inscription in Chinese declares: "Anyone who is treated with kindness and does not show gratitude is not worthy of being considered human."
It is a studio work of the Grand Genre type. Gallé defined as Grand Genre only works that were produced as one-off pieces or in small quantities, in which difficult techniques were often used and a great deal of time devoted to ensuring their artistic quality. They are masterpieces in which forms and decoration are fused into an indissoluble unity, and through which Gallé opened up new expressive possibilities for glass.
The vase is a transposition into glass of an Asian prototype, the Shishi lion typical of Japanese Bizen pottery. Gallé owned one of these lions, whose form coincides in detail with the version in glass. The choice of material was intended to evoke Chinese carvings in rock crystal. At the beginning of his artistic career Gallé's interest in Japonisme determined the style of his glassware: he saw the Oriental models as an unsurpassed example of the stylization of natural forms. In this sense Japonisme can be said to lie at the origin of much of Art Nouveau.
Signature or mark: "Emile Gallé Nanceiis fecit" engraved under the base, "[...]mile Gallé a Na[...]" painted, initials "EG" and the cross of Lorraine engraved.
Bibliography: *Silice e fuoco*, 1992, p. 57.

14
Emile Gallé
Vase painted in enamel
Gallé, Nancy, 1880
Mold-blown glass, decorated in enamel and gold,
h. 20.8 cm
Kunstmuseum, Düsseldorf
State of conservation: excellent

Vase in smoked glass blown into open mold with ribs; decorated with flowering branches and birds of paradise in polychrome enamels in relief, outlined in gold; finished with reliefs in silvered enamel.
Studio work in *demi-riche* or Grand Genre style. The decoration of the vase is closely connected with three designs that Gallé conceived in June 1880 (now in the Corning Museum of Glass). The form was used frequently between 1878 and *c.* 1900, with different decorations.
The Oriental origins of the ornamentation are evident.
Signature or mark: signed "EG" with the cross of Lorraine and "déposé Emile Gallé a Nancy" in italics in black enamel under the base.
Bibliography: Hilschenz-Mlynek, Ricke, 1985, no. 174; *Silice e fuoco*, 1992, no. 59; Ricke, 1995, no. 224.

13

14

15
Amethyst goblet with dragon
Fratelli Toso, Murano, *c.* 1880
Blown glass produced by the *mezza stampaura* or "half-molding" technique with applications, h. 32.5 cm
Rossella Junck Collection
State of conservation: restored

Goblet blown from amethyst glass with ribs in the lower part obtained by *mezza stampaura.* Irregular drips of gold-leaf glass descend from the rim. A dragon in amber-spotted crystal and with outstretched wings clings to the stem in gold-leaf crystal decorated with gold-leaf drips. Amethyst foot.
The dragon decorated with drips appears in many models produced by the Fratelli Toso for a period of over twenty years from the 1880s onward.
Bibliography: *Catalogo Fratelli Toso*, n.d., no. 41; Bova, Junck, Migliaccio, 2000, no. 108, p. 139.
(P.M.)

15

16
Filigree goblet with dragons and serpents
Salviati Dott. Antonio, Murano, *c.* 1885
Blown filigree glass, with applications,
h. 27 cm
Ruth Baljöhr Collection, Berlin
State of conservation: restored

Tulip goblet in spiral filigree known as *filigrana a retortoli* (or *zanfirico*) made of opaline and aventurine crystal. Two small dragons in blown aquamarine gold-leaf glass with lobed wings are perched symmetrically on the rim. At the base of the goblet are applied three aquamarine handles with chains inside. A serpent of aquamarine gold-leaf glass is wound around the stem of classical form. The foot is in *filigrana a retortoli.*
This model proved very popular and was produced in various versions by Salviati Dott. Antonio and other firms (Fratelli Toso, Compagnia di Venezia e Murano, Testolini, Candiani).
Bibliography: *Catalogo Salviati & C.*, n.d., no. 1099; Bova, Junck, Migliaccio, 2000, no. 116, p. 144.
(P.M.)

16

17

17
Ewer with dragon
Salviati Dott. Antonio, Murano, *c.* 1890
Blown glass with applications, h. 25 cm
Rossella Junck Collection
State of conservation: restored

Ewer in gold-leaf crystal coloured irregularly with ruby-red glass powder, with the body in the shape of an irregular sack with depressions. The surface is decorated with a mold-blown motif in relief *a baloton* (diamond pattern). A band of gold-leaf crystal closes the base of the neck. A ribbed dragon of crystal with eyes made of yellow-black *murrine*, the body of a serpent and lobed wings is applied to form a handle, while the tail winds around the neck.
There is a similar example coloured with green powder in the collection of the Cantor Center for Visual Arts at Stanford University, Palo Alto, California. It was donated by Maurizio Camerino, owner of the Salviati firm at the time, along with a collection of Salviati glassware from 1900-02, following the mosaic decoration of the church erected at Palo Alto by Senator Stanford, a decoration that was executed by Salviati's mosaicists.
Typological comparisons: Sarpellon, 1989, p. 20; Migliaccio, 1999, p. 36, no. 61.
Bibliography: *Catalogo Salviati & C.*, n.d., no. 1396.
(P.M.)

18

18
Carlo Scarpa
Chinese vase
Venini e C., 1940
Blown glass, h. 26 cm
Luciano Gemin Collection, Silea
State of conservation: excellent

Vase in opaque verd-antique glass. Like many aspects of Far Eastern culture, the forms of Chinese porcelain had always attracted Scarpa, who often took inspiration from them. From Scarpa's time down to the present day, the collection of Chinese vases has remained extremely popular. The forms are Chinese, the colours chromatic variants from the vast range offered by the Venini glassworks.
Signature or mark: etched signature "Venini Murano Italia."
Bibliography: *Gli artisti di Venini*, 1996, no. 108; Venini Diaz de Santillana, 2000, no. 100.

19
Francis Begou
Canopic vase
2000
Glass paste, 60 × 18 cm
Signed
Galerie Place des Arts Collection, Montpellier

19

20

21
22

22
Yoichi Ohira
White Gourd
Pasta Vitrea series, Murano, 2002
Blown glass web of white canes with two *murrine*, ground surface, h. 26.6 cm
Master glassworker Livio Serena
Master grinder Giacomo Barbini
Collection of the artist

Vase created by blowing a web of canes and *murrine* in which are inserted, in isolation, a small crystal tessera and a small red tessera. The brilliance of the surface has been toned down by grinding.
The choice of white as a colour is fundamental: the white is not dazzling but a shade of cream and over the course of the modelling the canes, previously uniform, have taken on lighter and darker tones. The absolute essentiality of the whole is disturbed by the unexpected presence of two *murrine*.
Typological comparisons: *Vetri veneziani*, 1998.

23
Ritsue Mishima
Hollow Gourd and Aureole
Murano, 2002
Blown crystal engraved on the grinding wheel, h. 19 cm, h. 34 cm
Collection of the artist

Two vases in blown crystal with a rounded and symmetrical structure finished on the surface with a dense mesh of incisions. Ritsue Mishima only uses colourless glass and his work is therefore in contrast with the current tendency in Murano and international glass. He takes the inspiration for his forms from natural organisms. They display a purity that recalls Zen gardens and Japanese architecture, but interpreted in the light of the quality of execution typical of Murano glass.
Typological comparisons: *Fusion*, 1999, no p. no.

20
Sunny Wang
Great Longevity, Great Longevity Orange
Canberra, 2000
Sanded and engraved cased glass, h. 30 cm, h. 27 cm
La Scaletta di Vetro, Milan

Vases in the form of squashed cylinders. The black surface has been sanded and engraved to bring out the inner layer, yellow in one and red in the other.
The engraving follows curved lines that are reminiscent of Chinese ideograms.
The sign and the drawing lie at the base of Sunny Wang's works and interact with the form of the blown glass.
Bibliography: *Glass Sunny Wang*, 2001.

21
Yoichi Ohira
Black Silhouettes
Pasta Vitrea series, Murano, 2002
Blown glass web of black and white canes with red *murrine*, ground surface, h. 23.5 cm
Master glassworker Livio Serena
Master grinder Giacomo Barbini
Collection of the artist

Shaped oblong vase with small neck, created by blowing an opaque glass web of white and black canes with red *murrine*. The brilliance of the surface has been toned down by grinding. The soft and essential form recalls classical models of Oriental pottery. In contrast it is decorated with a pattern of irregular black and red strokes on a white ground. The piece is an unusual one for Yoichi Ohira, but still displays the refinement that is a constant characteristic of his work.
Typological comparisons: *Vetri veneziani*, 1998.

23

24

24
Aldo Mondino
Iznik
1995
Oil on glass (installation: 4 pieces), 100 × 80 cm
Courtesy Galleria Astuni, Fano and Pietrasanta

In the works of Aldo Mondino there is no desire to scratch beneath the surface, to go deeply into the subject. He has no interest in revealing the motivation for the dance of the dervishes, the secrets of the Gnawa, the tribal logic of the corrida. The one thing that the artist would never do is decipher customs, demean the sacredness of the ritual. What interests him is the spectacle of culture, of traditions. The show must go on: the heart of the work lies in the preservation and sanctification of the performance. Sultans, bullfighters, dervishes, acrobats, jugglers, rabbis and odalisques all find a home in his works, since there is room there for anyone who knows how to put up a good show. The artist's ideal and favored theme is not the mysterious East, but the East of garish costumes, gaudy ornaments, the frenzied hubbub of the souk and objects on the edge of kitsch (or well over it). It is when life becomes a spectacle of colours, sounds and actions that the artist arrives: with his pictures and his tales. The *Iznik* cycle is devoted to the pottery, famous throughout the East, produced in the Turkish city of the same name. Mondino, who is also an enthusiastic collector of everything from vintage cars to autographs of great figures in history and art, would have liked to own some of those pots, the oldest and most valuable pieces. Given the impossibility of getting hold of them, he decided to paint his own, inventing a technique on glass that would have some of the brilliance and substantiality of the original material.

25
Aldo Mondino
Gnawa
2001
Crystal and shells, h. 44 cm, Ø 18 cm
Courtesy Galleria Astuni, Fano and Pietrasanta

The work of Aldo Mondino takes you on a trip round the world in images and figures. These range from Turkish tightrope walkers to matadors in Spanish arenas, from rabbis in synagogues to the elephants of the African tradition. All brought together and shaken up, over the course of the years, and presented in a style that is always direct and spontaneous, based on the immediacy of the vision. Sometimes they are tinged with mordant irony, at others shaded with subtle melancholy. In the paintings and sculptures of the artist from Turin we find the most diverse cultures – whirling dervishes and Gnawa dancers, Sufism and Judaism, the wisdom of the desert and the wisdom of the empire – but always on the understanding that they are symptoms of a profound sensibility, of a deep-rooted and captivating mysticism. And, within this general interest in human insights and customs, in all their diversity, the Orient has a special place, with its sultans and odalisques, its domes and its thousand and one stories. The *Gnawa* series of sculptures, made in glass and decorated with shells, is one of Mondino's paradoxes. While on the one hand the artist, reproducing the hats worn by Sufi mystics, pays tribute to the most cultured and spiritual part of Islam (in order to enter a state of ecstasy and draw near to God, the Gnawa dance themselves to exhaustion, twirling the pompons of their headgear), on the other he makes these otherwise sacred objects look absurd and incongruous. In fact, while the glass takes away the softness and elasticity of the hats, freezing their movement, the shells lend the whole thing a touch of the ridiculous and the extravagant.

25

26
Medhat Shafik
The Alchemist's Casket
2002
Mixed media on handmade paper,
142 × 200 cm
Spirale Arte, Milan

The son of a cotton merchant from al-Badari, a town on the Nile in the heart of Egypt, Medhat Shafik was born and grew up in an environment characterized by the stark contrast between the monotonous expanse of the sand dunes and the teeming life of the strip of fertile land that the river has wrested from the desert. On the one hand the void, on the other the Arab souk, with its voices, wares and odours. This contrast between full and empty, between nothing and everything, has never abandoned him and is a characteristic of his works. "In my pictures I have always sought of impose order on a material that does not want to keep still, like the sand of the Sahara," he declares. The theatre and the dubbing of animated cartoons have made a mark on him, and left him with a desire to tell stories, to fill his works with colours, graffiti and personages. "The telling of fables is not childish, and not even escapist. It is an emotional and gripping means of communication, necessary in an age of hi tech that threatens to turn us into aluminum," he says.
The works of Shafik assemble many images in a single picture, illustrate many episodes, one set next to the other, from the same story. Sometimes the overall effect is so chaotic that it may seem abstract picture, but this is not the case. There are always events and figures under the indiscriminate accumulation of signs. Some of his works illustrate scenes from the history of the Silk Road, others from the route of the trade in cashmere. And in this organized confusion, the pieces of glass inserted into *The Alchemist's Casket* lend the picture an additional touch of magic and mystery, as if they were some of the many gems embedded in the tales of the *Thousand and One Nights.*

26

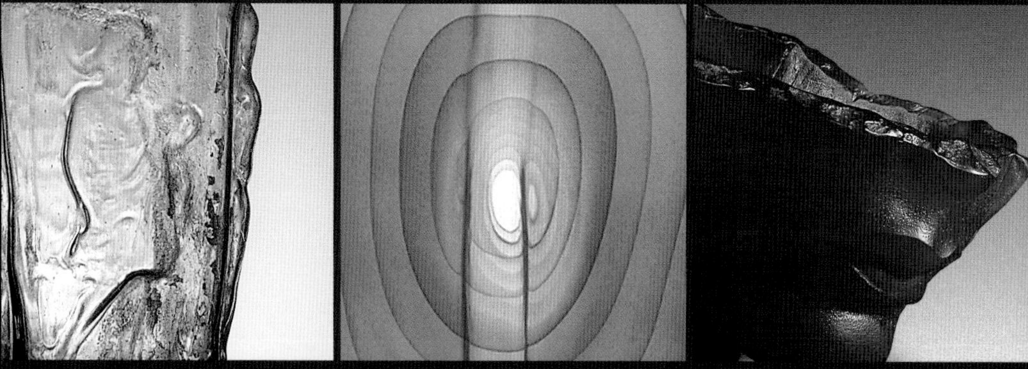

Room of the Sacred

ANCIENT GLASS

This room houses objects whose use or decoration is connected with the sphere of religion, whether pagan, Christian or others. In the practice of cremation that was widespread in the first two centuries of the Empire, cinerary urns and tubular *unguentaria*, the so-called tear bottles, were used as containers. A drinking glass from the Diageo Glass Collection portrays mythological subjects, framing them in architectural settings that are reminiscent of pagan temples. The *ampulla* produced by a Sidonian workshop, with a representation of ritual vases whose contents were intended for pilgrims on their way to the temple in Jerusalem, is linked to Sukkoth, the Jewish Feast of Tabernacles.

With the gradual spread of Christianity, evidence of the use of Christian symbology became more common. The bottom of a bowl from the 4th-5th century AD found in the Aosta Valley is stamped with the monogram of Constantine. Another remarkable find from Aosta is the celebratory drinking glass with an inscription of good wishes: VIVAS CVM TVIS OMNIBVS FELICITER IN DEO. It is decorated with a row of saints and apostles represented with the gold-leaf technique, and was probably made by a Roman workshop. Another reference to the Christian religion can be found in the *fondi d'oro* ("gold bottoms"), so-called for the presence of a figure in gold leaf between two layers of glass, which were placed in the tombs of early believers. Two cylindrical flasks from Zadar and Kiev were directly connected with religious rites: in all probability they contained a sacred liquid used in the celebration of services. Small *ampullae* from the so-called treasure of Theodelinda in Monza held oil from the lamps that used to burn in the tombs of martyrs. The small bottles in the Musée du Louvre with a representation of Saint Simeon the Stylite, venerated in a Syrian temple, speak to us of religious fervour and pilgrimages to the Holy Land. Another object evoking the realm of the sacred, the pectoral cross in blue-green glass and with tapering arms, is of Egyptian origin.

CREATORS OF GLASS

In the Venetian glassware of the second half of the 15th century and the early 16th century decorations with a religious theme were extremely rare and not very significant, with the exception of the oldest Venetian goblet decorated with polychrome enamels to have come down to us, the well-known *Blue Goblet* in the Museo Civico of Bologna, which it was not possible to transport to the exhibition. Instead, the decorations of that period tend to celebrate life, youth and love, along the lines of the poetic compositions of Lorenzo the Magnificent, or ideal values, like justice. Yet the themes of love cannot be considered profane. They are "courtly" loves, sanctioned by the bond of matrimony: most of these articles are marriage cups.

The glassworkers who most frequently tackled sacred themes were the excellent Bohemian engravers of the first half of the 19th century. Lovers of Italian Renaissance painting and fascinated by Raphael, they reproduced pictures on the walls of goblets of pure crystal or crystal cased in coloured and transparent glass, with a sculptural effect that was due to the optical illusion which makes figures cut deeply into glass look as if they are in bas-relief.

In the modern world of glass it is difficult, if not impossible, to speak of sacred art, while the theme of the profane has lost much of its provocative character. From an absolutely different cultural base and a tradition of design that is poles apart comes the work of Timo Sarpaneva, one of the greatest Nordic glassworkers of the last fifty years who has collaborated with the Murano craftsman Pino Signoretto: his work *Liber Mundi* suggests mysterious and totally secular reflections on the origins of life and the world, obscure but fascinating.

CONTEMPORARY ART

If for most of its history art has been placed at the service of the sacred, in the contemporary world an important part of it has been devoted to provocation. Over the last century and especially in recent years, the two themes have inevitably fused, in an irreverent revision of religious iconography. And while, on the one hand, the work of younger artists has verged on sacrilege and blasphemy (it suffices to think of Padre Pio transformed by Dario Arcidiacono into the McDonald's puppet of the Ultrapop, of Corrado Bonomi's dog's basket with a bell tower and bowl for offerings and of Maurizio Bertinetti's votive statues turned into bar tables), on the other even artists who received their training in the 1950s, 1960s and 1970s have not failed to subvert the emblems of the liturgy, although in a less aggressive and iconoclastic manner. Omar Galliani, for example, in his reinterpretation of Raphael's *Lady with a Unicorn*, places the emphasis on the pagan – and phallic – symbol of the mythical beast (rather than on the purity of the woman, in reality much faded), while Giuseppe Maraniello concentrates on the figure of the devil and old adversary, giving him a positive twist by setting him free of the red colour of damnation and presenting him as an allegory of the possibility of reexamining judgments that we take for granted. He makes use of glass in his works just as he does of all the other materials of contemporary art, without assigning it a precise significance, except perhaps as a contrast to the grandeur and imperishable resistance of marble and bronze.

1
Cinerary urn
end of 1st century AD
Blown glass,
h. 22.8 cm, ∅ of rim 20.3 cm, max. ∅ 21.1 cm, ∅ of base 8.5 cm
From T. 11, predial necropolis of Saint-Martin-de-Corléans, Aosta
Deposito della Sovrintendenza, Aosta Valley Autonomous Region, Aosta
cod. lab. 03-1305
State of conservation: reassembled with large gaps; superficial abrasions

Bubbly, transparent glass, blue in colour. Jar with an ovoid body, rim flattened and folded outward, flat, slightly concave bottom. The custom of burying the remains of cremated bodies in glass jars was not common in Aosta Valley and Piedmont, while it was widely practiced in the northeastern part of the peninsula. On the basis of the grave context, made up of Isings 43 plates, a shaped bottle (comparable to Isings 72) and a small *unguentarium*, as well as a bronze abacus and the remains of a small set of scales, a date in the late 1st century AD has been proposed.
Typological comparisons: Isings, 67a.
Bibliography: Isings, 1957, pp. 86-7; Lissia, 1994, pp. 94-6; Bonomi, 1996, no. 407, p. 180.
(R.M. - P.F.)

2
"Gotterbecher" drinking glass
1st century AD
Mold-blown glass,
h. 12.5 cm
From Pergamum
Diageo Glass Collection, Santa Vittoria d'Alba
State of conservation: excellent

This is one of a group of twenty examples in existence, whole or in fragments, of molded drinking glasses. The four figures, each in its own niche, probably refer to the seasons: Mercury holding a caduceus represents the fall, Diana the winter, Hercules carrying a calf the summer, and Hymen the spring. The drinking glass, found at Pergamum, is thought to have been made at Sidon.
Bibliography: Davidson Weinberg, 1972, pp. 29-30; *Vetri dei Cesari*, 1988, pp. 163-4, no. 85.
(P.L.)

2

1

3
Hexagonal flask
second half 1st century AD
Glass blown in two-part mold, apart from the neck,
h. 7 cm, max. ∅ 3.3 cm, ∅ of rim 2 cm
Necropolises of Zadar, Nona and Asseria, Museum of Saint Donat's, Zadar
Museo Vetrario di Murano, Venice, inv. no. IGVE 406
State of conservation: whole

The flask, in transparent green glass, has a flattened tubular rim, cylindrical neck, pear-shaped body and quadrangular flat bottom with two concentric circles in relief. The decoration of the body is complex: each of six rectangular panels, separated by columns, houses a ritual vase; above and below the central band is set an ovolo motif framed by festoons. The piece was originally in the Museum of Saint Donat's in Zadar, whose collections, transferred to Venice for reasons of safety during the Second World War, were assigned in part to Italy in 1961 after a long diplomatic dispute. Most of the material, on show since 1963 at the Museo Vetrario di Murano, comes from the necropolises of Aenona (Nona) and Jadera (Zadar), but is wholly devoid of context, as is the case with the finds made in many Dalmatian graveyards, excavated from middle of the nineteenth century onward often without adequate documentation (Ravagnan, 1994, pp. 10-11; Buora, 1998, pp. 57-8). The glassware of Zadar represents the finest production of the Mediterranean area. The flask with hexagonal walls we see here is an example of a type known from Neronian and Flavian contexts and is the product of an eastern workshop, probably in Syria-Palestine. In fact, it displays significant parallels with glassware signed by *Ennion*, also decorated with representations of ritual vases (Ravagnan, 1994, pp. 17, 47).
Typological comparisons: Isings, form 78, pp. 93-4; *Journal of Glass Studies*, 1962, no. 7, p. 140; *Journal of Glass Studies*, 1971, no. 10, p. 137; Hayes 1975, no. 84, p. 48, pl. 7; *Constable Maxwell*, 1979, nos. 70-2, pp. 52-3.
Bibliography: De Bersa, 1913, no. 224, p. 87; Forlati, Mariacher, 1963, no. 24, p. 14; Ravagnan, 1994, no. 68, p. 52; *Trasparenze imperiali*, 1998, no. 45, pp. 112 and 230.
(M.D.P.)

3

reflects the taste for ornamental symbolism of an allegorical character linked to the cult of martyrs.
The gilded drinking glass with rows of saints, of fine workmanship, was very probably a mark of prestige, presumably a commemorative gift made to an important personage.
The technical and morphological aspects recall the typical characteristics of 4th-century glassware. The decoration of the rim with a triple groove and the figurative repertoire, which finds precise iconographic parallels in the *fondi d'oro* in the collection of the Vatican Library, suggest a likely Roman provenance. Similarly, the acclamatory formula "Dignitas Amicorum" allows it to be inserted in the substantial group of *fondi d'oro* (Morey, 1959, nos. 37, 45, 47, 49, 58, 187, 236, 241, 271, 274, 285, 314, 329, 365, 378, 379, 388 and 450) produced by a definable workshop; further support for this origin is provided by the many stylistic analogies in the composition of the figures, the decoration of the surfaces, the physiognomic features and the themes of the symbolic ornamentation.
Typological comparisons: Isings, 106a.
Bibliography: Morey, 1959; Toth, 1969, pp. 47-9; *Vetri dei Cesari*, 1988, pp. 25-7; Mollo Mezzena, 1990, p. 292, no. 4e.4e.2C; Mollo Mezzena, 1992, p. 277, fig. 14; Paolucci, 1997, pp. 175-8.
(R.M.)

4
Beaker with row of saints
4th century AD
Blown glass with gold-leaf decoration applied on the outer surface. The finely engraved figures have the appearance of an abraded surface with a frosted effect. Grooves cut on wheel, h. 11.4 cm, ∅ of rim 11.4 cm, bottom 2.3 cm
From T. 17, predial necropolis of Saint-Martin-de-Corléans, Aosta
Deposito della Sovrintendenza, Aosta Valley Autonomous Region, Aosta
inv. no. SM/E 991
State of conservation: reassembled, incomplete, with numerous missing pieces. Only slight traces of the gilding have been preserved

Beaker in thin, colourless, transparent glass with a greenish nuance, body in the shape of a truncated cone, cut lip, rim underlined by three incised grooves; bottom slightly concave. Under the rim runs the acclamatory inscription VIVAS CVM TVIS OMNIBVS FELICITER IN DEO DIGNITAS AMICORVM, intercalated with roundish and leaf-like dividing points. From left to right runs a row of haloed saints and apostles, dressed in tunic and *pallium* draped around the body and adorned with *clavi* and *calliculae.*
The vertical division of the representation is underlined by elegant partitions of alternating plant and vine shoots.
The standing figures, represented in accordance with iconographic models typical of the 4th-century tradition, are identified by name: PETRVS, PAVLVS, SVSTVS, PIMOPEVS (TIMOTHEVS) and FL(OR)VS.
The depiction of the figures in the hortatory attitude of the *traditio legis,* as an exaltation of the evangelic mission underlined by the presence of *volumina*, does not depart from the canonical themes of the earliest period of Christianization.
From the compositional point of view the figures are grouped in pairs according to an association that is frequently encountered on *fondi d'oro* (Morey, 1959, Petrus-Paulus, nos. 88, 455, 449, 344, Sustus-Timotheus, nos. 55, 74, 258, 313). The filling of the surfaces with floral motifs – stylized budding wreaths (Morey, 1959, no. 67), schematic rosettes and vine shoots –

4

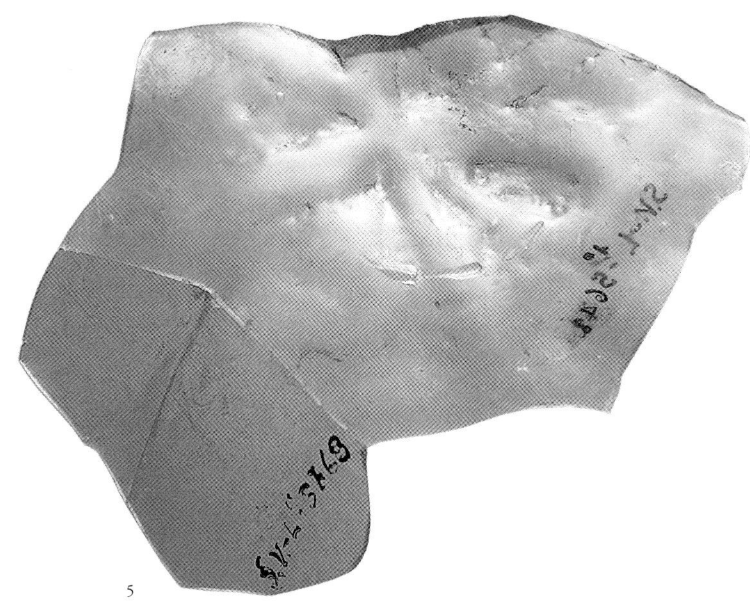
5

5
Fragment of cup
4th century AD
Blown glass with molded integration,
h. 1.9 cm, width 7.2 cm,
∅ of bottom 4.3 cm
From Saint-Vincent, excavation of parish church, level of destruction of the *praefurnium*
Deposito della Sovrintendenza, Aosta Valley Autonomous Region, Aosta inv. no. 5648
State of conservation: created by the union of three fragments

Bottom of small bowl or cup in thin, very pale green glass, to which is attached the beginning of a wall with indentations. The symbol of the christogram, fairly rare on the bottom of glass bowls, can be recognized in relief. It can be compared with a bowl from Mézières, in the north of France, where this motif appears in a similar position, in a frame of stylized plants. It is found more frequently on clay objects, such as early Christian oil lamps. The form of the bowl in thin clear glass has turned up fairly often in urban excavations at Aosta as well, especially in the layers of destruction. It is common at Aquileia and in the Rhineland.
Typological comparisons: Isings, 117.
Bibliography: Isings, 1957, pp. 147-8; Calvi, 1968, pp. 173-4, no. 347, pl. P.2; Périn, 1972, pp. 72 *et sqq.*; Mollo Mezzena, 1982, pp. 298-311.
(P.F.)

6
Fondo d'oro (“gold bottom”)
end of 4th century AD
Blown glass, inclusion of gold leaf between two layers of glass,
∅ 10.2 cm
Museo Nazionale del Bargello, Florence, inv. no. 32
State of conservation: broken along the edge, upper side concave; back convex

Bottom of bowl in whitish glass. A husband and wife crowned by a beardless Christ are represented in the central medallion, while the space around it is subdivided by columns supporting *tabulae ansatae* with the names of the saints represented between them: EPOLITVS, PETRVS, PAVLVS, LAVRENTIVS, SVSTVS and CIPRIANVS.
(from F.Z., 1969)

7
Cup
5th century AD
Blown glass,
h. 4 cm, ∅ of rim 18.8 cm
From Ittiri, context unknown
Deposito Museo Archeologico Nazionale, Cagliari, inv. 10666
State of conservation: whole

Bowl in transparent glass with slightly curved inward, straight rim. Body a segment of a sphere with no foot. The decoration is engraved on the outer surface inside two bands. At the centre stands the beardless figure of Christ, in the guise of lawgiver, with his head in profile turned to the right and haloed, dressed in tunic and *pallium*. In his right hand he holds an open *liber*, while the left is raised in the gesture of the *adlocutio*. The figure is framed at the sides by date palms, while four rhomboid gems are set in the background.
The stylistic characteristics of the working of the bowl, for which there are few parallels, distinguish it from those produced in Rome and Ravenna, but seem to have affinities with the products of workshops in the Syrian area.
Bibliography: Stiaffini, Borghetti, 1994, pp. 59-60, 124, no. 314, pls. 38-9.
(C.T.)

6

7

8
Cylindrical ampulla
4th century AD (?)
Free-blown glass, h. 18.2 cm, thickness 1.8 cm, Ø of rim 1.9 cm
From Zadar, Nona or Asseria
Arheološki Muzej, Zadar, inv. no. 5863
State of conservation: whole

Tubular ampulla in colourless greenish glass with thickened and flattened bottom and cylindrical body that broadens to form a disc in the vicinity of the neck. Sloping shoulder, narrow neck. Everted horizontal rim. On the inside and toward the bottom, the container narrows like a funnel.
Bibliography: *Trasparenze imperiali*, 1998, p. 212, no. 224.
(I.F.)

9
Flask
1st-4th century AD
Blown glass, h. 24.7 cm, Ø of rim 2.1 cm, Ø of bottom 1.5 cm
Northern Pricernomor'ja
From the S.N. Platonov Collection
The National Museum of History of Ukraine, Kiev, inv. no. 8524
State of conservation: the surface is covered with incrustations

Flask with spindle-shaped body and rounded bottom. The lip is everted and folded back. Tubular neck. Transparent glass, of greenish hue, containing numerous bubbles. In the Roman era terracotta vessels for incense and aromatic substances were replaced by glass toilet bottle. These articles were often used not only to hold perfumes, but also as ritual containers in funerary ceremonies. Flasks of similar form were common in Greece. In the whole of eastern Europe, however, only six such pieces have been found.
Typological comparisons: Kunina, Sorokina, 1972, pl. XIII, p. 168, type V.
Bibliography: Puklina, 2001, pp. 138-9.
(P.O.A.)

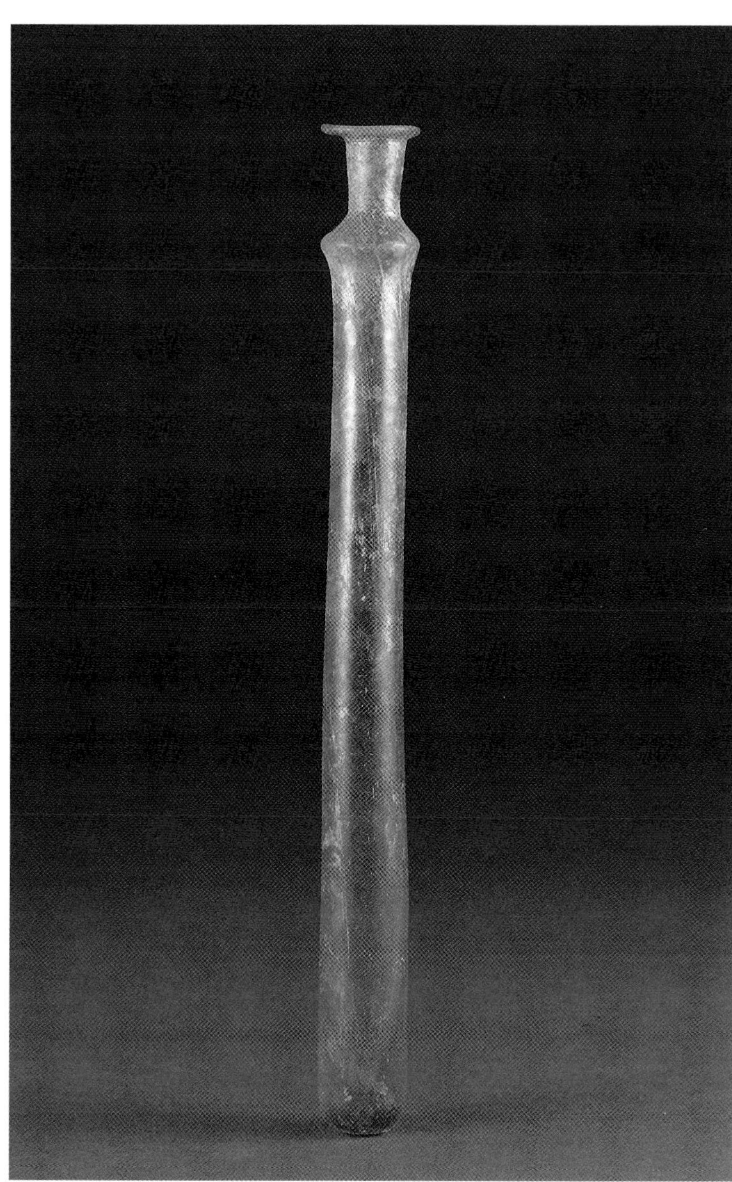
8

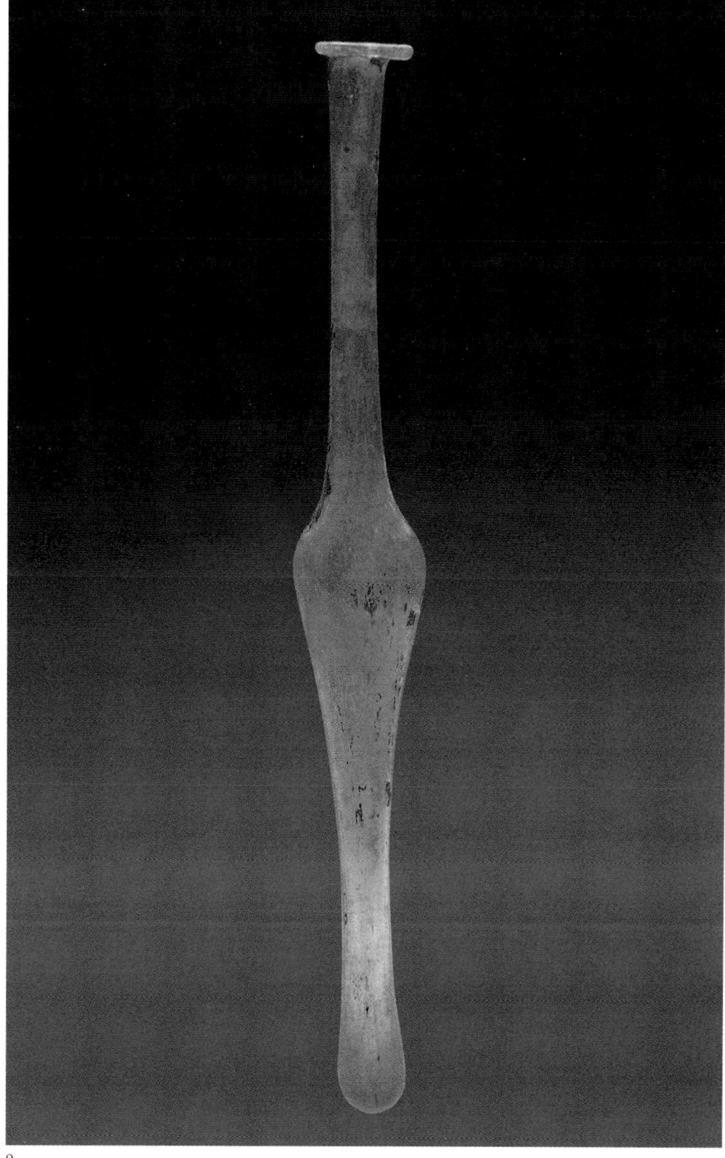
9

10a

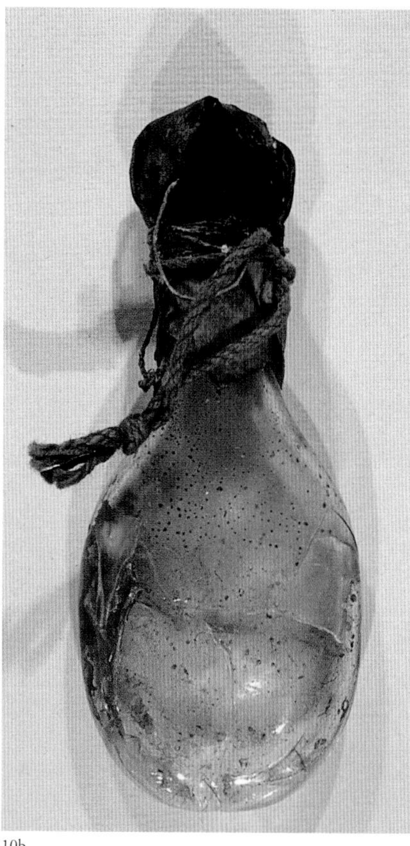
10b

11
Ampulla with representation of Saint Simeon the Stylite
Decorated part mold blown; shoulder and neck free blown; neck and handle applied, h. 15 cm, side 4.6 cm
Probably from Syria (acquired from an antique dealer in Cairo, in 1911)
Musée du Louvre, Paris, inv. no. OA 6417
State of conservation: good; one small hole on the shoulder

The greenish bottle, with a flat bottom, has a body in the shape of a parallelepiped and a low shoulder. The flared neck is ringed by a collar, an extension of the handle set on the shoulder. Each side is decorated in relief. On the side with the handle, there is a bird with the features of a wader looking to the right; the adjacent part has a Latin cross with groups of two small globes set between the arms; the opposite side is divided up into lozenges; finally, the side opposite the handle presents a schematic figure of Saint Simeon on his pillar; to the left is represented the ladder, with two rungs, while on the right there is a vertical row of five globes, like those that surround the cross. The stylites were hermits who chose to isolate themselves from the world by living on top of a pillar (*stylos* in Greek). This type of Christian ascetic was most common in Syria. Saint Simeon the Elder (around 389-459) was venerated at a great sanctuary, at Telanissus, now Qala'at Sema'an, in the north of the country. Large numbers of pilgrims went there to pray to the saint, bringing back bottles like this as a souvenir.
Typological comparisons: Eisen, pp. 483-4, pls. 12, 122; Klausen Nottmeyer, fig. b, pl. 126.
Bibliography: *Byzance*, 1992, no. 53, p. 99.
(D.B.)

10
Two small ampullae for holy oil
5th-6th century AD
Blown glass, 8.8 × 3.6 cm; 9.5 × 5 cm
From Rome
Museo del Duomo, Monza
State of conservation: each have pieces missing from the belly; restored

The two *ampullae* come from a group of twenty-six that belonged to the original collection of relics donated by the queen of the Longobards, Theodelinda, to the basilica of San Giovanni Battista in Monza. The *ampullae* can be divided morphologically into eight different types, with a number of variants, identified by Elisabetta Roffia (1995). The predominant colour is blue-green, the glass seedy with inclusions, the rim flattened and folded inward. The mark where the pontil was detached is visible. The example of type "1," with a squashed body, common throughout the Mediterranean area from the first centuries of the empire up until the 6th century, on show here still has its stopper of parchment and wax, with traces of oil on the walls, but part of one side is missing. The example of type "5," with a globular body, documented between the 4th and 7th century, we see here has a stopper made of linen and wax and contains substantial resinous residues. Two pieces are missing. The *ampullae* contained "holy oil" taken from the lamps that used to illuminate the tombs of martyrs in the Roman catacombs and which were brought to Monza during the pontificate of Gregory I by *Johannis indignus et peccator domne Theodelindae reginae de Rome*, as we are informed by the *Notula olearum*, an inventory written on papyrus between the 6th and 7th century and conserved in the treasury of Monza cathedral. The Johannis cited in the *Notula* may have been the abbot whose arrival was announced in Gregory's epistle to Theodelinda in the September of 593. Strips of papyrus (*pittacia*) bearing the names of the martyrs were tied to the necks of the ampullae. These were subsequently transcribed in the *Notula*, making it an important source of information on the topography of the Roman catacombs.
The group of twenty-six *ampullae* is also mentioned in an inventory of 1042, transcribed onto a sheet of *Alcuin's Bible* in the Chapter Library of Monza cathedral.
Typological comparisons: Roffia, 1995, type 1 and type 5.
(R.C.)

11

12

12
Pectoral cross
4th-6th century AD
Glass cast in mold and cut, h. 5.5 cm, width 4.5 cm
From Coptos (Egypt)
Civiche Raccolte Archeologiche, Milan, inv. no. A.0.9.1726. Formerly Seletti Collection (1019 GI)
State of conservation: piece missing from upper arm

Latin cross in blue-green, bubbly, opaque glass, with arms tapering toward the center. The break in the upper vertical arm, from which the end is missing, reveals the mark left by the hole where it was suspended. A fine line is engraved at the ends of the lower vertical arm and the horizontal arms.
Bibliography: Davidson, 1952, p. 258, no. 2075; Ross, 1962, p. 56; *Fitzwilliam Museum* 1978, p. 55, no. 112a.
(From E.R., 1993)

13
Glass paten
10th-11th century
Paten: cut glass; mounting: gilded silver, *cabochons* of glass paste, beads,
h. 8 cm, ∅ 26.5 cm
From Constantinople
Tesoro della Basilica di San Marco, Venice
State of conservation: good

Glass dish with greenish hues, decorated with cut polygonal elements of six or seven sides, more asymmetrical in the central part, more regular towards the edge, arranged in a honeycomb pattern. The green colour of the glass allows us to identify the object as the one listed as no. 16 in the third section of the Inventory of the Treasury of Saint Mark's compiled by the procurators Pietro Grimani and Angelo Mudazio in 1325: *"platinam unam viridem ornatam silver deaurato, quae dicitur esse de smeraldo, quod non credimus"* (Gallo, 1967, p. 278). The setting, in gilded silver, consists of a foot decorated with beading, four supports with a flat disc in the middle and a border with a series of alternating oval and rectangular bezels with *cabochons* of blue and green glass paste, imitating precious stones, between two rows of small beads, most of them made of blown glass. Some of the beads located at the sides of the bezels are broken. Grabar (1971, p. 73) expresses doubts about the liturgical function of this object, though it is traditionally considered a paten, i.e. the plate on which the bread is placed at the Eucharist, as well as the dating of the part in glass to the 6th century. Instead he thinks the dish and mounting to be contemporary, holding them to be the work of Constantinopolitan craftsmen of the 10th-11th century, when the imitation of antique vases in glass and semiprecious stones was one of the characteristics of the "Macedonian renaissance."
(M.d.V.U.)

13

14

Stained-glass windows in Aosta Valley

The stained-glass windows presented at this exhibition constitute a sample of the rich range of such decorations to be found in Aosta Valley, a genre which reached its peak in this area between the late 15th century and the beginning of the 16th. The restoration to which they have recently been subjected is part of the program of conservation and enhancement of the entire regional heritage promoted by the Department of Education and Culture.

14
Stained-glass window depicting the Madonna and Child
late 15th century - early 16th century
Stained-glass lead-mounted and tin-souldered, grisaille and silver yellow painted, *c.* 174 × 80 cm
The window is made up of two panels: the lower, rectangular in shape, measures 115 × 78 cm; the upper one with an arched top measures 57.5 × 78 cm
North side of nave, cathedral of Santa Maria Assunta, Aosta
State of conservation: restored in 1999-2001 by Laura Morandotti

The window, which has undergone many alterations over the course of time, is made up of two panels of different shape and size. Their reassembly, documented by a photograph in Toesca's catalogue of 1911, can in all probability be ascribed to a 19th-century intervention. The upper panel, grasaille and silver yellow painted presents a mythological scene in an exedra decorated with bean motifs and is bounded at the sides by *candelabre* wrapped in beaded festoons, while the lower one depicts the Madonna seated with the Child giving his blessing. It is possible that the Virgin – who has long flowing hair, two carnations in her right hand and an open book on her lap – was part of a diptych, whose left-hand side can be identified as the adjacent window, depicting *Saint Stephen with a Devotee*. The work is an example of the rich range of stained-glass to be found in Aosta Valley, which comprises, in addition to the twenty-three windows of the cathedral and those of the collegiate church of Santi Pietro e Orso, fragments from Avise, Arpuilles, Gignod, Saint-Vincent, Arnad and Challant-Saint-Victor, and two shutters from the castle of Issogne, now in the Museo Civico of Turin. The execution of the *Madonna and Child*, datable to between the end of the 15th century and the beginning of the 16th, was plausibly connected with the work of enlargement of Aosta cathedral, documented by a capitular resolution of 1493 and promoted by Bishop Francesco De Prez (Orlandoni, 1996, pp. 156-8). The cathedral's stained-glass windows demonstrate the complexity of the figurative culture of a region situated in the heart of the Alps, permeated by Franco-Flemish influences but not immune to ideas coming from the South, and should be seen in relation to those of the collegiate church of Sant'Orso, installed at the behest of George of Challant, on which worked the Genevan P. Vaser and Bodichino, Flemish by origin and Lyonese by training (Dolino, 2001, pp. 205-18). The panel with the Virgin shows affinities with the windows of Bourges cathedral, which present a similar modelling of the flesh tones by means of light glazes of "sanguigne" a technique of execution widely used by French artists, while the typology of the representation can be traced to a Lombard repertory derived from Foppa (Pirina, 1999).

Bibliography: Toesca, 1911, p. 26, section 22; Viale, 1939, p. 222, no. 19; Castelnuovo, 1954, pp. 38-47; Brizio, 1958, pp. 366-79; Castelnuovo, 1958, pp. 3-24; Gabrielli, 1958, pp. 393-421; Castelnuovo, 1961, p. 634; Viale, Viale Ferrero, 1967, pl. XXVI; Brunod, 1975, pp. 306-7; Barberi, 1988 (unpublished); Orlandoni, 1996, pp. 156-7; Pirina, 1999 (unpublished); Dolino, 2001, p. 217.

(D.J. - L.P.)

15

Stained-glass depicting Saint Stephen with Devotee

late 15th - early 16th century
Stained-glass lead-mounted and tin-souldered, grisaille and silver yellow painted, *c.* 165 × 78 cm
The window is made up of two panels
North side of nave, cathedral of Santa Maria Assunta, Aosta
State of conservation: restored in 1999-2001 by Laura Morandotti

Surrounded by modern panes of colourless glass, Saint Stephen is represented standing, holding a book in his left hand, on which are placed the stones of his martyrdom, and presenting a kneeling devotee with his right. The scene is set against a blue ground damasked with black. The donor has been hypothetically identified with the canon Bartolomeo Pensa, parish priest of the church of Santo Stefano and *magister fabricae* of the cathedral after the death of the canon Ugo Ferrein of Courmayeur in 1500 (Orlandoni, 1996, pp. 156-7). It is plausible that the window was the left-hand panel of a diptych of which the *Madonna and Child* was the right-hand part. This hypothesis is supported by the affinities of style and execution discernible in the two images: the soft and full modelling of the figures, represented with light glazes, are similar, as are the depiction of the locks of hair, whose dense yellow colour is achieved through the use of silver yellow, and the utilization of relatively wide pieces of glass (Pirina, 1999). The two windows in the cathedral, which show the influence of Franco-Flemish culture and have been compared to some of the stained-glass in Bourges cathedral, should be seen in relation to those of the collegiate church of Sant'Orso in Aosta, commissioned by the prior commendator George of Challant, in whose service the two stained-glass artists Bodichino and P. Vaser are documented.

15

Bibliography: Toesca, 1911, pp. 26-7, section 23; Viale, 1939, p. 221, no. 15, ill. 305; Castelnuovo, 1954, pp. 38-47; Gabrielli, 1956, p. 417; Brizio, 1958, pp. 367-79, ill. no. 3, p. 373; Castelnuovo, 1958, pp. 3-24; Castelnuovo, 1961, p. 634; Viale, Viale Ferrero, 1967, plate XXVI, ill. on p. 104; Brunod, 1975, p. 304, fig. 384; Barberi, 1988 (unpublished); Orlandoni, 1996, pp. 156-7, ill. 232; Pirina, 1999 (unpublished); Dolino, 2001, pp. 205-18.

(D.J. - L.P.)

16

16

16

16
Stained-glass depicting a bishop presenting an acolyte and the Crucifixion
1530
Stained-glass lead-mounted and tin-souldered, grisaille and silver yellow painted, *c.* 175 × 61 cm
The window is made up of three panels
Parish church of San Brizio, Avise, temporarily on show at Aosta cathedral
State of conservation: restored in 1996-97 under the direction of Laura Morandotti

The stained-glass window, from the parish church of San Brizio in Avise, is composed of three panels set one on top of the other and representing, from top to bottom, a bishop presenting an acolyte, the *Crucifixion* and a shutter, characterized by rhomboidal pieces of colourless glass framed by decorative floral motifs, that contains a scroll with the inscription "fecit fieri 1530." This precise chronological indication, fundamental not just for this particular window but also for the study of the whole corpus of stained-glass in Aosta Valley, was revealed during the recent restoration, as the lower panel of the window in Avise had been partially covered by the wall. The two figurative scenes, set in a similar architectural structure bounded at the sides by two columns, are characterized by a high level of quality as well as the use of relatively wide pieces of glass. From the historical and artistic point of view the window, executed at a later date than the cycles in the cathedral and the collegiate church of Sant'Orso in Aosta, has not yet been subjected to thorough critical analysis.
Bibliography: Barberi, 1988 (unpublished); Brunod, 1995, p. 15, fig. 5; Vicquéry, 1997, pp. 9-12; Pirina, 1999 (unpublished).
(D.V. - L.P.)

17
Fragment of stained-glass depicting a putto
late 15th - 16th century
Fragment of stained-glass lead-mounted and tin-souldered, grisaille and silver yellow painted,
20 × 16 cm
Chapel of Arpuilles, temporarily on show at Aosta cathedral
State of conservation: restored in 1997 by Laura Morandotti

The fragment, which arrived at an unknown date in the chapel of Arpuilles (Aosta), where it was inserted in a window made up of modern pieces of colourless glass, represents a putto holding a festoon grisaille and silver yellow painted. The delicate figure of the child was executed on a single piece of glass, which had been broken in the lower part and then reassembled with a heavy strip of lead. During the restoration, which has made the image legible again and revealed its high quality, the strips of lead have been eliminated and the breaks filled with epoxy resin by infiltration. The putto from Arpuilles must originally have been located at the top of a stained-glass window, where it formed the right-hand pinnacle of an aedicule, in accordance with a type of architectural framing that can be seen in a group of stained-glass windows in Aosta cathedral, datable to sometime between the late 15th century and the beginning of the 16th century, to which it can also be related stylistically.
Bibliography: Brunod, 1981, p. 301, fig. 242; Barberi, 1988 (unpublished); Vicquéry, 1997, p. 9; Pirina, 1999 (unpublished).
(D.V. - D.J.)

17

18

18
Goblet of the Madonna della Seggiola
Bohemia, 1850
Mold-blown, cut and engraved crystal,
h. 17.1 cm
Museum of Decorative Arts, Prague
State of conservation: excellent

Goblet on solid, multifoiled foot, short stem, tall cylindrical bowl, finished by cutting and engraved on the front with a reproduction of Raphael's *Madonna della Seggiola*.
The Italian painting of the Renaissance was a favourite source of models for Bohemian engravers. Raphael was particularly esteemed by the best of them who, from the 1820s and the works of the great engraver Dominik Biemanos onward, showed a special fondness for the *Madonna della Seggiola*.
Typological comparisons: Pazaurek, von Philippovich, 1976, p. 43; *Vetri europei dell'Ottocento*, 1980, no. 28 (*Sistine Madonna*); *Verres de Bohême*, 1989, no. 26; Drahotová, 1991, fig. 127; Drahotová, 2000, p. 67.

19
Timo Sarpaneva
Liber Mundi
1999
Sunk, solid, multicoloured glass
Collection of the artist, Murano

Sculpture made up of successive layers of glass modeled while hot into a vertical, flattened and curved shape. Timo Sarpaneva produced most of his glassware in Finland, but in the 1990s he designed models for Venini and, in 1999, created one-off pieces in glass in collaboration with Pino Signoretto, a craftsman on Murano whom he chose for his extraordinary ability in the modelling of plastic forms. The *Millennium* collection constitutes a synthesis between an aesthetics of essential but also organic character of Nordic origin and the manual skill typical of Venetian glasswork. Suggestive in their integration of delicate shades of colour and refined forms, they are the purest expression of Timo Sarpaneva's art and were presented at a special exhibition at the Finnish National Opera in Helsinki in the autumn of 2000.
Bibliography: *Millenium Meum*, 1999.

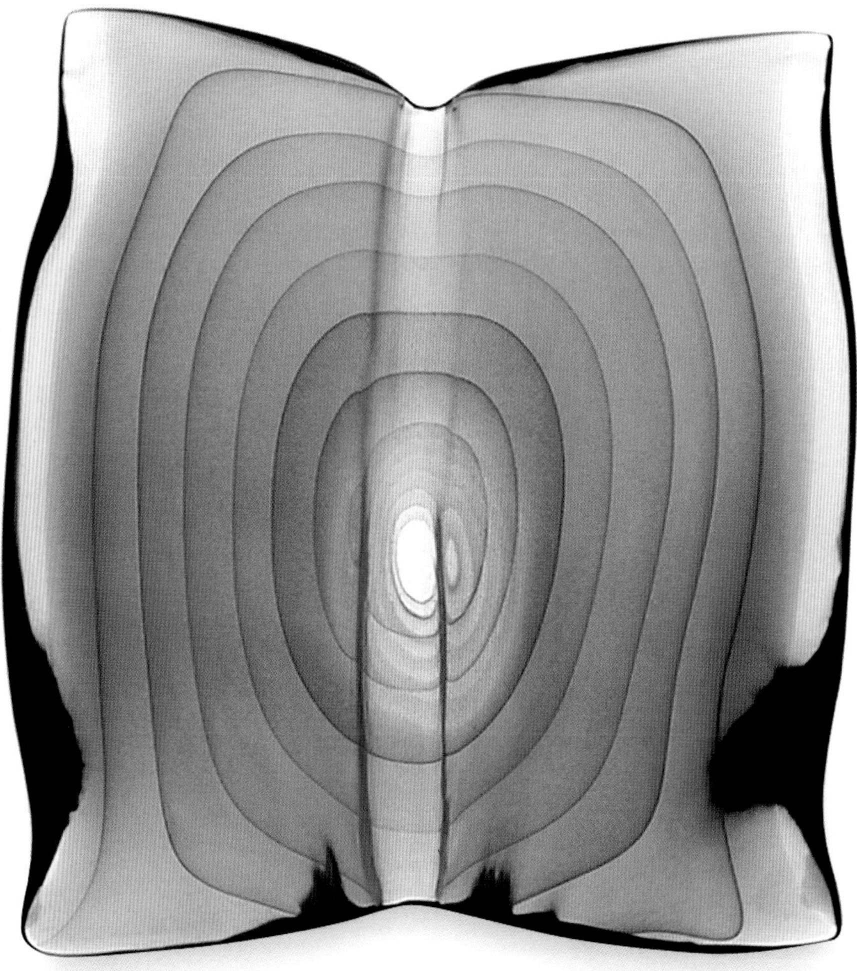

19

20
Lucio Bubacco
The Magic of Glass
2001
Flame-modeled glass, blown goblet,
h. 68 cm
Collection of the artist, Murano

Goblet with foot and bowl blown in the furnace and stem made up of a complex structure modeled in its entirety on the lamp. Diabolical figures in the act of working the glass while hot are applied to the branches of the structure, drawing a parallel between the fire of the furnace and that of hell.
Typological comparisons: Barovier Mentasti, 1992, fig. 167; Tosi, 2001, fig. 13.

20

21
Omar Galliani
Portrait of Lady with a Unicorn
1979
Pencil on panel, hide and glass,
145 × 252 cm
Laura Intilia Collection, Reggio Emilia

At the beginning of his career, when he was the youngest member of the anachronistic group promoted by Maurizio Calvesi and at a time when, in reaction to Arte Povera and purely conceptual art, a tendency toward citation and symbolism was emerging that was to lead at the end of the 1970s to the Transavanguardia and Magico Primario movements, Omar Galliani studied old drawings and paintings, reproducing details of masterpieces by Leonardo, Velázquez and Francisco de Zurbarán in pencil and pastel. The Emilian artist examined and copied the works of the masters in order to learn their syntax of image, and argued that "the perfect imitation is no longer an imitation, it is the thing itself." For the work *Ri-tratto di dama con unicorno* ("Portrait of Lady with a Unicorn"), displayed in the Room of the Sacred for its distinctly sacred and mythological iconography, Galliani took his inspiration from Raphael's celebrated painting *Portrait of a Young Woman* in the Galleria Borghese, also known as the *Lady with a Unicorn.* A few fragments spread out along an entire wall present the myth of the unicorn: a symbol of chastity, it was described in the *Physiologus* as similar in appearance to a kid, but fierce and stronger than any hunter. The only way to catch it was to place a virgin in front of it, get it to leap into a ring-amulet hanging at the girl's breast and allow it to suckle. In the installation, all that Galliani retains of Raphael's lady is a hazy and faded image of her face, while next to her he presents the presumed hide of the animal and the outline of its horn, in pure glass, another symbol of chastity.

22

21

22
Igor Mitoraj
Blue Saturnia
1990
Crystal paste,
19 × 28 × 27 cm
Private collection, Lucca

Igor Mitoraj is an indefatigable traveler. He has gone all over the world to learn the secrets of sculpture, studying Rodin, the Maya, Greek statuary. From his training in Cracow under Tadeusz Kantor to his studies in Paris and from his trips to Palenque, Ithaca and Delphi to his engagements in New York and Italy, every place he has visited has added something important to his work. In France he found force and grandeur, in Mexico monumentality, in Greece the human being and myth. For his sculptures with slanting eyes and high cheekbones he has looked further afield, perhaps to the Olmec heads of Central America, perhaps to the Turkish ones of Nemrut Dagi, or even the Cambodian statues of Angkor Wat. The two sculptures from his *Saturnia* series, presented in the Room of the Sacred since their principal reference is Greek mythology, are offspring of the ancient statues of Athens and Melos, mutilated by time. They are the Platonic dream of the excellent, beautiful and well-proportioned human being, who always ends up being shattered and overcome by events. A shattering which is underlined by the choice of glass as a material, conveying more effectively than bronze (because it is less resistant), the unattainable illusion of the perfect man. The artist often designs fragmented statues, busts and heads of marble, shields of bronze, that seem to come directly from the past but at the same time betray, by some obvious detail, their contemporary origin. From the stories of mythology he chooses the most contradictory and least Apollonian figures: Icarus, Ulysses, Eros, the Centaurs and the Gorgons.

23
Maurizio Bertinetti
Dumb waiter (red & blue)
2000
Painted statues, crystal, Absolut Vodka,
90 × 47 cm
Courtesy Absolut Vodka

Maurizio Bertinetti has always turned his sights on the self-righteous, fleeting fashions, religious fanaticism and the arrogance of power, heaping them with irony. A work from 2001, *Nutellas*, a reassessment of Manzoni's *Artist's Shit* – a pile of pages torn out of the magazine *Flash Art*, spread with chocolate and crumpled up, as if they had been used for purposes very different from reading – mocks the critical infallibility of certain specialist publications. A sculpture in granite from 2002, at once extremely heavy and insignificant, entitled *Souvenir*, makes fun of tourists who go round the world collecting useless objects… The work on show here (more profane than sacred, on the edge of blasphemy) – the pair of red and blue tables called *Dumb waiter*, made for the Absolut Vodka collection – targets religion and the do-it-yourself altars to be found in the homes of sanctimonious believers. The crystal table top, on which is set a bottle of liquor, is supported by statues of Christ and the Virgin, painted a metallic red or blue. As if to say, if you really have to have them in your apartment, then at least let them serve a useful purpose. Bertinetti uses mass-produced sheets of glass: the artist is interested in getting across a provocative idea, and not in technique.

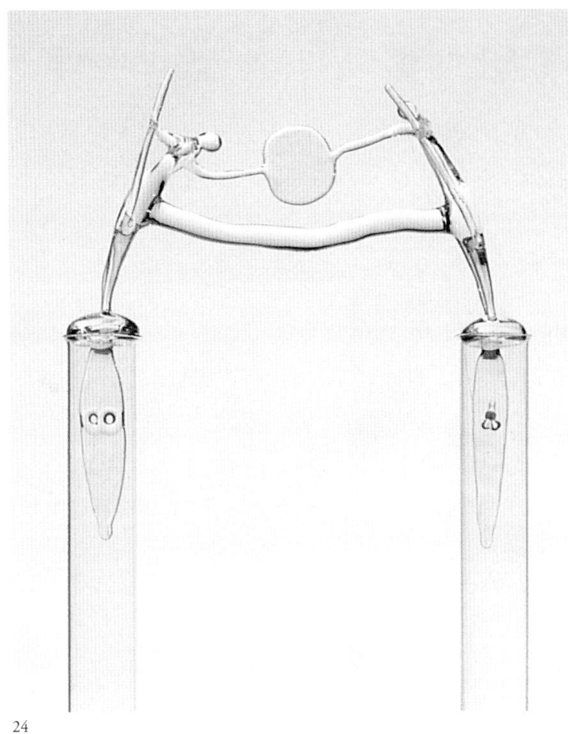
24

24
Giuseppe Maraniello
Rebis
2002
Glass,
180 × 50 × 35 cm
Galleria Flora Bigai, Venice

Giuseppe Maraniello's works are sometimes filled with archers, horsemen, divers and warriors who appear worthy of the Etruscan tradition and of the votive sculpture of the pre-Roman peoples; at others we find sketches made by the imaginative hand of a child, which in a few square centimetres illustrate battles, retreats, clashes, parades and flags. For *Glassway* the artist has created *Rebis*, a work in which he has used glass for the first time, completing a process of lightening that has led his sculpture from the dark tones of bronze first to those of silver and gold, then to monochrome white and finally to transparence. The work is presented in the Room of the Sacred for its resemblance to a hallowed portal, for its air of a threshold of initiation, in which the figures of the warriors seem to be indicating to the adept what, after abandoning the frivolity of adolescence, will be his new social role.

23 23

VI.

Room of the Fantastic

ANCIENT GLASS

In ancient times glass was not utilized for predominantly expressive purposes. Practical requirements, applying to all fields of the art, obliged craftsmen to rein in their creative impulses so as to produce functional forms, which answered to everyday needs. Yet originality and fantasy still played a part in limited cases and in a fairly controlled form. The emergence of the Rhenish school of glass onto the market introduced a new current of taste, remote from the staid classical tradition and outside the canons that had been respected hitherto. Thus original creations were proposed with the evident aim of arousing wonder. A small fish – which could function perfectly as a container – testifies to this caricatural and playful interpretation of glass, which also found expression in forms of more elaborate and bizarre conception.

CREATORS OF GLASS

Some works in glass stand out not just for their aesthetic and technical qualities but also for their spectacular effect, enhanced by particular lighting. Some of these are creations in which the glass is worked under "extreme" conditions, like Anna Skibska's three-dimensional cobwebs, or Markku Salo's lattices of glass which looks like ice, or Lucio Bubacco's flame-worked compositions resembling cathedrals, in which the fragile material is pushed to its limits. Others are multimedia works in which the effects of natural and artificial light are blended with sound. The term "fantastic" can be applied to Dale Chihuly's entire body of work: a theatrical designer who not coincidentally has worked successfully in the world of opera, though obviously in his own inimitable way, he plays with the most provocative colours, creating breathtaking compositions that catch the light in cunning ways.

CONTEMPORARY ART

After peopling the universe and repeatedly invading the Earth – in movies like *Invasion of the Body Snatchers, Blade Runner* and *Star Wars*, to mention just a few – androids, mutants and aliens have for some time had their designs on artistic production. After literature, the cinema, cartoons, television and video games, pictures, photographs, sculptures and installations (and we mustn't forget the videos of Chris Cunningham) have also been taken over by robots and extraterrestrials, by intergalactic species and "things" of the other world. All the genres of fantasy have without exception found an echo in the creations of the most recent generation of artists, who show a particular inclination to combine specialist research with those phenomena of mass culture – amongst which science fiction has been one of the most influential over the last forty years – that have left an unequivocal mark of the evolution of our age. Cosmic creatures or overgrown animals like Godzilla have made their way into the works of Bonomi, Ghibaudo, Hirst and Merrick, while the space parasites that contaminated earth organisms in the past (according to movies like *Species* and *The Puppet Masters*) seem also to have taken hold in the works of many contemporary artists, fond of suspense and the unpleasant surprise. Very many artists have chosen to present us with that recent past/immediate future that might await us following the apocalyptic events of *The Day After*. Glass, owing to its almost perverse fascination, its ability to be at once hard and soft, and to change from an opaque material into a transparent surface, is often the perfect medium for creating an effect of strangeness, for evoking the idea of mystery and wonder, as in Guzzetti's work peopled by twelve small aliens, animated and intrusive little creatures made out of glass. And as in the visionary and phantasmagorical worlds of Enrico T. De Paris.

1

1
Markku Salo
Transparent
2001
Glass paste,
h. 112 cm
Markku Salo Studio,
Nuutajärvi
Collection of the artist,
Nuutajärvi

Openwork drape created by fusing tiny slivers of glass together when hot to form a sort of lattice. It belongs to a series of extremely delicate one-off pieces, drapes and large bowls, that recall the ice of the Far North and stem from experimentation with a technique that is ancient but used in a totally new way, in order to exalt the extreme fragility of the glass. A drape of exceptional size was shown at *Aperto vetro* in Venice in 1998 and at the Global Art Glass Triennial, at Borgholm Castle in Sweden.
Typological comparisons: *Aperto Vetro*, 1998, p. 118; *Moderne Zeiten*, 1998, nos. 82-4; *Global Art Glass*, 1999, no p. no.

2
Dale Chihuly
Mosaic Blue Seaform Set
2001
Blown glass,
h. 30 cm
Seattle (Wash.), USA
La Scaletta di Vetro, Milan

Large bowl in the shape of an irregular shell made out of blue glass with repeated horizontal threads around the wall and a lip profiled in yellow. It contains nine smaller pieces, some of a similar form and others shaped like discs, making up a single work. Seaforms are among his favourites and he has been experimenting with them over the last two decades, coming up with new colourings and new decorative effects.
Typological comparisons: Frantz, 1989, p. 133.

3
Lucio Bubacco
Bucolic Seduction
2001
Flame-modeled glass, blown goblet,
h. 50.5 cm
Collection of the artist,
Murano

Goblet with foot and bowl blown in the furnace and stem made up of a complex structure completely modeled by flame. Classically modeled nude figures are applied on the branches of the structure, creating the scene of a bacchanal. Erotic themes are not infrequent in Bubacco's work. He tackles them with amusement and irony and they also provide him with an opportunity to make the most of his great skill in the modeling of the nude.
Typological comparisons: *Aperto vetro*, 1998, p. 61; Tosi, 2001, figs. 6, 9.

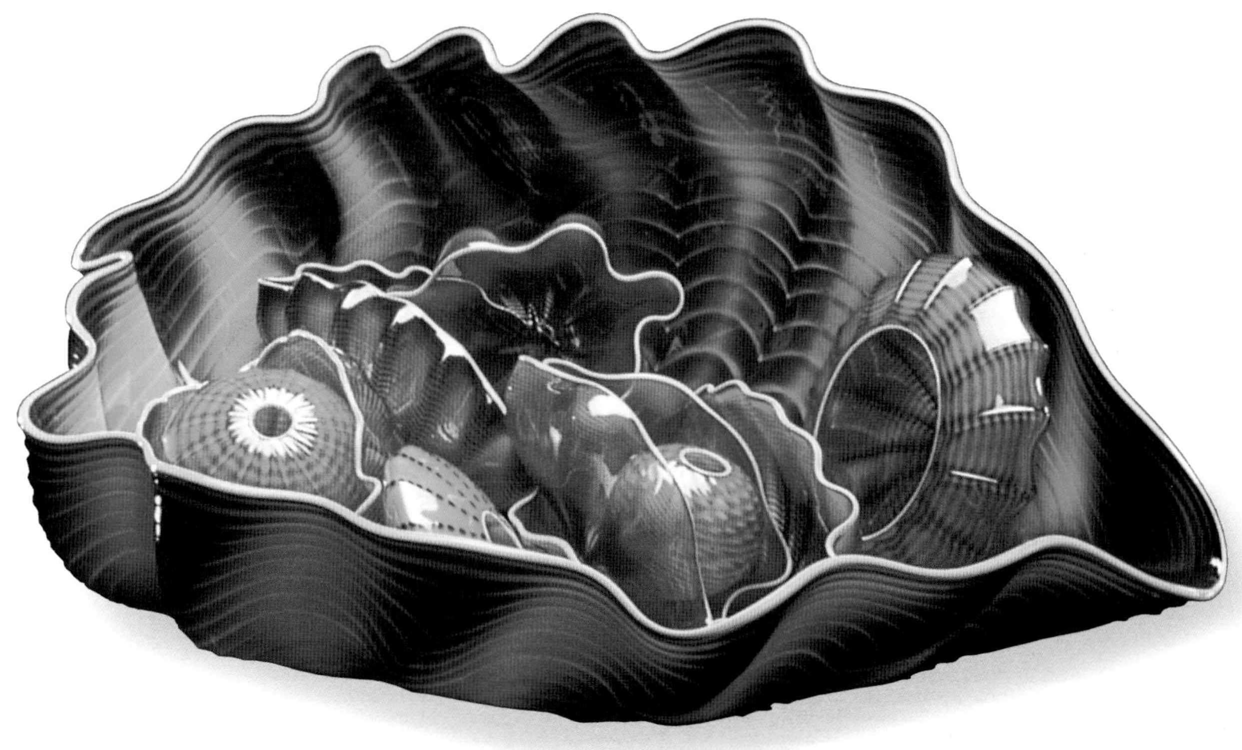

2

3

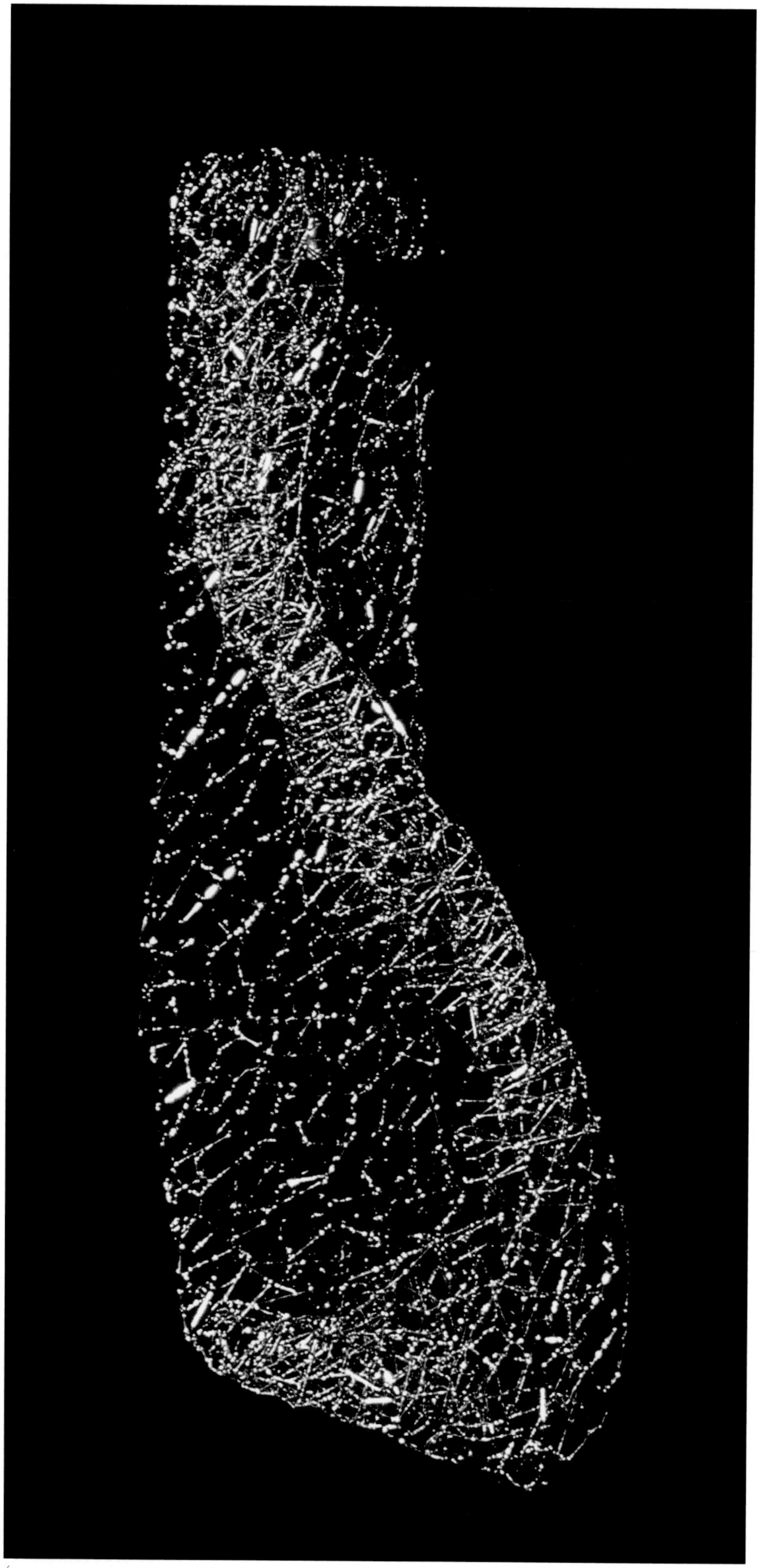

4
Anna Skibska
S. 1
2002
Flame-worked glass,
h. 150 cm; l. 200 cm
Collection of the artist,
Venice

Hanging sculpture made up of a light three-dimensional lattice of flame-worked glass. Technically, Skibska's works are astonishing: all she needs to make them is a cane of glass, a gas flame and a pair of tweezers, but there is much more to them than that. The artist has described her works as "traps of light" and in effect these lattices, which can be several meters long, catch the light and reflect it like iridescent cobwebs. They are also linked to their surroundings by the ever-changing shadows they cast on walls. They are often conceived in relationship to the environment and the form, which is not necessarily regular, is designed by the artist on the basis of this relationship.
Typological comparisons: Wichert, 1999, pp. 31-5; Kangas, 2000, pp. 24-31; Redaelli, 2000; Ricke, 2000; Toso Fei, 2000, p. 61.

5a
Lino Tagliapietra
Bilbao
Seattle, 2000-01
Blown *incalmo* glass, *battuto* and engraved finishing; blown *zanfirico* canes of glass,
h. 44 cm
Collection of the artist

5b
Lino Tagliapietra
Basel
Blown *incalmo* glass, *battuto* and engraved finishing; blown *zanfirico* canes of glass,
h. 63 cm
Collection of the artist

Vase of rounded shape with pieces made out of monochrome glass and out of twisted canes (*zanfirico*) of different colours, joined together by the *incalmo* technique and then engraved to create a *battuto* or "beaten" effect and incisions. Slender vase with a shaped neck of red glass with inserts of multicoloured *zanfirico* canes. These two works are emblematic of the masterly skill and elegant design of Lino Tagliapietra, one of the finest glassworkers in the world. He sometimes makes use of cold finishing, but in any case his work adapts the techniques of the Murano tradition to produce absolutely contemporary results.

5a

4

5b

6

6
Ale Guzzetti
Northward - Westward
1999
Flame-blown glass and electronic circuits (12 pieces), 50 × 100 × 500 cm
Private collection, Turin

Over the last fifteen years, in Italy and abroad, new genres have appeared on the horizon of artistic research. Alongside traditional ones like the landscape, still life, seascape and portrait, decidedly in crisis, other subjects have caught the attention of experts and occasional observers. Among them, almost all inherited from the study of other creative disciplines such as cinema and literature, there is science fiction. Many artists have drawn, for their creations, on the popular imagery made up of spaceships, aliens, UFO sightings and galactic battles whose Bibles are the *Star Trek* series, *2001: A Space Odyssey* and the covers of science-fiction paperbacks. Ale Guzzetti is one of these artists, filling galleries and museums with strange personages, disquieting presences in the manner of the *X-Files*, and very often making use of glass for its at once fascinating, mysterious and threatening properties. Properties that allow it to enchant, hypnotize and convince. This work – for obvious reasons in the Room of the Fantastic – is a collection of tiny creatures that are activated in the presence of spectators. Equipped with sensors, these little aliens made of glass start to emit sounds when someone approaches, turning from apparently immobile knickknacks into living things, capable of communicating and eager to make contact with civilizations decidedly different from their own. Owing to the function of the glass in the work – as skin, scale and body of the alien presence – the working of the material is a significant aspect of Guzzetti's work. He exploits all its chromatic and technical qualities, following a deep-rooted tradition of artists working in glass but without abandoning the freer and less artisan territory of contemporary art.

7
Peter Fischer
Repellus
1998
Metal, wood, glass,
150 × 150 × 150 cm
Courtesy Gabriel Soucheyre, Videoformes

Peter Fischer puts the show on show. He constructs complicated and delicately balanced machinery to render spectacular a moment – the projection of a film – that familiarity has stripped of its magic and enchantment. In *Repellus*, included in the Room of the Fantastic because it sets out to give the cinema back its old fascination, every puff of air or tiny shock makes the image move, causing it to vibrate and lending it a breath of life. The glass is present as the material needed to construct lenses and projectors, as a medium that is extraordinary in its ability to give an event, whatever it may be, a sense of wonder and enchantment.

8
Marcel Duchamp
A l'Infinitif (The White Box)
1966
Plexiglas box and silk-screen,
33 × 28 × 3 cm
Camerone Collection, Turin

Marcel Duchamp is the father of contemporary research, someone who still has to be reckoned with even today by any artist who sets out to create a form. The realization of *Fountain*, in 1917, changed the nature of art. After this work everything became possible, irony and paradox made their triumphal entry into the world of art. And sculpture took a road that would have been inconceivable before it. Duchamp often used glass in his pieces, from *Paris Air* – the ampoule containing 50 cc of the city's presumed atmosphere – to his most imposing work, left incomplete, *The Large Glass* (and neither should we forget the *Studies on Glass* he made for this). The piece proposed in the Room of the Fantastic – owing to its utopian aspect– is *A l'Infinitif*, also known as *The White Box*, a sort of study or portable version of the *Large Glass*. Constructed along the lines of the *Boîte-en-valise*, the work brings all the great creator's imagery together in a box. On the never-finished work and its surrogates, he wrote: "It has always been my intention to reduce the glass to an extremely succinct illustration of all the ideas of the box, which should be a sort of catalogue of these ideas. In other words, the glass should not be looked at for its own sake but only in relation to the catalogue that I have never made."

7

8

9a

9
Enrico Tommaso De Paris
a) **Pieces of Universe no. 1**
2002
Mixed media: steel structure and glass ampullae,
60 × 190 × 60 cm
Private collection, Milan

b) **Pieces of Universe no. 2**
2002
Mixed media: steel structure and glass ampullae,
60 × 90 × 60 cm
Private collection, Milan

c) **Pieces of Universe no. 3**
2002
Mixed media: steel structure and glass ampullae,
60 × 190 × 60 cm
Private collection, Milan

Often drawing on the imagery of the cartoon strip and the media, the research of Enrico Tommaso De Paris has deeper and more distant roots. It represents a reinterpretation, in a contemporary key and therefore one that is also conditioned by the graphics of cartoons and the themes proposed by the mass media, of the painting and the fantastic imagery of past centuries. From the formal point of view his referents, for their hallucinatory landscapes, the emotionality of their horizons, their maze of signs and their symbolic value, cannot be anything but Hieronymus Bosch and Pieter Bruegel the Elder. In his works the source of the density of the constructions, and with it the absurdity of the urban settings, cannot be limited to cartoon strips, but must be extended to the skylines of cities like New York, Hong Kong, Manila and Toronto. *Pieces of Universe*, a series of three visionary sculptures, recreates on a small scale the original Big Bang, an explosion of matter and forms that seems to be able to procreate new life and new space. The bright colours allude to the playful aspect of creation, but at the same time the atomic or molecular structure of the works, the concentration of suggestions and symbols, is an avowal of a desire to reconstruct, or at least to imagine, the logic of creation.

10
Silvano Rubino
Urn 3
2001
Blown glass - Vase/sculpture in black glass and ribbons of opaline glass,
76 × 25 cm
Collection of the artist, Venice

In his work Silvano Rubino, who has a great passion for scenography, utilizes videos, installations and photographs, in a line of research that focuses on chromatic contrast and memory. In the diptych *Story-Board*, a print of 1996, he juxtaposes the half-naked body of a girl with a handwritten page, filled with changes of mind and corrections. She is wearing nothing but a skirt, whose pattern echoes the handwriting on the page. In the installation *Dans le temps, dans la mémoire*, he places two red beds in a white room, and three photographs – a self-portrait and pictures of his father and daughter – on the wall to create a chamber of reminiscence. The artist's work is always based on solid colours, with no shading, as when he dresses a model in a blue drape and photographs her against a completely black background. Solid colours and memories are also to be found in the three works presented here, all from the same series of *Urns*. Rubino works the glass in such a way that it preserves its appearance of lightness, but eliminates refractions and transparencies so that it takes on the severity and the hieratic character of heavier, darker materials, suited to holding the ashes of the dead, like marble or bronze. Yet the form of the vases almost contradicts the object's function: the lid turns into an animal, coming alive and looking as if it could move away from the container of its own accord. And, in a fantastic dimension, as if it could carry off the soul to a new life.

10

9a

9b

9c

VII.

Room of the Everyday

ANCIENT GLASS

Ideal for the conservation of foodstuffs and liquids, as Trimalchio points out in Petronius's *Satyricon*, the use of glass became common in the home, both in the larder and on the table, especially with the spread of the technique of glassblowing in the Augustan era. This room is filled with a great range of objects of functional character, not so very different from the ones we use today. In the 1st century ordinary blue glass in open and closed forms came into widespread use. The numerous products made for the table – plates, bowls, drinking glasses, ewers and bottles – make up true dinner services that often drew their inspiration from traditional objects in terracotta or precious metals. Other services are characterized by the choice of opaque azure or black glass (Adria).
The room houses a number of vessels connected with eating habits typical of the Roman world, such as the small *amphoriskos* used for the fish sauce called *garum*, the *modiolus* cup used as a scoop and the various little bowls known as *acetabula*, *trullae* and *askoi*.
At the same time, glassware of Hellenistic derivation was much sought after, representing a sort of status symbol for its fortunate possessors. At the end of the century a type of production derived from metal models, originating in the East and called "honeycomb," came onto the scene. This faceted and colourless glass was used to make table services of some complexity (Sassari, Sarsina and Zara). In the 3rd century the workshops of the Rhine Valley gained a substantial share of the glass market, producing fine articles in colourless glass to which stylized decorations were applied. After a period of stagnation, a new shift in taste occurred in late antiquity, with the emergence of a style in which a few, select forms were privileged. These included goblets, drinking glasses on feet with decorations that also appear on vessels used for serving (Kiev, Kerch).
A group of oil lamps attests to the use of glass for lighting.

CREATORS OF GLASS

After the fall of the Roman empire the decline in specialized craft techniques in Europe resulted in a reduction in the number and quality of objects made out of glass. Around the year 1000, however, and increasingly in the first few centuries of the second millennium of the Christian era, Venice took up the legacy of Rome, handed down through Islamic and Byzantine centres of glassworking. The city's workshops produced glassware for practical use, especially drinking glasses, bottles (*inghistere*) and lamps, documented in paintings and by the fragments found in considerable quantity in the lagoon. The types of objects for everyday use remained unchanged for centuries. There were glassworks in other parts of Italy, in particular at Altare (Savona), which took on ever increasing importance from the Renaissance onward. The craftsmen of Altare built up a reputation for quality production and for articles for daily use, including some toward the end of the 19th century that were designed to serve some quite peculiar purposes. A considerable improvement in quality took place in the 20th century, from the 1930s onward, with the entrance of modern design into the factory. Architects and designers came up with functional models – Wilhelm Wagenfeld's "cube" refrigerator set and Aino Aalto's Bolgeblick dinner service are significant examples – which in numerous versions and imitations still enrich our daily lives. Yet there is another category of functional glassware: the refined products of highly skilled craftsmen, an area in which Venice has been the pioneer. When Venice lost its monopoly of the market at the end of the 17th century, new styles of glassware emerged, such as those of Bohemia and England. Today the tableware made by famous Venetian, French, Irish and Finnish glassworks are true status symbols, as well as miniature masterpieces of craftsmanship and creative imagination, such as the eccentric objects of Maria Grazia Rosin and Richard Marquis.

CONTEMPORARY ART

Paintings, photographs, videos. The last few years have seen the triumph of the everyday in the field of contemporary art, and an explosion of interest in the banal, the routine, the nullity of daily life. Works executed in the most varied media, and in every corner of the world, have given up describing curious situations, have stopped imagining captivating stories, have forgotten all about inventing epic tales, so as to concentrate instead on the familiar drudgery that, whether we like it or not, enmeshes and imprisons us all. Or at least the majority of people. These works speak of how they live their lives, of what people are really like, seeking to break down the barriers between truth and representation. This propensity, which has now become a runaway tendency, has been able to emerge in part thanks to previous experiments that had already brought ordinary life and the world of everyday experience onto the scene of art. In his *Tableaux-pièges* Daniel Spoerri has long captured, in frozen and unreal images, the leftovers of meals that have absolutely nothing exceptional about them, preserving for posterity the memory of an occasion at which nothing worth remembering occurred, while Silvia Levenson has often created impossible scenes in which the horror of domestic life seems to have remained attached to the skin of the objects, to the forms of all the things.

1
Quadrangular jar
1st century AD
Mold-blown glass,
h. 15.7 cm, ∅ of rim 8 cm, width of base 8.5 cm
From T. 39, western necropolis (Cantiere ex Polveriera), Aosta
Deposito della Sovrintendenza, Aosta Valley Autonomous Region, Aosta, cod. lab. 03-487
State of conservation: reassembled; small pieces missing from rim and body

Blue glass with marks of the mold on the walls. Quadrangular body and rounded shoulder. Vertical rim with double hollow tube. On the flat bottom, hard-to-distinguish concentric circles occupy the whole of the surface. The square jar, intended for the storage of solid food, had a wide distribution both to the north and the south of the Alps. The flattened rim has been associated with the Italian production of the 1st century. According to Taborelli (1983), the concentric circles in relief are a sort of trademark, indicating the producers of the contents of the vessel.
Typological comparisons: Isings, 62; Trier, 102; Scatozza, 55.
Bibliography: Isings, 1957; Calvi, 1968, group Bß, p. 89; Goethert-Polaschek, 1977; Maccabruni, 1983, p. 93; Scatozza Horicht, 1986, p. 68; Biaggio Simona, 1991, pp. 161-3, pl. 27; Roffia, 1993, p. 171; Bonomi, 1996, no. 381, p. 172; Paolucci, 2000, p. 100. (P.F.)

2
Two-handled jar with lid
second half of 1st century AD
Free-blown glass,
h. 29 cm, ∅ of belly 25 cm; lid: h. 8.5 cm, ∅ 14 cm
From tomb 759, northeastern necropolis of the Via Annia, excavation 1970, Altino (Venice)
Museo Archeologico Nazionale, Altino, inv. no. AL. 3917
State of conservation: reassembled

Wide mouth with rounded, expanded and flattened rim. Short neck with throat, broad shoulder, ovoid belly, concave bottom. W-shaped handles applied on the shoulder. Lid with conical body and forked handle. Blue-green transparent glass. Made in northeastern Italy. The jar-ossuary was deposited inside the sawn-off upper half of an amphora, fixed in the ground by the neck, and covered by the lower half of another amphora of larger size. The *olla* contained grave goods, mixed up with the cremated remains: an unidentifiable as, an iron *fibula* and a glass inkwell covered with gilded silver foil and engraved and embossed with a representation of a horserace.
Typological comparisons: jar: Isings, 1957, form 64; Calvi, 1968, group Aß, pp. 88-91; lid: Isings, 1957, form 66d; Calvi, 1968, type d, p. 89; Tirelli, 1994, cat. no. 1, p. 5. (M.T.)

1

2

3
Jar
second half of 1st - 2nd century AD
Blown glass,
h. 27.5 cm, ∅ of belly 22 cm; lid: h. 5 cm, ∅ 13 cm
Civiche Raccolte Archeologiche, Milan, inv. no. A.0.9.1352; formerly Seletti Collection (324 GI)
State of conservation: whole; slight traces of alteration; lid whole, inner surface with pitting and patches of iridescence

Fairly thin, transparent, blue glass, with bubbles. Wide mouth, with expanded lip and rounded rim, sloping inward. Broad, almost horizontal shoulder. Elongated, ovoid belly, with foot made by pushing the wall outward. Concave bottom. Curved strap handles, with double ribs, set on the shoulder and fused to the neck, under the lip. Flat lid, with rim folded slightly downward, cut to form a sharp edge. Button knob. Western production.
Bibliography: *Glass from the Ancient*, 1957, p. 119, no. 204; Fogolari, Scarfì, 1970, p. 87, no. 67.
(from E.R., 1993)

4
Ovoid jar with handles
1st-2nd century AD
Opaque violet glass, blown freehand,
h. 23.2 cm, ∅ of mouth 16 cm, ∅ of foot 11.1 cm
Provenance unknown; formerly Palagi Collection
Museo Civico Archeologico, Bologna
State of conservation: holes in body; one handle missing; surfaces devoid of iridescence

Rim rounded and folded outward; broad flared lip with pronounced edging on which to place the lid; short, throated neck; roundish ovoid body; foot in the shape of a truncated cone with concave bottom; small omega-shaped handles set on the shoulder. Perhaps used originally as a container for ashes in a grave, this jar stands out from the more usual production of cinerary urns for its deep violet colour. Typologically, it finds parallels in examples from a tomb at Este-Morlungo and from Adria, both produced by workshops in northeastern Italy, although it differs from these in the small size of the handles, a fairly rare morphological feature.
Typological comparisons: Isings, 64; Bonomi, 1996, p. 174, no. 388; Toniolo, 2000, p. 132, no. 309 and p. 136, no. 322 (for the colour).
Bibliography: Bologna, 1959, p. 33, no. 71; Mariacher, 1960, pl. 15; Bologna, 1976, p. 335, no. 343; Meconcelli Notarianni, 1979, p. 84, no. 79; Bologna, 1999, p. 47, no. 193.
(M.M.)

3

4

5

6

5
Cylindrical jar with lid
1st century AD
Blown glass,
h. 28.5 cm, ∅ of rim 13.3 cm; lid: h. 1.5 cm, ∅ 10 cm
From the southwestern necropolis of the Via Annia, 1952 excavation, Altino
Museo Archeologico Nazionale, Altino, inv. nos. AL. 1386-7
State of conservation: whole

Rim folded out and flattened, short neck, rounded shoulder, cylindrical body decorated with twelve bands of very fine engravings, separated by regular gaps of two centimetres, concave bottom. Transparent blue-green glass. The jar is closed by a small dish-shaped lid, also made of transparent blue-green glass, of the type with a folded back rim, slightly flaring vertical wall and flat base with a hollow at the centre. Typologically, there are no comparisons that can be made with the *olla*, apart from one specimen, but with two handles and a different rim, from Trier, dated to the first half of the 2nd century AD (Goethert-Polaschek 1977, form 104, pp. 182-3).
The jar, used as an ossuary, was placed inside an urn of white marble in the shape of a truncated cone and in turn contained, mixed up with the cremated remains, numerous melon-shaped beads in blue *faïence*, a bronze *fibula*, a small ring and pin made of gold, four gems and five asses. The grave goods were subsequently dispersed, but six beads and an as of Tiberius for *Divus Augustus* datable to 15-16 AD have been preserved.
Typological comparisons: Goethert-Polaschek, 1977; lid: Isings, 1957, form 46; Calvi, 1968, group B, pp. 93-5.
Bibliography: Marcello, 1956, pp. 71-2, fig. 45.
(M.T.)

6
Amphoriskos
1st century AD
Blown glass,
h. 41.5 cm, ∅ of rim 8.1 cm
Deposito Museo Archeologico Nazionale, Naples, inv. no. 13501
State of conservation: whole with internal cracks

Amphoriskos with rounded extremity and drop-shaped appendage, tall, elongated ovoid belly, marked shoulder and cylindrical neck. Acute-angled, forked handles, running from three-quarters of the way up the neck down to the shoulder. Everted lip with convex profile. This object, especially in view of its unusual dimensions, is clearly inspired by the better-known Roman amphorae used to transport wine and in all probability represents a particular kind of tableware, used to hold liquids of a certain value.
Typological comparisons: Isings, 60a; Calvi, Bα; De Tommaso, 59.
Bibliography: *Collezioni Napoli*, 1986, pp. 224-5, no. 40.
(C.Z.)

7

8

7
Bottle with one handle
second half of 1st century AD
Mold-blown glass,
h. 11.5 cm, sides 6 × 6 cm
From the northeastern necropolis of the Via Annia, tomb 89, 1966 excavation, Altino
Museo Archeologico Nazionale, Altino, AL. 1717
State of conservation: whole

Folded-back, horizontal rim, cylindrical neck, broad strap handle with two ribs, bent at an acute angle, sloping shoulder, cubic body decorated with a series of concentric circles in relief, flat base. Produced by a workshop in northeastern Italy.
The cremation grave, protected by a sawed half-amphora resting on a brick, included among its burial goods a second glass bottle, in addition to this one, several necklace beads, four melon-shaped beads, two faience pendants, other amber and glass paste beads, and a Claudian as for Germanico, dating from between 50 and 54 AD.
Typological comparisons: Isings, 1957, form 50; Calvi, 1968, group Ca, pp. 82-3; Biaggio Simona, 1991, type 10.2.2.1., pp. 177-82.
Bibliography: Tirelli, 1995, cat. no. 16.1, p. 17.
(M.T.)

8
Bowl
late 1st century BC
- early 1st century AD
Mold-pressed glass,
h. 4.5 cm, ∅ of rim 15.9 cm
From tomb 16, necropolis of the Canal Bianco, Adria
Museo Archeologico Nazionale, Adria, inv. no. IG AD 232
State of conservation: reassembled from numerous fragments

Low bowl of thick, dark-yellow and translucent glass, with cut and rounded rim, curved wall and slightly concave base. The only decoration consists of a pair of deep incisions cut with the grinding wheel, located under the rim. The bowl belongs to a craft tradition, of Hellenistic origin, typical of the glassworks of central and southern Italy.
Typological comparisons: Isings, 18.
Bibliography: Bonomi, 1996, p. 153, no. 337.
(S.B.)

9
Hemispherical bowl
first half of 1st century AD
Glass paste varying in colour from dark to pale violet, mould-pressed by the "mosaic" technique,
h. 5.5 cm, thickness 17.8 cm
From Zadar (Iader)
Arheološki Muzej, Zadar, inv. no. 694
State of conservation: glued and integrated

Bowl with hemispheroidal body. The delicately rounded rim follows the line of the body. On the walls, twenty-three ribs in relief run from the slightly concave bottom to the edge.
Typological comparisons: Morin-Jean, 1922-23, form 68; Marconi, 1932, p. 37; *Glass from the Ancient,* 1957, pp. 80-1; Isings, 1957, form 3a; Berger, 1960, pl. 2:18.2a; Tamaro Forlati, Mariacher, 1963, 8; Mariacher, 1966, 24; Doppelfed, 1966, fig. 86; Subic, 1976, p. 47, fig. 15; Goethert-Polaschek, 1977, form 3 A; Goldstein, 1979, p. 188, no. 501; De Maine, 1983, p. 85; Kirigin, 1984, p. 123, nos. 2-3; Lith, Randsborg, 1985, pp. 416, 429; Scatozza Horicht, 1986, form 2 A; Harden, 1988, p. 51, no. 27.
Bibliography: Marconi, 1932, p. 37.
(I.F.)

9

10
Small amphora
first half of 1st century AD
Free-blown glass,
h. 21.7 cm, ∅ of mouth 6.0 cm, ∅ of foot 6.5 cm, max. ∅ 10.7 cm
From Zanirato Collection, Adria
Museo Archeologico Nazionale, Adria, inv. no. IG AD 9001
State of conservation: whole

Small amphora of opaque azure glass with folded-back and flared rim, high neck to which two vertical handles with three ribs are attached, pear-shaped body and ring foot. The exceptional character of this piece lies in the material: completely opaque coloured glassware is quite rare, in fact, and seems to have been a peculiarity of northeastern Italy.
Typological comparisons: Isings, 15.
Bibliography: Bonomi, 1996, p. 23, no. 3.
(S.B.)

11
Small plate
first half of 1st century AD
Free-blown glass,
h. 2 cm, max. ∅ 10 cm
From Zanirato Collection, Adria
Museo Archeologico Nazionale, Adria, inv. no. IG AD 9002
State of conservation: whole

The plate has a very simple form: slightly thickened and rounded rim, low convex wall and ring foot made from base. Its peculiarity lies in the opaque azure glass from which it has been made. It constituted a set, along with the small amphora from Adria, IG AD 9001, of the same material and with an identical plate, and formed part of the contents of a grave which entered the Zanirato Collection in Adria.
Typological comparisons: Isings, 47.
Bibliography: Bonomi, 1996, p. 194, no. 445.
(S.B.)

12-13

12
Cup
early 1st century AD
Glass cast in mold and finished on wheel,
h. 5.8 cm, ∅ of rim 11.8 cm, ∅ of foot 5.8 cm
From Bocchi Collection, Adria
Museo Archeologico Nazionale, Adria, inv. no. IG AD 21519
State of conservation: whole

Hemispherical cup of thick, opaque black glass, with rounded and slightly everted rim and flared ring foot. This is a rare example of the glass known as *obsianum*, an imitation of obsidian, mentioned by Pliny the Elder (*Nat. Hist.*, XXXVI, 196).
Typological comparisons: Isings, 20.
Bibliography: Bonomi, 1996, p. 155, no. 345.
(S.B.)

13
Small cup
first half of 1st century AD
Free-blown glass; tool-worked and finished on the wheel, h. 3.5 cm, ∅ of rim 7.3 cm, ∅ of foot 5.5 cm
From tomb 34, necropolis of the Canal Bianco, Adria
Museo Archeologico Nazionale, Adria, inv. no. IG AD 431
State of conservation: whole

Small cup of thick, opaque black glass, with heavy flared and rounded rim, underlined by a molding made by bending the wall, short body in the shape of a truncated cone and disc foot. This too is an example of *obsianum* glass, imitating the volcanic glass, but this time blown rather than cast.
Typological comparisons: Isings, 69d.
Bibliography: Bonomi, 1996, p. 164, no. 372.
(S.B.)

10 11

14
Dish
1st century AD
Mould-pressed glass,
l. 23.8 cm, width 11.4 cm
Pompeii (I, 14, 11.15)
Deposito Archeologico,
Pompeii, inv. no. 12242
State of conservation:
reassembled with gaps

Rectangular dish with raised and slightly everted rim. At the side, two rectangular handles with arched edges terminate in two stylized volutes. The rare find from Vesuvius, part of a dinner service used to carry food or containers for drinks, is derived from and only has close parallels with similar objects in silver.
(E.D.C.)

15
Skyphos
1st century AD
Mould-blown glass, h. 11.2,
∅ of mouth 9.2 cm
From the House of the
Moralist, Pompeii (III, 4, 2)
Deposito Archeologico,
Pompeii, inv. no. 2540
State of conservation:
reassembled, with some gaps

Skyphos with deep ovoid bowl decorated with scales and slender goblet-style foot. Vertical ring handles with flat tongue set at the height of the rim and on the wall. The precious object, directly derived from similar examples in silver, is unique among the glassware found in the Vesuvian area. In fact the most pertinent comparisons are with elegant *skyphoi* in the service of silverware found in the House of Menander at Pompeii and with two other finds, perhaps from Herculaneum, in which the bowl is decorated with ivy shoots. Further examples of *skyphoi* but with less deep bowls and short goblet-style feet, also datable to the 1st century AD, have been discovered in other locations outside the Vesuvian area.
Typological comparisons: Calvi, 1968, pp. 63-4, no. 160, pl. 7, no. 1; Meconcelli Notarianni, 1979, p. 38, no. 21; *Collezioni Napoli*, 1986, p. 207, nos. 5b-6b, and p. 213, nos. 52-3.
(E.D.C.)

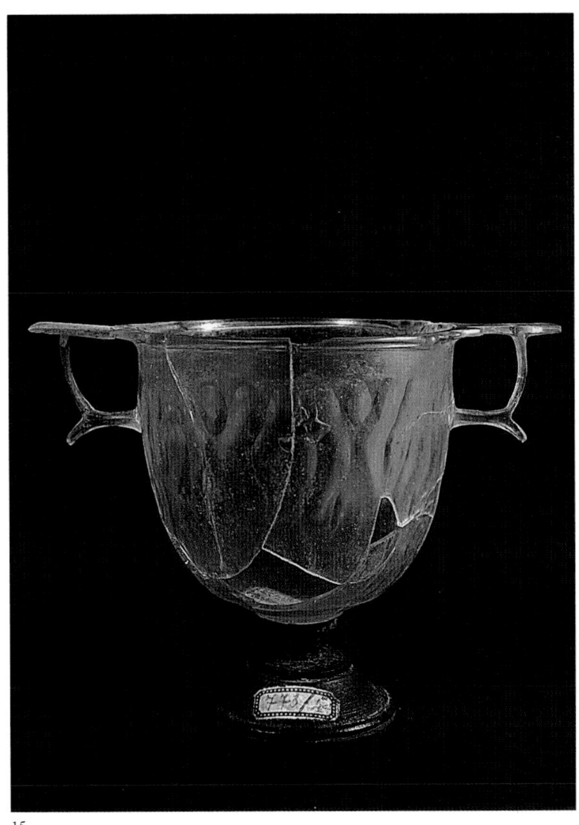

15

14

16
Kantharos
second half of 1st century AD
Blown glass,
h. 14 cm, ∅ of rim 15 cm
From Altino, without precise data of provenance
Museo Archeologico Nazionale, Altino, inv. no. AL. 6341
State of conservation: reassembled and integrated

Large krater-shaped bowl in transparent blue-green glass with thickened rim to which are attached two strap handles with tongue-shaped protuberances, standing on the middle of the wall. Short foot in the shape of a truncated cone. Handles and foot were modeled separately and applied when hot. The specimen, whose form is clearly inspired by silver and bronze models, was in all likelihood made in northeastern Italy.
Typological comparisons: Isings, 1957, form 39.
Bibliography: Tirelli, 1995, cat. no. 15, p. 17; Tirelli, 2000.
(M.T.)

17
Ribbed cup with threads
second quarter of 1st century AD
Mold- and free-blown glass, applied threads of glass paste,
max. h. 6.1 cm, ∅ of rim 6.7 cm, bottom 4.7 cm
From T. 49, western necropolis (Cantiere Gomiero), Aosta
Deposito della Sovrintendenza, Aosta Valley Autonomous Region, Aosta, cod. lab. 03-260
State of conservation: rim missing, outer surface completely altered by fire, including the threads, which have almost vanished

Small cup in thin aqua green glass. The hemispherical body tends to narrow toward the flared and cut rim; flat bottom. Twenty-two slender threads are interrupted at the height of the base. Fine trails of white glass paste encircle the neck and bowl, terminating in a spiral on the bottom.
A common type in various colourings, amber yellow, blue, azure and pale green, found in the urban layers of Aosta up until the Flavian era. Probably produced in the northwestern area, where many glassworks were active, it shows concrete affinities in its working with the ball-shaped *unguentaria*, Isings 10, also adorned with trails.
Typological comparisons: Isings, 17.
Bibliography: Isings, 1957, pp. 35-6; Calvi, 1968, form G, pp. 70-1, with previous bibl.; Carazzetti, Biaggio Simona, 1988, p. 51, pl. 12, no. 30; Biaggio Simona, 1991, pp. 71-4, pl. 4; Filippi, 1997, no. 318, pl. 1.3, p. 279.
(R.M.)

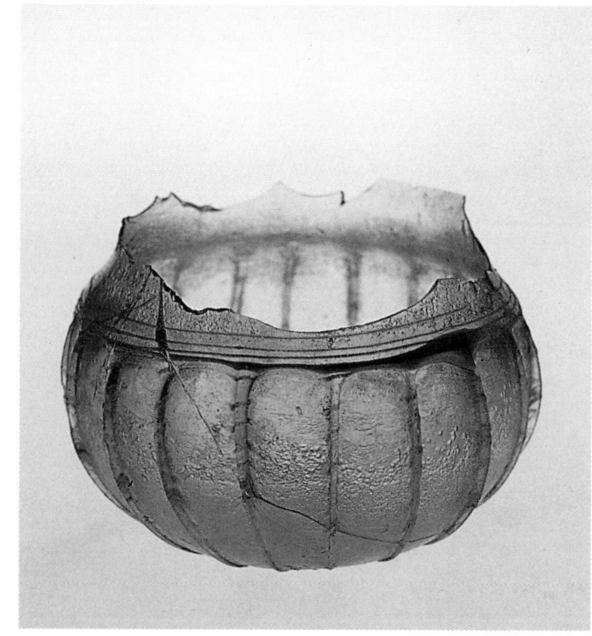
17

16

18
Small bottle decorated with speckles
middle of 1st century AD
Blown and decorated glass with speckles, applied handle,
h. 10.6 cm, ∅ of rim 3 cm, ∅ of belly 7.5 cm
From T. 49, western necropolis (Cantiere Gomiero), Aosta
Deposito della Sovrintendenza, Aosta Valley Autonomous Region, Aosta, cod. lab. 03-186
State of conservation: whole, apart from small piece missing near rim

Small bottle in thin, opaque blue glass, rounded conical body, cylindrical neck with constriction, rounded rim folded inward; elbow-shaped handle with three ribs and three terminal appendages, folded back at the attachment to the neck; flat bottom. The example from Aosta is decorated entirely with white

18

19

speckles and with yellow spots, more frequent on the neck and shoulder.
Olpai decorated with speckles are present in Northern Italy in the contexts of the first half of the 1st century. They were products of value, reserved for an élite. Similar examples have been found in the Pavia region (Maccabruni) and Canton Ticino (Biaggio). The type may represent a simplification of more refined products in polychrome mosaic glass (Grose).
Typological comparisons: Isings, 14.
Bibliography: Isings, 1957; Grose, 1983, p. 101; Maccabruni, 1983, no. 36, p. 64 (from Zerbolò); Biaggio Simona, 1991, fig. 18, p. 189; Bonomi, 1996, no. 314, p. 137.
(P.F.)

19
Small ewer
middle of 1st century AD
Blown glass,
h. 10.5 cm, ∅ of rim 5.1 cm, max. ∅ of belly 7.2 cm
From T. 49, western necropolis (Cantiere Gomiero), Aosta
(AO-GOM 2)
Deposito della Sovrintendenza, Aosta Valley Autonomous Region, Aosta, cod. lab. 03-283
State of conservation: whole, superficial alterations

Thin, transparent yellowish glass. Biconical body, wide cylindrical, expanded neck, finished with a tubular rim folded back internally; curved rod handle with terminal appendage. Concave bottom. One of the most ancient forms, derived from metal working, it was found in association with the small blue, speckled *olpe* and with the small Isings 17 cup. An example of refined execution, a substitute for metal objects.
Typological comparisons: comparable to Isings, 58.
Bibliography: Calvi, 1968, pp. 59-61, no. 154; Bonomi, 1996, no. 329, p. 144; Facchini, 1999, no. 382, p. 167; Brecciaroli Taborelli, 2000, pl. 344, pl. 70, pp. 294-5.
(R.M.)

20
Bottle with one handle and conical body
middle of 1st century AD
Blown glass, applied handle,
h. 16.9 cm, ∅ 3.3 cm,
max. ∅ 9.1 cm
From the context of a tomb at Pignet, Saint-Christophe
Deposito della Sovrintendenza, Aosta Valley Autonomous Region, Aosta, inv. no. 56 PG 1583-2238, 17
State of conservation: whole

Bottle in transparent blue glass, with a conical body and very broad concave base; cylindrical neck with slight constriction at the bottom. Rim with a triangular section, folded back externally and flattened. Handle with two ribs, folded back at the top, extending at the bottom in two tangs. The production of these glass vessels for domestic use does not appear to have been widespread in northern Italy, as was that of the more common bottles with cubic and cylindrical bodies. Probably of western production, in the dated contexts of Canton Ticino and the Novara region, bottles with a conical body can be ascribed to the period between the Claudio-Neronian era and sometime well into the first century. The principal comparisons are with objects from Canton Ticino (Locarno, level a 44), (Ascona, tomb s. 3) and the Piedmont region (tomb 8, Gravellona Toce, Carpignano and Cesto). So far glass *olpai* with conical bodies are poorly represented in the necropolises and urban deposits of *Augusta Praetoria*.
Typological comparisons: Isings, 55a, pp. 72-4.
Bibliography: Vescoz, 1909, p. 41; Barocelli, 1926, p. 93; Lamboglia, 1943, pp. 163-94; Barocelli, 1948, col. 197; Isings, 1957, pp. 72-4; Donati, 1987, pp. 59-60, 84 *et sqq.* ; Uglietti, 1991, p. 128; Mollo Mezzena, 1995, pp. 111-8.
(R.M.)

20

21
Ewer
1st century AD
Blown glass,
h. 12 cm, ∅ of rim 4,8 cm,
∅ of body 11.3 cm
Place of discovery unknown
The National Museum of History of Ukraine, Kiev, inv. no. 27-2781
State of conservation: incrustations on surface

Ewer with wide conical body and broad profiled lip. The short and cylindrical neck has a constriction at the point of contact with the body. Wide strap handle that curves to form an acute angle. The bottom is flat. The body is decorated with five bands of engraved lines. Transparent glass, with bluish tinges, containing numerous bubbles. These containers were used to pour and store small quantities of liquid. Similar vessels were common in the ancient cities of northern Pricernomor'ja. They were made in the workshops of the eastern Mediterranean.
Typological comparisons: Sorokina, 1978, p. 268, drawing 1.4.; Kunina, 1997, cat. no. 239.
(P.O.A.)

22
Cup
1st century AD
Blown glass,
h. 8 cm, ∅ of rim 14.3 cm,
∅ of bottom 5.4 cm
Northern Pricernomor'ja
From the S.N. Platonov Collection
The National Museum of History of Ukraine, Kiev, inv. no. 8518
State of conservation: the surface is covered with incrustations. A piece is missing from the foot

Cup with high profiled and protruding lip. Body with rounded walls, narrowing toward the bottom, on conical foot. Transparent glass, with greenish cast. Signs of the pontil are visible on the bottom. Such bowls were used for drinking. In northern Pricernomor'ja these cups have been found in the necropolis of Pantikapey. The area of production for similar containers was the eastern Mediterranean. They are based on the form of cups in *sigillata* pottery, which were common in those times.
Typological comparisons: Vessberg, 1952, pl. IX, pp. 40-1; Isings, 1957, form 69a; Kunina, 1997, p. 311, cat. nos. 285-6.
Bibliography: Puklina, 2001, pp. 138-9; Var. Authors, 2001, p. 32, ill. 57.
(P.O.A.)

21

22

23

24

23
Ewer
end of 1st century AD
Blown glass, handle cast separately and applied,
h. 21.9 cm, ∅ of rim 7.4 cm, max. ∅ 12.3 cm
From T. 11, predial necropolis of Saint-Martin-de-Corléans, Aosta
Deposito della Sovrintendenza, Aosta Valley Autonomous Region, Aosta, inv. no. 03-595
State of conservation: reassembled from many fragments, with gaps

Ewer in thin, transparent, pale-blue glass, with an ovoid body, rounded shoulder, neck in the shape of a truncated cone and broad everted tubular rim, rounded and folded back internally. Curved handle with double ribbing, fused to the rim with a roundish protuberance, and truncated-cone foot, with concave base. Derived from metal models, the specimen, a less common variant of better-known and more widespread types, can be ascribed to a northern Italian workshop. The most specific parallels are with footless ewers from Aquileia (Calvi, 1968, group A, plate B 9, cat. no. 155) and the Veneto region in general (Bonomi, 1996, cat. no. 329).
Typological comparisons: Isings, form 58.
Bibliography: Isings, 1957, pp. 76-7; Calvi, 1968, p. 60, pl. 8.4.
(R.M.)

24
Small cylindrical cup with grooves
second half of 1st century AD
Blown glass, cut on grinding wheel,
h. 6.3 cm, ∅ of rim 8.2 cm
From T. 36, western necropolis (Cantiere Gomiero), Aosta
Deposito della Sovrintendenza, Aosta Valley Autonomous Region, Aosta, cod. lab. 03-605
State of conservation: reassembled, pieces missing from rim and altered surface

Small cup in semi-opaque greenish glass. Cylindrical body, rounded toward the flat bottom. The rim, slightly indented and cut, is underlined by a groove; two more broad grooves adorn the wall. A very widespread drinking glass, it represents a simple variant of Isings form 12, influenced by articles in metal.
Typological comparisons: Isings, 12.
Bibliography: Isings, 1957, pp. 27-9; Calvi, 1968, group A, pp. 52-3, pl. B, 1; Facchini 1999, no. 397.
(P.F.)

25

26

25
Hourglass-shaped beaker
second half of 1st century AD
Free-blown glass,
h. 11.5 cm, ∅ of rim 7.9 cm, ∅ of bottom 6.5 cm
From tomb 45, necropolis of the Canal Bianco, Adria
Museo Archeologico Nazionale, Adria, inv. no. IG AD 639
State of conservation: whole

Beaker of thin, colourless, transparent glass, with indistinct, simply cut rim, underlined by a line engraved on the grinding wheel; body in the shape of a double truncated cone; flat base. There are no precise comparisons with the piece, but its form recalls mold-blown examples, including one from the same necropolis in Adria (Bonomi, 1996, no. 282, p. 124). In the current state of our knowledge there are no elements that serve to attribute the piece to a particular workshop with any certainty.
Bibliography: Bonomi, 1996, no. 288, p. 126.
(S.B.)

26
Small amphora
1st century AD
Free-blown glass; handles worked separately and applied,
h. 19 cm; ∅ of mouth 6 cm
From tomb 41, feeder-road necropolis, 1982 excavation, Altino
Museo Archeologico Nazionale, Altino, inv. no. AL. 21340
State of conservation: reassembled

Small amphora in transparent, pale green glass decorated with white and red speckles. Rim folded back and flared, vertical handles with two ribs set on the body and fused to the upper part of the neck, flared neck, pear-shaped body, ring foot. Produced by a workshop in northern Italy. The tomb with the cremated remains was contained inside half an amphora of small size and closed by a bowl-shaped lid in gray pottery. The remains were at the bottom of the container, along with a coin, an unidentifiable as. Above were deposited in succession, all turned upside down, two glass *unguentaria*, the small amphora in question and two bottles, one made of blue-green glass, the other of yellow.
Typological comparisons: Isings, 1957, form 15; Calvi, 1968, type Aa, pp. 22-3, pls. A:1 and 1:7.
Bibliography: Tirelli, 1994, p. 19, fig. 20.
(M.T.)

27
Jar
second half of 1st century AD
Free-blown glass,
h. 18.8 cm, ∅ of mouth 14.5 cm
From tomb 701, northeastern necropolis of the Via Annia, 1969 excavation, Altino
Museo Archeologico Nazionale, Altino, inv. no. AL. 3348
State of conservation: reassembled and integrated

Folded-back, horizontal rim, broad shoulder, ovoid body, concave bottom. Translucent, violet glass decorated with white speckles. Produced in northern Italy. The jar, used as an ossuary, contained a Claudian as, datable to between 41 and 54 AD, among the cremated remains.
Typological comparisons: Isings, 1957, form 67a; Calvi, 1968, group A, pp. 88-91.
(M.T.)

27

28
Small jar
second half of 1st century AD
Free-blown glass,
h. 12.5 cm, ∅ of mouth 12 cm
From tomb 883, northeastern necropolis of the Via Annia, 1970 excavation, Altino
Museo Archeologico Nazionale, Altino, inv. no. AL. 4336
State of conservation: reassembled and integrated

Folded-back horizontal rim, broad shoulder, ovoid body, concave bottom. Transparent yellow glass. Made in northeastern Italy. The tomb with the cremated remains was protected by an amphora sawn in half. The small jar, probably used as the ossuary of a child, contained grave goods among the cremated remains: an iron *fibula* and an as that is not identifiable owing to its heavy corrosion.
Typological comparisons: Isings, 1957, form 67a; Calvi, 1968, group A, pp. 88-91.
(M.T.)

29
Bowl with omega-shaped handles
1st century AD
Blown glass with applied handles,
h. 5.4 cm, ∅ of rim 15.3 cm, foot 5.6 cm
From T. 36, western necropolis (Cantiere ex Polveriera), Aosta
Deposito della Sovrintendenza, Aosta Valley Autonomous Region, Aosta, cod. lab. 03-604
State of conservation: reassembled with numerous gaps

Olive-green glass with many impurities and some bubbles. Hemispherical bowl with tubular rim, indented and folded back outward. Two small omega-shaped handles set against the wall and irregularly modeled: one protrudes above the rim; low ring foot, thickened and slightly raised bottom. Derived from bronze models, mostly produced in the central and southern area, the bowl finds a precise parallel in an example from the Pavia region (Dorno-Battera) assigned by C. Maccabruni to no later than the Flavian era. The colouring of the glass suggests the bowl found in Aosta was produced on the northern side of the Alps.
Typological comparisons: Trier, 21.
Bibliography: Goerthert-Polaschek, 1977, no. 91, pl. 33; Fremersdorf, IV, pl. 71; Maccabruni, 1983, pp. 40-1, no. 14, p. 49.
(P.F.)

29

30

28

30
Askós
1st century AD
Mold-blown colourless glass,
10.5 × 15.5 cm
From Pompeii
Deposito Museo Archeologico Nazionale, Naples, inv. no. s.n. 2
State of conservation: whole with many cracks inside

Small, elongated, ring foot, swollen belly with gadrooned, irregularly projecting rim. Small angular handle raised above the lip and decorated with an engraved herringbone pattern bounded by horizontal incisions. Upper attachment in the form of a flat strap with a cuspidate incision, pointed lower attachment with double lateral fins. The object is an imitation in glass of the well-known ceramic and metal form. This specimen, unfortunately lacking an inventory number but probably from Pompeii – as suggested in the bibliography – combines the quality of the raw material – a fairly thin and pure colourless glass – with a high technical level of working. In fact the gadroon decoration of the belly was attained by mold blowing while the decorative motifs of the small handle, made separately, were produced by engraving and polishing. The type has been found in the cities of the Vesuvius area in blue and blue-white glass as well.
Typological comparisons: Isings, 59.
Bibliography: Isings, 1957, p. 77; Var. Authors, 1986, pp. 224-5, no. 39.
(C.Z.)

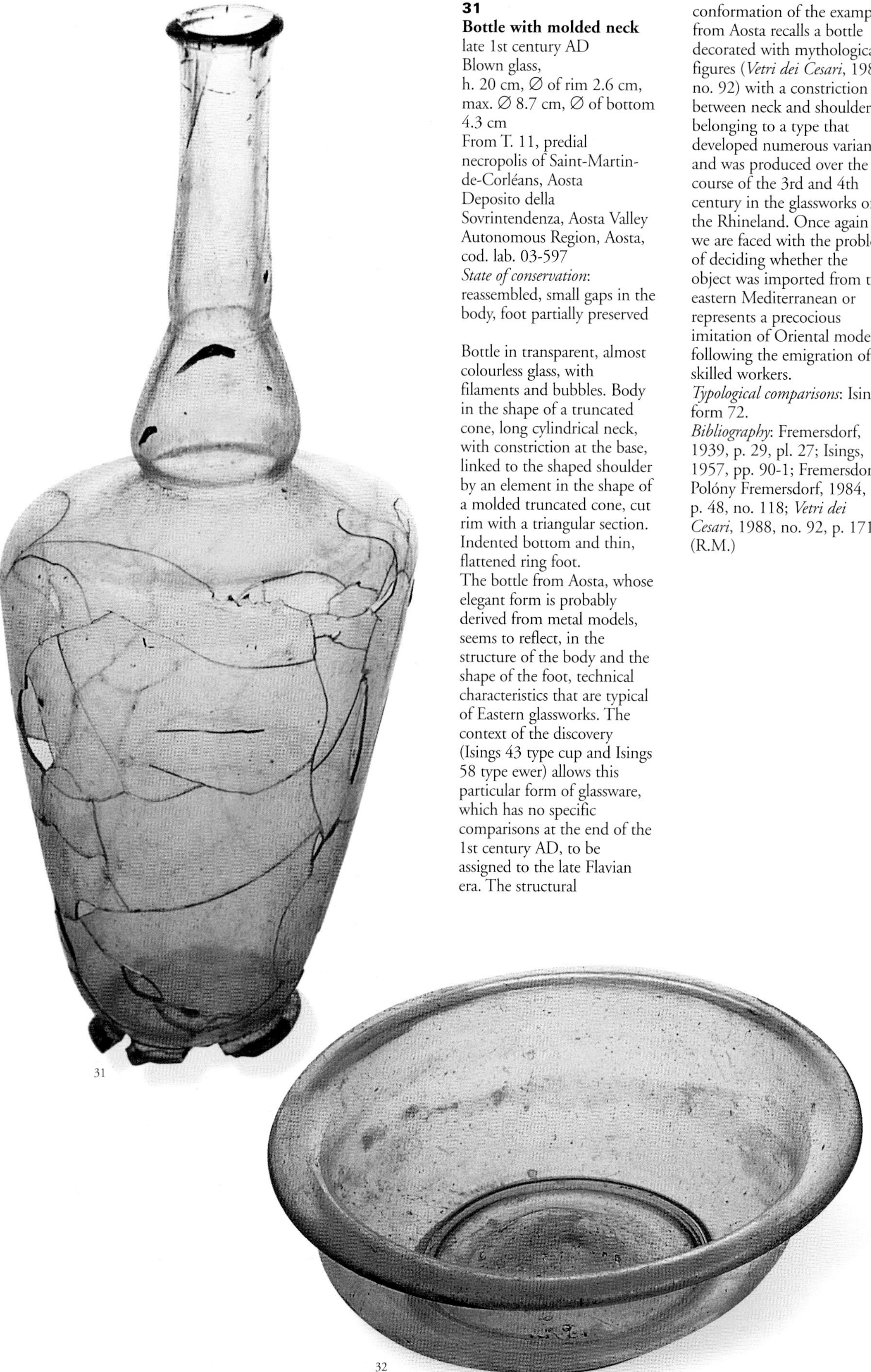

31

32

31
Bottle with molded neck
late 1st century AD
Blown glass,
h. 20 cm, ∅ of rim 2.6 cm, max. ∅ 8.7 cm, ∅ of bottom 4.3 cm
From T. 11, predial necropolis of Saint-Martin-de-Corléans, Aosta
Deposito della Sovrintendenza, Aosta Valley Autonomous Region, Aosta, cod. lab. 03-597
State of conservation: reassembled, small gaps in the body, foot partially preserved

Bottle in transparent, almost colourless glass, with filaments and bubbles. Body in the shape of a truncated cone, long cylindrical neck, with constriction at the base, linked to the shaped shoulder by an element in the shape of a molded truncated cone, cut rim with a triangular section. Indented bottom and thin, flattened ring foot.
The bottle from Aosta, whose elegant form is probably derived from metal models, seems to reflect, in the structure of the body and the shape of the foot, technical characteristics that are typical of Eastern glassworks. The context of the discovery (Isings 43 type cup and Isings 58 type ewer) allows this particular form of glassware, which has no specific comparisons at the end of the 1st century AD, to be assigned to the late Flavian era. The structural conformation of the example from Aosta recalls a bottle decorated with mythological figures (*Vetri dei Cesari*, 1988, no. 92) with a constriction between neck and shoulder, belonging to a type that developed numerous variants and was produced over the course of the 3rd and 4th century in the glassworks of the Rhineland. Once again we are faced with the problem of deciding whether the object was imported from the eastern Mediterranean or represents a precocious imitation of Oriental models following the emigration of skilled workers.
Typological comparisons: Isings, form 72.
Bibliography: Fremersdorf, 1939, p. 29, pl. 27; Isings, 1957, pp. 90-1; Fremersdorf, Polóny Fremersdorf, 1984, p. 48, no. 118; *Vetri dei Cesari*, 1988, no. 92, p. 171.
(R.M.)

32
Carinate cup
late 1st century AD
Blown glass,
h. 4 cm, ∅ of rim 13.5 cm, ∅ of foot 6 cm
From T. 11, predial necropolis of Saint-Martin-de-Corléans, Aosta
Deposito della Sovrintendenza, Aosta Valley Autonomous Region, Aosta, cod. lab. 03-594
State of conservation: whole, streaked at the rim

Cup in colourless, transparent glass, with tiny bubbles. Carinate bowl, wide, horizontal, everted, cut and rounded rim and ring foot. Indented bottom with mark of the punty.
The cup, which formed a set with a morphologically similar cup and a bottle of Isings type 72, is a contemporary variant of Isings form 43, with no festoon but a cut and rounded rim. The same morphological characteristics are displayed by glassware found in the Syrio-Palestinian area, such as the plates from Capernaum (Roffia, 2000, cat. nos. 4-6). Close formal analogies are also to be found in western examples from Canton Ticino and Piedmont (tomb 15, Asti), datable to between the late 1st and early 2nd century AD. For this type of plate and cup, present in various localities of northern Italy, the problem is also raised of the centres of production and their connection with the areas of distribution of plates with festoon handles, Isings form 43.
Typological comparisons: Isings, form 43.
Bibliography: Isings, 1957, p. 59; Mollo Mezzena, 1981, fig. 62, pp. 116-17; Biaggio Simona, 1991, p. 55; Zanda *et al.*, 1994, p. 179, no. 5, pl. XLVI, 5.
(R.M.)

33

33
Carinate beaker
second half of 1st - early 2nd century AD
Blown glass, finished on grinding wheel,
h. 5.9 cm, ∅ of rim 8.2 cm, ∅ of foot 2.7 cm
From the area of the destroyed tombs, eastern San Rocco necropolis, Aosta
Deposito della Sovrintendenza, Aosta Valley Autonomous Region, Aosta, cod. lab. 03-1401
State of conservation: reassembled, small gaps in the upper part of the body

Beaker in thin, semitransparent, colourless glass, with ground surface. Carinate body, high wall, slightly expanded rim, slender ring foot. A double border in relief marks the rim and carination.
The drinking glass, in opaque, colourless glass, is undoubtedly a product of great value that is difficult to fit into the classification usually adopted. The example from Aosta finds generic affinities in the western production of glassware that began to spread through the region in the second half of the 1st century AD (cf. Biaggio Simona, 1991, pp. 103-4), in the overall form of the body, flared at the top and carinate at the bottom. A number of differences, such the ornamental disposition of the border in relief and the particular treatment of the glass, appear to suggest an eastern origin or a direct derivation from Oriental prototypes.
Bibliography: Coarelli, 1963, pp. 74-6; Price, 1987, pp. 33-4; Biaggio Simona, 1991, p. 103, 7.3.3., pl. 10 (139.2.030); Paolucci, 1999, pp. 70, 81, no. 30.
(R.M.)

34
Ewer
1st century AD
Mold-blown glass, h. 13.5 cm, ∅ of bottom 4.6 cm
Museo Nazionale G. A. Sanna, Sassari, inv. no. 3724
State of conservation: fragmentary; iridescent surfaces

Opaque glass of medium thickness and pale-green colour. Squashed globular body on which the cylindrical neck is set with a continuous profile; trefoil mouth with rim folded back to form a tubular edging, flattened inward; flat, unstable base; strap handle, bent into a right angle, set on the shoulder and fused to the rim, folded into a vertical eye above the upper attachment. Body and bottom decorated with a "honeycomb" pattern. The technique used to obtain this decoration, blowing into a mold, suggests a probable eastern origin for the ewer in the Sassari Museum. A similar decoration to that of the ewer can be found on a piece of glassware from Cornus, now in the Museo Archeologico of Cagliari. The example, considered one of the oldest bowls made by the technique of the pressing into a mold, is datable from sometime between the pre-Roman period and the 1st century AD. The bowl, like the trefoil ewer, reproduces not just the form but also the embossed decoration of metal prototypes of particular value (*Museo di Cagliari*, 1994, p. 73, cat. no. 359, pl. 80, p. 228).
Typological comparisons: Isings, form 56, pp. 74-5.
Bibliography: Lissia, 2000, cat. no. 48, pp. 57, 65-6.
(D.L.)

34

35

36
Ewer
1st-2nd century AD
Blown glass,
h. 23 cm, ∅ of rim 5.5 cm,
∅ of bottom 6.3 cm
Northern Pricernomor'ja
From the S.N. Platonov Collection
The National Museum of History of Ukraine, Kiev,
inv. no. 8520
State of conservation: cracks are present on various parts of the body. The surface is covered with incrustations

Ewer in transparent glass with ovoid body on ring foot, the lip is folded back and everted. The funnel-shaped neck is decorated with doubly-twisted glass threads. Wide strap handle, which curves to form a right angle with a protuberance above the lip. The bottom is visibly concave; the marks left by the pontil are visible. These ewers were used to pour and store small quantities of liquid. Similar vessels were widespread in the ancient cities of northern Pricernomor'ja. They were made in the workshops of the eastern Mediterranean.
Typological comparisons: Kunina, 1997, p. 305, cat. no. 254.
Bibliography: Puklina, 2001, pp. 138-9.
(P.O.A.)

35
Beaker
Blown and engraved colourless glass,
h. 13 cm, ∅ 14.6 cm
From tomb 50, Sarsina (Forlì)
Deposito Museo Archeologico Nazionale, Ferrara,
inv. no. S 48
State of conservation: reassembled and integrated

Beaker in the shape of a truncated cone, low flared foot, with a height almost equal to the diameter, central part with six rows of "honeycomb" facets bounded at the top and bottom by a border in relief (for the technique see Lierke, 1999, pp. 97-109, fig. 273B).
No solution has yet been found to the problem of the place of production of these pieces engraved with a geometric motif, luxury articles which reflect the high rank of their purchasers and of the tombs in which they are found (Paolucci, 1997, pp. 63-8, fig. 28: according to the author, the colourless "honeycomb" glassware of the Flavian era can be attributed to eastern and in particular Egyptian workshops).
Thus the tradition of the studies (Oliver, 1984; Rütti, 1988, pp. 54-7, 863, pl. II and fig. 34; Rütti, 1991, p. 69), suggests an Oriental origin (Syria and Egypt), but Rütti does not exclude the possibility of a technique developed in the East having been adopted in western glassworks (for a comparison with the famous glassware of Begram and extensive previous bibliography see Menninger, 1996, pp. 32-8, pl. 8, type A).
The incineration tomb, *alla cappuccina* (covered with sloping tiles), dates from the beginning of the 2nd century AD, but the drinking glass can be ascribed to as far back as the Flavian era, although it is attested up to the early decades of the 2nd century.
Typological comparisons: Isings, form 21.
Bibliography: *Giornale di Scavo*, 1930, tomb 50; Ortalli, 1998b, pp. 78-9.
(G.M.N.)

36

37

37
Globular bottle with one handle
2nd century AD
Blown glass, handle modeled and applied,
h. 15.9 cm, ∅ of rim 5 cm, ∅ of belly 12.1 cm, ∅ of foot 7.6 cm
From T. 14, former Hotel du Mont Blanc necropolis, Aosta, Deposito della Sovrintendenza, Aosta Valley Autonomous Region, Aosta, cod. lab. 03-1331
State of conservation: reassembled, gaps in the body, in the rim and on the handle; diffuse incrustations, frequent bubbles and streaks

Bottle in very thin and milky glass. Spheroidal body, raised belly, short cylindrical neck and wide rim, folded back and flattened at the top. Broad strap handle bent at an acute angle and running from shoulder to neck. Foot in the shape of a truncated cone with a concave base. This is a type of *olpe* with a spherical belly in the undecorated version, found in the Rhineland and the former Yugoslavia. The variant with a short neck is attested in the western Po Valley and more rarely finds parallels in Ticino and the Pavia and Piedmont areas.
Typological comparisons: Isings, 52.
Bibliography: Isings, 1957, pp. 69-70; Plesnicar Gec, 1972, p. 205; Goethert-Polaschek, 1977, pp. 190-1; Maccabruni, 1983, nos. 32, 35; Biaggio Simona, 1991, pp. 196-7, pl. 41; Caramella, De Giuli, 1993, pl. XXXIX, 3; Gabucci, 1997, figs. 1, 25.
(R.M.)

38
Cylindrical bottle with incisions
second half of 2nd century AD
Mold-blown glass, incisions made on grinding wheel,
h. 25.2 cm, ∅ 6.9 cm, max. ∅ 11.4 cm
From T. 327, western necropolis (former Hotel du Mont Blanc), Aosta
Deposito della Sovrintendenza, Aosta Valley Autonomous Region, Aosta, cod. lab. 03-602
State of conservation: reassembled, small integrations

Bottle in thin, semitransparent glass with greenish cast and minute bubbles. Tall cylindrical body, decorated with four bands of incisions set at unequal distances. Cylindrical, slightly tapered neck, funnel-shaped rim with thickened and molded lip; long strap handle with narrow vertical grooves, bent at an acute angle. Flat bottom with slight concavity. The bottle has morphological parallels with an example from Sardinia decorated with bands of horizontal incisions (Maccabruni, 1983, no. 64). A type common in the Western provinces over the course of the 2nd to 3rd century AD, it is comparable in its refinement of execution and elegance of form to the bottle from Cornus (Fortuna Canivet, 1969, pp. 99-100), which is hypothesized to be an import from the eastern Mediterranean area. The bottles present in the Canton Ticino differ in the outline of the rim and the conformation of the handle (Biaggio Simona, 1991, p. 187).
Typological comparisons: Maccabruni, 1983, no. 64.
Bibliography: Fremersdorf, 1965-66, p. 34; Fortuna Canivet, 1969, pp. 99-100; Fremersdorf, Polóny Fremersdorf, 1984, pp. 75-80, no. 174; Biaggio Simona, 1991, p. 187.
(R.M.)

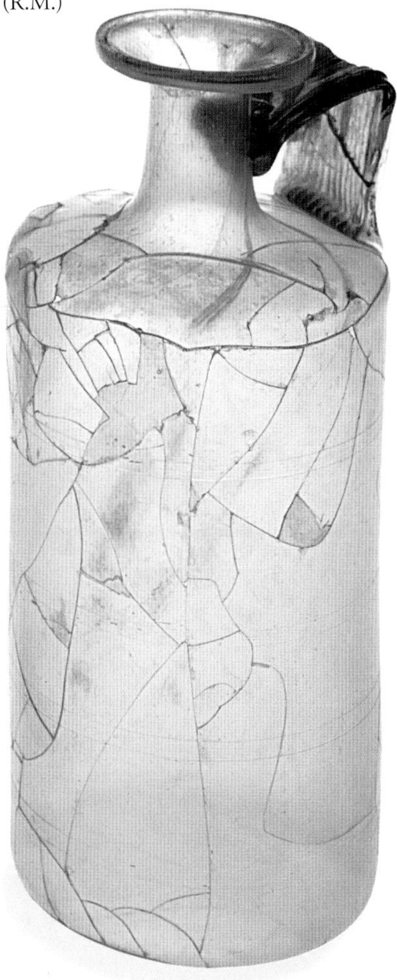

38

39
Plate with horizontal rim
second half of 2nd century AD
Blown and cut glass,
h. 3.4 cm, ∅ 24.4 cm, bottom 12.9 cm
From Tomb 327, western necropolis (former Hotel du Mont Blanc), Aosta
Deposito della Sovrintendenza, Aosta Valley Autonomous Region, Aosta, cod. lab. 03-603
State of conservation: reassembled and integrated at the rim, cracks

Plate in transparent, light green glass, with sparse, point-like bubbles. Carinate bowl, thickened and raised bottom, wide ring foot with mark of the pontil on the bottom. Along the slightly molded brim run a series of cuts and elongated notches. The decoration of vertical facet-cut that characterizes the upper face of the plate's rim seems to present a fairly close parallel with a plate/bowl from Alba (Gabucci, 1997, p. 467, figs. 2-4), dated to the beginning of 2nd century AD. The fact that the plate from Aosta comes from a funerary context datable to sometime in the 2nd century AD seems to fit into the chronological framework proposed for decorations of cuts and facets (Paolucci, 1997, pp. 108-11).
Typological comparisons: Isings, 97a.
Bibliography: Isings, 1957, pp. 116-17; Ravagnan, 1994, no. 467, p. 231; Gabucci, 1997, p. 468; Paolucci, 1997, pp. 108-11.
(R.M.)

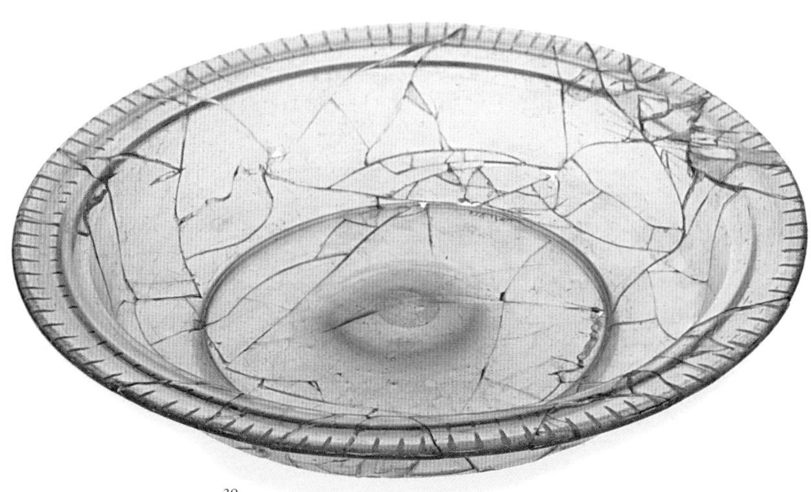

39

40

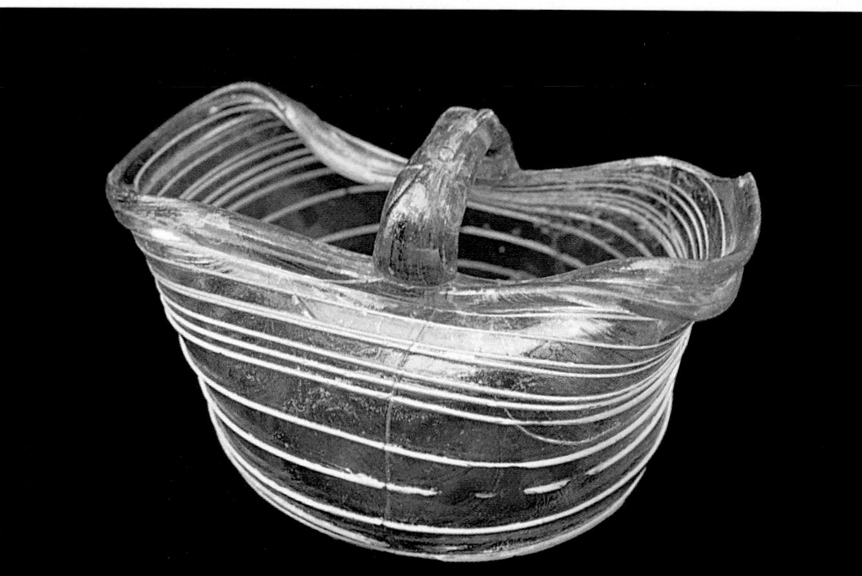

41

43

40
Plate
3rd century AD
Blown glass,
h. 5.4/4.8 cm; ∅ of rim 20 cm; ∅ of foot 7.8 cm
A. Personeni Collection
Civiche Raccolte Archeologiche, Milan,
inv. no. A 998.01.97
State of conservation: whole, mark of punty

Plate in pale-blue, thin and transparent glass with numerous bubbles and streaks. The piece is inclined as a result of irregular working. Bowl with round wall, tubular rim, folded outward. Concave bottom, small ring foot formed by folding of the wall.
Presents numerous parallels with specimens from the eastern Mediterranean and dating from the 2nd to 3rd century AD.
Typological comparisons: Hayes, 1975, p. 63, no. 177; Platz-Horster 1976, p. 62, no. 116; Roffia, 1993, p. 94, no. 94.
Bibliography: *Constable Maxwell*, 1979, p. 162, no. 284.
(from E.R., 2000)

41
Basket-shaped vessel
2nd century AD
Free-blown glass, with applied white threads and handle,
h. 7 cm, thickness 13 × 9 cm
From west necropolis of Salona, 1827 excavation,
Solin (Salona)
Arheološki Muzej, Split,
inv. no. G 45
State of conservation: glued, a small part of the border is missing

Vessel made of pale-blue glass in the shape of a basket with a ring handle in the middle of the narrow part of the body. Flat bottom. White glass threads applied around the body.
Typological comparisons: approximate analogies: Kisa, 1908, form 435; Morin-Jean, 1922-23, form 138; Doppelfeld, 1966, p. 119; *Constable Maxwell*, 1979, p. 69, no. 108.
Bibliography: Saldern, 1964, p. 44, no. 7.
(I.F.)

42
Ewer and trulla
3rd century AD
Blown glass with applications of threads,
ewer: h. 11.4 cm, pan: l. 19 cm, ∅ 13.5 cm
From tomb 166, Roman necropolis in the Luxemburger Strasse, Cologne
Römisch-Germanisches Museum, Cologne, inv. nos. L 668, L 667
State of conservation: ewer: whole, opaque glass. Pan with handle slightly rounded at the edge

Ewer in colourless glass with trefoil spout, body with wide handle in the shape of a ribbon. The applied, alternating opaque blue and white threads repeat four times the ornamental motifs typical of glass vessels from Cologne. They are characterized by a horizontal decoration of undulating filaments, bending upward to the left and downward to the right and running horizontally above and below the ripples and bending again to end in a spiral. An undulating blue ribbon is applied to the handle. A pan with a handle of colourless and transparent glass was found with the ewer. The border of the spout is folded outward. The end of the handle of blue-green glass has been flattened with a pincer. Ewer and pan with handle – *vas et trulleum* – were a typical combination of functional tableware in the Roman period, used for washing hands, especially at banquets. In practice terracotta vessels were used, or as a more costly variant, metal ones, the most precious made out of silver. On the basis of the finds made in the Rhineland, it has to be assumed that this type of glassware was produced in large quantities. The form and technique are more or less the same in all the examples. The miniature glass vessels found along with ewers and pans are undoubtedly just ornamental elements.
Typological comparisons: ewer: Kisa, 1908, p. 467; pan: Fremersdorf, 1959, pls. 50-2; Harden, 1988, p. 128, no. 58; Follmann-Schulz, 1992, p. 57 no. 32, p. 60 no. 33.
Bibliography: Hagen, 1906, p. 412; Isings, 1957, form 75a; Fremersdorf, 1959, p. 51, pls. 53, 55; Fremersdorf, 1961, p. 29, pl. 27.
(H.G.)

43
Two-handled cup
3rd century AD
Free-blown glass, handles pressed in mold and applied, h. 6.8 cm, thickness 10.7 cm, ∅ of lip 8.2 cm
Dalj (*Teutoburgium*)
Arheološki Muzej, Zagreb, inv. no. 11860
State of conservation: whole

Cup in colourless glass with a yellowish cast, flat bottom and cylindrical body. Slightly everted, cut rim. Two small handles in the shape of a lion's head in relief are set diametrically opposite, halfway up the cylindrical body.
Bibliography: Šaranović-Svetek, 1986, group 2:4.
(I.F.)

42

44
Two-handled bottle with applied threads
3rd century AD
Blown glass, applied handles and threads,
h. 24.7 cm; ∅ of rim 5 cm, max. ∅ 12.5 cm,
∅ of bottom 7.5 cm
From Aosta
Deposito della Sovrintendenza, Aosta Valley Autonomous Region, Aosta, inv. no. 1956
State of conservation: restored and integrated. Foot incomplete, small gaps and numerous imperfections

Bottle in glass of greenish colour, with point-like bubbles and filaments. Globular body, long cylindrical neck, funnel-shaped mouth with rounded edge. Ring foot molded and rounded on the outside, indented bottom with mark of the pontil. The handles, in opaque green glass, are set on the body, bent to an angle and joined to the neck by a ring; a thread in the same colour winds around the mouth. As far as the working is concerned, the example belongs to the category of

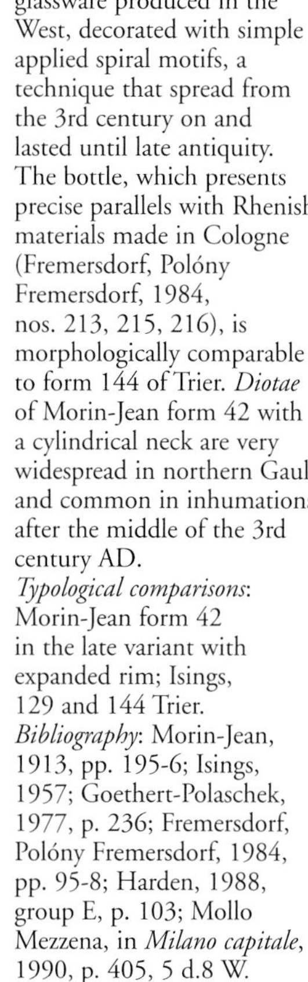
glassware produced in the West, decorated with simple applied spiral motifs, a technique that spread from the 3rd century on and lasted until late antiquity. The bottle, which presents precise parallels with Rhenish materials made in Cologne (Fremersdorf, Polóny Fremersdorf, 1984, nos. 213, 215, 216), is morphologically comparable to form 144 of Trier. *Diotae* of Morin-Jean form 42 with a cylindrical neck are very widespread in northern Gaul and common in inhumations after the middle of the 3rd century AD.
Typological comparisons: Morin-Jean form 42 in the late variant with expanded rim; Isings, 129 and 144 Trier.
Bibliography: Morin-Jean, 1913, pp. 195-6; Isings, 1957; Goethert-Polaschek, 1977, p. 236; Fremersdorf, Polóny Fremersdorf, 1984, pp. 95-8; Harden, 1988, group E, p. 103; Mollo Mezzena, in *Milano capitale*, 1990, p. 405, 5 d.8 W.
(R.M.)

44

45

45
Cup on stem
4th century and first half of 5th century AD
Blown glass,
h. 9.6 cm, ∅ of rim 6.9 cm, of foot 3.8 cm
Tomb 125, necropolis of the “Lilac Bay” country estate, Pricernomor’ja. Bosphorus region. Excavations of the archeological expedition to eastern Crimea, carried out by Dr. of Historical Sciences A.A. Maslennikov
KGIKZ collections, State Historico-Cultural Reserve, Kerch, inv. no. Кл 145797
State of conservation: alterations of the glass

Bowl with body of cylindrical form and rounded foot. Lip slightly folded back externally. Low foot with a not very marked constriction. Concave bottom. The body has decorations in relief made up of large oval blobs of blue glass, comprised between two bands of double engraved lines. Transparent glass, with olive-green hue. The regions where glassware with decorations of blue blobs are attested are Pricernomor’ja and the eastern Mediterranean, in the 4th-5th centuries AD. Drinking glasses, produced in an older style, are often found in the Bosphorus region.
Typological comparisons: Sorokina, 1971, p. 86, d. 1; Kunina, 1997.
Bibliography: Maslennikov, 2000, no. 3, pp. 144, 178, pl. III.4.
(A.Z.)

46
Ewer
5th century AD
Blown glass,
h. 28.5 cm, ∅ of rim 7.4 cm, max. ∅ 9.9 cm
Tomb 13, necropolis of the "Lilac Bay" rural settlement, Pricernomor'ja, to the northeast of the Kerch peninsula. Excavations of the archeological expedition to eastern Crimea, carried out by Dr. of Historical Sciences A.A. Maslennikov
KGIKZ Collections, State Historico-Cultural Reserve, Kerch, inv. no. KMAC - 1171
State of conservation: areas on surface where the glass is altered

Ewer with pear-shaped body, no shoulders, very tall neck, broadening toward the bottom, and a funnel-shaped lip. The foot is conical. Flat and ribbed handle, bent to form an acute angle, with a plastic protuberance above the lip. Four threads are set one above the other on the rim, while the everted lip is thick. There is a modeled tube on the neck. The marks left by the pontil are visible on the bottom. Transparent glass, with a pale-green cast and small bubbles. Such articles were widespread in Pricernomor'ja and the eastern Mediterranean in the 4th-5th centuries AD. Ewers of a similar form are found in the necropolises of the Bosphorus region.
Typological comparisons: Kunina, 1997, pp. 330-2, cat. nos. 398-9.
Bibliography: Maslennikov, 1997, pp. 15, 80, d. 28.1.
(A.Z.)

46

47

48

47
Lamp
1st century AD
Blown glass,
l. 11 cm, h. 4 cm,
∅ of disc 8 cm
From Pompeii (I, 11, 16)
Deposito Archeologico,
Pompeii, inv. no. 12714
State of conservation: handle missing

Oil lamp with lenticular body and no distinction between the shoulder and disc; the hole used to pour in the oil is large and circular, the cylindrical nozzle is short and turned upward, the bottom is ring shaped. Glass oil lamps, unlike those in terracotta and bronze, are very rare; there is another oil lamp with the same shaped body in the Museo Archeologico Nazionale of Naples. Glass oil lamps of this shape can be compared with bronze oil lamps of the type with a short and raised nozzle, deriving from Hellenistic prototypes of the 2nd-1st century BC and attested in the 1st century AD in the Vesuvian area.
Bibliography: *Homo Faber*, 1999, p. 208, no. 273.
(E.D.C.)

48
Conical lamp
second half of 4th century AD
Colourless glass with a greenish cast, blown freehand and polished, lip cut,
h. 13.3 cm, thickness 8.2 cm
From Solin (*Salona*)
Arheološki Muzej, Split, inv. no. G 1771
State of conservation: whole

The markedly conical body of the oil lamp widens from the narrow rounded bottom toward the cut lip. Three broad horizontal lines are engraved around body and under the folded back lip.
Typological comparisons: Morin-Jean, 1922-23, form 107; Sunkowski, 1956, fig. 11a; Isings, 1957, 106A; *Trois millénaires*, 1958, p. 51, no. 60; Berger, 1960, pp. 228-9; Isings, 1975, no. 477; Cermanović-Kuzmanović, 1976, p. 190, no. 3; Šubic, 1976, p. 61, no. 58; Goethert-Polaschek, 1977, form 54; Šaranović-Svetek, 1986, group 3:8 A; Barkóczi, 1988, pp. 99-106; Lith, 1988, p. 63; Friedhoff, 1989, p. 39, fig. 1:15.
Bibliography: Buljević, 1994, p. 262, no. 13.
(I.F.)

49
Beaker - lamp
4th-5th century AD
Blown glass,
h. 16 cm, Ø of rim 7.8 cm
Northern Pricernomor'ja
From the S.N. Platonov Collection
The National Museum of History of Ukraine, Kiev
inv. no. 8529
State of conservation: the surface is covered with incrustations

Beaker with a conical body narrowing toward the small bottom with a rounded tip. The edges are smooth and cut. The body is adorned with four bands of engraved lines. Transparent glass. These vessels were used for drinking, but their form also made it possible for them to be utilized as oil lamps in hanging candelabra. Such cups were common in Egypt, Syria and northern Pricernomor'ja and have often been found in the burial tumuli of the Chernikovsk culture. Possible places of production of these vessels are Egypt and Syria.
Typological comparisons: Harden, 1936, p. 157; Sorokina, 1971, no. 4, pp. 85-100, type III, ds. 3-5; Kunina, 1997, p. 337, cat. nos. 424-5.
Bibliography: Puklina, 2001, pp. 138-9.
(P.O.A.)

50
Lamp
5th-6th century AD
Very thin, transparent, pale-yellow glass, with bubbles,
h. 7 cm, Ø of lip 9.4 cm
Civiche Raccolte Archeologiche, Milan, inv. no. A.0.9.1339. Formerly Seletti Collection (1413 GI)
State of conservation: one handle almost completely missing, another reattached. Surface with altered patches and concretions

Tubular lip, formed by folding the wall out and flattening it. Body in the shape of a truncated cone; bottom very concave at the centre. Mark of the pontil on the bottom. Three strap handles, bent to form acute angles, applied vertically above the lip at equal distances. Western production (central-southern Italy?).
Bibliography: Roffia, 1981-83, pp. 214-15; Stiaffini, 1985, p. 673, form D1, pls. 1, 5; Stevenson, 1988, p. 201.
(From E.R., 1993)

49

50

51

52

51
Bowl
Venice, early 16th century
Blown glass *a mezza stampaura*, enameled, with gold graffito,
h. 8 cm
Museo Ala Ponzone, Cremona
State of conservation: excellent

Bowl on foot of amethyst colour decorated with a dense series of radial ribs obtained by the *mezza stampaura* or "half-molding" technique. A thread of amethyst is applied around the ribs and a band of gold leaf with a graffito inscription in capital letters runs around the border.
A specimen of great refinement rendered extremely rare by the presence of the inscription. There is another example in the British Museum and two in the Museum of Decorative Arts in Prague.
The bowl was part of the original nucleus of the Ala Ponzone collection, prior to 1840.
Typological comparisons: *Catalogue Venetian Glass*, 1973, cat. nos. 8, 10; Tait, 1979, no. 28.

52
Ribbed bowl
Venice, early decades of 16th century
Blown crystal with ribs *a mezza stampaura*,
h. 12.9 cm
Museo Ala Ponzone, Cremona,
State of conservation: excellent

Bowl on amethyst-coloured foot with radial ribs and a thread of amethyst glass applied to the outside. The border is profiled by a blue thread. The type corresponds to a model relatively common at the beginning of the 16th century, which in a version without a foot is also documented in a painting: Pietro di Cosimo, *Madonna and Child*, Royal Collections of Stockholm.
The bowl was part of a bequest from the antiquarian Vincenzo Favenza, active in Venice in the second half of the 19th century.
Typological comparisons: *Mille anni*, 1982, p. 123.

53
Goblet
Murano, second half of 16th century
Mold-blown, *filigrana a retortoli* glass,
h. 14.5 cm
Civici Musei d'Arte e Storia, Brescia,
State of conservation: excellent

Goblet on foot with folded-back rim made from alternate straight and twisted canes of crystal and the opaque white glass known as *lattimo*, linking avolio in crystal, baluster stem of straight and twisted canes. The bowl, also made from a filigree of alternate straight and twisted canes, is blown into a mold with a rusticated pattern that results in an undulation of the canes. The technique of *filigrana a retortoli*, using twisted rods of glass, was patented on Murano by Filippo Cattani in 1527 and has remained in use ever since. The elegant and balanced form of this goblet corresponds to the finest period of Venetian Renaissance glassware and can be seen in numerous paintings by great Italian artists, from Veronese to Caravaggio. There is an almost identical example in the Corning Museum of Glass, but with no rustication of the bowl.
Typological comparisons: Barovier Mentasti, 1982, figs. 68, 86, 88; *Mille anni*, 1982, no. 169 (diamond-point engraved); *Venezianisches Glass der Veste Coburg*, 1994, no. 259.
Bibliography: Mariacher, 1965, p. 21; *Vetri nelle collezioni bresciane*, 1987, no. 33b.

53

54
Jug with dragons
Venice, second half of 16th century
Mold-blown, *filigrana a retortoli* glass,
h. 27.4 cm
Museo Ala Ponzone, Cremona
State of conservation: excellent

Jug in *filigrana a retortoli* of crystal and *lattimo* with applied foot with folded-back rim, blown linking node, mold-blown body with dragons in relief and bean motifs in the upper part. Trefoil mouth, handle raised above the mouth. These proportions are typical of the finest period of Venetian Renaissance glassware and are documented in paintings of the time, by Titian and Paris Bordone among others, but in pure crystal. There are a relatively large number of examples in *filigrana* of the same form, blown in the mold, clearly demonstrating the popularity of the model. The jug was part of the original nucleus of the Ala Ponzone collection, prior to 1840.
Typological comparisons: Omodeo, 1970, fig. 11; Tait, 1979, nos. 156, 158, 159; *Wunderkammer siciliana*, 2001.

55
Dish
Catalonia or Venice, 16th century
Blown glass, applied thread, ∅ 29.5 cm
Museo Ala Ponzone, Vincenzo Favenza Donation, Cremona
State of conservation: excellent

Dish in slightly smoked crystal with radial molded ribs and *lattimo* thread applied in a spiral, broken into short segments over the course of the working. This technique was very common

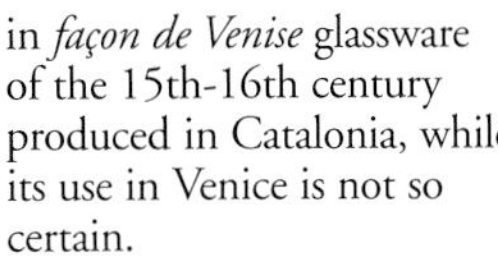

in *façon de Venise* glassware of the 15th-16th century produced in Catalonia, while its use in Venice is not so certain.
Typological comparisons: Barovier Mentasti, 1982, figs. 75-6; Mariacher, 1983, nos. 55-6; Lanmon, Whitehouse, 1993, no. 39.

54

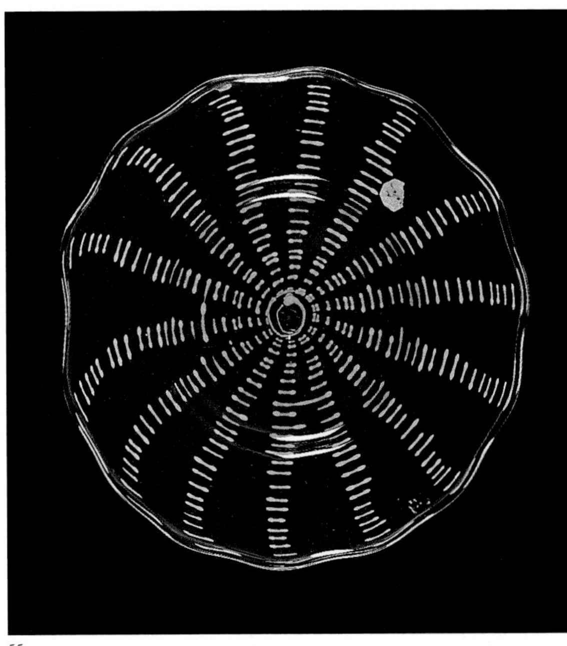

55

56

56
Small two-handled bowl
Venice, late 17th - early 18th century
Blown crystal,
h. 7.9 cm
Museo Ala Ponzone, Cremona
State of conservation: excellent

Blown and hand-modeled crystal bowl, in the shape of a segment of a sphere on applied foot, with two lateral, curled handles. The model was extensively produced in crystal, opalescent glass, chalcedony glass and, more rarely, *filigrana*. It presents numerous variants in the details: the handles can be decorated with *morise*, the bowl decorated with ribs. A useful clue to the date is provided by the presence of this model in the collection at the Rosenborg Palace in Copenhagen, of Venetian origin and dated to the winter of 1708-09. The model can also be found in still lives of the early 18th century, including one by Cristoforo Munari.
Typological comparisons: Boesen, 1960, nos. 37, 61, 84; Barovier Mentasti, 1982, figs. 150, 159; *Venezianisches Glass der Veste Coburg*, 1994, nos. 91, 92, 94.

57
Graffito goblet
Murano, end 17th - early 18th century
Blown crystal, diamond-point graffito,
h. 13.2 cm
Civici Musei d'Arte e Storia, Brescia,
State of conservation: excellent

Crystal goblet on wide foot with folded-back rim and diamond-point graffito decoration with plant elements. Blown baluster stem, hemispherical bowl of crystal engraved with flowers and two peacocks. Diamond-point decoration, first used on blown glass in 1549, became naturalistic in the baroque period. The bowl is in the shape of a bell-mouthed hemisphere and is mounted on a column-shaped stem with a small intermediate sphere and a slightly convex base with a folded back border. The bowl and the foot are decorated in diamond point with foliage, flowers and two peacocks. This type of goblet often has fin handles and the floral decorations are sometimes accompanied by inscriptions.
Typological comparisons: Mariacher, 1983, no. 68, 69; *Venezianisches Glass der Veste Coburg*, 1994, nos. 297-9; Mori, 1996, p. 40.
Bibliography: *Vetri nelle collezioni bresciane*, 1987, no. 25b.

58
Goblet with lid
Silesia or Bohemia, 1720-40
Blown, engraved and cut crystal,
h. 25.8 cm
Civiche Raccolte d'Arte Applicata, Castello Sforzesco, Milan
State of conservation: excellent

Crystal goblet on wide foot with modeled stem cut into facets. Bowl faceted at the bottom and engraved on the upper part with a plant motif and, in a rosette at the back, a scene of a cupid fleeing from two serpents; the rosette at the front frames a scene of a cupid seated between two trees, with an inscription in German which translates as: "much better to be alone." The convex lid is engraved with volutes of leaves and the double knob is cut into facets.
Bibliography: Mori, 1996, p. 41.

57

58

59
Goblet with the coat of arms of Princess Anne
Newcastle, England, 1740
Blown and hand-modeled glass, engraved on the wheel, h. 23 cm
Diageo Glass Collection, Santa Vittoria d'Alba
State of conservation: excellent

Goblet on wide foot, with long stem modeled in the upper part and conical bowl with the finely engraved coat of arms of Princess Anne, daughter of George II, before her marriage to William IV of Orange. The engraving presents the white horse of Hanover, above the princess's crown and coat of arms. Thus this goblet belonged to a member of the ruling house of Hanover, rivals to the purchasers of the "Amen" goblets, the Stuarts. The fineness of the wheel engraving is evident and undoubtedly necessary, given the high rank of the person for whom it was intended.
Typological comparisons: Charleston, pl. 36b.
Bibliography: *Cinzano Glass Collection*, 1974, no p. no.

59

60

61

60
Amen goblet
England, 1725
Blown and hand-modeled crystal, engraved with diamond point,
h. 19.1 cm
Diageo Glass Collection, Santa Vittoria d'Alba
State of conservation: excellent

Slender conical goblet, wide foot with folded-back rim, long and thick stem with an internal drop of air that widens to form the bowl. The bowl is diamond-point engraved with a crown surmounting the interlaced initials J.R., alluding to King James VII of Scotland. On the sides and back it is engraved with a complete Jacobite hymn, along with the inscription " To His Royal Highness/PRINCE HENRY/Duke of Albany & York." Beneath the royal initials the word "Amen" framed by plant volutes. At the sides the date "March 6th, 1725." Diamond-point engraving, much in vogue in the 17th century, was still used in the first half of the 18th. Some goblets were used as vehicles for political ideas, including the group known as "Amen" glasses because of the recurrence of the word in the engravings. The unknown author of the diamond-point inscriptions on the "Amen" goblets praised the house of Stuart, and in particular King James VII and his son Prince Charles Edward. The slender form is typical of the period. The main variations are to be found in the modeling of the stem: no longer in the shape of a baluster, it became decidedly elongated, and in its simplest and most economic form, straight, as in this case.
Typological comparisons: Charleston, 1984, p. 139, p. 150; *Storia del vetro*, 1984, p. 130; Liefkes, 1997, p. 94.
Bibliography: *Cinzano Glass Collection*, 1974, no p. no.

61
Spoon
Venice, early 18th century
Hot-modeled glass,
l. 21.3 cm
Vincenzo Favenza Donation, Museo Ala Ponzone, Cremona
State of conservation: excellent

Spoon in crystal with applied twisted handle and application at the end. Examples of flatware in glass, and spoons in particular, were produced at the beginning of the 18th century and are documented in *filigrana* in the Rosenborg Collection in Copenhagen, dated to 1708-09 and of Venetian provenance.
Typological comparisons: Boesen, 1960, no. 32.

62

63
Altare Glassworkers
Petrol lamp
mid-19th century
Blown and hand-modeled glass,
h. 31 cm, Ø 11 cm
Istituto per lo Studio del Vetro e dell'Arte Vetraria, Altare, inv. no. 130

62
Service of the counts Desfours-Walderode
Harrach Glassworks, Nový Svět, *c.* 1840
Engraved uranium-tinted glass, decorated with enamel,
h. 31 cm, h. 28.5 cm,
h. 21.5 cm, h. 13.5 cm,
l. 46 cm
Museum of Decorative Arts, Prague
State of conservation: excellent

Tray, two bottles, sugar bowl and goblet in uranium-tinted, fluorescent yellow glass (*Annagelb*).
The five pieces are deeply engraved and decorated on the inside with a medallion bearing the coat of arms of the counts Desfours-Walderode in polychrome enamel and gold. The service was probably a gift from the count of Harrach to Francis Vincenci Desfours-Walderode in 1839. It is an exceptional piece for the quality of the glass, the refinement of the cutting and the enamel decoration. The robust forms and cuts in relief are typical of Bohemian Biedermeier glassware, as is the uranium-tinted glass that took its name *Annagelb* ("Anna yellow") from the wife of its inventor, the Bohemian Josef Riedel. He also invented the equally fluorescent *Annagrün* glass. Uranium-tinted yellow glass was introduced almost simultaneously in the Harrach glassworks and in southern Bohemia. The medallion was an imitation of the "incrustations," medallions of porcelain inserted in glass, that were produced in France and England.
Typological comparisons: Pazaurek, von Philippovich, 1976, fig. 2, pp. 278-91.
Bibliography: *Czechoslovakian Glass*, 1980, no. 52; *Storia del vetro*, 1984, p. 174; *Verres de Bohême*, 1989, no. 37; *Bohemian Glass*, 1991, p. 78.

63

64
Altare Glassworkers
Meat cover
last quarter of 19th century
Blown and hand-modeled white glass,
h. 19 cm
Istituto per lo Studio del Vetro e dell'Arte Vetraria, Altare, inv. no. 173

65
Altare Glassworkers
Breast pump with reservoir
last quarter of 19th century
Blown and hand-modeled glass,
h. 10 cm
Istituto per lo Studio del Vetro e dell'Arte Vetraria, Altare, inv. no. 209

66
Altare Glassworkers
Bohemian bottle with umbrella stopper
last quarter of 19th century
Blown and fluted glass,
h. 30 cm
Istituto per lo Studio del Vetro e dell'Arte Vetraria, Altare, inv. no. 55

67
Altare Glassworkers
Watch stand
last quarter of 19th century
Blown and hand-modeled glass,
h. 14 cm
Istituto per lo Studio del Vetro e dell'Arte Vetraria, Altare, inv. no. 289

68
Altare Glassworkers
Drinking trough for birds
first quarter of 20th century
Blown and hand-modeled glass,
h. 17.5 cm
Istituto per lo Studio del Vetro e dell'Arte Vetraria, Altare, inv. no. 208

64

65

66

67

68

69

69
Altare Glassworkers
Kipp's apparatus
first quarter of 20th century
Mold-blown and ground glass,
h. 53 cm
Istituto per lo Studio del Vetro e dell'Arte Vetraria, Altare, inv. no. 97

70
Altare Glassworkers
Witt's apparatus
first quarter of 20th century
Mold-blown and ground glass,
h. 28 cm
Istituto per lo Studio del Vetro e dell'Arte Vetraria, Altare, inv. no. 92

71
Altare Glassworkers
Scheibler's desiccator
first quarter of 20th century
Transparent white glass with lid and cock,
h. 44 cm
Istituto per lo Studio del Vetro e dell'Arte Vetraria, Altare, inv. no. 91

70

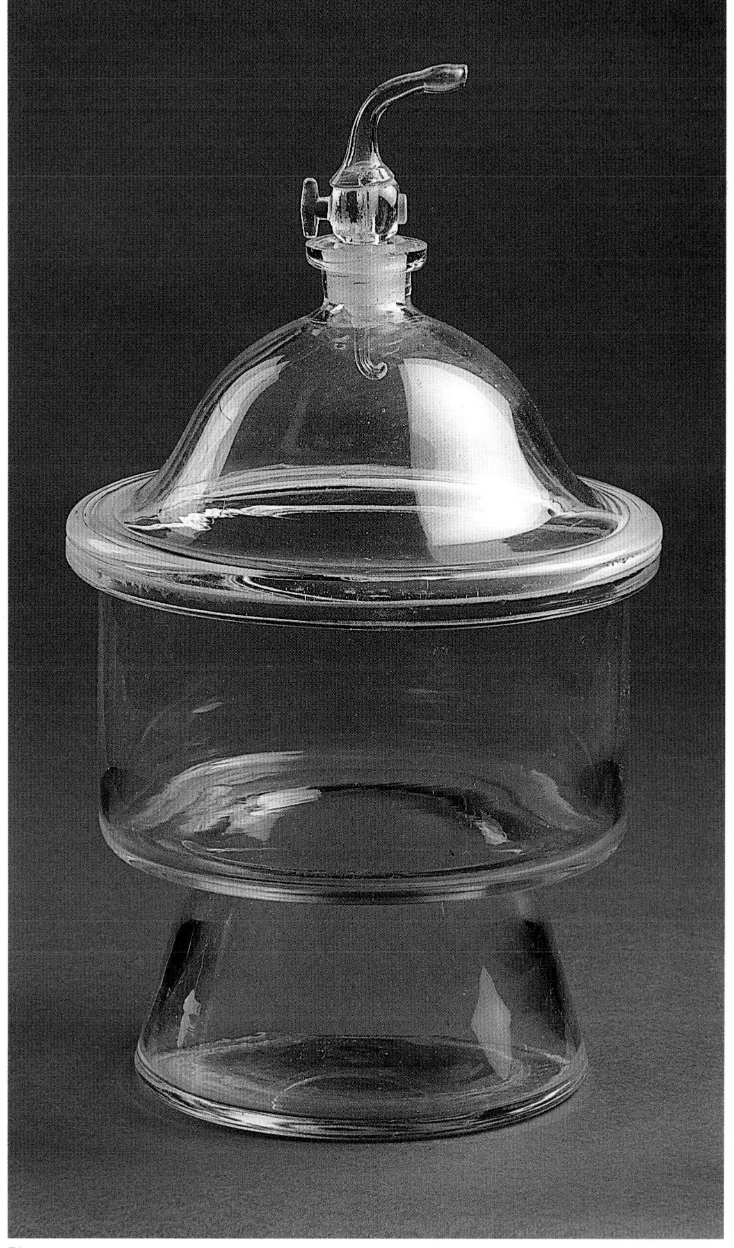
71

72

72
Altare glassworkers
Vase for confectionery
first quarter of 20th century
Blown and fluted glass,
h. 45 cm
Istituto per lo Studio del
Vetro e dell'Arte Vetraria,
Altare, inv. no. 45

73
Umberto Nason
Two-colour drinking glasses
1955
Cased, mold-blown glass, h. 8.5 cm
Nason & Moretti, Murano
State of conservation: excellent

Six mold-blown drinking glasses with straight walls, in coloured glass cased in *lattimo*. The inner colour is different for each drinking glass. Service awarded the Compasso d'Oro in 1955. *Bibliography*: La Rinascente, Compasso d'Oro, 1955; *Stile Industria*, Feb. 1956, no. 6, p. 25; *Il vetro a Milano*, 1998, no. 155.

73

74

74
Marc Lalique and Marie-Claude Lalique
Roxanne hollowware
Cristallerie Lalique & Cie, France, 1968-93
Molded crystal, satin finish
h. 32.5 cm, h. 20 cm, h. 19 cm, h. 17 cm
Lalique Italia Srl, Milan

Table service in mold-blown crystal with stem modeled in mold and partly given a satin finish. The refinement of the Lalique pieces derives from the fact that the modernity of their design still fully reflects the technical and stylistic tradition of the brand, and from the quality of the molds used, capable of reproducing perfectly the details of the figurative or abstract motif that characterizes the stems of the goblets and the stoppers of the bottles.
This collection was designed by Marc Lalique (1900-1977), son of the great René, and Marie-Claude (1935), Marc's daughter.
Bibliography: Lalique, 1988, p. 618.

75
Tapio Wirkkala
Ultima Thule
Iittala, 1968
Mold-blown glass,
max. h. of drinking glasses 15 cm, h. of carafe 20.7 cm
Suomen Lasimuseo (Finlands Glassmuseum), Riihimäki

Set of drinking glasses, carafes, dishes and bowls in mold-blown transparent glass. Originally designed for use in first class on the transoceanic flights of the airline Finnair. Wirkkala created a type of glass surface with a corrugated finish that had appendages resembling icicles at the base, inspired by the nature of the Far North of which he was so fond, a theme to which both he and his imitators returned to again and again. The collection included wine carafes and caviar dishes. Wirkkala made the graphite molds for the prototypes himself; subsequently metal molds were used, though these too were hollowed out by hand. Today the molds are made by machine and the manufacture of the glassware is completely automated. The *Ultima Thule* series is the most famous in the entire history of the Iittala glassworks.
Bibliography: *European Glass*, 1994, p. 182; *Autriche, Suède et Finlande*, 1995, p. 46; *Moderne Zeiten*, 1998, p. 27, no. 22; *Tapio Wirkkala, eye...*, 2000, p. 120, p. 316.

76
Pietro Pelzel
Drinking glass that cannot be tipped over
Vetreria Vetrelco, Treviso, 1969
Glass blown in wooden mold, h. 7.5 cm
Collection of the artist

Drinking glass made of transparent, steel-coloured glass. It is distinguished by the fact that it can be tilted to an angle of about 40° without spilling any liquid in the lower part. Its practicality is also demonstrated by its ease of handling. The model is an example of the quest for functionality that was one of the principal marks of Italian design in the 1960s.
Signature or mark: P. 69.

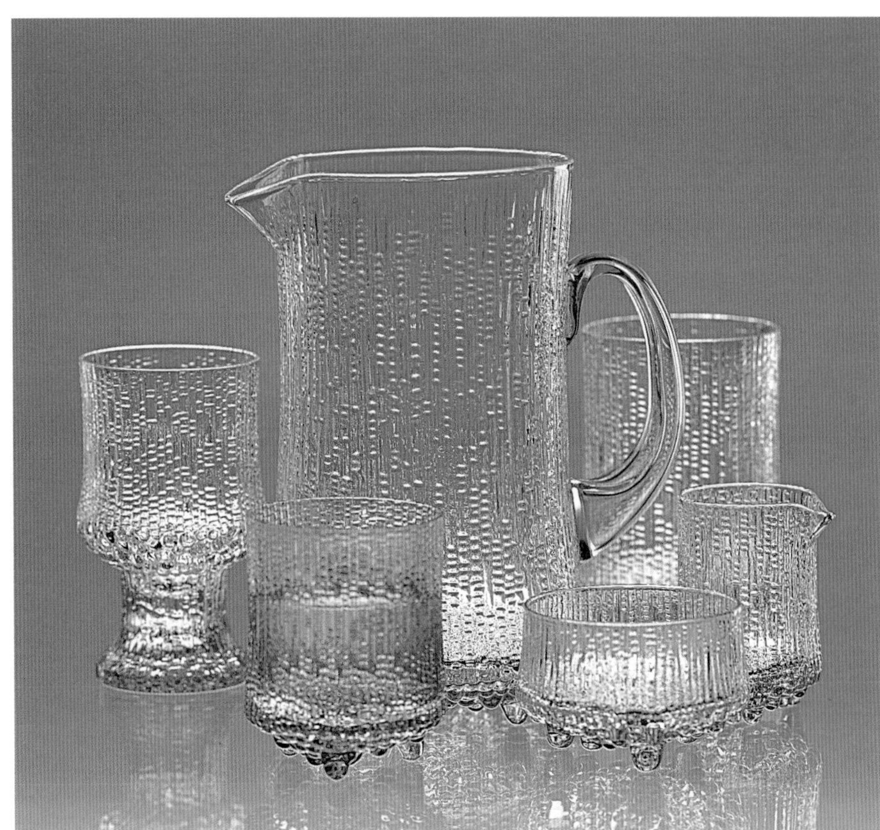
75

76

77

77
Fulvio Bianconi
Gust of Wind
Toso Vetri d'Arte, Murano, 1983
Blown glass,
h. 5.25 cm, h. 27 cm, h. 29 cm, h. 28 cm
Piero Cicutto Collection, Venice

Series of four goblets. Very thin blown glass with green or amethyst stems and applications of *lattimo* modeled into figures. In a progressive series, the goblets are increasingly bent over, and therefore rendered unusable, as if struck by a gust of wind. The designer, returning to Murano after an absence of fifteen years, showed that he had maintained intact the imagination and irony that had characterized his works in the 1950s.
Typological comparisons: Dorigato, 1983, no. 146; Barovier Mentasti, 1992, fig. 162; Barovier Mentasti, 1993, p. 34; *I vetri di Fulvio Bianconi*, 1993.

78

78
Kerttu Nurminen
World
1988
Mold-blown glass,
various dimensions
Tehtaan Museo
(Glassmuseum), Iittala

Table service: decanter and goblets of colourless glass with lower part of the stem and foot in green glass. The mold-blown bowl is attached directly to the stem, and a new technique made possible a smooth transition from transparent glass to green glass. It was exhibited at the *Finland Designs* exhibition and a year later was already in the catalogue of the Museum of Modern Art in New York.
Bibliography: *Autriche, Suède et Finlande*, 1995, no. 118; *Finnish Post-war Glass*, 1996, pl. 47; *Moderne Zeiten*, 1998, p. 50.

79
Richard Marquis
Granular Vase - Anvil with Rubber Rooster
Seattle, 1998
Blown *murrine* glass, elements in wood and rubber,
h. 91 cm
Galleria d'Arte e di Vetro, Bergamo

Vase made by blowing a sheet of polychrome *murrine*. The installation includes a wooden anvil and toy rooster made of rubber. In the installation the perfection of Richard Marquis's glasswork in Venetian-style *murrine* is playfully set alongside the modest material of the *objets trouvés* that he likes to collect and insert in his works, as an ironic tribute to the kitsch that makes up so much of our daily lives.
Typological comparisons: Oldknow, 1997; Tognon, 2001, pp. 8-13.
Bibliography: *Global Art Glass*, 1999, no p. no.

79

80

80
Richard Marquis
Granular Shelf Lighthouse
Seattle, Wash., 1998
Installation with shelf, *murrine* objects and painted seascape,
h. 41 cm
Galleria d'Arte e di Vetro, Bergamo

Nine objects blown from polychrome *murrine* glass hanging from or set on a small wooden shelf; in the background a seascape is painted on panel.
Typological comparisons: *Aperto vetro*, 1996, p. 131.
Bibliography: Tognon, 2001, p. 9, fig. 2.

81
Andrea Zilio
The Personages
Murano, Glassworks Amphora, 1999
Blown cane glass,
h. 47 cm, h. 41 cm, h. 36 cm, h. 35 cm, h. 34 cm

Five goblets in two-colour blown glass formed from opaque diagonal canes. The goblets stand on a blown intermediate node fused to a tall conical foot. They constitute a modern and highly stylized interpretation of the traditional Venetian goblet. Their brilliant colours make them decorative objects, but they have also been proposed as tableware.

82
Maria Grazia Rosin
Detergents
Murano, 2000
Blown glass,
h. 35 cm
Galleria d'Arte e di Vetro, Bergamo

Bottles in the shape of detergent containers made of coloured bands of glass blown in the furnace, with flame modeled tops. Ever since her first experiments with glass, Maria Grazia Rosin has played with the theme of the plastic detergent container, using a brilliant polychrome glass blown with the most sophisticated of Murano techniques, an ironic homage to the objects of everyday life.
Typological comparisons: *Progetto Glass*, 1992.
Bibliography: *Strano ma vetro*, 2000, pp. 42-53.

81

82

83
Carlo Moretti
Six collector's wineglasses
Murano, 2002
Blown and hand-modeled translucent glass with applications,
h. 27.2 cm
Collection of the artist

Flutes in opalescent glass with different applications on each model: spirals, canes, coloured inserts, *murrine*. Every year Carlo Moretti designs for his glassworks a different set of six collector's wineglasses, in which the form of the bowl and the dimension remain constant. Hence the collection is virtually unlimited. However, the denomination as "collector's items" does not exclude them from being used for a practical purpose, i.e. for the table.
Signature or mark: Carlo Moretti 2002.
Typological comparisons: *Carlo Moretti*, 1998, p. 200.
Bibliography: *Domina*, December 2001, February 2002.

83

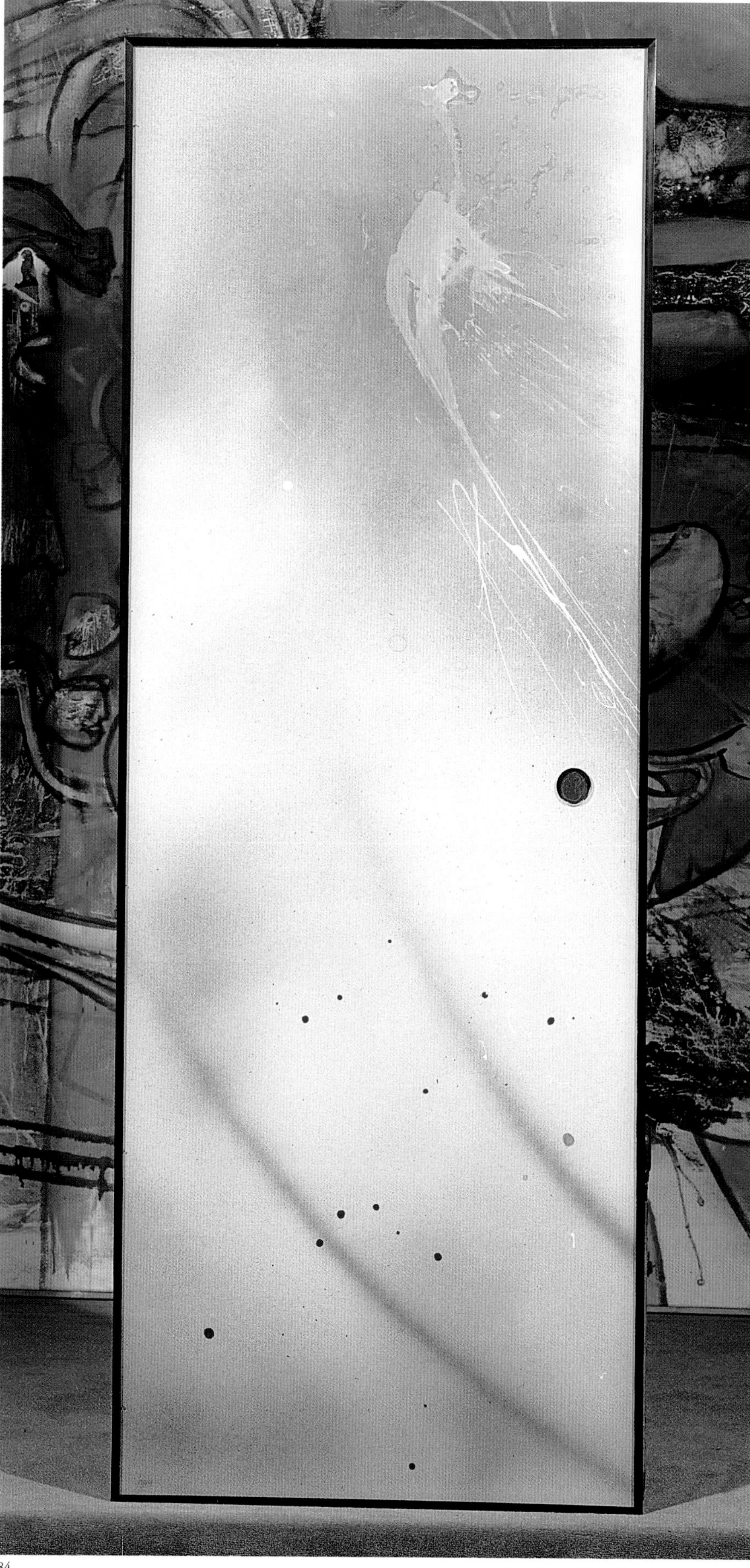

84

84
Lucio Fontana
Decoration for Closet Door
1952-53
Mixed media on tempered crystal no. 1,
163 × 60 cm
Courtesy Tornabuoni Arte, Florence

Lucio Fontana, one of the fathers of contemporary research and an artist whose insights have opened up directions that are still being followed today (it suffices to think of the way he has modified our perception of spaces), often made use of glass in his compositions. From his *Spatial Concepts* to his environments, the artist utilized the material in fragments, as if it were an artificial stone mixed in with the oil paint of the canvases, or inserted bubbles of blown material and industrial neon bulbs into his works. The decoration for a closet door, for obvious reasons in the Room of the Everyday, echoes some of the themes and signs typical of the artist's production, but relates them to a functional object and a structure with deep roots in the craft tradition.

85
Silvia Levenson
It's Raining Knives
1999
Glass cast in molds,
variable dimensions
Collection of the artist, Pavia

The subtle, continual and unmotivated violence that often takes place in the home, and in people's daily lives, is one of the recurrent themes in the work of Silvia Levenson. Her works often denounce the abuse that women are subjected to in an undeniably male-chauvinistic society, and do not confine themselves to the brutalities of marriage. The artist also turns her sights on the impositions of fashion, the iniquities of custom and the persecutions of convention, which drive many people into anorexia, loneliness and depression. *It's Raining Knives*, an installation consisting of a large number of kitchen knives made of glass, hung from the ceiling and pointing threateningly at anyone who rashly passes underneath, is a work that speaks of family tensions, of the anxiety and aggressiveness that are often to be found in a relationship that has gone wrong, or just not particularly well. The kitchen can be the heart of a shared life, but if knives are used to symbolize it this means that something is out of kilter. At times, hidden behind the perfect furnishings, the latest generation of television set, the rigid and conventional relations with neighbours and friends, there are unresolved problems, dissatisfactions and abuses of power that threaten to break out into open conflict at any time. In this piece glass is not used, as so often happens in contemporary art, as a symbol of fragility, but for its disturbing ability to cut, stab and wound.

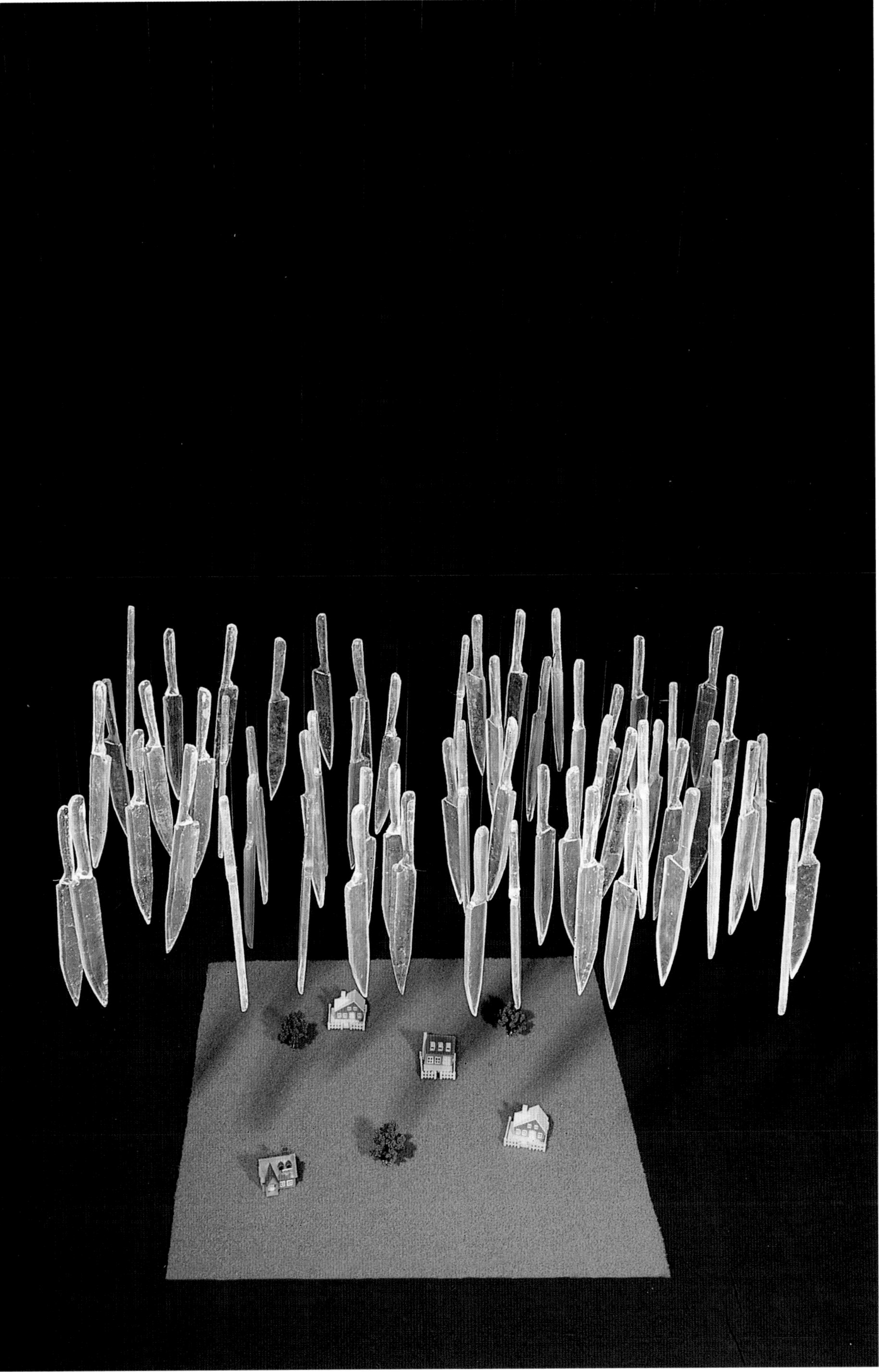

85

86
Daniel Spoerri
The Drunkard
Tableau piège (assemblage on table),
60 × 60 cm
Private collection, Milan

A prominent exponent of Nouveau Réalisme, Daniel Spoerri has been aptly defined as a sort of "archeologist of the present." Like real archeologists, he studies sites and finds, and attempts to reconstruct customs and cultures on the basis of objective situations that he has uncovered and catalogued. Unlike real archeologists, who have to overcome great difficulties to find their evidence, he is able to choose from hundreds of possible alternatives. In the 1960s, when he started to produce his *Tableaux-pièges* ("Snare Pictures"), his Paestum, Pompeii and Athens were the restaurants he frequented, or the dining rooms in the houses of his friends. Those works were born out of chance: rejecting the idea of individual creativity, the artist stuck onto a base everything that was left on the table at the end of a meal, from empty bottles to dirty plates to ashtrays filled with cigarette butts. Sometimes even objects like compact cameras, if they happened to still be there when everyone got up. "Art only interests me in so far as it represents a visual lesson," he declared in a meeting-interview with Dominique Star, "and the visual lesson has to consist in drawing attention to the situations of our daily life that are never or almost never noticed." Glass, obviously, turns up very frequently in Spoerri's propositions, as it is a material in very common use, and the work *The Drunkard*, presented in the Room of the Everyday (as it freezes forever a situation lifted from daily life), is particularly rich in it, given that it consists of a group of bottles, some broken and some whole, abandoned after a binge.

86

87
Gianfranco Baruchello
High Altitude Epinafico
1967
Wood, glass, paint, Plexiglas, 51 × 36 cm
Private collection, Milan

Notes and sketches jotted down in a notebook, ideas dashed off quickly in order to keep up with the flow of thought, or out of haste. Gianfranco Baruchello's work *High Altitude Epinafico* – presented in the Room of the Everyday, given that it is a haphazard collection of scribbles and scrawls of an intimate character – reflects the chaotic nature of ideas, and the artist's attempt to give them a complete form, to understand and classify them. Only the notebook is no ordinary one. It is not made of paper, and not written on with a pen. Each page is a sheet, not of paper, but of glass. In fact it is not a notebook at all, but a pile of sheets of glass used as pages. And so, given their transparency, the notes and sketches are superimposed, mixed up, forced to hold a dialogue even when speaking different tongues, like a miniature and portable version of the Tower of Babel. And the chaos is revealed as a gigantic harmony, a perfection that human beings cannot understand and reproduce, but only admire.

87

VIII.

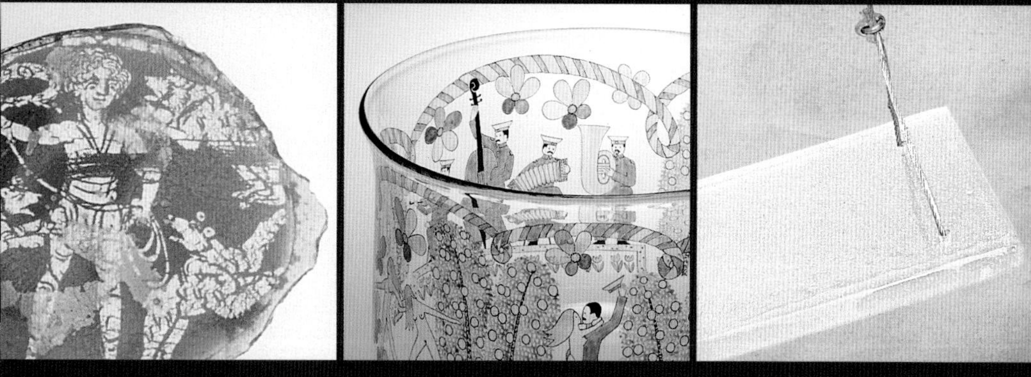

Room of Play

ANCIENT GLASS

In this particular field, glass and to an even greater extent glass paste are used to make toys and games, things to play with. According to Pliny, the majority of Romans of both sexes spent a great deal of time playing *latrunculi*, a sort of war game. The pieces traditionally used in the game, of various shapes and colours, from black to white, from yellow to blue and sometimes even made of murrine glass, were moved around on often makeshift boards.
There is no lack of figurative references to games in the broad sense, as they were understood in the classical world. Athletic contests, fights between gladiators and chariot races at the circus: the protagonists of these games are often depicted on bowls and drinking glasses, either painted or stamped in molds, as in the glass from Aosta and the fragments of a bowl from Barcelona. Connected with this spirit of competition are the drinking glasses decorated with laurel wreaths and celebratory inscriptions singing the praises of victory.
The theatrical masks that adorn the base of a "almond"-shaped beaker from Murano allude to a more cultural kind of entertainment, and one that is almost completely opposite in tone to the animal tamer represented on a medallion in the act of capturing wild beasts with a rope, during thrilling spectacles staged in the arena (Museo Civico Archeologico, Bologna).

CREATORS OF GLASS

One of the most common and least expensive children's toys of the modern era is the multicoloured marble. We have all played with these objects, and our children still do, bartering them with the same passion as they do picture cards. They have been in use since time immemorial and are frequently mentioned in the children's literature of the 19th and 20th century.
Glass toys of refined craftsmanship, on the other hand, have been exceptional products, usually made to order. In the second half of the 19th century prestigious small tables with inlays of coloured enamel and aventurine, sometimes with checkerboard patterns, were produced in Venice for expositions. The memory has been handed down in the Venini family of a chess set with glass pieces of extraordinary quality, executed to the commission of some sheikh or other.
A special category is that of the playful and mocking drinking glasses made in the baroque period: goblets with bowls shaped in such a way as to spill water or wine on the incautious drinker, goblets superimposed in a sort of glass "labour of Hercules" and complicated structures designed to create plays of water, as documented in the drawings of Medicean artists conserved in the Gabinetto Disegni e Stampe of the Uffizi. More common, especially in the 20th century, are figurative decorations that have games, sports or amusements as their theme. The techniques of painting in enamel and engraving were used to produce attractive and lively objects in Swedish as well as Venetian glassworks: significant examples are the works of Guido Balsamo Stella, Eugenio Fegarotti, Franz Pelzel for SALIR and Gunnar Cyrén for Orrefors. Who has best interpreted the playful side of life in the sector of the unique work of art in glass is the American Richard Meitner, who lives and works in Amsterdam. His creations in blown borosilicate glass and glass blown in the furnace, irrational, dreamlike and always new and stimulating, could only be embodied in this mutable and insubstantial material, glass.

CONTEMPORARY ART

During the 1980s and 1990s the international art scene, although dominated by figurative and abstract painting, by photography and by the conceptual, was enriched by a very particular line of research, which has introduced a new language, extraordinarily close to the creativity of children and adolescents. A line of research – emerging in part from the teachings and intuitions of Bruno Munari, Pino Pascali, Alighiero Boetti, Gino De Dominicis, Yves Klein, Errò and Ronnie Cutrone – ideally suited to artists and members of the public who have never been completely able to shake off the Peter Pan syndrome, and who are still convinced, like Bill Watterson, that "the majority of people get old without growing up, and that at the bottom of every adult there is a kid who wants everything his own way." The keywords of this heterogeneous movement have been irony, play, childhood, fun and imagination, but in a sense that is anything but light and superficial. Many artists have brought the structural and relational logic of cartoon strips and toys into western and eastern art, ripping away the veil of seriousness typical of the majority of contemporary tendencies, which have forgotten the most profound lesson of Dadaism. They have given rise to a series of works that have the same freshness and bite as a Peanuts cartoon, as an exchange between Calvin and Hobbes. These interpreters of the Ars Ludica – who include Arienti, Bonomi, Borghi, Cockrill, Delvoye, Dingle, Di Piazza, Koons, Murakami, Pinna, Riello and Tung Lu Hung – have also used glass whenever they felt the need, and often in a paradoxical manner, playing above all with its presumed fragility. Delvoye, for example, has used it to make the net of a goal for a game of soccer. And while Bonomi has constructed a Meccano set out of it, Riello has preferred to utilize it to design and make nails to bang in the wall. All in the name of uselessness.

1

2

3

1
Polychrome gaming piece
first half of 1st century AD
Glass canes,
max. Ø 2.5 cm,
thickness 0.6 cm
From layers IV-V, Giardino dei Ragazzi excavation, Aosta
Deposito della Sovrintendenza, Aosta Valley Autonomous Region, Aosta, cod. lab. 03-151
State of conservation: broken roughly in half, devitrified

Counter in mosaic glass with a plano-convex section. Dark-green ground, variegated with pale green and with sections of pale yellow canes with a green centre.
(P.F.)

2
Gaming pieces
1st-2nd century AD
Glass cast in mold,
Ø 3.3 cm, thickness 0.7 cm
Collection of the Accademia of Sant'Anselmo, Aosta
State of conservation: whole, signs of wear

Black glass paste. Pair of large gaming pieces with a plano-convex section; traces of detachment from the mold.
Typological comparisons: Albenga, 1999, p. 144, no. 133.
(P.F.)

3
Gaming pieces
1st century AD
Glass cast in mold,
Ø from 1.1 to 1.8 cm
From layers VI A and B, V B, III, and I B, Giardino dei Ragazzi excavation, Aosta
Deposito della Sovrintendenza, Aosta Valley Autonomous Region, Aosta, cod. lab. 03-396/399; 03-401/403; 03-410/416
State of conservation: whole, signs of wear and devitrification

Group of gaming pieces in coloured glass paste, all circular except no. 03-398, which is oval. Plano-convex section. The colours of the pieces found are white, yellow, turquoise, dark azure, blue and above all black.
(P.F.)

4
Painted beaker
late 1st century AD
Blown and cut glass, painted in enamel,
h. 10.5 cm, Ø of rim 6.7 cm, Ø of foot 3.5 cm
From T. 9, predial necropolis of Saint-Martin-de-Corléans, Aosta
Deposito della Sovrintendenza, Aosta Valley Autonomous Region, Aosta, cod. lab. 03-250
State of conservation: reassembled, integrated, much of rim missing, painting faded

Beaker in transparent, colourless glass with minute bubbles and impurities. Body in the shape of an elongated truncated cone, decorated with four symmetrically arranged indentations; expanded rim underlined by two borders in relief; thin and flattened ring foot.
The painted decoration occupies the central part: this is divided into four panels framed by a reticular geometric pattern, originally painted in yellow, enclosed by a thin red line. The bottom, underneath the low carination, was also painted.
In each of the four panels is set the figure of an athlete-juggler in rapid movement. The figures form two pairs, and are dressed in Oriental costume.
In upright postures, they have a certain three-dimensional quality, emphasized by the thickened outline and the developed shoulders; each figure wears a waistcloth and a Phrygian cap and holds two slender rods, crossed over.
As far as the subject of the painted decoration is concerned, it is very likely a rare representation of an acrobatic display or a dance connected with a theatrical *ludus* or cultic event.
Dancers holding crossed sticks are depicted in a relief at Ariccia (Lembke, 1994, pl. 31), while dancers wearing caps are frescoed on the sign of a shop in Pompeii (De Carolis, 1997, p. 42), from the middle of the 1st century AD.
Of Oriental, probably Alexandrine production, something that is also indicated by the technical and morphological characteristics, the beaker from Aosta is datable to the late Flavian era, partly on the basis of the dated contexts (Scatozza, 1999, nos. 6861 and 7013) and grave goods with which it is associated.
With regard to the problem of the distribution of the glassware from Egypt and found in the regions of the eastern Mediterranean as well as in the western part of the empire, it should be pointed out that in the late 1st century AD the *ager* of *Augusta Praetoria* was a territory with a strategic location at the western end of the Po Valley, in the vicinity of the mountain passes on an important transalpine trade route.
Typological comparisons: Isings, form 35.
Bibliography: Kisa, 1908, vol. III, p. 811; Harden, 1936, pp. 136, 145 *et sqq*.; Vessberg, 1952, p. 124; Adriani, 1955, pp. 129-32; Harden, 1956, vol. II, p. 324; Isings, 1957, pp. 49-50; Coarelli, 1963, pp. 61-85; Painter, 1988,

4

pp. 259-62; Roffia, 1993, p. 85; De Carolis, 1997, pp. 42-4; Scatozza, 1999, p. 101, pls. V, VI, nos. 6861, 7013. (P.F.-R.M.)

5
Cup
second half of 1st century AD
Mold-blown glass, h. 5.1 cm, l. 7.1 cm
Empúries (Girona)
Museu d'Arqueologia de Catalunya, Barcelona, inv. no. NIG 2200
State of conservation: fragmentary

Fragment in two pieces of a cylindrical cup depicting chariot races on two rows. Made from a paste tending to blue, it was blown in a mold composed of three parts: the first two for the zone of the inscription and the strips with the figures, the third for the lower part and base.
The upper part is inscribed with the words [Î]NCITATEVA ICARE V in slight relief. In the band underneath are represented various elements of the *spina* of a circus, doubtless based on the *Circus Maximus* in Rome. From left to right it is possible to make out the following figures: part of an obelisk, a rampant lion, the three pyramids of the *metae* crowned by a sphere, a column with a statue and a base. All that can be seen on the lower band is part of the base of the *metae*, made up of three large quadrangular blocks.
Typological comparisons: Sennequier, type B; Berger, nos. 154-5; Sternini, no. 256; Morin, 83.
Bibliography: Morin-Jean, 1922-23, p. 83; Gudiol Ricart, 1941, p. 9; Almagro, 1952, pp. 187-8, nos. 153, 156; Berger, 1960, pp. 56-7, pl. 9, figs. D, E, nos. 154-5; Darder, 1988, pp. 287-300; Sternini, 1991, p. 131, pl. 50, no. 256; Fabre, Mayer, Rodà, 2002, pp. 206-7, no. 178. (T.C.R.)

6
Inscripted beaker
1st century AD
Mold-blown glass, h. 8 cm, ∅ of rim 7.2 cm
From Cornus (Santa Caterina di Pittinuri), context unknown
Deposito Museo Archeologico Nazionale, Cagliari, inv. no. 33947
State of conservation: whole

The green drinking glass has a cylindrical form with a slanting and sharp rim. The main decoration is an inscription in Greek letters ΚΑΤΑΞΑΙΠΕ ΚΑΙ ΕΨϘΠΑΙΝΟΨ, set in a band divided vertically by two palm leaves. At the top are set two pairs of horizontal palm leaves surmounted by two small fillets in relief. At the bottom run two more borders in relief, with two rows of leaves underneath. Flat bottom with three concentric circles in relief.
The inscription on this drinking glass finds parallels chiefly in the Middle East. In particular, it is taken from the same mold as a similar example in the Louvre and found on Cyprus. Harden suggests that the workshop was located at Sidon.
Typological comparisons: Harden, 1935, pp. 163-86, 172-3.
Bibliography: *Museo di Cagliari*, 1994, pp. 78-80, 140, no. 425, pl. 104. (C.T.)

7
Medallion
first half of 4th century AD
Engraved gold leaf between two layers of blown glass, the upper transparent, the lower blue, h. 3.1 cm, width 3.7 cm
Provenance unknown; formerly Bologna University Collection
Museo Civico Archeologico, Bologna
State of conservation: fractured irregularly along the edge; small patches of iridescence on the upper face

Probably a fragment of a bowl, with a convex lower disc, on which is depicted, inside a simple circular frame, a young *venator*, dressed in a short tunic with a high belt around the waist, leather gaiters and boots and armed with a lasso (*laqueus*). At the sides of the hunter's legs and to the left of his shoulder are represented three bears with gaping jaws, about to leap on him. To the right of his head is set a bejeweled crown.
Discussion of this object, for which the date proposed by Zanchi Roppo has now been unanimously accepted, has focused largely on the interpretation of the theme of the figuration, fairly rare in the iconographic repertoire of late-classical so-called *fondi d'oro*, and in particular on the identity of the male figure. Defined variously by scholars as an "animal tamer," a "keeper of wild beasts" or simply a hunter surrounded by his dogs, he is more likely to be an *ursarius*, as Raeck has recently pointed out. In other words a gladiator armed with a lasso for capture of the bears that were used in the hunting spectacles of the late-classical period, when the *venationes* turned into acrobatic displays with tamed animals, instead of real combats between man and beast. In fact the iconography of the hunter with a lasso is known chiefly from north African mosaics of the 3rd-4th century AD and, later on, from consular diptychs of the 6th century AD.
Bibliography: Ducati, 1929, p. 246, no. 9; Zanchi Roppo, 1969, pp. 15 *et sqq.*, no. 6, fig. 5; Meconcelli Notarianni, 1979, p. 164, no. 225; Raeck, 1992, p. 4; Rasmussen, 1996. (M.M.)

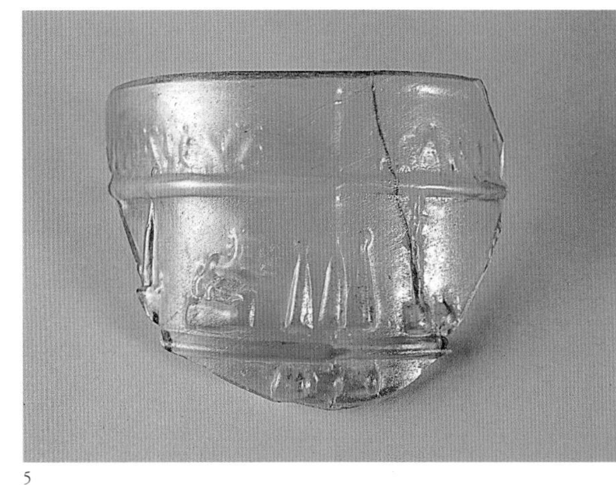
5

6

7

8

8
Table triumph
Bohemia or *façon de Bohême*, second half of 18th century
Blown crystal, engraved with wheel,
h. 53 cm
Museo Nazionale del Bargello, Florence
State of conservation: excellent

A series of three superimposed goblets, identical in shape but progressively decreasing in size from bottom to top. The base element has a broad foot with a wheel-engraved decoration of foliage, a stem worked into a variety of forms and a bowl in the shape of a segment of a sphere with a plant decoration and the Medici coat of arms engraved at the centre.
The lid of this element constitutes the base for the intermediate element, otherwise identical to the previous one. The third and smallest element is identical to the middle one, but has a lid ending in a ring-shaped handle.
Central piece of a table triumph made up of several elements, including a number of bottles now in Florentine private collections. Other elements of this triumph are in the same museum and in the Istituto e Museo di Storia della Scienza, also in Florence.

9
Guido Balsamo Stella
Cup of the Skiers
SALIR, Murano, 1930
Blown crystal, engraved on the wheel,
h. 33 cm
SALIR Snc Collection, Murano
State of conservation: excellent

Crystal cup of cylindrical form widening toward the mouth, wheel-engraved with figures of skiers.
Presented at the Milan Triennale of 1930.
It is a piece of great quality, both for the graceful and ironic decorative design and for the refined technique of engraving, executed by the master craftsman Franz Pelzel. The elegance of the figures that stemmed from the collaboration between Guido Balsamo Star and Franz Pelzel is evident in scenes on a contemporary theme as well as those on a classical one.
Bibliography: Felice, 1930, pl. 78; Felice, 1931, p. 318; *Il vetro a Milano*, 1998, no. 45.

10
Eugenio Fegarotti
Merry-Go-Round Vase
SALIR, Murano, 1936
Blown and engraved smoked glass,
h. 72 cm
Luciano Colantonio Collection, Brescia
State of conservation: excellent

Large vase in blown and hand-modeled straw-yellow glass, on applied large and rounded foot. With conical lid surmounted by a weathervane. The wall is decorated with oblique lines and engraved with a stylized representation of a merry-go-round. Presented at the Milan Triennale in 1936. In a decade in which wheel engraving attained great popularity, lively and playful subjects started to appear alongside more traditional ones.
Bibliography: Fotografia Archivio Triennale, nos. 817, 823; *L'artigianato d'Italia*, 1936, no. 114; *Il vetro a Milano*, 1998, no. 79.

9

10

11
Franz Pelzel
Roller Coaster
1952
Wheel-engraved with polished parts,
h. 22 cm
Private collection, Murano
State of conservation: good

Crystal vase decorated with wittily stylized "roller coasters." The decoration runs all the way round the cylindrical wall of the vase, exploiting its curvature. Stylized and often humorous or caricatural decorations, engraved or painted, were common in the applied art of the 1950s.
Signature or mark: F.P. 1952
Bibliography: Barovier Mentasti, 1995.

12
Gunnar Cyrén
In the Full Flower of Youth
Glasbruk, Orrefors, 1968
Mold-blown glass painted in enamel,
h. 15.8 cm
Smålands Museum Collection, Växjö

Cylindrical crystal bowl painted in polychrome enamel. Running all round the wall is a decoration made up of lively nude girls dancing and amusing themselves with sailors in uniform, in a park where a band is playing.
This work stands out for the extraordinary freshness of the naïve decoration, while in other works by the same artist the decoration is more complex in its colours and composition and in some cases echoes Pop Art.

12

11

13
Fernando Agostinho
The Dragster
2002
Blown glass,
45 × 16 × 14 cm
Signed
Galerie Place des Arts Collection, Montpellier

14
Richard Meitner
Installation: Toy, Lamp, Art
2002
Blown black borosilicate glass, with period Electra light bulbs,
h. 65 cm
Galleria d'Arte e di Vetro, Bergamo

Articulated toy figures, each assembled out of elements of flame-blown black borosilicate glass, surmounted by period Electra light bulbs. If connected to the power supply, the work lights up. Play and provocation, invention and rediscovery of obsolete objects constitute the dimension in which Richard Meitner moves. This installation is conceived as a child's toy to be constructed according to the whim of the moment. In this sense it is something new in Meitner's work.
Typological comparisons: *Aperto vetro*, 1996, pp. 74, 75; *Richard Meitner*, 2001.

13

14

15

15
Silvia Levenson
She's Flown Away
1999
Glass cast by lost-wax technique and steel cable,
300 × 47 cm
Collection of the artist, Pavia

Silvia Levenson, an Argentinean artist who has been living in Italy for years, often recalls in her works the bloody events that took place in her native country during the years of military dictatorship. She never refers directly to the violence of that period, but lets us read between the lines, bringing it to our minds through associations of ideas, assonances and similarities between the underlying meaning of the works and the history of South America. For anyone who has experienced at firsthand the tragedy of the *desaparecidos*, and heard the protests and cries of the mothers of Plaza De Majo, the absence or mere distance of a loved one can evoke deep, unhealed wounds. The work *She's Flown Away* is a terse presentation of the collective drama of a people that can no longer take itself for granted, destined to discover, for a long time to come, that there is always going to be someone missing. Someone whose sad fate can be imagined, but not known with certainty. In this work-cum-stage set, with a swing and the shoes of a little girl made out of glass, perhaps to remind us of the fragility of existence, the protagonist is absent, erased by a cruelty of which only human beings are capable. A child protagonist who would have loved to go on playing, having fun, swinging through the air, but who cannot. The work is included in the Room of Play as a counterweight to the amused and amusing works of Bonomi and Delvoye and serves as a reminder that the experience of play can sometimes be a painful initiation into life and death.

16

16
Corrado Bonomi
From the series of Impossible Toys: Glass Meccano
1996
Mixed media, glass and wood,
30 × 35 × 5 cm
Collection of the artist, Novara

The artist is an exponent of that ironic Italian vein of Conceptualism who, in spite of being perfectly in tune with an important part of international artistic research (it suffices to think of the sculptures of Tom Sacks, Wim Delvoye and Takashi Murakami), has not enjoyed the attention he deserves in his home country. Corrado Bonomi has always tried to create a short circuit between the image and the support, between the figure, usually drawn from popular imagery, and the material out of which it is made (or on which it is drawn). *Glass Meccano*, a legitimate heir of certain sarcastic and caustic creations by Bruno Munari, Pino Pascali and Alighiero Boetti, undermines the very meaning of one of the best-known and most widely sold toys in history. The construction set most popular with children – whose pieces and tools are, in the original version, made out of strong and resistant steel, capable of standing up to the sometimes violent enthusiasm of the young – is proposed by the artist in an improbable and extremely delicate, coloured glass, which renders it totally absurd and unusable. A deliberately provocative work, Bonomi's *Meccano* – presented in the Room of Play because it is an exact reproduction, apart from the material, of the venerable toy – is a real contradiction in terms between the purpose of the product and the method of its fabrication. The work is a follow-up to two earlier ones produced by the artist from Novara for the same series of *Impossible Toys*: *Model Trains*, miniature locomotives and cars that can be taken apart and put back together again like the scale models made by Lima and Rivarossi, painted in oil on pages torn from railroad schedules, and the toy soldiers of *Non omnis moriar*, similar to the playthings for children but engaged in apparently real and dramatic battles.

17
Wim Delvoye
Untitled
early 1990s
Glass,
70 × 30 cm
B & B Arte, Mantua

Wim Delvoye has tattooed chickens and pigs, disguised old gas bottles as precious pieces of Delft pottery and drawn fake maps of unlikely continents in the shapes of a teapot, penis or hammer. His letters bear not the romantic impression of a kiss left by lipstick but that of a butt. He is an *enfant terrible*, a Huckleberry Finn of art, a worthy heir to the caustic spirit of Manzoni. And in fact his most recent work, *Cloaca*, is a tribute to that great master, a monumental and technological revisitation of the famous *Artist's Shit*. "I am not a troublemaker," he claims, "but a healthy virus in a sick system." But all his work is in the key of mockery and provocation, from the large wooden sculptures that reproduce embarrassing cement mixers to ironing boards transformed into medieval shields. When he works with glass he exploits its properties of fragility and transparency and its decorative characteristics, short-circuiting the materials by substituting one absurdly for another. In his series of works inspired by sport (but non avowedly), he replaces the net of a soccer goal with the mock-Gothic stained-glass window of a cathedral, leaving us to imagine the shattering effect of the first ball to be kicked on target. In the same manner, he replaces the gut strings of a tennis racket with decorated glass, as charming as it is useless and contradictory in such an implement. Challenge, competition and contest are rendered impossible by the modifications made by Delvoye, who in the Room of Play brings into question the very logic of sport.

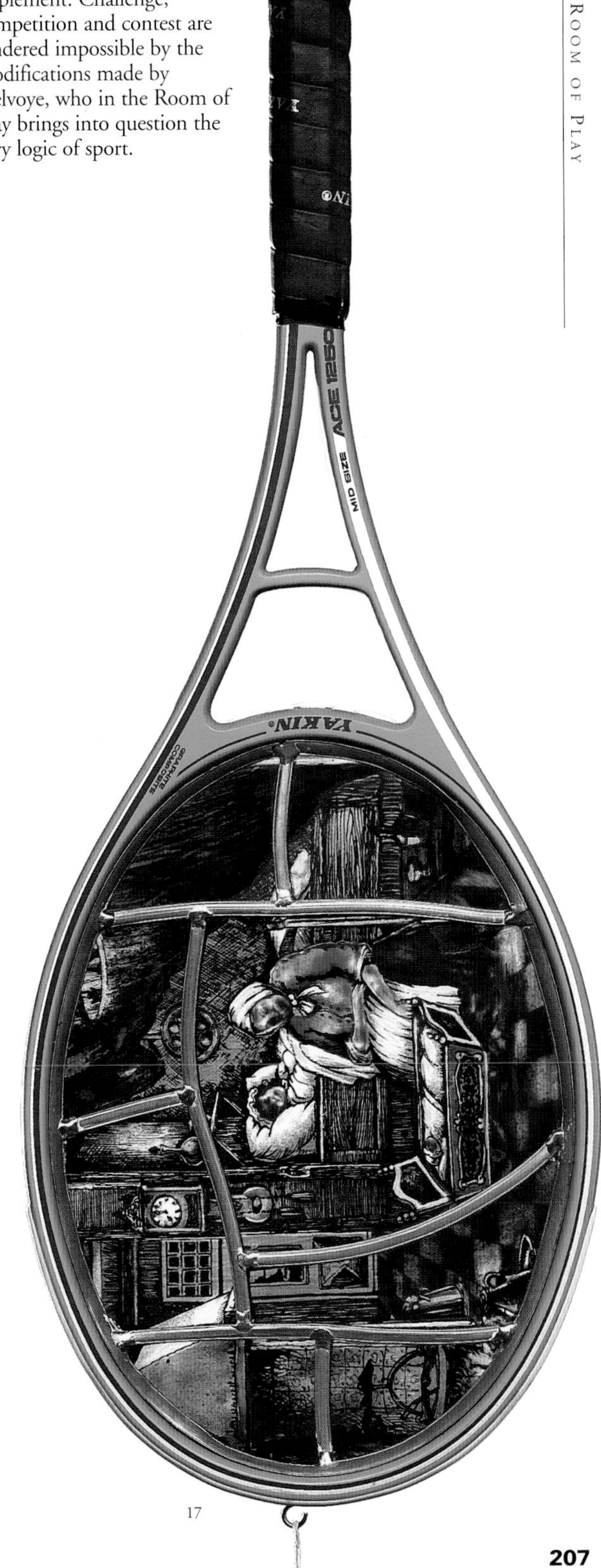

17

18

18
Arman
Dolls
Parts of dolls under glass,
30 × 20 cm
Private collection, Milan

Light bulbs, electric razors, puppets, rubber stamps, small electric appliances, cogs, brushes, tubes of paint. Anything can end up, and perhaps already has, in Arman's *Accumulations.* A prominent exponent of Nouveau Réalisme, the current centering on the critic Pierre Restany, the artist, like his associates in the movement, from César to Rotella to Tinguely, has always been fascinated by the mass-produced goods of consumer society and by the waste that is dumped in such large quantities in the contemporary era. Creativity can give new life to these objects, reutilizing them in a different way and seeing them from a different point of view. And, above all, valuing them not for their original function, but only for their aesthetic presence. *Dolls* is an accumulation of pieces of plastic dolls in a glass case, a work that, perhaps involuntarily, speaks to us of a lost childhood, of a carefree state that has given way to the preoccupations of adulthood, of a world that soon obliges us to leave our playthings behind us. And it also speaks of a metropolitan pace of life which grinds up everything that is no longer of any use, claiming victims among objects as well as human beings.

19
Man Ray
Le Voyeur
1972
Wood, glass,
11 × 17 × 3.5 cm
Private collection, Turin

In this work by Man Ray the glass is there but you don't see it (paradoxically, given the title of the work!). It is part of the peephole set in that block of wood simulating an insurmountable barrier. Here the Dadaist artist, who played a leading role in the great cultural revolution of the avant-garde, but who was above all a genius of innovation and provocation, exploits the innate curiosity of the human being, often tinged by a slight (or perhaps powerful) vein of perversion. The title suggests that there is something titillating to be seen through the peephole, and the observer is inevitably infected by the desire to see what it is, to bend down, lean over and place his or her eye to the hole. Obviously, in the pure spirit of Dada, there is nothing to see but... the space behind the work, just like behind the door of any house. Only that, in this case, it would be possible to find that out without looking through the... keyhole. The work is housed in the Room of Play because of the playful spirit that often, and especially in this case, characterizes the great creations of Man Ray, Duchamp and Co.

19

IX.

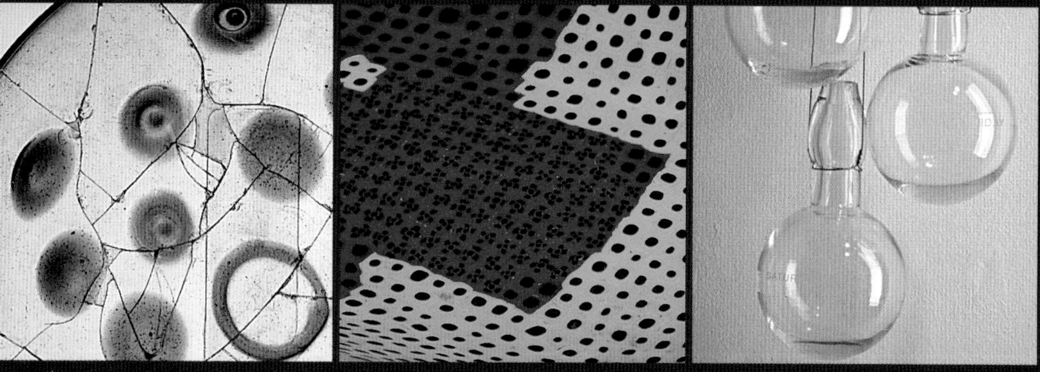

Room of Geometry

ANCIENT GLASS

Among the products of antiquity we find a number of vases of essential shape and refined elegance that, along with others, could be described as geometric in their form and decoration. The lace-mosaic (*reticello*) bowl from Ancona and its imitations in central and southern Italy can be traced back to Hellenistic production: they are open forms in which the technique of working brings out a modularly repeated geometric pattern. The process of making objects from canes of glass of different colours set side by side was used to produce plates and bowls, very common in the Augustan period, with symmetrical and polychrome designs, as in the example from Adria. The two-colour checkerboard bowl from Aosta, although fragmentary, displays an elegant schematism.
With the advent of the technique of mold blowing it became possible to make closed forms inspired by geometric solids and their infinite combinations, as the bottles of modern appearance, with elongated and conical shapes, from Zadar, Cologne and Turin testify. Other productions, again exploiting the mold technique, were embellished on the surface with additional geometrical decorations of spirals or meanders.
Geometry also provided inspiration for the technique of engraving that characterized products of high value in the 3rd century, such as the plate in the Split Museum, adorned with a uniform grid of diamonds and circles.
The production of Cologne of the 3rd and 4th century AD pursued original lines of decoration, openly contrasting with one another. Ingenious serpentine motifs wind around the bodies of bottles of essential form set on feet, while simple coloured blobs stand out against the transparent ground of bowls and bottles.

CREATORS OF GLASS

There have been moments in the history of glass in which the use of geometric designs has reached levels of absolute originality, or in which particular artists have made geometry the distinctive feature of their creations.
In the Middle Ages, at the time of the Sassanid dynasty and during the early Islamic period, cut glass with geometric motifs, mostly circular or oval, of astonishing modernity was produced in the regions of the Middle East. This glassware was closely linked, from the technical as well as aesthetic point of view, with objects carved out of rock crystal.
Geometry came into the foreground at the time of the Wiener Werkstätte as well: the Viennese firm J. and L. Lobmeyr began to work closely with Josef Hoffmann, Koloman Moser, Michael Powolny, Otto Prutscher and their pupils. Like their designs for architecture and furnishings, these items of glassware relied on effects of two-dimensional geometry and on contrasts of black and white.
Blown *murrina* and mosaic glass are also based on geometric patterns and colour contrasts. This was true of the Roman *murrine* as well as those produced on Murano following the rediscovery of the technique in the last quarter of the 19th century. In 1940 the Venetian Carlo Scarpa designed brightly coloured *murrine* of a square shape for Venini that are almost ethnic in appearance. In the 1950s and 1960s several glassworkers on Murano, including Ercole Barovier and Luciano Gaspari, produced blown *murrine* and mosaic glass in an Op Art style.
A geometric essentiality of structure, emphasized by the color, is a fundamental part of the language of Ettore Sottsass, and more recently of Michele Burato and Mieke Groot. The generation of Bohemian glassworkers trained after the Second World War has tended to accentuate the sculptural qualities of glass, in geometricized structures. Those of Stanislav Libenský, who has recently died, are particularly splendid.

CONTEMPORARY ART

From the Bauhaus to Swiss Concrete Art and from van Doesburg to Max Bill, geometry and structural rigor have played a fundamental role in the art of the second half of the 20th century, a role that has been a stimulating and provocative one where both figuration and poetic abstraction are concerned. In Italy for example, from the MAC to Optical Art and Programmed Art, many have sought to establish a relationship with the rigid expressiveness of orthogonal lines, the distinct tones of primary colours, the clear and precise signs of mathematics. Over the last few decades artists, who have always been susceptible to the allure of geometry, have for the most part thrown off the shackles of the absolute laws they had imposed on themselves, and have roamed the universe of points, segments, lines, flat figures and solids with greater freedom and creativity, permitting themselves frequent exceptions to the rules and combining gestural intuitions with almost arithmetical rhythms. In the Room of Geometry Rosanna Rossi, who has often constructed her regular volumes out of glass, so that the irregular gleams of the material are able to undermine the severe and static quality of the form from the inside, exhibits an apparently perfect parallelepiped, but one that is in fact made up of such uncontrollable, different and variable elements as bottles, rendering paradoxical the work's aspiration to present itself as a new version of Brancusi's *Endless Column*.

1

1
"Reticello" bowl
150-100 BC
Modeled in mold, transparent blue glass, translucent, white and opaque glass and colourless glass with small roundish bubbles, worked in multiple canes with windings in the same direction. Horizontal, close-set and fine marks on the whole inner and outer surface,
h. 6.8 cm, ∅ of rim 13.7 cm
From tomb on Corso Amendola at the junction with Via C. Battisti, Ancona (1951 excavation)
Museo Archeologico Nazionale delle Marche, Ancona (storehouse), inv. no. 6904
State of conservation: whole, with iridescent whitish patina on the inside of the bottom and partially on the outside

Concave, not very deep bowl, formed out of four colourless canes, terminating in a spiral at the bottom and each wrapped with a double white thread. Rounded indistinct rim, formed out of a single blue cane wound with white thread.
Bibliography: Mercando, 1976, p. 166, fig. 51, and, for a critical perspective and comparisons, Colivicchi, 1999, pp. 110 *et sqq.*, figs. 3 and 13.
(G.B.)

2
"Reticello" bowl
late 1st century BC - early 1st century AD
Composition of canes modeled in mold,
h. 5 cm, ∅ of rim 18.5 cm
From Cuora, Cavarzere, Museo Archeologico Nazionale, Adria, inv. no. IG AD 9094
State of conservation: reassembled from two fragments

Wide bowl with rim made from an applied tube of green colour, an oblique wall and slightly concave base. Each of the canes of transparent glass contains a twisted thread of white glass paste and they are arranged in parallel rows. The piece is a typical example of the version of the Hellenistic lace-mosaic technique adopted in the Roman era by the glassworks of central and southern Italy.
Typological comparisons: Isings, 18.
Bibliography: Bonomi, 1996, nos. 3, 49, p. 157.
(S.B.)

3
Bowl made from polychrome canes
late 1st century BC - early 1st century AD
Quadripartite composition of polychrome canes modeled in mold,
h. 5.2 cm, ∅ of rim 12.2 cm
From Cuora, Cavarzere
Museo Archeologico Nazionale, Adria, inv. no. IG AD 9096
State of conservation: whole

Hemispherical bowl with rim made from an applied tube of blue colour and a flat base. The polychrome canes are arranged in quarters identified by two canes of green colour that form a cross, marked by a central piece of *millefiori* glass. Tubes containing twisted threads of glass paste alternating with ribbons of solid colour in a fixed order: white, blue, yellow, white, dark violet, yellow, blue, white, blue, green, yellow, blue and white. It is the refined product of the glassworks in central or southern Italy, which took up and developed a well-known technique of Hellenistic invention.
Typological comparisons: Isings, 1.
Bibliography: Bonomi, 1996, no. 348, p. 156.
(S.B.)

2

3

4
Bottle with spiral ribs
end of 1st century AD
(late Flavian era)
Glass blown in mold and subsequently rotated,
h. 28.1 cm, max. ∅ 8.2 cm, ∅ of base 4.4 cm, ∅ of neck 3 cm
From predial necropolis of Saint-Martin-de-Corléans, to the northeast of T. 10 (*ustrinum* 16), Aosta
Deposito della Sovrintendenza, Aosta Valley Autonomous Region, Aosta, inv. no. AO-SM 49
State of conservation: reassembled, small integrations and gaps in the body, rim missing. Faint mesh of superficial *craquelures* caused by heat

Bottle in transparent, colourless glass with greenish-yellow hues, numerous bubbles and filaments. Elongated and flattened pear-shaped body, decorated with thin ribs in a spiral pattern that delimit the neck, presumably funnel-shaped. Small expanded foot, rounded base.
Rare example of a glass bottle with a spiral pattern, probably of Oriental origin given the quality of the glass, the elaborate structure and the refinement of the decoration, that is attested in the Mediterranean basin, in the Syrio-Palestinian area. Generic comparisons, especially as far as the decoration is concerned, can be made with a pear-shaped bottle from the necropolis of Albingaunum (Paolucci, 1999, cat. 49), referable to Rütti type AR 153, of the late 1st - early 2nd century AD. The technique of glassware decorated with spiral ribs, developed in the East, seems to have been introduced into the West at the end of the 1st century AD (Harden, *Vetri dei Cesari*, 1988, pp. 103-8), but not to have spread to the workshops of the Rhineland until between the 3rd and 4th century AD.
Bibliography: Fremersdorf, 1961, pp. 61-2, pl. 123; *Vetri dei Cesari*, 1988, p. 141; Rütti, 1991, pp. 185 *et sqq.*; Maccabruni, 1999, p. 164; Paolucci, 1999, p. 92.
(R.M.)

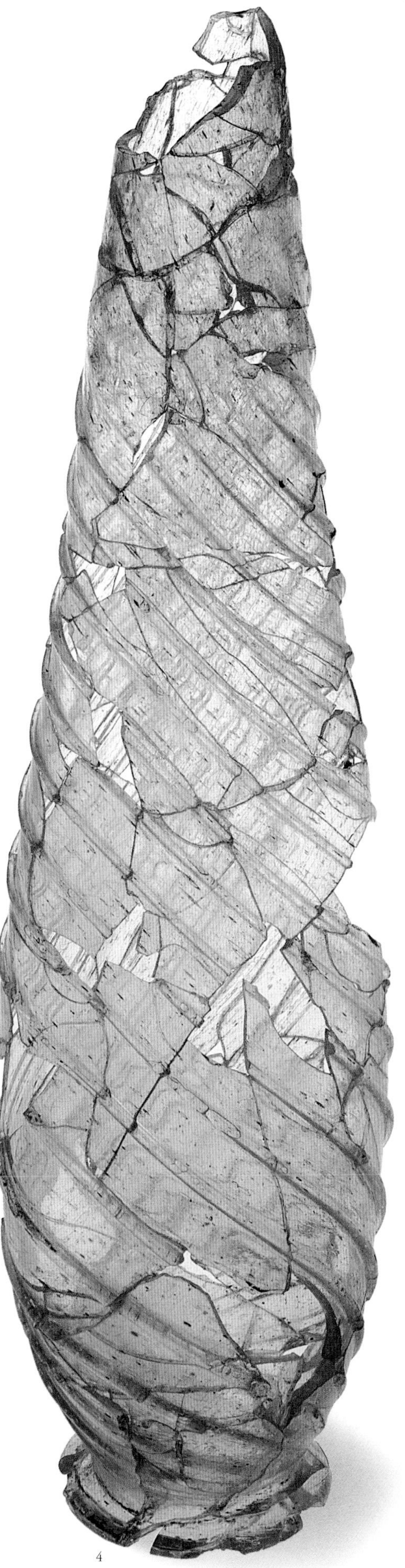

4

5
Plate
3rd century AD
Pale greenish-yellow glass, molded and polished, cut lip,
h. 4.2 cm,
∅ 17.2 cm
From Solin (*Solana*)
Arheološki Muzej, Split, inv. no. G 37
State of conservation: whole

The body and bottom of the plate are rounded. The body terminates in a cut lip. The whole plate, apart from the lip, is decorated with polished circles set in octagons, square on the inside, regularly distributed at the sides. A diamond and two triangles are engraved on the edge of each side. The ornamentation suggests a lavish "honeycomb".

Typological comparisons: Kisa, 1908, figs. 238, 240; Isings, 1957, pp. 114-6; Šubic, 1976, p. 58, p. 32; De Maine, 1983, p. 83; Lith, Randsborg, 1985, p. 430; Barkóczi, 1988, pp. 64-5, nos. 39-42.
Bibliography: Saldern, 1964, p. 46, no. 11.
(I.F.)

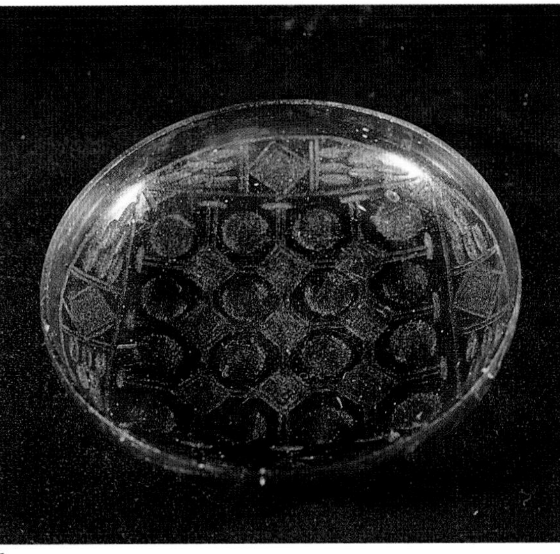

5

6
Flattened flask on foot
late 2nd century - early 3rd century AD
Blown glass with applied decoration,
h. 25.3 cm
From a Roman tomb in Cologne
Römisch-Germanisches Museum, Cologne, glass inv. no. 232
State of conservation: container intact, now appears opaque. Base partly remade

Flattened flask on transparent base with profiled stem and foot, long tubular neck and funnel-shaped mouth. The belly is decorated on the outer surface with serpentine motifs of threads and on the sides with loops, both engraved. The neck is wrapped with several turns of a fine, transparent thread.
The decorations were applied to the body of the container while it was still hot and not yet been modeled. Similar vessels with artistic serpentine motifs of threads were produced, apart from a few exceptions, in the West, in Roman Cologne.
Typological comparisons: Kisa, 1908, fig. 126; *Römer am Rhein*, 1967, p. 263, no. D 42; Whitehouse, 2001, p. 224, no. 795.
Bibliography: Poppelreuter, 1911, p. 98; Fremersdorf, 1959, p. 43, no. 232, pl. 23; Doppelfeld, 1966, fig. 113; *Römer am Rhein*, 1967, p. 262, no. D 38.
(H.G.)

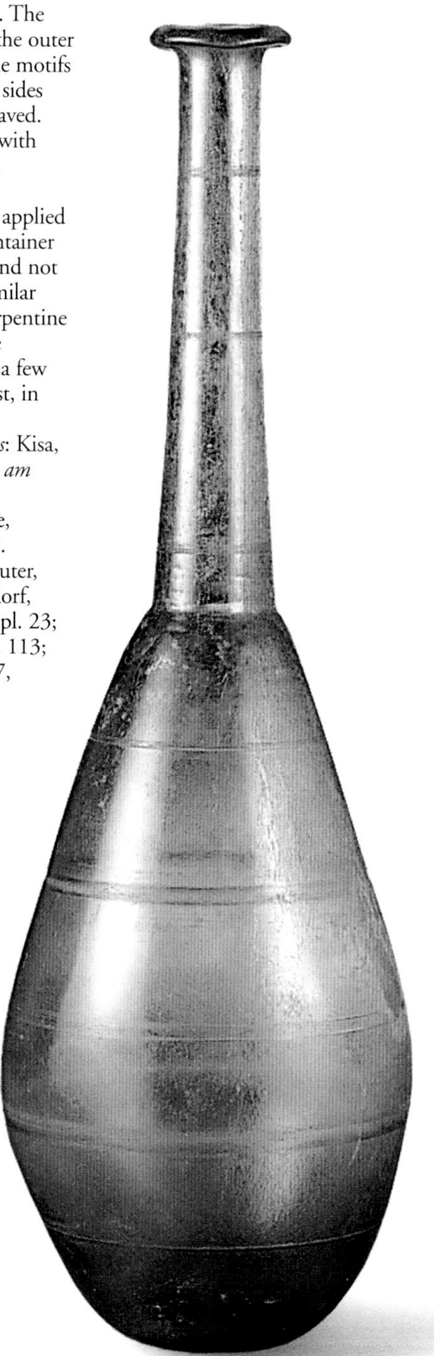

6

7

7
Conical bottle
middle of 2nd century AD
Free-blown glass, horizontal grooves cut while hot,
h. 24.5 cm, thickness 7.8 cm, ∅ of rim 2.6 cm, ∅ of neck 1.8 cm
From Zadar, Nona or Asseria
Arheološki Muzej, Zadar, inv. no. 665
State of conservation: whole

Bottle with conical body in greenish-yellow glass that narrows considerably toward the cylindrical and very long neck. The body and neck are about the same length. The neck ends in an everted and folded back rim. Slightly concave bottom. Five horizontal grooves engraved around the body and three around the neck.
Typological comparisons: Calvi, 1968, 145, group A beta 1; Hayes, 1975, 145; Fadić, 1986, 26, no. 51, form 6; Fadić, 1989a, p. 25, no. 51, form 6; Ravagnan, 1994, 153, no. 297.
(I.F.)

8
Bottle
2nd century AD
Blown glass,
h. 19.5 cm, ∅ of shoulder 6.9 cm, ∅ of foot 3.9 cm
From a tomb in the Roman necropolis on Luxemburger Strasse, Cologne
Römisch-Germanisches Museum, Cologne, inv. no. N 524
State of conservation: whole

Bottle with long and slightly eccentric neck, projecting shoulder. The body of the vase narrows toward the bottom and then widens again near the base, creating a slightly concave profile. The surface is decorated with horizontal grooves.
Only a few examples of bottles like this have been found in 1st- and 2nd-century AD contexts. A very similar specimen comes from Tunisia (now in the Corning Museum of Glass): the body of this vase is also decorated with cut grooves, but does not widen at the base. Undecorated and typologically similar bottles have been found in the Roman provinces along the Rhine.
Typological comparisons: Froehner, 1879, pl. X, no. 60; Isings, 1957, form 72 (with comparisons); Fremersdorf, 1958b, p. 42, no. 304, pl. 87; Whitehouse, 1997, p. 231, no. 392.
Bibliography: *Niessen*, 1911, p. 46, no. 524, pl. 38; Fremersdorf, 1965-66, p. 33, pl. 12.6.
(H.G.)

8

9

10

9
Bottle
second half of 3rd century - 4th century AD
Free-blown glass,
h. 19.4 cm, Ø of rim 2.5 cm, Ø of bottom 6 cm
Museo Nazionale G. A. Sanna, Sassari, inv. no. 3754
State of conservation: whole; iridescent surfaces, with traces of calcareous incrustations

Semi-opaque glass of considerable thickness, pale green in colour. Spherical body and neck with a constriction at the base, tapering a little toward the top. Indistinct rim; flat, slightly indented bottom. The decoration on the surface of the belly is made up of four concentric circles, formed out of bands of engraved lines. The form, probably of eastern origin, was also widespread in the West.
An example from the second half of the 3rd century AD (Isings, 1957, p. 122) with a decoration similar to that of the bottle in the Sassari Museum comes from tomb 35 of the necropolis of Saint Severinus in Cologne. A bottle from the 3rd century AD was found in T. 7/84 of the necropolis on Corso Magenta in Brescia (Mariotti, 1988, p. 100, pl. XXVIII, no. 1). The globular bottle in the Personeni Collection at Sondrio, dated to the 3rd-4th century AD (Roffia, 2000, p. 24, no. 38; p. 74, pl. VI), is of eastern origin. Examples without decoration are typical of the production of Aquileia. Bottles have also been found that are decorated with painted or engravings of landscapes, such as the ones produced as souvenirs for visitors to Pozzuoli: the city's harbour is depicted on one of these (Calvi, 1968, pp. 146-7).
Typological comparisons: Isings, form 103, pp. 121-2.
Bibliography: Lissia, 2000, cat. no. 56, pp. 60-1, 73.
(D.L.)

10
Flask with "spinning-top" body
3rd-4th century AD
Blown glass decorated with engraving,
h. 13.5 cm, max. Ø 13 cm
Museo di Antichità, Turin, inv. no. 3321
State of conservation: whole

Bottle with squashed biconical body on ring foot. The funnel-shaped neck, very wide at the mouth, narrows slightly in the middle and swells noticeably at the base. It stands on a pronounced shoulder, marked at the base by "whirling" engravings traced on the upper part of the body. The rim and centre of the neck are underlined by pairs of engraved lines. Very pale and not perfectly transparent green glass.
Typological comparisons: similar form in Whitehouse, 1997, p. 181, no. 319 (with bibliography).
(A.B.)

11
Bottle with lenticular body
late 3rd - early 4th century AD
Blown and pressed glass,
h. 30 cm, max. Ø 24 cm, thickness 12 cm
From the environs of Turin
Museo di Antichità, Turin, inv. no. 3843
State of conservation: whole

Large flask with lenticular body and showing gross irregularities of manufacture. It has a slightly concave bottom and a neck set on an almost horizontal shoulder. Made of thicker glass, the neck has the shape of a gently tapering cylinder, with a slight constriction at the base. Pale, not perfectly transparent green glass with conspicuous incrustations; bubbles of air, especially in the neck.
Typological comparisons: similar in form, but with a globular body, is the Isings 103 bottle; cf. too Kisa, 1908, p. 331, no. 5.
(A.B.)

11

12

13
Two-handled globular bottle
first half of 4th century AD
Blown-glass bottle with applied blobs,
h. 32 cm, Ø of body 19.5 cm
From tomb in the Roman necropolis on Neusser Strasse, Cologne
Römisch-Germanisches Museum, Cologne,
inv. no. N 133, formerly Niessen Collection
State of conservation: reassembled from fragments, with several completions on the body of the vase

Tall bottle of spherical form made of transparent greenish glass with applied blue blobs. Threads run around the top and bottom of the part of the vase's body that is decorated with blue glass. During the decoration process the body of the vase and the mass of glass were still so hot that the blobs sank into the wall and fused with it. Two handles have been applied to the back: they form broad arches stretching upward and linked by a horizontal, projecting and fixed ring. The tall cylindrical neck terminates in a sharp and chipped rim. The form of the vessel is defined by Horace (*Carm.* I.9.7) as *diota* ("two ears"). Bottles of the same type from dated contexts are attributed to the 4th century AD. Bowls and drinking glasses in particular were decorated with blobs from the 1st century onward in northern and central Italy; the spherical bottle from Cologne represents a typological exception. From the middle of the 3rd century AD on, drinking glasses with blobs were also produced in the Rhineland, especially at Cologne. Finds have been made from as late as the end of the 4th century AD.
Typological comparisons: Fremersdorf, 1933, p. 97, pl. 56; Haberey, 1942, pp. 259, 263, fig. 3, pl. 29, no. 1; Isings, 1957, p. 159, form 129; Haupt, 1976, pp. 51-7, pl. 15.2; Whitehouse, 1997, p. 254, no. 435.
Bibliography: Kisa, 1908, fig. 147; *Niessen*, 1911, p. 16, no. 133, pl. XI; Fremersdorf, 1937, pl. 55; Fremersdorf, 1962, p. 37, pl. 55; Harden, 1988, pp. 102, 114, no. 47; Fleming, 1999, p. 108, fig. E.50, c.
(H.G.)

12
Bowl with blobs
first half of 4th century AD
Blown glass with applied blobs,
h. 5.3 cm, Ø 22.8 cm
From a tomb in the Roman necropolis on Luxemburger Strasse, Cologne
Römisch-Germanisches Museum, Cologne,
inv. no. N 150, formerly Niessen Collection
State of conservation: reassembled from several fragments; parts missing from the bottom and edge of the bowl have been integrated

Bowl of coloured, transparent glass, with slightly arched border, cut subsequently, with an application of threads of golden brown glass forming a flat ring-shaped base. Large moss-green and golden brown oval blobs are fused to the underside of the bowl; most of them are umbilicate and distributed in an irregular manner.
Vessels decorated with blobs in a solid, usually blue colour date from as early as the 1st century AD. Drinking glasses with blobs of various colours appear in the 3rd century AD, but only in the western provinces of the Roman empire. This was probably connected with the influx of Teutonic tribes. The movement of population was on such a scale that it prompted craftsmen to produce vessels that met the distinctive taste of the Teutons, i.e. with richer colouring. Typologically comparable bowls can be dated to the 4th century: it is supposed that Cologne was the place of origin.
Typological comparisons: Fremersdorf, 1962, p. 33, pl. 45.
Bibliography: *Niessen*, 1911, p. 17, no. 150, pl. XIII; Fremersdorf, 1962, p. 33, pls. 46-7; Harden, 1988, pp. 102, 115, no. 48; Fleming, 1999, p. 108 fig. E.50, e.
(H.G.)

13

14

15

14
Sassanid art, cut bowl
6th century AD
Glass blown into mold and wheel cut,
h. 7.5 cm
From Iran
Kunstmuseum, Düsseldorf
State of conservation: whole

Semispherical bowl in colourless glass of great thickness, mold-blown and wheel cut. It is a model typical of Sassanid glassware (247-645 AD), deeply cut like similar models in rock crystal.
The dating, to the 4th century, is confirmed by an identical bowl found in the tomb of the Emperor Ankan (550-600 AD), now in the National Museum of Tokyo.
Typological comparisons: Tait, 1991, fig. 138.
Bibliography: Saldern, 1974, no. 271; Ricke, 1995, no. 47.

15
Sassanid art, cut bowl
7th-8th century AD
Glass blown into mold and wheel cut,
h. 11.2 cm
From Iran or Iraq
Kunstmuseum, Düsseldorf
State of conservation: large integrations in the wall

Bowl with spheroidal body, in colourless slightly yellowish glass, mold-blown and finished on the wheel with decorative spheroidal and umbilicate elements in relief. There are similar works in the Treasury of Saint Mark's Basilica in Venice.
Typological comparisons: Saldern, 1968, p. 33.
Bibliography: Saldern, 1974, no. 274; Ricke, 1980, p. V-5; Ricke, 1995, no. 48.

16
Josef Hoffmann
Wineglass, champagne glass, drinking glass for water
"Bronzit B" collection, 1914
Blown glass, rendered opaque with acid and decorated by the "bronzit" process, black enamel with a bronze effect,
h. 13.5 cm, h. 12 cm,
h. 10 cm
J. and L. Lobmeyr, Vienna
State of conservation: whole

The blown drinking glass and goblets have a strictly geometric decoration, consisting of absolutely regular, alternately vertical and horizontal lines of black enamel with a bronze effect. This decoration contrasted markedly with earlier artistic glassware, whose forms and decorations were mostly based on stylizations of natural organisms. These new proposals were perfectly in line with the new artistic language of the Wiener Werkstätte.
In 1910, the year in which the firm J. and L. Lobmeyr won the Gran Prix at the International Exposition in Buenos Aires, the glassworks, which liked to keep right up to date in the style of its products, started to commission designs from exponents of the Viennese Sezession, and later from members of the Wiener Werkstätte as well: Joseph Hoffmann, Koloman Moser, Michael Powolny, Otto Prutscher and their pupils. Hoffmann used a new type of decorative technique called *Schwarzbronzit* and adapted it to his own style, characterized by geometric forms or highly stylized floral and animal motifs set flat against a black ground. They were fully in keeping with the rest of Hoffmann's design work, with the geometric limpidity of his modern furniture and with his conviction that close links between architecture, furnishing and decoration were indispensable to the new art.
Bibliography: Arwas, 1987, p. 201; *Silice e fuoco*, 1992, p. 161, no. 224; *Autriche, Suède et Finlande,* 1995, p. 74, no. 4.

16

17
Josef Hoffmann
“Animals” oval vase
J. and L. Lobmeyr, Vienna, 1914-16
Blown crystal, etched and decorated by the “bronzit” process, black enamel with a bronze effect,
h. 10 cm
J. and L. Lobmeyer, Vienna

Design of the form: Josef Hoffmann; geometric decoration: Urban Janke; animal decoration: Ludwig Heinrich Jungnickel.
This series of vases and *jardinières* is characterized by a decoration of geometric motifs, mostly on a quadrangular module, the trademark of the Wiener Werkstätte and a reaction to the curved lines of Art Nouveau. Thus they are works emblematic, in spite of their small dimensions, of the aesthetic approach of the Wiener Werkstätte.
Around 1900 the Steinschönau Academy in Bohemia had developed a technique that produced a decorative metallic effect by covering the glass with a special paste, known as “bronzit,” applying a coat of paint and finally etching it with acid.
Lobmeyr acquired this technique and exploited it, entrusting the design to members of the Wiener Werkstätte and fusing the technical tradition of Bohemian glassworkers and decorators with Viennese stylistic innovations.

Bibliography: Arwas, 1987, p. 201; *Silice e fuoco* 1992, p. 161, no. 224; *Autriche, Suède et Finlande,* 1995, p. 74, no. 4.

18
Altare Glassworkers
Yellow drop vase
second quarter of 20th century
Blown and hand-modeled glass,
h. 67 cm, ∅ 18 cm
Istituto per lo Studio del Vetro e dell’Arte Vetraria, Altare, inv. no. 652

17

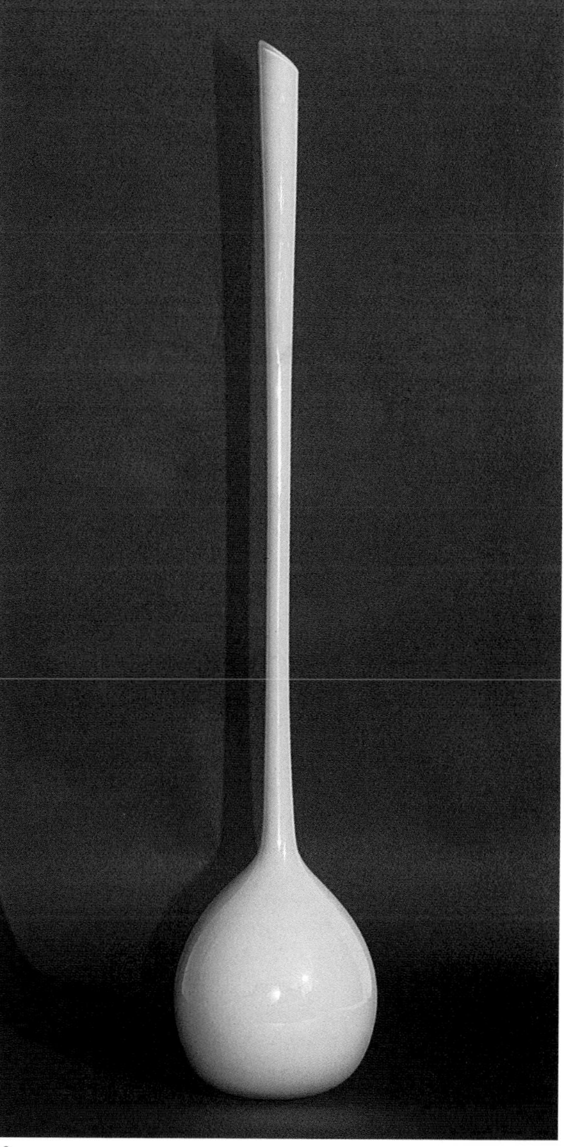

18

19

19
Napoleone Martinuzzi
Red vase
Vetri Artistici e Mosaici, Murano, 1934
Cased and blown glass, h. 19 cm, Ø 16 cm
Zecchin Martinuzzi, Murano, Fondazione Cassa di Risparmio, Venice

Blown vase in thin, "veiled" opaque red glass (*lattimo* cased in transparent red glass), spheroidal in form with a cylindrical neck wrapped with a thread of "veiled" opaque red glass. The base ring is made of similar, applied thread.
The works designed by Martinuzzi for the Zecchin Martinuzzi firm were of essential and often geometric form, and generally much more up to date than the distinctly Novecento ones that he had designed for Venini between 1925 and 1931.
Typological comparisons: Barovier Mentasti, 1992, fig. 58; *Napoleone Martinuzzi*, 1992, nos. 40-6.
Bibliography: Barovier Mentasti, 1994, no. 23; *L'art du verre à Murano*, 1995, p. 21.

20
Carlo Scarpa
Murrine dish
Venini e C., Murano, 1940
Murrino tesserae fused without blowing,
h. 5 cm, 30 × 18 cm
Kunstmuseum, Düsseldorf

Rectangular dish divided into two zones, one in red and black *murrine*, the other in aquamarine and black *murrine*. The central part contains a rectangle formed from *murrine* with a different decorative pattern.
Each of Carlo Scarpa's *murrine* presents variations in the tesserae and their arrangement, and, apart from the serpent model, are one-off pieces. In the sector of the *murrina* Scarpa renewed the Roman technique that had been revived on Murano in the 19th century in an absolutely contemporary key.
Bibliography: *Gli artisti di Venini*, 1996, p. 104, no. 110; Barovier, 1997, no. 238; Venini Diaz de Santillana, 2000, fig. 106.

20

21
Ercole Barovier
Inlaid bowl
Vetreria Barovier & Toso, Murano, 1962
Blown glass made up of tesserae,
h. 12 cm
Fondazione Cassa di Risparmio, Venice

Bowl in the shape of a truncated cone with walls made of alternating triangular tesserae of amethyst and green glass.
Ercole Barovier, a great creator of glass although not a glassworker himself, developed two lines of production after the Second World War, one which set out to make the most of materials characterized by special internal effects, often with heterogeneous inclusions, and the other, more in keeping with the times, based on highly geometric arrangements of tesserae.
Signature or mark: label with inscription "Biennale 1962 V/77."
Typological comparisons: Dorigato, 1989, figs. 106-7.
Bibliography: Barovier Mentasti, 1994, no. 64.

22
Luciano Gaspari
Op dish
Vetreria Salviati & C., Murano, 1966
Murrino glass,
width 37 cm
Fondazione Cassa di Risparmio, Venice

Oval dish in *murrino* glass with circles of yellow and green crystal glass on a black ground. It is one of the finest works designed by Luciano Gaspari for Salviati. For the most part, he favored the technique of sunk glass, consistent with his style of painting, but in 1966 he designed a series of *murrino* dishes and vases that were very up to date in their absolutely geometric decorative motifs.
Signature or mark: Salviati n. 12 disegno L. Gaspari.
Typological comparisons: *Il vetro alle Biennali*, 1995.
Bibliography: Barovier Mentasti, 1992, fig. 122; Barovier Mentasti, 1994, no. 85; *L'art du verre à Murano*, 1995, p. 29.

21

22

23

23
Ettore Sottsass
Yemen
Venini Spa, Murano, 1994
Blown glass with *incalmi*,
h. 31 cm
Collection Barile, Turin

Blown and hand-modeled vase in opaque black glass, with upper part in the shape of a truncated cone made of opaque red glass and base also in the shape of a truncated cone made of transparent green glass. The joints between the three parts are marked by threads of *lattimo*. Sottsass first tried his hand with glass immediately after the war and returned to Murano in the 1980s and 1990s, designing objects made up of superimposed geometric elements, each brilliantly coloured. They have been widely imitated.
Bibliography: *Catalogo Venini*, no. 787.00; *Gli artisti di Venini*, 1996, no. 271.

24
Stanislav Libenský and Jaroslava Brychtová
Head T
Prague, 1996-97
Gray glass cast in open mold and partially cut,
h. 90 cm
Galleria d'Arte e di Vetro, Bergamo

In the form of a dome flattened at the front and rear, hollow on the inside with a T-shaped cut on the front part. Made of rough gray glass resembling stone, the object takes on different chromatic tones with variations in the light. It belongs to a series of works inspired by a visit Libenský and Brychtová made to an exhibition of antique armor in Japan.
Bibliography: *I grandi vetri*, 1998, p. 79; *Libenský - Brychtová*, 2000, no p. no.

25
Stanislav Libenský and Jaroslava Brychtová
Lying Angel
Prague, 1999-2000
Gray glass cast in open mold and partially cut,
h. 58 cm
Galleria d'Arte e di Vetro, Bergamo

The stereometric form obtained by casting in a mold recalls the figure of a reclining angel. After an early abstract phase the work of Libenský and Brychtová has returned to figurative forms in recent times. The figure of the standing angel dates from the last few years but the *Lying Angel* is their last work, from just before Stanislav Libenský's death in 2002. The rough surface of the glass accentuates the dramatic character of the work while the dark colour, resembling that of stone, picks up and reflects the light, revealing the essence of the material.
Typological comparisons: *Libenský - Brychtová*, 2000.
Bibliography: *Libenský - Brychtová*, 2002, cover.

24

25

26

26
Michele Burato
Oval vase
Murano, 2000
Sections of Bullseye coloured glass fused into a sheet and blown,
h. 16 cm
Courtesy Galleria Rossella Junck, Venice

Ovoid vase made by blowing a sheet of glass made from a mixture of pieces of coloured glass, some of them dichroic. Michele Burato uses the Venetian *murrina* technique, but with glass, often with dichroic properties, produced by the American firm Bullseye. The coloured patterns are exalted by the blown geometric forms.
Signature or mark: Michele Burato, 2000
Bibliography: True Color, 2000, no p. no.

27
Michele Burato
Goliath
Murano, 2001
Sections of coloured glass fused into a sheet and blown,
h. 30 cm
Courtesy Galleria Rossella Junck, Venice

Disc-shaped vase made by blowing a sheet of fused pieces of polychrome glass
Signature or mark: Golia Michele Burato 2001
Typological comparisons: *True Color*, 2000, no p. no.

28
Mieke Groot
Untitled: three vases
Amsterdam, 2002
Blown glass, successive layers of enamel mixed with sand,
h. 32 cm, h. 28 cm, h. 16 cm
Galleria d'Arte e di Vetro, Bergamo

Vases in blown gray glass with spikes in relief and a surface made of successive layers of red vitreous enamel to create a rough effect.
Mieke Groot has developed a highly personal technique that entails adding successive layers of enamel mixed with sand, producing works that are consistent, in their form and the alternation of coloured parts of the surface, with the geometric propensity of Dutch design.
Typological comparisons: *Mieke Groot*, 2000, nos. 84, 50; *Aperto Vetro*, 1996, p. 115.

27

28

29
Monica Guggisberg and Philip Baldwin
Puzzled Watcher
Paris - Murano, 2002
Blown glass with double layer of colour, cut,
h. 30 cm
Collection of the artist

Vase in the shape of a squashed sphere with two layers of glass of different colours. A pattern of irregularly intersecting segments is cut into the upper blue layer so as to reveal the underlying layer of green.

30
Monica Guggisberg and Philip Baldwin
Rough Road Sentinel
Paris - Murano, 2002
Blown glass with layers of colour, cut,
h. 60 cm
Collection of the artist

Oval vase with two layers of glass of different colours. The surface of the outer opaque red layer is cut so as to reveal parts of the layer of transparent fuchsia underneath. The cuts are rectangular in shape but the fuchsia-coloured areas that emerge are round, thanks to the curvature of the wall. The "Sentinels" collection commenced with an installation of oblong forms on tall metal stems entitled *Courtiers and Guardians*, shown at *Aperto Vetro* in 1998 and, even earlier, with a series of uncut vases in 1994.
Typological comparisons: *Battuto*, 2002.

30

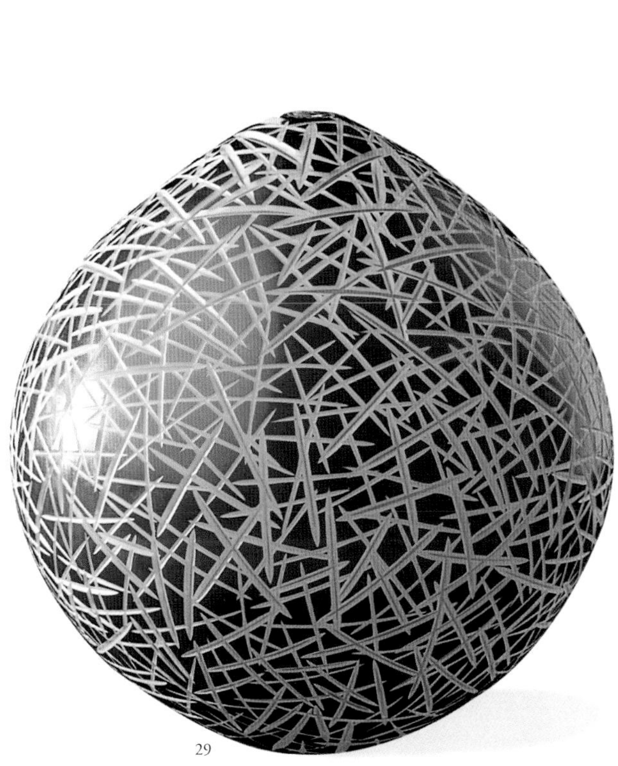

29

31
Louise Bourgeois
Untitled (Hommage à Duras)
1995
Wood, metal and glass, 56.5 × 45 × 11.4 cm
Courtesy Galleria Karsten Greve, Cologne

In the work of Louise Bourgeois, doyenne of the art world, continue to surface the nightmares and tensions of a difficult adolescence and life, much of it spent in the midst of acute family conflict, partly as a consequence of her mother's long illness. Her imagery – bursting with the harsh and unpleasant reality of daily life – is filled with jugs and bottles, in which she collected the salves and liniments used to treat her mother, and female torsos constructed brutally out of cloth and defeated by violence, anguish and mutilation, as if in a patchwork whose pattern is dictated more by pain than by an aesthetic idea. The bodies made by the artist always lean on unsteady crutches, have lost their limbs or heads or display deep and lacerating wounds, and out of their painful past emerge Kafkaesque monsters and phantoms, jailers in the shape of terrible spiders and victims who bear the marks of injustice and evil. Bourgeois's work often speaks of the body, and describes a universe similar to the one to be found in the pages of *The Naked Lunch* or the movie *Scanners*. Where it is impossible to escape from hallucinatory memories and from the fear of what is to come.

32
Mauro Staccioli
Untitled
1999-2000
Cor-Ten steel and blown glass, 90 × 90 × 30 cm (two elements)
Collection of the artist, Milan

Mauro Staccioli is one of the Italian masters of environmental art. Ever since his first significant works, at the turn of the 1960s, he has paid attention to the realities of the natural and urban world, inserting his sculptures into existing situations and relating them to what goes on around. Even when he has tackled the spaces of museums and galleries he has avoided obvious and banal choices, intervening in areas and surfaces and modifying them radically. His works, of which the most emblematic are still the wall he built on the main pathway of the Gardens at the Venice Biennale of 1978 and the gigantic arch constructed in the Square of the Games at the Seoul Olympics of 1988, are principally geometric signs – plinths, sections of circles, triangles, arcs – that seem to want to impart order to the spontaneous growth of the environment. The work presented in the Room of Geometry given its rigorous and absolute lines, marks the artist's first use of glass. A fragile and transparent element that contrasts with the strength, which he has always favoured, of concrete, steel and wood and creates new expressive possibilities for his research.

31

32

33

33
Jaume Plensa
Sunday, Monday, Tuesday, Wednesday, Thursday, Friday, Saturday
2000
Glass, stainless steel,
36 × 45 cm (variable)
Collection of the artist,
Barcelona

Two decades of environmental installations, walls of crystal, spheres, gongs and lasers. First heavy and menacing works, made of solid iron, resembling old implements of war, and then ever lighter and more appealing works, transparent and suspended in the air, made out of glass or brass. Sometimes even immaterial, created out of the nighttime illumination of the city and laser beams. At others contradictory, like the 1990 sculpture *Nächtlich*, formed from a pair of tall bronze cylinders, looking like industrial containers but enclosing the image of animals walking in the light of dawn. Jaume Plensa makes extensive use of transparency and glows of light in his creations, and for this reason often turns to glass, which also puts in an appearance through his frequent citations of Oriental and Islamic culture, where mirrors and chandeliers abound. A series of recent works, stemming from the artist's visits to places of worship in the Middle East, presents a sequence of rooms with transparent walls – of glass, resin or alabaster – containing nothing but the excessive luxury of chandeliers of drop crystal or the excessive reflections of mirrored surfaces. The work *Sunday, Monday, Tuesday, Wednesday, Thursday, Friday, Saturday*, presented in the Room of Geometry for the rigour of its forms and composition, encapsulates the repetitive nature of daily life. The spheres of glass, resembling drops that fall and pass away one after the other, inexorably, evoke the passing of the hours, and with the hours the days, and with the days the weeks, without anything much actually changing in our lives.

34
Rosanna Rossi
Untitled
2000-02
Stainless steel and bottles,
245 × 106 × 60 cm
Collection of the artist,
Cagliari

Rosanna Rossi, with experience in optical research and other areas behind her, has for a long time used glass for its chromatic properties, for the possibility it offers of modifying colour in relation to the illumination. On the wall of a building in Cagliari, an enormous mosaic made up of pieces of broken bottles changes colour as time passes, depending on the inclination and strength of the sun's rays. This work is a sort of Tower of Babel, an homage to Brancusi's *Endless Column* but reevaluated and corrected in the light of modern consumption and the creative design of the contemporary world. The artist has had crates for bottles made that closely resemble the ones used by industry, but on cleaner and more rigorous lines. In the containers she has placed a variety of coloured glass containers, grouped by shade. The crates, piled one on top of the other, form a gigantic abstract-geometric picture, made up of blocks of red, green, blue and white. Moving around the column, the blocks are superimposed, the colours mixing and forming secondary shades, as if it were an original kind of kaleidoscope.

34

Room of the Fragment

ANCIENT GLASS

The fragment as such began to play an important part in archeological studies of a scientific character at least as far back as the middle of the 19th century. Since then generations of archeologists have applied themselves to the study of fragments, learning to extract from them information about the development of material culture in the various civilizations. And if found in a layer of ground, the piece of glass can contribute, like all other fragments, to the determination of an absolute chronology. When compiling statistics on the quantities of glass present in a given context, it is necessary to bear in mind that the people in the past used to collect fragments and melt them down, where they did not simply reutilize them. In our own day ancient glass is the object of intense study and finds its way into museums, where it is conserved and restored. Notwithstanding the tendency to recycle glass for economic reasons, some special objects were preserved for their beauty and collected. An example of restoration in the past is provided by the famous vase in cameo glass, repaired using a portion of a similar piece of glassware, the so-called Portland disc.
An example of the taste for reutilization, relating to the Renaissance period this time, is the bottom of a bowl engraved with Heracles and the Nemean lion, which was turned into a medallion.
Interest in the fragment in antiquity gave rise to techniques that made use of it in particular productions, of limited diffusion. Vessels were made in northern Italy that were studded at random with chunks or grains of coloured glass, sometimes even pieces of large size as in the specimen from Adria.

CREATORS OF GLASS

The fragment of glass is precious. Many books on the history of glass are based on the study of fragments, which can tell us a great about the composition of glass in the past. Scraps and rejects from the manufacturing process can provide evidence for the existence of glassworks in the places where they are found. The most eminent historian of Venetian glass, Luigi Zecchin, made extensive use of old fragments, which he was able to interpret in the light of the documents he studied in the archives. Another historian of glass, the Frenchman James Barrelet, used to frequent a certain antique store in Venice, where fragments of ancient glass found in the lagoon were set aside for him. Fragments of glass can be melted down and transformed into new and beautiful objects. The recycling of glass is not a product of the modern concern for the environment. On the contrary, it is a very old tradition. Those in the past who did not know how to make their own glass used to import broken glass and melt it down. It is also a longstanding practice in glassworks to mix scraps with the frit, or glass constituents, to facilitate their melting and save energy. The scraps can modify the composition of the frit: in the 17th and 18th centuries the glassmakers of Murano used to introduce potash into their glass by adding *roti de Boemia*, or broken pieces of Bohemian glass, in an attempt to reproduce the brilliance of the northern European crystal. Fragments are fascinating: in the 19th-century pieces of ancient Roman *murrine* were mounted in gilded metal, to emphasize their value. Skilled craftsmen in Rome used fragments of ancient *murrine* to create splendid inlaid tops for tables. Some designers and artists have played with the fragility of glass and the way it can take on new life. While Federica Marangoni is well known for her use of broken glass in challenging multimedia works, the glassware of some of the most famous contemporary designers, from Fulvio Bianconi to Mario Bellini and Gaetano Pesce are also provocative in character.

CONTEMPORARY ART

Ever since the avant-garde movements of the early 20th century, construction has not been the sole protagonist of art. The deconstruction, destruction and progressive dismantling of form have entered the scene as well. Christo, for example, wraps up buildings to conceal their architectural form, Arman gathers and displays the junk of industrial civilization and César, with his crumpled automobiles rescued from the scrap yard, presents us with a negation of the perfect and finished figure. It is obvious that, in this context, the idea of fragment, scrap and sliver has taken on ever greater importance. It is obvious that glass, whose intrinsic fragility makes it a perfect symbol of the shattering of form, plays an ever greater part in creations that focus on the definition of imperfection, incompleteness and disruption.

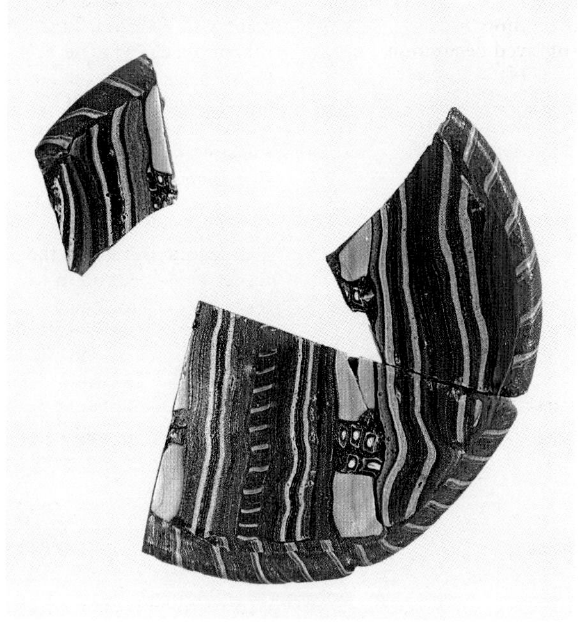

1

2

3

1
Small "plate" with polychrome ribbons
late 1st century BC - early 1st century AD
Canes worked and modeled in mold,
max. ∅ 7.2 cm, thickness 0.3 cm
From Regione Consolata (Barello excavation), to the west of shaft 5, layer IV b (SB 2246), Aosta
Deposito della Sovrintendenza, Aosta Valley Autonomous Region, Aosta, cod. lab. 03-174
State of conservation: reassembled, conserved in part

Portion of small "plate" in polychrome glass on a blue ground. The median axis is marked by a white spiral motif, similar to the one running around the rim. Symmetrical bands of yellow, red and green alternate, intercalated by two white stripes that are themselves interrupted by small squares with a motif of circular canes. It is an example of the application of the mosaic glass technique, exploiting its fanciful colours and rhythmic patterns. Its small dimensions limit the field of possible functional interpretations, not in any case very clear, but such objects were clearly appreciated, given their reutilization up until the early Middle Ages. Finds are fairly rare, even in northeastern Italy. An example from *Salona*, with the use of various colour combinations, is considered of certain Egyptian provenance (Fadić).
Bibliography: Negro Ponzi Mancini, 1988, pp. 70-1; Fadić, 1997, no. 173, p. 89; Facchini, 1998, p. 30.
(P.F. - R.M.)

2
Plate in mosaic glass
late 1st century BC - early 1st century AD
Worked canes,
max. dimensions 5.3 × 3.4 cm, 5.2 × 2.5 cm, thickness 0.25 cm
From insula 51, Giardino dei Ragazzi excavation, layer VI (Ao Gdr 46), Aosta
Deposito della Sovrintendenza, Aosta Valley Autonomous Region, Aosta, cod. lab. 03-154
State of conservation: fragments that do not fit together

Two fragments of the base of a plate with a flat, low and wide bottom. Two canes of glass paste with a sub-rectangular section, brown and whitish in colour, have been utilized. Both fragments bear a modest incision in the form of an arc of a circle on the underside, indicating the size of the diameter. Examples of mosaic glass in a checkerboard pattern are rare and hardly ever intact.
Typological comparisons: Czurda-Ruth, 1979, pl. 17.5; Roffia, 1993, no. 29, p. 57.
(R.M. - P.F.)

3
Beaker with grains
first half of 1st century AD
Free-blown glass,
h. 8.6 cm, Ø of rim 6.7 cm,
Ø of base 2.8 cm
From tomb 147, necropolis of the Canal Bianco, Adria
Museo Archeologico Nazionale, Adria,
IG AD 1939
State of conservation: whole; deformed

Small beaker glass of transparent, dark-violet glass with flared rim folded back to form a collar; ovoid body; flat base. The body is studded with large grains of white glass paste. This particular technique of decoration should perhaps be attributed to workshops in northern Italy specializing in the production of speckled glassware, which entailed the initial use of grains of glass paste, which were then heated, marbleized and turned into spots with the blowing of the vessel.
Bibliography: Bonomi, 1996, p. 127, no. 290.
(S.B.)

4
Funnel-shaped flask
4th century AD
Blown glass,
h. 14 cm, Ø of mouth 3 cm, max. Ø 9.4 cm, Ø of bottom 5 cm
From T. 16, predial necropolis of Saint-Martin-de-Corléans (former nursery school, Corso Europa), Aosta
Deposito della Sovrintendenza, Aosta Valley Autonomous Region, Aosta, inv. no. SM/E 987
State of conservation: reassembled, part of neck missing

Flask made of thin, light green glass with a globular body, funnel-shaped neck, slightly concave base and no foot.
Morphologically similar flasks, datable to between the second half of the 3rd century and the 4th century AD, are attested in northern Italy (Brescia, Ostiglia, Aquileia, Milan, Modena, Ravenna), but are more common in the former regions of Gaul and the Rhineland.
Typological comparisons: Isings, 104b, comparable to Goethert-Polaschek, form 101b.
Bibliography: Isings, 1957, pp. 123-4; Calvi, 1968, p. 145 pl. 23, M 6 Group a; Goethert-Polaschek, 1977, p. 16; De Tommaso 1986, pp. 111-12; *Milano capitale*, 1990, p. 291, nos. 4e4, 4e4C.1, p. 405, 5d.8v; Roffia, 1990, p. 398, 501.8a.
(R.M.)

5
Medallion with engraved decoration
15th-16th century
Blown white glass of great thickness, with deep wheel engraving,
Ø 7.6 cm
Museo Civico Archeologico, Bologna
State of conservation: reassembled from two fragments; no iridescence; a few small chips

Medallion of slightly squashed circular form, with irregularly chipped outer edge, suggesting that the medallion was originally part of an object of larger size, perhaps a bowl or a plate.
The engraved scene represents the struggle between Heracles and the Nemean lion: the hero, kneeling, clasps the animal's muzzle with his arms, sinking his head into its thick mane; the lion, in an attempt to escape his grip, arches its body, pushing with its paws against Heracles's legs and arms.
The iconographic scheme, characterized by a unity of composition that the makes it particularly well suited to use on a round support, is widely documented in the coinage of Heraclea, Taras (Taranto) and Syracuse between the end of the 5th and the 3rd century BC, and would be taken up again by the artists of the Renaissance, who were fascinated by the theme of the labours of Heracles.
The stylistic features of the scene, as a whole and in its individual details, find a close parallel in several small bronze plaques now in Padua and attributed to Moderno, an artist active between the 15th and 16th century. There is a striking resemblance in the anatomical representation of the bodies of the hero and the animal, which are in the same position on all the different objects, and even in some "incongruities" of the composition, such as the skinniness of Heracles's legs with respect to the powerful frame of his bust.
Typological comparisons: Gorini, Parise Labadessa, Saccocci, 1991, p. 78, fig. 39 (for Moderno's plaques).
Bibliography: Meconcelli Notarianni, 1979, p. 44, no. 31.
(M.M.)

4

5

6

7

8
Two stems of goblets
Murano, 16th century
Glass blown and modeled freehand; glass blown in mold,
h. 6 cm, h. 6.5 cm
Private collection
State of conservation: fragments

The foot in crystal with a stem made up of two solid spheres is one of the numerous variants of the stalks of 16th-century goblets that can be seen in museums, have been found in the lagoon and are reproduced by numerous Renaissance painters. The mold-blown stem in the shape of a lion's head is also very common, and in particular can be seen with the same connecting discs at the top and bottom in a drinking glass found on a Venetian ship that sank off the coast of Dalmatia around 1583.
Typological comparisons: Tait, 1979, no. 88, no. 90; *Mille anni*, 1982, no. 199.

6
Fragment of drinking glass
Murano, *c.* 1500
Rosette glass,
h. 6 cm
Private collection
State of conservation: fragment

Fragment of drinking glass with ribs obtained by mold blowing. Pieces of rosette polychrome cane (with concentric layers of different colours forming a typical star or rosette motif) are incorporated into the wall of crystal. There are not many whole specimens in the museums, but a large number of fragments have been found in the lagoon. These articles are mentioned in the records of late 15th-century Murano.
Typological comparisons: Tait, 1979, nos. 162, 166.
Bibliography: Barovier Mentasti, 1982, fig. 22.

7
Bottleneck
Murano, 16th century
Glass blown *a rigadin ritorto*,
h. 7 cm
Private collection
State of conservation: fragment

Neck of bottle in glass blown *a rigadin ritorto*, i.e. into a mold with thin ribs and then twisted to make a spiral pattern. The fragment was found in the lagoon alongside shards of 16th-century pottery. It was part of an *inghistera*, a typical bottle with or without a foot that had a rounded and squashed body and a long neck, found throughout Italy from the Middle Ages to the 18th century. They were bottles in common use and of varying quality. A whole specimen with a smooth neck was found in a walled-up niche above a brick bearing the date 1492 in the church of San Sigismondo at Cremona. These *inghistere a rigadin ritorto* are frequently depicted in paintings, from Benozzo Gozzoli to Titian and beyond.

8a

8b

9
Three bases of bottles
Murano, 16th century
Blown crystal, blown crystal, *mezza filigrana*,
h. 5 cm, h. 1.5 cm,
h. 4.5 cm
Private collection
State of conservation:
fragments

The three bases represent three different kinds of base used for the *inghistera*, the typical bottle with a rounded and squashed body and long neck that was in use all over Italy from the Middle Ages to the 18th century. All, however, are of the *siambola cavada* type, i.e. a base in the shape of a truncated cone made by folding back the wall of the body. One crystal base has a flat bottom, the other a marked conical indentation. The third base also has a conical indentation, but is in *mezza filigrana* glass, i.e. made out of canes of *lattimo* and crystal. The three bases were found in the lagoon along with pieces of 16th-century pottery.

10
Fulvio Bianconi
Fragments
Vetreria Ferro Galliano,
Murano, 1966
Blown glass with applications
h. 14 cm, ∅ 14 cm
Fondazione Cassa di Risparmio, Venice,
inv. no. 0056

Vase from the *Fragments* series in thin yellow glass with an intermediate band of glass threads woven into an irregular pattern and applied hot.
Bibliography: Barovier Mentasti, 1994.

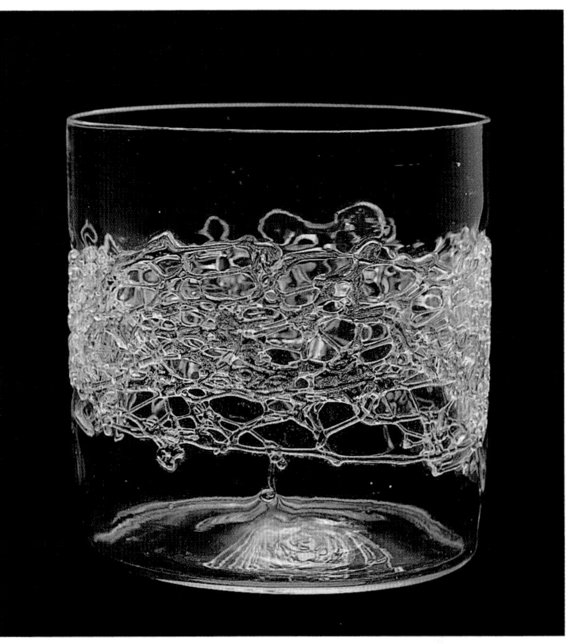
10

9

11
Gaetano Pesce
Cul-de-Sac
CIRVA, Marseilles, 1989
Industrial glass thermoformed on mold, rubber spheres,
h. 16.5 cm
Galleria d'Arte e di Vetro, Bergamo

Three sheets of green, red and periwinkle blue industrial glass, superimposed and thermoformed on a mold. They rest on three rubber balls. The one-off piece belongs to an experimental collection produced between 1988 and 1992 at the CIRVA in Marseilles, an international centre of research into glass and the visual arts that is more interested in contemporary art than in the tradition of handcrafted glass. CIRVA offers painters, sculptors and designers an opportunity to work with the material with the assistance of highly-qualified technicians. In the eighty works in the series Gaetano Pesce spurned the tradition of blown glass to experiment with new and different techniques, in some ways closer to his work with resins, plastics and silicon. The result is extraordinary and provocative but absolutely in keeping with the essence of the material.
Bibliography: *Gaetano Pesce*, 1992, no. 37; *Aperto Vetro*, 1998, p. 225.

12
Mario Bellini
Shattered Dreams
Venini, Venice, 1992
Blown glass,
h. 49.5 cm, ∅ 35 cm
La Scaletta di Vetro, Milan

Blown and hand-worked with applications of multicoloured and iridescent glass. A series of salvaged pieces of glass or discards from manufacture have been applied to the top of the bowl to create a vase sculpture. In glass nothing is lost: even scrap from the furnace can be given new life.
Bibliography: *Aperto Vetro*, 2000, p. 70; *Glass Objects*.

11

12

13
Antonio Trotta
Dew
1998
Bronze and pieces of crystal, 3 × 120 × 90 cm
Courtesy Galleria Astuni, Fano and Pietrasanta

An exponent first of Minimalism and then of Classicism, Antonio Trotta favours bronze and marble. His work, consisting chiefly of sculpture and mosaic, combines traditional techniques with contemporary and provocative themes, as when, in a Neo-Pop key, he carves a monumental rolled-up sock out of stone, or when, fascinated by gleams of light, he uses mosaic tesserae to design a gigantic vinyl disc. The artist often creates a contradiction between the heaviness of the material and the lightness of the figures sculpted in it. An illuminating example, in this sense, is the work *Fountain of Peace*, shown at the Venice Biennale in 1990: a large and heavy net of bronze, reproduced in every particular, with every mesh, that appears to be lifted by two doves, producing an overall impression which cancels out all the rigidity and heaviness of the elements. Glass often appears in Trotta's work, where it is treated with spontaneity and simplicity, exploiting the brilliance that makes it resemble water. The enormous drops caught by the net of *Dew*, the work presented in the Room of the Fragment, are made of glass. The mesh has caught and, now hauled up, reveals its treasure: some of the simplest and most inimitable gems in the world, those produced every morning by the dew.

14a
Piergiorgio Colombara
Secret Lies
2001
Glass and steel, 150 × 34 cm
Collection of the artist, Genoa

14b
Piergiorgio Colombara
Secret Lies
2001
Glass and steel, 150 × 24 cm
Collection of the artist, Genoa

To produce his works, some of which were exhibited at the Venice Biennale of 1993, Piergiorgio Colombara draws his inspiration from the Middle Ages, its symbols, its customs and traditions. A coherent and logical choice for an artist who was born and grew up in the historic centre of Genoa, who lives a stone's throw from the cathedral of San Lorenzo, who is always surrounded by the black and white of an ancient, gloomy city. Where to rekindle a sense of pomp and glory it is necessary to go back in the mind to the centuries of the Superba, of the Doria, Fieschi and Spinola families. Even the choice of materials – lead, silver, brass and glass – is influenced by his passion for the year 1000 and thereabouts. The cycle of sculptures *Secret Lies* – exhibited in the Room of the Fragmen since at the heart of each work is set a broken piece of an old suit of armor, well protected by long drops of glass – re-proposes the classical and venerable form of the chandelier, circular, adorned with drops of crystal, that is still so often to be found hanging at the centre of the great halls of disused castles. Glass, whose intrinsic beauty contemporary art has so often been ignored in order to concentrate on its material characteristics, is used in this case to embellish the object, to create reflections and transparencies, and in this way recover a historic use of the element, one that is no longer common in the current panorama of the visual arts.

13

14a

14b

15
Chiara Dynys
Entr'acte Series
1999
Murano glass, ash, gold, oxide and pigments
Danna Olgiati, Volker Feierabend and Manoli Traxler Collections

Chiara Dynys is not an artist of glass, in the sense that she possesses no personal mastery of the techniques required to work it or any secret recipe for treating the material in an original way. But she is one of the figures on the national and international art scene who, along with Cragg, Corsini and Vercruysse, has most often made use of it in her creations. She has cut it like a diamond, she has transformed it into a mirror, she has exploited its transparency and brilliance. The works of the "Entr'acte" series, whose title recalls René Clair's celebrated film starring Picabia, Man Ray, Duchamp and Satie, a diatribe against bourgeois academicism and "prescribed" art, contain the ashes of the artist's old diaries in a shell of Murano glass. Once again, as in the Dadaist film, there is a funeral involved. Dynys cremates her old thoughts, the desires of the past, the hopes and disappointments entrusted in solitude, and thus in total sincerity, to pen and paper, and gives the task of preserving without ever revealing them to the transparency of glass. Observers are tempted to imagine what those ashes once concealed, and the transparency of the material sharpens their irrational appetite, as if it were still possible to make out something in those carbonized fragments, to steal a phrase or a sigh.

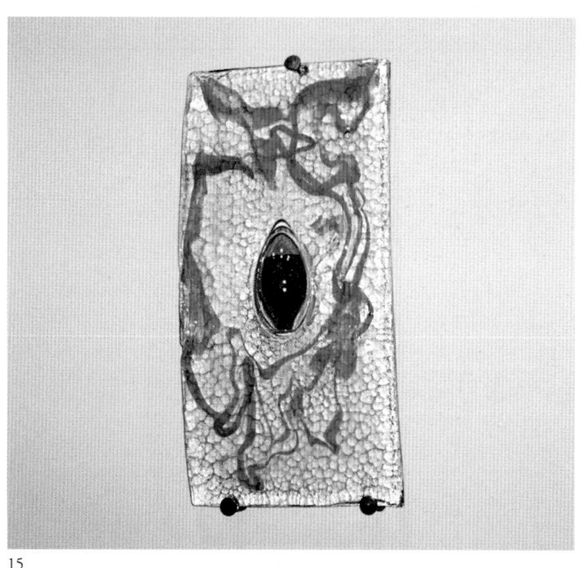
15

15

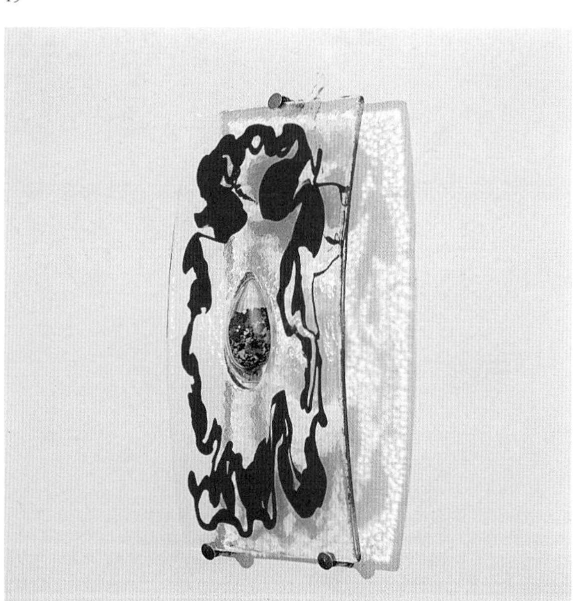
15

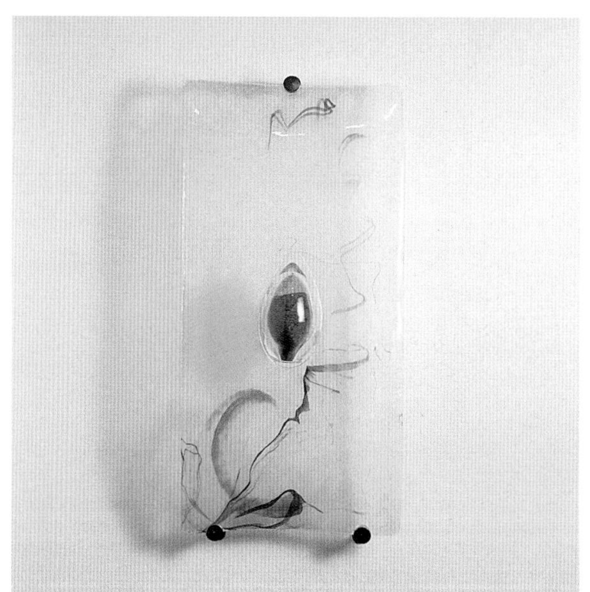
15

16a
Thorsten Kirchhoff
Life Size
1999
Oil on glass,
50 × 75 cm
Private collection, Turin

16b
Thorsten Kirchhoff
Pilot
2000
Oil on glass,
50 × 75 cm
Private collection, Turin

16c
Thorsten Kirchhoff
Twilight Zone
2000
Oil on glass,
65 × 55 cm
Galleria Alberto Peola, Turin

16d
Thorsten Kirchhoff
Twilight Zone
2000
Oil on glass,
65 × 55 cm
Galleria Alberto Peola, Turin

In Thorsten Kirchhoff's work truth is often mixed with fiction, and the effect is that of an alienating, absurd, frenzied humor. His painting, strictly in black and white, like the clips from the historic films from which it sometimes seems to draw its inspiration, like the lines and contrasts of the Nordic design that characterizes the world in which the artist grew up, often encounters real objects, rendering the functions that these normally perform disquieting or ironic. In *Everyone Can Sing*, from 1993, the songs of the band Ivor Axeglovitch, to which Kirchhoff himself belonged in the 1980s, are played on a tape recorder and the sound emitted by an endless series of speakers on which the faces of people singing are drawn. In *Long Playing*, again from 1993, the faces of four artists, including Kirchhoff, are painted – as if they were those of the Beatles – on a vinyl disc that revolves, always stuck in the same groove, on a record player. *Hardware* – from the series of oils on glass, as are *Twilight Zone*, *Pilot* and *Life Size* – presents a highly cinematographic close-up of the face of a man wearing glasses, but the glass of the support on which the image is painted is broken, as if by the impact of a stone, at the point corresponding to the left lens of the spectacles. Reality wins out over fantasy, the material on which the artist works makes itself felt and prevails over the fruit of his imagination. And that crack in the glass unites the destinies of fiction and the real world in an unforgettable way.

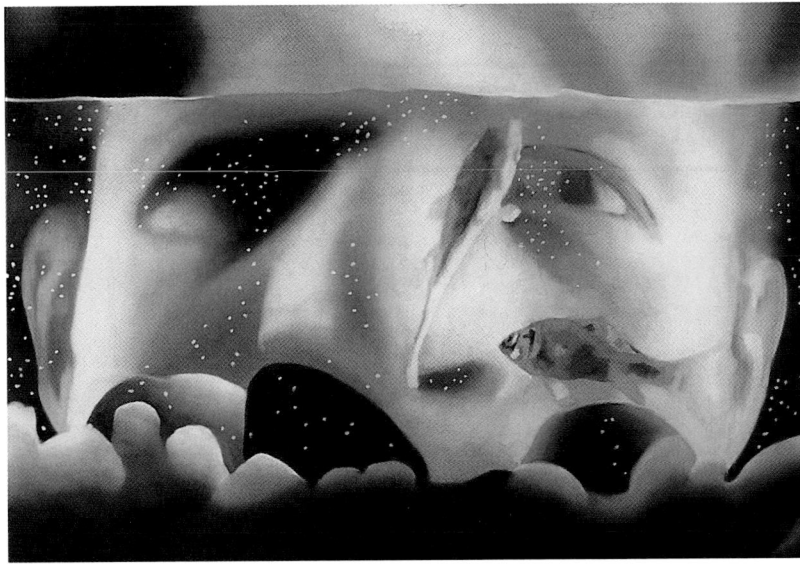
16a

16c

16b

16d

17a

17a
Luca Pancrazzi
Bulborundum
2001
Glass, silicon, light bulb and electric system,
23 × 15 × 15 cm
Galleria d'Arte Emilio Mazzoli, Modena

17b
Luca Pancrazzi
750 ml
2001
Glass, silicon,
30 × 15 × 15 cm
Galleria d'Arte Emilio Mazzoli, Modena

An eclectic artist, Luca Pancrazzi is capable of passing from sculpture to photography, from the installation to the painting, without losing the thread of his discourse. On the contrary, he enriches the same theme with new facets. With the series of works shown at Emilio Mazzoli's gallery in Modena in 2001 and now at Aosta, he continues a line of research he has been pursuing for years. Using oil and stains in his monochrome canvases, using correcting fluid on photographs clipped from newspapers, using splinters of glass on objects of everyday use, such as light bulbs, chairs and bottles, the artist breaks down familiar images and forms, rendered reassuring by their constant appearance in daily life, and turns them into objects that are harder to define. The eye recognizes the shapes, but the vibrant surface of the works prevents it from bringing them into focus, from being sure of what it sees. And in this way even the most obvious and repetitive of visions can be transformed into an out-of-the-ordinary experience.
As the artist declares in the catalogue *Intruso-Estruso*, published in 2001, the two works presented at *Glassway* were born many years ago and stem from his curiosity as a child. Walking around, he used to wonder what was the purpose of those pieces of glass, those splinters lined up on top of walls, like scales on the back of mutant dinosaurs. When the reason was explained to him, he accepted – in that absolute way that only a child can – the logic of defense or attack, without any possible middle course, and understood that the pieces of glass were there to stop the wall from being climbed, and that all that was left for him was to try to climb it. Now, after much time has passed, he presents us with this defensive strategy of things, which in order to preserve themselves threaten anyone who approaches like a porcupine.

17b

Techniques and Materials

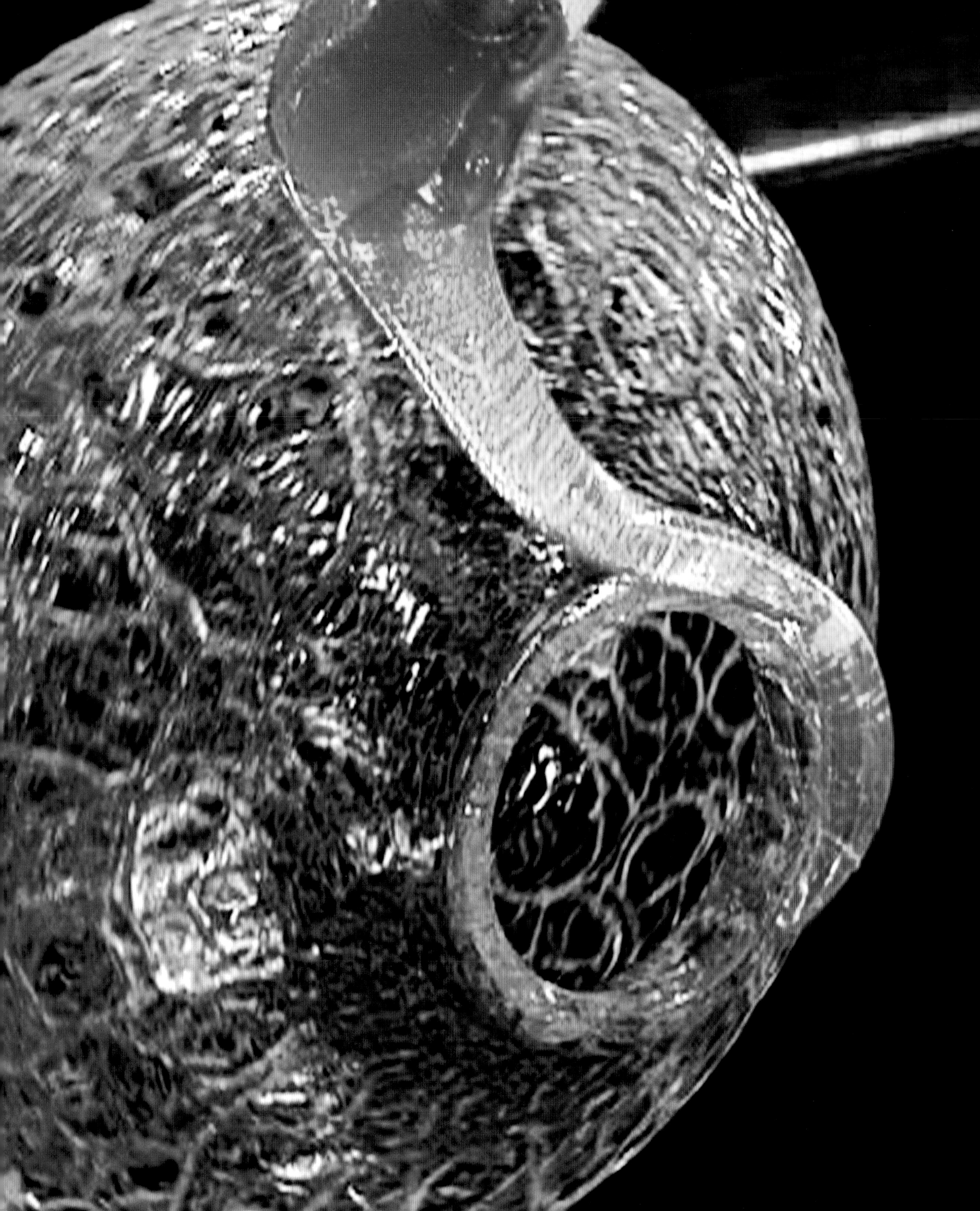

From the Magic of Fused Glass to Intelligent Glass

Anna Geotti

Glass: history and main characteristics

Glass is a solid with unique features: it has an amorphous structure and not a crystalline one, in other words, the molecules constituting it are not ordered in a regular way according to repetitive sequences, but in a spatially disordered way similar to liquid molecules.

There are also natural glass compounds called tektites: small dark-coloured vitreous material having an almost spherical shape. There are different theories regarding the origin of tektites; according to some they are small meteorites formed by fusion as they enter the Earth's atmosphere, others believe they are Earth rocks formed by fusion from the heat of impact with a meteorite.

The first tektites were found in Texas and Lebanon in the 1930s. Silica makes up 80% of a tektite, and in terms of age research has established that they were recently formed; they range from being circa 0.7 million years old (Australian tektites), to almost circa 33 million years old (North American tektites).

The raw material that creates glass through fusion is a mixture of mainly glass formers, flux or melting agents, stabilizers and other allied substances – refining agents, decolourants, colourants and opacifiers that are added based on the desired final product.

The glass former is generally silica, in the form of quartzose sand. The most valued sands are those with a low metal content, in particular iron; metals give glass a colour that ranges from yellow-brown to green. In order to reduce the fusion temperature of the mixture, substances called flux or melting agents are added to allow the mixture to remain "liquid" at lower temperatures. Melting agents are also called reticulation modifiers because the atoms that dissociate from these molecules weave their way into the silica molecules, interrupting their interaction and giving them a certain mobility in temperatures sometimes lower than 1600°C. Sodic glass has a small defect – it dissolves in water, that is, when in contact with water for an extended time it removes sodium atoms from the solid, causing material opacification and weakening. To rectify this, compounds called stabilizers are added, the most common being calcium salt: this alkaline earth metal, thanks to its chemical qualities, is more resistant to attack from water and so stabilizes the whole structure. Sodium carbonate, together with calcium carbonate, is commonly used (common glass sodium-calcic).

Other stabilizers are barium carbonate and lead and aluminium oxide, selected and added according to the specific strength required for the glass.

Refining agents are substances that tend to dissolve in the molten mixture, developing large gaseous bubbles that remove lumps, small bubbles and potential impurities.

Colorants and opacifiers are characterized by the way they interact with the molecules of the molten mass: the first form soluble compounds which colour the glass but leave it translucent; the latter initially dissolve in the molten mass but separate during cooling, forming small crystals with refraction indexes that differ from that of glass, resulting in opacity.

These are the identifiable raw materials. The chemical laws connected to transformation during fusion are the same, but in glass production there are

The picture on the opposite page and the ones on the following pages are taken from the video Glassway *(2002) by Giuliana Cunéaz. Edging of ice glass*

differences between artisan methods and industrial processes.
In artisan production, old refractory furnaces continue to be used. They contain crucibles in which the batch is prepared during the night. The base mixture, with the addition of additives and/or colourants, is made based on the artisan's experience and after trials on casting samples; any necessary corrections to the colour are then made.
The instruments used have also changed very little with time, especially in glassworks producing specific products. Metal shears, tongs, and paddles are used to mix the material.
The shift to industrial production reduced time and increased quality. In industrial fusion processes for the mass production of bottles, sheets and other objects, the dosage of raw materials is mainly automatic, while the balance of the additives is added manually after weighing.
However, quality greatly increased with the introduction of tank furnaces, which replaced crucible furnaces and enabled continuous production cycles. Crucible furnaces continue to be used in artisan production and in industrial production of objects requiring specific uniformity in the molten mixture.
Glass is a fragile material, that is, it breaks if it is subjected to violent mechanical or thermal stress: it is a common and sometimes harmful experience because glass breaks into sharp pieces. This problem can be rectified in some cases because there are specific glass products that when broken do not produce pieces that can cut. For example, kitchen glass is made specifically so that it can be put in ovens or in contact with a flame ("Pyrex" glass); so called "shatterproof" glass when broken forms minute fragments that can be collected by hand without injury; and technology has produced glass and polycarbonate sheets that when smashed the glass remains attached to the sheet.
Glass objects, like all manner of everyday use objects, eventually break and become waste.
From the beginnings of mass production to the middle of last century, breaking an object generally meant throwing it away and replacing it with a similar object, perhaps a more practical one or one with better accessories. In the later part of the 20th century society began to change; the system began to call us to order, pointing out that consumption of materials and energy to create objects that did not last long was irresponsible. No one had taken into account that the environment has quantitative and qualitative limits to its powers to absorb waste.
Very gradually waste became an issue to be dealt with and experts began focus-

Preparation of glass blown from zanfirico *rods*

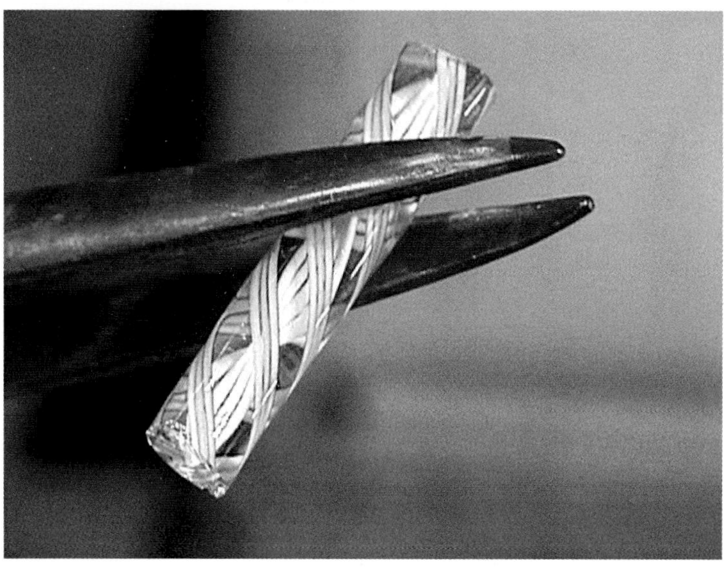

ing on finding the best ways to manage it. Results were not immediate, but it was acknowledged that the best way to manage waste was to produce less of it and also to reuse as much as possible the material that forms waste.

Common glass objects, such as bottles, glasses, containers and other kitchen objects and window glass panes, also contain variable quantities of metal (aluminium surrounds for panes or the rings around bottle necks), paper (labels on bottles), and sometimes plastic film. These common glass objects are excellent recyclable objects. In point of fact glass, appropriately ground and added to the raw compound of primary materials ready for melting, reduces the temperature of a batch, enabling a saving in both raw materials and thermal energy. This is not a modern invention; old Murano glassworks used their own scrap material to prepare new batches.

In order to thoroughly understand the organization of activities in a glass-recycling centre it is necessary to keep in mind that recycling material to its full potential depends on how much the material is contaminated by other material. When separation of materials is necessary, the amount of recyclable material is naturally reduced and in the end may not be economically advantageous.

For this reason, companies collecting glass waste, known as cullet, separate the scrap according to where it comes from. The recycling centre therefore has distinct areas: sheet glass, mirrors, car windscreen glass, pharmaceutical phials, bottles, and glass from urban street collection. Some industries, such as furniture factories, producers of window frames, companies producing drinks and bottles, distributors of bottled products, and hospitals with regards to phials, produce relatively homogeneous glass, which can be ground and returned to that particular production cycle, unless it requires the application of specific technology. On the other hand, glass from street collection is highly contaminated and requires a thorough separation treatment to eliminate chiefly metal and ceramic fragments. Metal or ceramic material can cause problems in two ways. It can trigger fractures in the batch glass itself, and it can damage the equipment in which the glass is being created, as metal granules in the batch corrode furnace refractory slabs.

Production of sheet glass

We will now look at the development of industrial sheet glass.

The first system used to produce glass in sheets was based on the system for blowing glass. This manual system, used until the first years of the 19th century, was the so-called Crown glass that involved a series of operations that called for precision, physical strength and determination as well as an in-depth knowledge of the materials involved.

A certain quantity of glass was blown and, when the glass master saw fit, it was turned at high speed inside the furnace until it formed a disk. It was then detached from the rod and cooled, producing a disk with a maximum diameter of 150 cm, or less when cut into a square or rectangle. The name came from the crown shaped imprint that was left on the glass after the rod had been detached.

To make larger sheets the cylinder system was developed: the glass was blown downward into a tube so as to produce a cylinder varying in size according to the quantity and how it was worked. The ends were then cut from this cylinder and it was opened out creating a rectangle the size of the cylinder surface.

At the end of the 17th century a system was invented in France producing sheet glass by rolling.

The molten glass was poured out of the melting pot onto a smooth metal surface and was spread by a large cylinder rolling along two side guides to ensure uniform thickness. This system had the advantage of being able to produce

larger sheets than with the cylinder method. The sheets were subsequently ground and polished to remove irregularities.
The development of the building industry in the 19th century brought an increase in sheet glass factories but also led the market to demand better quality products, especially regarding uniformity of thickness. The solution was a device for double rolling: the molten glass was poured out onto a flat surface and at later stages was rolled between different pairs of cylinders into a relatively uniform thickness; subsequent grinding and polishing was necessary.
The system used today is lamination by the Float process, which produces a finished sheet directly without final grinding and polishing.
After lamination the sheet is spread onto a vat of molten tin and over which there is a set of nozzles producing downward flames. On contact with the molten tin the sheet becomes perfectly smooth and the upper surface is made smooth thanks to the flames.
After forming the sheets must be cooled at the right speed to avoid the creation of tensions that would interfere with subsequent cutting. This phase is called annealing and is carried out in tunnel kilns where the temperature is gradually brought down to normal environment temperature.
From the simple sheet, products have been developed for specific usages ranging from tempered glass to layered or reinforced products, specially designed products for the building industry such as double glazing or innovative products that modulate solar radiation, and more recent products that are still being studied, so-called "intelligent glass" which can change their colour according to the levels of solar radiation.
Tempering is a process that consists in heating the glass to 600°C and subsequent cooling of the surface with cold air jets: in this way the surface cools and contracts faster than the internal part of the glass creating a system of tensions which holds until the glass is struck: the impact releases these tensions causing the sheet of glass to literally explode into minute rounded fragments, completely harmless to the skin. The advantage is self evident when compared to the dangerous splinters that are the normal result of breakage.
The other products listed are obtained by combining sheet glass with other materials, plastic sheets or coatings with vaporized metals.
It appears that laminated glass was discovered by chance by the French chemist Edouard Benedictus at the beginning of the last century: while working in his laboratory he dropped a bottle that seemed to be empty and it broke but the fragments did not detach from one another. Finding that this was an interesting phenomenon he kept the bottle, noted the incident, and returned to his work. Later he was struck by the fact that in numerous driving accidents the victims often died or were left horribly disfigured by the breaking windscreen, he had a stroke of genius, he analyzed the content of the bottle and found that it contained cellulose nitrate. He applied this substance between two sheets of glass creating the first laminated glass, which was called "triplex": its first usage was during the First World War for gas masks (cfr. Dri, 1994).
Creativity coupled with the evolution of technology has permitted the development of ever more specialized products for the most varied applications. Especially in the building sector where at the same time lighting and thermal conditions have been optimized: particularly significant in this sense is so-called "intelligent glass."
Varilite is a special type of glass that can be turned opaque or transparent with the simple flick of a switch. This instant transformation not only varies visibility through the glass panel but also modulates the quantity of light that is transmitted. The important element here is a film of liquid crystals inserted between two sheets of glass by means of

a vacuum lamination in an autoclave. In their normal state the molecules of liquid crystals have a casual layout that appears opaline. This state allows light diffusion to be amplified but vision through the panel is totally impeded. When alimented however, the molecules are immediately directed in an orthogonal direction to the observation point thus making the panel perfectly transparent and without any deviation of light rays.
Cromalite is a panel of stratified glass with a special organic conductive composite that can change colour with a low voltage electrical impulse. It is an experimental product at present and has yet to be put into mass production. The colour depends on the composition of the composite so that a neutral or slightly amber tint can be changed into blue, green or another colour.
The choice of glass type in building is based on aesthetics and optimal environmental comfort, considering factors such as illumination and acoustic and thermal insulation. Sometimes windows with high solar control, which are optimal in summer, can screen excessively in winter to such an extent that artificial illumination is required even during the day. A solution to this problem could be found in special products such as electrochromic glass: at present this product is still in the experimental stage but if market conditions are favourable it is foreseeable that it will be soon developed on an industrial scale.
Energy Saving Glass is principally used during the summer when solar radiation is strong and it is necessary to reduce the transmission of infrared rays without reducing light transmission. By inserting a film of particular metal between the sheets of glass infrared rays are reflected, thus reducing summer overheating. Combining this type of product with low emission glass (low-e) summer protection from heat can be combined with winter thermal insulation, creating a balance between optic and energetic parameters.

Techniques for bottle manufacture

The history of bottle-like containers can be traced back to 1500 BC in the Middle East. Bottles were made in Greece, Egypt and Syria by covering a core made of sand and clay in molten glass and then using a rod to roll it on a flat stone until the surface was smooth. After annealing the inside core was dug out. The blowpipe was discovered around 50 BC in Syria and obviously led to much faster production of bottles and with a greater variety of forms obtainable.
The Roman period, up to 400 AD was very rich in bottle production; the blowpipe made it possible to produce bottles of thinner glass, phials and small bottles of different sizes for various uses. There was a certain variation in the colours available from shades of blue to amber. Decoration was also noteworthy with seals and masks being impressed on the bottles and some were also engraved.
The technical essentials of bottle production using glass blowing have remained the same both in artistic glass and in some particular industrial production methods.
In the first half of the 12th century the German monk Theophilus Presbyter describes how to make a long necked bottle in his treatise *Schedula diversum*: take a gather of glass on the blowpipe and blow it into a broad shaped form, then rotate this over the head as if one were about to throw it, until the part close to the blowpipe is extended. Detach it from the blowpipe and put it into the annealing furnace. The mixture was made with two parts of sand and one of wood ash fused in two successive stages, first a sintering stage followed by a real fusion in a different melting pot. Cullet was often added.
Venice and Altare were the principal European centres of glass production in the 13th century while France and Great Britain became the main centres in the 14th: James I issued an edict in England in 1615 prohibiting the use of wood for glass furnaces; it appears that

to produce one kilogram of glass two and a half tons of wood were required!
Modern bottle production began in Europe during the 18th century, forms and consistency changed, the dark glassed cylindrical bottle was adopted, the common type used today for ordinary drinks (wine, beer and mineral water).
In 1821 Henry Ricketts of Bristol invented a system to produce bottles with a three-part mould and he patented it. This mould created the complete form of the bottle while the mouth was finished in a second phase; this new discovery was a revolution and made mass production possible. The system spread throughout Europe and is still, at least in principle, the same system as is used today.
The industrial revolution of the second half of the 19th century led to the mechanization of bottle production; in 1865 Belgian Ernest Solvay managed to produce sodium bicarbonate on an industrial scale for the manufacture of glass and soap; this caused the price of sodium bicarbonate to drop and made it possible to produce mechanical and optical glass of a decidedly better quality. In 1867 Friedrik Siemens invented the first furnace for the industrial production of bottles: from that date to the early 20th century several different patents were issued for machines for making bottles in France and Germany.
The automatic production of bottles followed the same sequence as manual production by blowing or moulding: the necessary gather is taken onto the blowpipe, the surface is cooled, worked into the appropriate shape, placed in the mould and blown into its final shape.
In mechanical production two moulds are used, one to make a preliminary form and one for the definitive shape: the so-called "pre-form" is produced in a mould with a drop of molten glass in the first phase; the mould is then opened and the glass is re-heated and moves on to the second moulding after which it is annealed.
The process is extremely complex with many steps following each other rapidly: in the Individual Section (IS) version it is possible to produce bottles of different shapes at the same time as each drop of glass in the moulds follows a particular path through the process.
Seeing these machines in operation recalls images of the first industrial plants: a series of contrasting colours and rapidly moving parts against the black background of the machine; we see the flashing of incandescent drops of glass falling into the lined up moulds. At the end of the line we see the black moulds that open up to release the finished bottles, they are no longer incandescent but are rather of an uncertain colour betraying the thermal energy still within, which deters the temptation to touch them, lightly vibrating they move on to the annealing phase.
In this system as a whole, the function of the moulds is important, they must allow the bottle to cool while maintaining good surface quality, without sticking. They must also be made of substances, which are mechanically and chemically resistant while having good thermal conductivity. Cast iron possesses these qualities. Moulds need regular maintenance because of the physical-mechanical stress involved. Perfectly functional moulds are essential for quality products, each mould is specially designed to produce the final product and a bottle factory can have thousands of moulds in its warehouse.

Lenses or the bottoms of bottles?

It seems that a Venetian in the 13th century was responsible for inventing lenses for spectacles. Certainly in earlier centuries various methods were used for magnifying: certain types of glass, mirrors with a particular curvature, or transparent containers filled with liquid, but the idea of using these improvised devices to correct vision was still distant.
The ancient Greeks and Romans used

magnifying systems, but in the medical treatises of the time there are no references to eyesight problems. This was only possible after the discovery of refraction and reflection laws.

The first step to attaining a correcting lens was of course knowledge of magnification: a lens used in contact with an object "corrected" it by magnifying it, while a lens used in contact with an eye corrects the defect of the eye and allows the eye to see the real object. One of the first magnifying systems was perhaps the concave mirror, which enlarged and inverted an object. Magnifying lenses appeared in the 12th century, and spectacles arrived shortly afterwards.

Placing together two magnifying lenses with a hinge at the base of a handle was perhaps what first suggested a physiological affinity with the eye. This gave birth to the prototype for spectacles. In the next few centuries this discovery became widespread in Italy and particularly in Tuscany. At the same time, the development of the spectacle frame began, from the hinge to the bridge frame. In the 18th century, oval lenses appeared and became widespread, and France developed the system for fixing spectacles to the nose, the *pince-nez*. The 18th century also saw the invention of the frame sidepiece that fixed spectacles to the ears (this probably came from Spain).

The spread of glasses to correct vision was greatly increased by the invention of printing machines, which produced books and documents with words written in small characters.

At the close of the 18th century Benjamin Franklin invented the bifocal lens, which enabled people with myopia to read by lowering their gaze and see what was in front of them without needing to change glasses.

In addition to correcting eyesight, lenses are used in the production of scientific instruments to study very distant objects, for example the spyglass and the telescope, and also to study very close and small objects, for example, the microscope. They function by correctly arranging groups of lenses together.

Lens production is problematic because the glass must be completely transparent and without defects. There are two distinct types of glass used in lens production: Crown glass and Flint glass. They differ in terms of chemical composition and density. Up to the 19th century lenses were made from common glass, often from the bottom of bottles; then in France in the first half of the 19th century a method was developed which produced high quality optical glass. Following this, the first company specifically producing lenses was born.

Up to the first half of last century, a discontinuous system was used for lens

Bottles emerging on the conveyer belt

production, which had a success rate of between 20% and 50%. After the first stage of melting and cooling, the product was removed from the crucible in pieces varying from 1 to 10 kilograms; those pieces containing visible defects such as bubbles and batch stone were removed, and the remaining pieces were reheated at dropping temperatures in refractory pans. They were then transferred to analogous metal pans and pressed to mould their shape. After annealing, which eliminated mechanical stress built up in the glass, a further selection process removed more defect pieces. Following this, mechanical abrasion created the desired shape and size; this was carried out manually piece-by-piece, or in a series by fixing the pieces on a block under an abrasion apparatus. The abrasives were used in granulometric sequence, from the largest to the finest grade, which enabled elimination of scratches and surface defects. This was followed by successive washing with water and drying, and finally quality control to identify the presence of any defects and to grade the exact power of the lens with a focometer.

Today, production is continuous and carried out in tank furnaces, which are lined with inert metal (platinum). The process requires very long melting times in order to guarantee optimum homogeneity. Glass cylinders are "cored" from the amalgam, in general by extrusion. Following a long period of cooling they are cut with a diamond saw into smaller rolls called blanks; these are then subjected to abrasion to produce a lens.

Current processes certainly have a greater success rate with respect to the raw material used but very expensive systems and instruments are required so as not to contaminate the glass. And although the process is partly automated, it is still very complex.

Processes and techniques for artistic glass making

The point of departure in examining the techniques used for glass making is beyond doubt the Roman period even though the earliest techniques and their subsequent evolution were located in the eastern part of the Mediterranean where the oldest glass artefacts have been found (about 1500 BC). The composition of the mixture was simpler, less refined because knowledge of the materials was prevalently empirical. The primary components were glass formers and flux, in other words silicates, alkalis and carbonates, and the secondary components, colourants and glass cullet (recycled glass).

These primary elements were obtained from sand or lumps of mineral such as sandstone, quartzite for the silicates; vegetable combustion ash (ferns and beech) or mineral soda for the alkalis; the shells naturally present in the sand provided the calcium necessary to make the glass less soluble in water. The secondary components were various metal oxides added for colour; indeed some oxides, ferric oxide in particular, are already found in the primary materials and give their colour to the glass and this can be changed by addition of other minerals. In fact the colour could also be eliminated thus obtaining transparent glass using the so-called "glass-makers' soap" which consists of antimony salts or manganese dioxide.

As for techniques, the invention of glass blowing (around 1st century BC) clearly divides the production techniques into two categories.

Before glass blowing a casting technique was used: a cavity was created in a container in the form of the object to be modelled.

A method that has been traced back to the Hellenistic period is "modelling in an upturned form." It was used to make hemispheric bowls that were both uniformly coloured or decorated. An upturned hemisphere of mineral substance was positioned between two compact supports of resistant material or two slightly higher stones than the hemispherical form. A quantity of glass was placed in the furnace until the fragments melted into a relatively thick disk. This disk was then cooled until it returned to a solid state. It was then placed on the supports of the device described above and heated again until the central part of the disk began to soften and descend onto the hemispherical form. The supports were then removed and the disk took on the shape of the model. Once cool, it was only necessary to smooth out the inside and edges of the bowl.

To create coloured bowls the initial mass of glass was composed of coloured canes placed side by side on a plate, so that they would melt evenly from the centre out, thus forming a rudimentary disk already when cold. After the first melting of these elements a strip of glass was placed around the disk to complete the rim. The second melting was carried out over the form as described above. The colour scheme of the final result depended on the composition of the initial rods.

Another form (mosaic glass) was obtained using the same technique but using coloured glass roundels taken from canes rather than the canes themselves. The canes were obtained by soldering small different coloured cylinders of glass together to obtain a greater diameter. These were heated, drawn and transformed into thin canes from which the basic roundels for the bowl were cut. In this case too, after the initial melting into a disk, perhaps with the addition of a rim, the disk was melted onto a hemispherical form to produce the final result.

The technique must have been different for the production of ribbed bowls, a bowl where the rim is characterized by ribs which meet at the base; different hypotheses have been advanced on the methods used: lost wax casting, modelling or using a lathe.

The first technique presumably involved a dome-shaped mould of heat-resistant material on which a layer of wax was spread with the ribs moulded in relief, once the wax had been shaped a second layer of clay was set over it leaving only the upper part open. This device was then reheated so that the outer layer of clay hardened and the wax on the contrary melted away through the opening leaving a cavity between the inner and outer layers. Through this same opening the cavity was filled with pieces of glass and was brought to melting point. Once cooled the bowl was extracted by breaking the outer layer and digging out the inner layer.

Modelling involved the principle described above with a disk of glass. The disk was taken when still soft and with a radial ribbed stamp the form of the ribbing was pressed onto the malleable glass. Placing the disk on a domed mould and bringing up the temperature again, a bowl shape was obtained without losing the external ribbed effect.

The third hypothesis involved using a lathe: the base dome-shaped form was placed on the lathe and a disk of glass that was still malleable was placed on top, spinning the lathe the ribbing was made using a suitable instrument. In all three cases particular care would have been given to smoothing the edges.

Glass blowing, which seems to have been discovered in the 1st century BC was a revolution in glass production; indeed it made production faster and led to a more widespread use of glass objects which up to that point had been used only by those who could afford it. Glass containers were preferred not only for their aesthetic qualities but also for their hygienic qualities as containers for liquid foodstuffs (oil, wine, etc.).

The production of particular shaped containers led to the invention of the technique of mould blowing: the container was blown into a mould, extracted and completed with the addition of a rim and if desired a stem and handles. Decoration was executed by engraving, carving, application and surface work using pincers.

Wheel engraving and stipple engraving were the methods used: especially for high relief decorations, notable exam-

ples of which come from the 1st and 3rd century BC, an economy method was used on an exceptionally thick piece of glass with decorative motifs inspired by nature or geometry.
Application consisted in attaching filaments or pieces of glass while hot onto the surface of the object: spiral filaments wound around vases were made already in the 2nd millennium BC; they could also be interlaced or in sinuous curves, while flakes or pieces of glass were lightly soldered onto the hot glass remaining in relief unless they were flattened and fused into coloured blotches. In particular drop-like decoration was made applying pieces of glass before re-melting and blowing, subsequent blowing created elongated drop-like shapes of coloured glass.
Another embellishment obtained by application and subsequent working while hot is *piumatura* (feathering): strips of opaque coloured glass are applied to the surface of the vase and lengthen during rotation and blowing to form spiral-like forms.
A type of decoration common during the 5th century AD was the application of coloured lozenges by pressing: the blown vase, though not yet hot, was rotated over lozenges of coloured glass laid out on a worktop so that they attached to it. These pieces could be geometric or in the shape of animals.
A speedy form of decoration was to draw the glass with a pincers making protuberances, which could be refined later.
We will now examine some examples of techniques employed by Venetian glass masters from the 15th century.
The principal technique used for the production of artistic glass such as glasses, goblets and containers in general was blowing. First the proportions of the object were established in a sketch, a gather of molten glass is taken on the end of the blowpipe and kept in rotation on a metal slab known at the time as "bronzin." This phase is very important as it determines the subsequent compactness and homogeneity necessary to obtain the correct thickness. The glass is then lengthened with a tongs, always kept in rotation on the glassmakers chair, until it is time to begin blowing: this proceeds in alternation with shaping using the necessary instruments for the object desired. In the case of goblets and glasses, tongs and forks are used to finish the glass in the smoothest way possible. Once the "container" has been made the annealing process is begun and the glass master proceeds with the creation of any handles and stems that need to be added. The process is always a matter of working a gather of glass with tongs and pincers shaping it into the desired form. These operations are always carried out next to the furnace so the object can be immediately re-heated, always rotating the blowpipe. Once completed, stems and handles are applied to the body controlling the symmetry and alignment and the entire object undergoes the annealing process.
Two types of glass that were produced in Murano in the 15th century were *cristallo* (crystal) and *lattimo* (opaline).
Crystal is a particularly transparent glass invented by Angelo Barovier. This transparency is obtained by only using the purest material. Glass formers are derived from Ticino quartz river pebbles heat-treated, washed and sifted. The flux (sodium carbonate) consists of soda ash, purified through a lengthy process and crystallized. The glass former was calcined in a furnace and then fused with manganese dioxide. This fusion was repeatedly transferred through water and fused again until it reached the desired level of purity. This type of glass was also made in Great Britain and in Bohemia but with different compositions. Venetian crystal is sodic-calcic, while the English version is made adding about 30% lead oxide to the mixture and the Bohemian has high concentrations of barium oxide and potassium.
Lattimo is an opaque type of glass, it is also known as milk-glass, which was made adding lead, lime or tin lime. To-

day it is made adding calcium fluoride and sodium, which creates the opaque effect because of their separate dispersion phases during the cooling process.
Another opaque type of glass is so-called "chalcedony," it was obtained by melting a mixture of opaque and transparent glass cullet and at successive stages adding silver nitrate, cobalt oxide, potassium bichromate and other salts. Once these additions have been made the glass is brought to working temperature and the resulting product looks very much the stone known as chalcedony used as a precious or semi-precious stone.
Glass blowing technique was varied by using moulds: for example, to obtain a ribbed effect a cap of glass is applied to the base of a piece and the composition is blown into an open ribbed mould.
Mould blowing gives special forms to objects; moulds were made of clay, wood, stone or metal and could be either in one single piece or several pieces depending on the object to be moulded.
In the 15th century it was popular to decorate glass objects with enamel. This enamel was made with powdered coloured glass mixed with pigments, metallic oxides and grease; it was applied to the glass by brush and fired at 800-900°C, this heat sometimes caused unwanted flaws in the decoration. Today the enamel used can be fired at 500°C thus avoiding this problem.
One of the most refined decoration techniques was introduced in the 16th century: filigree.
Filigree is obtained during the normal blowing process with glass containing rods with threads of coloured or opaline glass. The rods are made taking a gather of coloured or opaline glass and forming a cone, which is then dipped into a melting pot of transparent glass, and again forming a cone. With the help of another glass master the cone is then drawn out in opposite directions to form a long cane with coloured glass inside transparent glass.
Once cooled the glass is cut into suitably long canes and placed on a plate in the desired order, brought to melting temperature: the plate is then taken out of the furnace and a bubble of glass is passed over them so that the canes stick to it. This cylinder is reheated and worked on the bench until it is ready for blowing, after cutting off the necessary amount with a shears.
Variations of filigree include *reticello* (netted filigree) and *retortoli* (twisted filigree).
The first is made using two filigree canes, which are entwined singly, placed on each other and subsequently blown so that the two form a netting effect.
Retortoli is made the same way except that the process begins with canes containing threads that have already been entwined. These canes are made from canes containing opaline or coloured glass: the canes are laid out according to the desired effect on a plate or heat resistant material and heated. A gather of prepared glass is then rolled over these. This composition is worked on the bench and reheated until ready and then dipped into a melting pot of colourless transparent glass encasing the coloured glass within two layers. Re-working this on the bench a cylinder is again formed: the cylinder is then drawn out and twisted at the same time. The rods are then attached to a gather and blown as desired.
Another special effect obtained was so-called *vetro ghiaccio* (ice glass) where the surface seems irregularly cracked though remaining transparent. This effect was obtained immersing the half worked object in cold water and putting it immediately into the furnace again so that the superficial cracks were closed. After the effect had been created the piece could be blown and worked normally.
Typical products of the 17th century were *avventurina* and *vetro girasole* (sunflower) and some decorations taken from ancient Roman tradition.
Avventurina is a transparent glass in which copper crystals are evenly dispersed during cooling. It seems that

this technique was discovered by chance, probably because of an error in preparing the mixture, but it was not easy to optimize the metallic sheen, and thus it acquired the name avventurina from the word *avventura*, that means adventure. It was made by adding copper salts and reducing agents such as iron, silica or carbon and then cooling the entire mass very slowly: when the process was executed well it produced crystals of up to one millimetre in length.
Vetro girasole is an opaque or translucent glass, which is used to make carafes; like all opaque glass it is made by adding substances that separate from the glass during cooling with a different refraction index, it is usually made with lead arsenate. This particular salt gives glass the curious effect of being blue when viewed in reflected light but light brown or pink when seen in transmitted light.
The 18th century was the century of mirrors. In ancient times mirrors were made of polished metal though it would appear that in ancient Egypt there were mirrors of silver plated glass and the Romans had mirrors of glass and tin. Manufacturing mirrors involved firstly the production of the glass plate to support the mirror and then the metal surface. In the 16th century the method used by the Venetians was the cylinder method: a sphere of crystal was elongated by force of gravity from the blowpipe until it took on a cylinder shape with a hemispherical base. The two ends were cut off and the remaining cylinder opened lengthwise to form a sheet of glass. Another method used at the time was the crown method: by the centrifugal force of rapid rotation a sphere of glass was transformed into a disk of considerable diameter. This disk was tempered and then cut into a rectangular shape; passing from disk to rectangle implied considerable waste. Both systems were replaced by the drawing technique at the beginning of the 17th century.
As far as decoration was concerned, the 17th century brought an evolution in engraving techniques with semi-precious stones and new systems were developed for engraving: a copper wheel mounted on a lathe. Wheels with different profiles were used depending on the type of engraving to be carried out and were trailed with a leather tongue which applied abrasive powder mixed with grease onto the wheel.
In the 19th century the Venetians revived the production of *murrine* as imitations of ancient vases: the Venetians produced the originals in the 14th century as an attempt to imitate the murrah vases of the Roman epoch from which the name originates. Work in *murrina* style implies first the production of canes such as those described for filigree: the initial gather of glass, the centre of the cane, is worked into a cylinder shape and then covered with a layer of a different colour and by using a mould is given a star-shaped form. Then successive layers are added shaped as desired so as to achieve a symmetrical form and the whole is coated in a final layer. The resulting cylinder is again worked at the bench until another rod is attached to the free end and two glass masters draw it out into a long cane of limited diameter but with the inside pattern intact. The cane is now cut into roundels of 10 to 20 millimetres in thickness and these are known as *murrine*. These tiny disks are the basic unit of which the final product is composed: selected and polished the *murrine* are placed on a metal plate, the space between the circular pieces is filled in with pieces of glass, it is all put into the furnace and the single elements become fused together. This composition is then taken from the furnace and re-worked to make it compact and to eliminate any gaps. It is then put into a pre-heated frame or form and is again heated. As it heats, the material adapts to the form, for example a bowl or plate and after it has been cooled it is completed by polishing and grinding.
But *murrine* can also be blown: in this

case it is best to start using *murrine* that fit together as close as possible so as to avoid gaps between the single elements, then the chosen pattern is heated until fusion begins. In the meantime a cylinder of blown molten glass is prepared and rolled over the composition of *murrine* so that they adhere to it and sink into its surface. When this cylinder is reheated and blown into the desired shape the *murrine* are transformed dilating and deforming the single elements.

Four typical techniques of the 20th century were: *incalmo*, *vetro primavera*, *vetro pulegoso* and *vetro sommerso*.

The *incalmo* is a technique that allows two different colours of glass to be put together in one single piece: the two elements are worked separately and then united by *incalmo* technique which is to say the two parts are united by welding the two together. It is a very delicate process as the welding should not be visible in the final result, the two parts should be worked in a way that they fit together perfectly. First the two parts are worked singly making sure that the dimensions of the borders are the same: they are then united and heated by flame to initiate the welding process and the rod is detached from one of the pieces. The united piece is then worked on the bench revolving it quickly on a metal plate so that the surface becomes uniform and finally it is blown into its final form.

Vetro primavera and *vetro pulegoso* are two different processes invented respectively by Venetian masters Ercole Barovier and Napoleone Martinuzzi. *Vetro primavera* is made using a technique similar to that used for "ice glass," the surface is translucent and covered in cracks; *vetro pulegoso* is opaque thanks to the very large number of different sized bubbles in the glass. *Vetro pulegoso* is made by adding organic substances such as petroleum, which releases gas while decomposing, during the melting stage.

The *vetro sommerso* technique enables the creation of pieces of incredible thickness, which also convey a sense of depth. An initial gather of glass, is blown into an approximate version of the final work, it is then dipped into a melting pot of transparent glass, extracted and the excess is let drip off. It is then reworked and any necessary applications are added and the entire object may then be coated again and blown. By working on transparency and colour of successive layers an effect of relief and depth is obtained.

Another technique, which involves the interaction of glass with other materials, is the manufacture of glass pearls.

Pearls are made by means of a second fusion of coloured glass fashioned into canes: melted on a flame the glass drips onto a small rod of metal, covered in white powder to facilitate detachment once the process has been completed. They are then worked into the desired form; either spherical or cubic using metal pincers and finally they are decorated. The *perlere*, the women who make the pearls at the glassworks, work at a flame called *lume* which burns against a sheet of refractory material: the metal rod on which the glass is collected is kept in constant rotation between the mouth of the flame and the refractory sheet. Skill and knowledge of the materials involved is required to make even the most ordinary pieces: dexterity enables them to create forms and decorations using finer rods, once they have been softened on the flame they are plied into relief decorations or entwined around a chip of coloured glass and, re-covered with transparent glass, create an impression of material depth; yet again the pearl can be covered with gold leaf and finished with relief decorations. Once they have been detached from the tube, different cooling systems are used according to the type of pearl in question. They can be cooled inside a metal container full of inorganic material, or cooled in sand in which they will cool slowly.

The production of tesserae for mosaics involves three different elements: glass paste, enamel and metal leaf tesserae.

Glass paste tesserae are produced in a

limited number of colours, starting from a glass mix without lead oxide and components which disperse into the mix during the dispersion phase but do not melt in it making the glass opaque and coloured.

Enamels are products of glass mix fusion containing lead oxide and can be made in many different very brilliant colours.

Today enamels and glass paste are still the principal elements used by artists making mosaics.

To blend the right colour for an enamel involves melting an initial mixture of base colour, mixing small quantities of coloured powder into the melting pot with a long metal rod: after a certain amount of working a small quantity is taken from the melting pot and is hand pressed using a metal plate. The result is a disk about a half centimetre thick, which changes colour rapidly within the first minutes of cooling and then stabilizes. It is cooled in water and broken to check colour consistency and is compared with a reference sample to see if more colour needs to be added or if the glass can be poured. Using a type of ladle some molten glass is taken from the melting pot and spread onto a metal sheet with a roller mounted on it. Thanks to the movement of the sheet under the roller the glass becomes a plate and before it solidifies completely it is put into an annealing oven to slowly cool. These plates are then stored or transformed into tesserae: after being sawn into smaller pieces the pieces are further reduced by using a small chisel. The metal leaf tesserae are made using a more complex process as they consist of two glass layers with gold or silver leaf between them. The first usage of this type of tessera dates from the 4th century AD in Spain and Greece.

The thicker glass layer is made using a process similar to that used for the production of enamels and glass pastes starting from a mixture for transparent coloured or colourless glass.

The very thin transparent glass leaf called *cristallina* is obtained by a glassblowing technique called *sbuffi* or puffs. Oblong bubbles of transparent or coloured glass are blown and when broken produce slightly curved fragments: the *cristallina* mentioned above. The gold or silver leaf is, according to the technique used, attached first to one or the other layer of glass, is closed inside the two layers and the resulting composition is placed on a metal plate and put into the furnace until the glass layers soften. When it is extracted it is pressed to better bind the layers together. After heating and annealing the more or less round matrix is about one centimetre thick with the leaf in the centre. It is cut into tesserae by using a grid and a blade first to cut the part without metal leaf which is then simply removed by pressing it with the fingers. The remaining part is the tessera.

The major difficulty is in trying to maintain the right conditions to have a perfect stable union between the layers because the structures and processes involved are not easy to control, for example the chemical characteristics and the thickness of the metal leaf or the chemical and thermal conditions of the furnace.

Glass pearls made in Murano

Problems connected to glass restoration

In the field of the conservation of historic-artistic materials, glass indubitably presents an interesting case. It is clearly a difficult material to wholly preserve because of the variety of components that constitute it and its fragility. The following example illustrates this point. Works in glass from antiquity were "lucky": they remained buried and hence preserved for centuries in anomalous but effective containers such as tombs.

Damage to glass relates not only to its physical shape, but also to the play of translucency and opaqueness. External agents can disturb these important corollary qualities of glass, to the point that the piece, although intact, loses its aesthetic quality.

From this point of view, one of the most aggressive agents is a widespread environmental element: water, in particular in the form of humidity. In fact water, which is even more aggressive when it contains saline compounds and dissolved gasses, can extract part of the essential components from glass, causing opacification and reduction of impact resistance.

Details of the dynamics of this phenomenon of deterioration are complex because of the synergy of each environmental factor and the unique composition of glass. If for example, a new glass piece has contact with atmosphere containing a certain amount of humidity and dissolved gas, and then an antique piece, which has been extracted from a balanced physical-chemical environment where it has lain for centuries, is put into contact with the same environment, the consequences will be very different. Humidity that has contact with surfaces that have become porous due to lack of original compounds tends to fix itself to the structure, modifying its consistency and appearance.

Restoration also involves the difficulty of selecting the right materials to use during the process of repair.

The technical procedures can generally be divided into two precise stages: cleaning and gluing. Cleaning can and generally does relate to all glass objects, given that even glass museum pieces need to be cleaned if only from dust

Tesserae for mosaics

that can cause grime and opacity. This activity, which may seem banal, is not to be taken lightly, especially with regards to choosing a methodology and proceeding according to the state of repair of the original material. The most widely used material is of course water, but as we have seen, water must be used prudently and accurately, taking into account the level of the water's purity, in particular with regard to the presence of dissolved salts that can later generate surface deposits. Other fluids can be used for cleaning, above all in those cases where there are deposits of fatty substances. In this case, surface-active agents and organic solvents can be added to the water. The latter are much more suitable but often more toxic to the restorer.

In relation to glass cleaning, the so called dry cleaning methods, that is, those using special tools for removing surface dirt, are generally avoided. These can cause the dirt to scratch the surface, and also abrasion that can later cause further conservation problems.

In recent times attempts have been made to apply laser techniques, which have been successfully used to clean marble work and in some cases glass, but there are considerable limitations relating to using it on large-scale works. Firstly, this technology expends a great

deal of energy and secondly, there are problems in terms of removing "only" the dirt and not the glass particles. Glass which is particularly sensitive risks being weakened further, or can even shatter during this treatment. In addition, the technique is more suitable to cleaning small objects that can be easily handled, rather than large objects such as stained-glass windows.
If future developments in laser technology produce laser instruments which are more flexible, easier to handle and above all with better energy flow control, then this technology will be of enormous benefit in this field, as it will eliminate the necessity of applying chemical products.
In the same way that cleaning presents delicate problems that are often solved only with a measure of good sense, the same can be said for the process of gluing together fragments of a broken glass object. To be precise, the difficulties do not relate to the action of gluing but to the interaction of glue with the glass surface and, eventually, the way in which the two different components age. In fact, a gluing operation may seem successful on completion, but after a few years the seam could appear in the structure's membrane when the aging glue begins to change colour. It is easy to imagine how this can be a serious problem when valuable objects are displayed in museum cases. As such, it is possible that a new gluing operation may be required after some time, and the old glue removed. In these cases it is necessary to remove the old glue as soon as possible from the object so that the fragments do not incur further damage.
Today the resins on the market that give the best performers in terms of reversibility are the epoxy resins. These resins tend to turn yellow over time depending on the conditions to which the object is exposed, and the repair seam is left visible. However, they are easily removed by heating the object from room temperature to 180°C in a very gradual way in order to avoid thermal shock. In addition, their visibility depends on the type of glass; they cannot be seen on transparent glass but on red and blue glass.
The possibility of using silicon resins, used for some time now in building, has recently been proposed. However, experiments on samples have not yet been undertaken.
A further characteristic of glue is its fragility, in the sense that the seam of the repair must be able to bear the energy of a potential impact in order to safeguard the glued fragments from further breakage.
With regards to the restoration of stained-glass windows, the problems differ in that the single elements to be cleaned and glued are later rejoined to the leads and form part of a complex architectural composition. The process involves eliminating the leading, cleaning the pieces and reconstructing the cracked pieces using glue.

Modern alchemy: from waste to product

In the Middle Ages, alchemists spent their whole lives searching for a process that would transform base metals into gold, linking this transformation to their own spiritual rebirth. As confirmation of the fact that "a leopard cannot change its spots," modern chemists have not lost this odd penchant for trying to transform matter, even though they practise their activity for clearly less spiritual reasons. In the same way, many exponents of this group, in varying fields of activity, have committed themselves to searching for processes and techniques that transform waste into useful products that would otherwise have required pure raw materials to produce.
Today waste management is one of the most patent environmental problems of urban areas. The solution to curbing this problem is acting on several fronts at the same time:
- making products that, from their production to their use and disposal, have a limited quantity of non-reusable residues and reducing their specific harmfulness;

- favouring waste product differentiation as much as possible;
- identifying waste treatment technology that makes use of the residues of materials as much as possible.

This process is fraught with political, economic and also social difficulties. The uncontrolled disposal of waste in general, but above all of dangerous waste, causes incalculable economic harm to the health of a population and the integrity of a country's resources.

Incineration is a means of waste disposal that enables recycling of thermal energy, which if properly converted can be transformed into electrical energy. This process results in a considerable reduction in the volume of waste: nonetheless a part of the slag which results from this process is composed of very porous carbonaceous material that chemically fixes heavy metals and organic micro-pollutants and is thus generally classified as dangerous waste.

In particular, elements such as lead, chromium, cadmium, nickel, and arsenic, etc., present in industrial waste in different chemical forms, even though in small concentrations, cause substantial pollution if dispersed in the environment. When such elements are used in glass (as a glass former, flux or stabilizer) after a process of waste fusion, the risk of interaction between them and the environment is almost entirely erased. For the same reason, the vitrification process completely destroys the fibrous coating of asbestos minerals that is the main cause of toxicity, while the characteristic elements of these minerals are used to construct the new amorphous structure of vitreous material. For many years, the process used initially had the exclusive aim of fixing the harmful compounds in the vitreous structure in a stable way, in order to destroy the dangerous effects of waste by making them inert. The product resulting from this treatment nonetheless remained a waste.

The revolutionary idea is that of balancing the various waste, consisting of different kind of ashes, in a properly experimented blend that when used in the vitrification process produces an inert material that can be used for the production of marketable products. The following products could result from this process:
- short reinforcing fibre suitable for thermal and acoustic insulation and long fibre that can be utilised as reinforcing framework for cement, plastic and rubber;
- foamed glass that can be used as a base for catalysers, thermal insulators and ion exchanger supports;
- crystallized glass-ceramics obtained in various physical forms, that can be sintered to obtain cladding with high chemical and mechanical benefits.

The process in its entirety involves identifying waste components through chemical analysis, defining the composition of the mixture to be vitrified by establishing the optimal proportion for each type of waste, correcting the mixture with appropriate additives if necessary, fusion and production of the material in the predetermined form. The material obtained from this process, which is checked for chemical stability, has had positive results following the method indicated in the regulations.

Glass channels for transmitting signals: optic fibres

The use of optic fibres for transmission began around 1970 in the course of military research by the USA and the USSR.

For the fibre system to be competitive against the traditional copper system, it was necessary to find a way of reducing the optical attenuation of glass fibre, which was very high in the early stages, reaching thousands of decibels per kilometre. It was necessary to reduce attenuation to 20 dB/km, therefore less than what was possible at the time. Progress in production techniques reduced attenuation to 0.19 dB/km, almost equal to the innate limits deriving from the physical properties of the materials used. The technology enabling this rapid development was based on the process of CVD (chemical vapour deposition). An optic fibre is like a thin thread of glass, but in reality it is a composite system: a concentric sheathing or shell, the cladding, surrounds a cylindrical nucleus, the core or optic nucleus. The core consists of transparent material having visible or near infrared refractive index; the cladding has a refractive index less than that of the core. The difference between the refractive index of the materials that make up the core and cladding is one of the critical parameters of optic fibre mechanics: because of this convenient difference, the electromagnetic signal entering the core in a certain direction continues to be reflected inside it, without any dispersion, exiting at the opposite end. The creation of optimal refraction indexes is obtained by adding small quantities of appropriate rare elements called doping agents to the optical nucleus composition.

There are two types of optic fibres, multimodal and monomodal, which differ in relation to the size of the nucleus and the difference between the refraction index: the first have a diameter of circa 0.050 mm and allow the contemporaneous transmission of electromagnetic signals with different trajectories, the second have a smaller diameter of 0.008 mm, and allow the propagation of only one ray.

The process of optic fibre production can be divided essentially into two fundamental phases: production of preform or preform fibres, and the application of covering.

The term "preform" means a processed intermediate product that has all the requisites for the fibre: a nucleus (*core*) having a high refraction index surrounded by sheathing (*cladding*) having a reduced refraction index: the refraction index profile of the nucleus and the sheathing, like the ratio between their diameters, remains the same in the transformation from preform to fibre. The only difference between preform and fibre relates to size.

The silica used for optic fibres in telecommunications is generally produced synthetically via processes that guarantee a high level of purity in the final product.

The transmission of signals with optic fibre systems offers the following advantages: very high data transmission speeds, low sensitivity to interference, low attenuation (it is therefore possible to cover distances up to 200 km without the need for amplifiers), reduced cost of materials, and safety in relation to extraction or loss of data.

The introduction of these products in recent decades has revolutionized the telecommunications industry: indeed, with respect to transmission technology involving copper cables or through the air, optic fibre systems enable a very high transmission power at low cost. Optic fibre technology has paved the way for highly innovative services. Experimentation in the application phase is leading to the design and development of optic fibres that are conceived and optimized for a specific use.

Glass biocompatibility

The use of non-biological materials to replace bones was known in the pre-Christian era: at that time pure metals, copper or metallic alloys and bronze were generally used to attach fractured bone parts. The success of such repairs was undermined by the immediate rejection of the foreign part and, in cases where this did not occur, by the possibility of a slow, but not less dangerous, poisoning from the dissolution of the metal in the body.

Nonetheless, up to the 19th century, bronze and copper continued to be used almost exclusively for external prosthesis. In 1880, ivory fastened with cement and rosin was used for an internal prosthesis. In 1902 the precious metal gold was used to create a capsule placed between two joints. In fact gold was found to be particularly suitable because of its inert qualities.

Not very much later, around 1920, the first attempts were made to use glass to create joint capsules, but with little success due to the fragility of the material. At the same time experiments were being undertaken into the possibility of spraying melted glass on metal supports. Limited technology and materials that did not work at melting temperatures restricted these attempts. Up to the middle of last century there were no significant innovations in the field; prostheses used were in metal and had to be periodically replaced due to corrosion appearing along the metal contact points of the joints. To remedy this problem attempts were made to use plastic materials with acrylic (1948), thus Teflon (1961) and finally polyethylene (1970, though the first attempt to use it was in 1950). In experiments on laboratory animals, polyethylene was found to have alarming carcinogenetic properties and so its use was abandoned.

In the early 1970s a number of researchers directed their attention to metal oxides, aluminium oxide, zirconium oxide and calcium aluminate. The first positive results were achieved with sintered alumina and from 1973 the Italian Nicolini began to experiment using glass-ceramic, which was found to be superior to other materials being used.

Biomedical ceramic materials are classified according to their potential biological compatibility as bioinert or bioactive, in relation to their capacity to activate chemical-biological alterations in contact with the body. Aluminium oxide has good bioinert properties, that is, it does not cause transformations in the biological material, and this makes it suitable for replacing hard tissue. It is fragile though and so can be used to replace small bones that are not carrying a heavy weight. Bioceramics and bioglass, on the other hand, are bioactive materials, that is, they trigger transformation reactions when in contact with biological tissue.

The interaction between an organism and foreign substances triggers a series of reactions in which the biological molecules attempt to neutralize the presence of foreign compounds. The sum of these reactions involves a series of consecutive changes that develop towards a point of equilibrium that depends on the result in each stage. In this sense the human is like any other part of the natural system: he or she develops via successive changes and adjustments until the optimal conditions for operating in the surrounding environment are reached; in these conditions he/she is willing to absorb and neutralize the consequences of events that are unexpected and foreign to the overall equilibrium, provided they are limited in terms of size and duration. The more these events are disruptive to the system, the more the system's reaction will be destabilizing and thus harmful to it overall.

Glass collecting centre

Hydroxyapatite and bioglass, though in a different way, put in contact with the body stimulated a positive response from the organism.

Hydroxyapatite, a calcium hydroxide phosphate, is formed by wet treatment of the calcium phosphate at 900°C. This material has chemical-physical components that are similar to those in bones and so it is very biocompatible: the bone recognizes this material as similar to its own and creates a stable new equilibrium. In other words, the insertion of hydroxyapatite in the bone

causes local changes of limited intensity that are neutralized in a relatively short time.
The working principle of bioactive glass is different, in that the components of the material gradually change in contact with newly formed bone tissue. There are two types of bioactive glass: bioglass and ceramic bioglass. The various types of bioglass in turn can be distinguished by porosity: porous bioglass should, as a rule, be able to guarantee greater penetration of the biological transformation reactions in the biological-bioglass tissue interface. The mechanics of its production is based on systems able to create the most uniform and mechanically resistant porous structure; the size and distribution of pores appear to be critical factors ensuring rapid transformation of the interface surface.
In relation to the composition of the mixture and fusion techniques, bioglass is similar to common glass. A mixture of very pure oxides, silica, sodium oxide, calcium oxide and phosphorus pentoxide, are heated to a very high temperature (1300°C-1600°C) forming a uniform batch. The bond of glass and bone tissue appears to be the result of a reaction between the glass and blood plasma, in which, following the migration of phosphorus, calcium and silica, a specific phase is formed at the interface that is very ionium (OH) rich.
This is the ideal matrix for the development of calcium phosphate. As this substance is one of the components of bone tissue, it is recognized by the system of cells that has the role of reconstructing tissue, and is thus assimilated through the formation of chemical bonds; in this way, no clearly separating surface can be found between the bone tissue and glass material, only a continuously evolving tissue system.
There is thus a difference in principle between the choice of using a prosthesis covered in hydroxyapatite and a titanium prosthesis covered in bioglass: hydroxyapatite is an inorganic synthesis material that is recognized by the organism and "accepted," while bioglass when in contact with the tissue gradually disappears as it is biodegradable and has a very fine physical form, ensuring high surface contact, and is replaced by newly formed bone tissue in direct contact with titanium. The transformation takes about six months and the analytical test of this development is obtained by observing the reduction of silica throughout the period, which after a period of six months from the implant can hardly be detected.

(The paragraph about restoration was written in collaboration with Lorenzo Appolonia and Laura Morandotti)

Fiberglass produced from incinerated waste

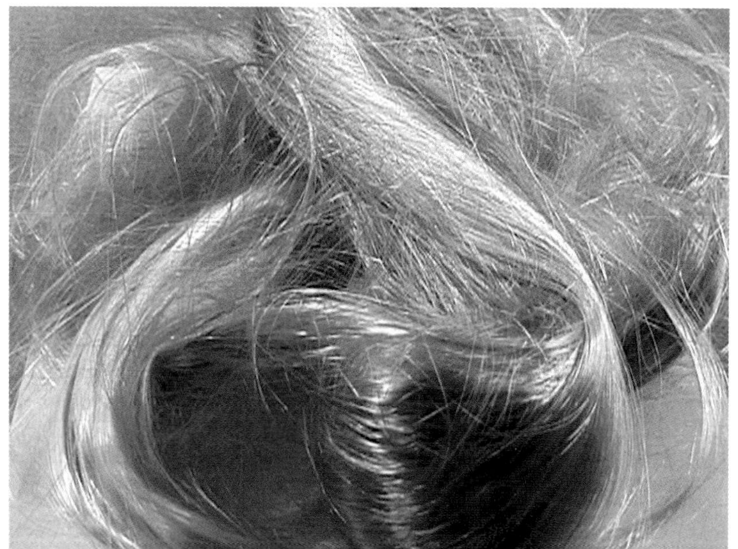

Annexes

Artists, Designers and Glass Masters - Biographies

Edited by Antonella Crippa and Silvana Gubetta

Alvar Aalto (1898-1976)
Alvar Aalto was one of the most important architects and designers of the 20th century. He was born in 1898 in Kuortane (Finland), and graduated from the University of Technology, Helsinki in 1921. He opened his studio in 1923 and in 1924 he married Aino Marsio who was his principal collaborator both in furniture design in Artek and in architecture, up to 1949 the year she died. From the 1920s he produced a series of noteworthy projects in both public and private sectors; apart from the aesthetic quality these projects were characterized by greater attention given to the social and cultural aspects of the intended users. Works by Alvar Aalto have been defined as being "inside and outside of time" and also rational-functional yet poetic. He was at the avant-garde of Rationalism, overcoming the geometric lines of the early Rationalist movement and he led the way for Scandinavian architecture and design. Each architectural project by Alvar Aalto was completed with the design and production of furniture, illumination and glass conceived as mobile components of the buildings for which they were designed. Though these objects are but a fragment of the architect's vision they possess a life of their own.

Arman (1928)
Arman (Armand Fernadez) was born in Nice (France) in 1928. Along with Yves Klein, Spoerri and Tinguely, he was co-founder of Nouveau Réalisme that formed around Pierre Restany. Arman expanded the idea of collecting objects and including them in art works, following the ideas of Duchamp. In 1959 he began creating canvasses with marks of objects in ink, in 1960 he created the *Poubelles*, *Colères* and *Accumulations*, complex structures formed by accumulations of similar-type objects (guns, pistols, nails, light bulbs, paint tubes), sometimes immersed in transparent containers (of Plexiglas or glass), the whole thickened with brushstrokes of colour and glue. Decorated with the Légion d'honneur in 1987 and a traveller and collector of African art, Arman has had numerous exhibitions, including a first retrospective at the Stedelijk Museum in Amsterdam (1964) and participation in the French pavilion at the 1964 Venice Biennale. A catalogue of his works was published in 1991. He lives and works in New York and Vence (France).

Emmanuel Babled (1967)
Emmanuel Babled was born in 1967 in Ambilly (France). He studied at the European Institute of Design in Milan and initially collaborated with the Galerie Ives Gastou in Paris. He set up his studio in Milan and from here he designs projects for companies like Wedgwood, Rosenthal and Venini. He created his first works in glass for Venini in 1992. He has had his collections manufactured in several furnaces in Murano and also works in other sectors of furniture and art works. Both his glass works and works in other materials have a very personal touch making use of curved lines and chromatic contrasts. His work therefore seems to flow along one single line.

**Philip Baldwin (1947)
and Monica Guggisberg (1955)**
Philip Baldwin was born in New York in 1947; he took a Bachelor of Art degree at the American University, Washington DC. Monica Guggisberg was born in Bern (Switzerland) in 1955. From 1974 to 1977 she followed a course in lamp technique in Zofingen (Switzerland). In 1978 she opened her own studio in Bern. Guggisberg and Baldwin met at Orrefors Glaskolan, Orrefors (Sweden), where they were studying thanks to scholarships in 1979-80. From 1979 to 1981 they were assistants to glass artists Wilke Adolfsson and Ann Wolff, in Transjö (Sweden). In 1982 they opened their own studio in Nonfoux in Switzerland, initially devoting themselves to the production of works in small series that they designed and produced personally, these works had a Nordic character, with essential forms and brilliant colours. From 1986 they began to produce unique once-off pieces, blown sometimes in two layers and sand blasted. Between 1993 and 1994 they worked with glass master Lino Tagliapietra in their studio in Nonfoux creating vases using *incalmo* and filigree techniques while remaining faithful to their essential geometric forms. Since 1994 they have created almost exclusively once-off pieces of exceptionally high quality where Scandinavian essentiality is animated by chromatic effects and vivid engravings, which are the result of a very personal reading of engraving history influenced by Carlo Scarpa. Since 1985 they have frequently collaborated with Rosenthal, Steuben, Hergiswil Glas and Venini in refined designs. In 2001 they moved their studio to Paris.

Guido Balsamo Stella (1882-1941)
Guido Balsamo Stella was born in Turin (Italy) in 1882 and died in 1941. Graduating from the city's academy, he tried his hand at Symbolist painting and showed his works at Brera in 1902 and at the Venice Biennale in 1907. He then devoted himself chiefly to graphic art, participating in numerous national and international exhibitions and establishing a reputation as a refined author of bookplates. In 1908 he married the Swedish painter Anna Akerdhal and during his frequent stays in her homeland got to know Edward Hald and Simon Gate. In 1922 he opened a workshop at Colle Val d'Elsa producing artistic glassware, engraved by the Bohemian master Franz Pelzel. These works were exhibited at the Triennali in Monza from 1923 onward and at the International Exhibition of Decorative Arts held in Paris in 1925, where he represented Italian glass alongside the works of Venini. In 1925 Balsamo Stella and Pelzel moved to Venice, where they opened a workshop on Giudecca. In 1927 they joined the SALIR glassworks on Murano, where Balsamo Stella became artistic director and Franz Pelzel head engraver. They created refined blown glass engraved with both classical themes and more up-to-date ones. For the Biennale and Triennale of 1930 Balsamo Stella designed splendid engraved glassware, animals and vases that were blown at the SAIAR Ferro Toso glassworks. After that year he only collaborated with SALIR on an occasional basis. He was also very active as a teacher: from 1924 to 1927 he directed the Istituto di Arti Applicate at Ortisei, from 1927 to 1929 the Scuola Industriale Pietro Selvatico in Padua, from 1930 to 1937 the Istituto Superiore delle Arti Decorative in Monza and, finally, the Istituto Statale d'Arte in Venice.

Alfredo Barbini (1912)
Alfredo Barbini was born in Murano (Italy) in 1912 into a family of glass masters dating back to the 17th century. He studied design for glass masters at the Abate Zanetti school of Murano and worked form his early years in the Murano furnaces. From 1925 to 1929 he worked at SAIAR Ferro Toso, where he became a master at the age of seventeen. From 1929 to 1932 he was a master at the Vetreria Fianchetti and the Vetreria San Marco in Milan. From 1932 to 1936 he worked for Zecchin-Martinuzzi and began to collaborate with Napoleone Martinuzzi, an experience Barbini considers to be fundamental to his artistic training, especially as a sculptor. In 1936 he also undertook a short collaboration with Seguso Vetri d'Arte where he worked with the designer Flavio Poli and in '37 he was the first master at VAMSA, specialized in the *morbido sommerso* manner with a particularly precious "smokey" effect. In the post-war years he became a partner in the Vetreria Vistosi, therefore underwent a period of study and research into glass experimentation under Martinuzzi thanks to a grant from the USA. From 1947 to 1950 he was a partner, artistic director and first glass master at Gino Cenedese & Co.: at the 1948 Biennale he exhibited works in "corroded glass" such as *Torso* and *Collasso* which were imbued in carnality and emotional tension. He opened his own glass factory, Alfredo Barbini, in 1950 and continues to this day to create countless abstract and figurative masterpieces also using other techniques such as blown glass and *murrina*. He exhibits in international galleries and museums. Now, in his 90s, he continues to be creative and works daily with his own hands.

Ercole Barovier (1889-1974)
Ercole Barovier was born in Murano (Italy) into a family with a long tradition of glass making; he began to work in the family business in 1919 when it took on the name Vetreria Artistica Barovier. In the mid 1920s he became artistic director of the company and co-manager with his brother Nicolò in 1926. When in 1932 he became the sole manager he formed a partnership with Decio and Artemio Toso which was called Ferro Toso Barovier, and later Barovier & Toso. He remained artistic manager until 1972. Among his outstanding works in Art Deco style are the large *murrine* (1924-25), glass-blown animals (1928-1930) and the *Primavera* pieces (1929-1930); his 20th-century style works include crystals and glass with "colorazione a caldo senza fusione" (coloured hot without fusion). From after the war until his last works of 1972 he designed "primitive" glass pieces coloured without fusion and polychromatic pieces in tesserae and *murrine*.

Gianfranco Baruchello (1927)
Gianfranco Baruchello was born in Livorno (Italy) in 1927. The year 1959 marked the beginning of his experiments on a series of works using found objects. In 1962 he began painting large canvasses: white surfaces grooved with a few marks and lines traced with dabs of colour. At this time he also began creating his first Plexiglas works, consisting of layers of transparent material over cardboard or metal remnants. He also began working as a film director. In the early 1970s he started experimenting with the electronic image and the concept of loss of quality (the use of a photocopy and a photocopy of a photocopy). Baruchello has used many materials, including aluminium, steel, glass and plastic. He has participated in numerous solo and group shows, including exhibitions at the Casa del Mantegna in Mantua (1982), the *Tour Fromage* in Aosta (1992) and at the Museo Laboratorio of La Sapienza University in Rome (1997). He took part in the Venice Biennale in 1976, 1984, 1988, 1990 and 1993. He was invited to take part in the sixth edition of *Documenta* (Kassel, 1977). He lives in Rome and Paris.

Mario Bellini (1936)
Mario Bellini was born in 1936 in Milan (Italy) where he graduated in architecture from the Polytechnic in 1959 and in 1963 he opened his studio in the same city. From 1986 to 1991 he was editor of *Domus* magazine. He specialized in the "product and furniture design" sector, a sector in which, from the second half of the 1960s, he has become one of the most important exponents of Milanese design. He has worked for Olivetti, B&B, Brionvega, Rosenthal and Vitra and thanks to these companies he has been awarded seven Compassi D'Oro. Since the end of the 1980s he has also worked as an architect both in Italy and abroad representing a midway point between Rationalism and Post-modern trends. He has held teaching posts at the Istituto Superiore del Disegno Industriale in Venice, at the Hochschule für Angewandte Kunst in Vienna, and at the Domus Accademy in Milan. Some of his furniture and illumination projects have become reference models in the design world and are still produced today.

Carlo Benvenuto (1966)
Carlo Benvenuto was born in Stresa (Italy) in 1966. He belongs to the latest generation of Italian artists. He works with photography, painting and installation. His experiments centre on the home and its contents, which are his favoured themes. His works have a subtle surreal quality: a cup is perfectly balanced on the edge of a table, a glass is turned over with water in it, a table rests on flimsy Bic caps. He uses glass intermittently: in his last solo show (Galleria Mazzoli, Modena) he created small transparent glasses engraved with self-portraits. He participated in the first Biennale in Valencia in Spain, in *Il dono* and *De Gustibus* exhibitions at the Palazzo delle Papesse in Siena and in the Contemporary Art Triennial in New Delhi, in addition to exhibiting in many Italian and overseas galleries. He lives and works in Milan.

Maurizio Bertinetti (1955)
Maurizio Bertinetti was born in Turin (Italy) in 1955. Growing up in those years, he was attracted to the poetics of Pascali, Boetti and Mondino, preferring an "ironic conceptualism" to the Arte Povera option. Defined as an art terrorist and saboteur, he is one of a number of Italian artists whose work addresses the inherent problems in the art system and its market. The most recent and outstanding of his many solo shows in Italy were at the Galleria d'Arte Moderna - Villa Serena in Bologna (2000), at the Galleria Carbone (2001) and at the Centro Lingotto in Turin (2001). He lives and works at Palazzo Galimberti in Verrua Savoia (Turin).

Joseph Beuys (1921-1986)
Joseph Beuys was born in Krefeld (Germany) in 1921 and died in 1986. After the war, where he saw direct action as a Luftwaffe pilot, Beuys attended the Academy in Düsseldorf. In the 1960s, Bueys was attracted to Nam June Paik and the Fluxus group, whose public concerts and events blurred the distinction between literature, music, visual art, performance and life experience. He was one of the major figures of Conceptual art and was also a reference point for his activism: he always believed that artistic practice was, or should be, revolutionary in itself, and that every individual, whatever his or her experience, had a duty to be a part of this. He made large installations alongside small objects created in the most varied materials. He was one of the first artists to create multiple works. Beuys represented Germany at the Venice Biennale in 1976 and 1980. A large retrospective of the artist's work was held at the Guggenheim Museum in New York in 1979. During the inauguration of *Documenta* in 1982, Beuys planted the first of 7,000 oak trees and repeated this in many cities for many years, with clear ecological concerns. Harald Szeeman dedicated a small retrospective to him at the 2001 Venice Biennale. Between 2001 and May 2002 the Beuysian year was celebrated (marking eighty years since the artist's birth) with exhibitions and publications, including those of MART, Palazzo delle Albere in Trento.

Fulvio Bianconi (1915-1996)
Fulvio Bianconi was born in Padua (Italy) in 1915 and died in 1996. He attended the Istituto d'Arte and the Accademia di Belle Arti in Venice. While still very young he started to decorate glassware with enamel for Salviati under the guidance of Michele Pinto, as well as to work as a caricaturist. At the age of twenty he experimented with the art of window-dressing in Milan and designed perfume bottles for G.V.M., Visconti di Modrone. In 1935 he started to work for the Mondadori and Rizzoli publishing houses as an illustrator, a profession that he never abandoned. From 1947 onward he collaborated with Venini, creating some of the most interesting collections of the 20th century for the Murano glassworks: stylized figurines and polychrome vases. He collaborated with Venini again in 1967 and in 1989. In the 1950s he worked with Cenedese, in 1958 with the Galleria Danese in Milan, on glassware made at the Vetreria IVR Mazzega, and in 1963 with the Vetreria Vistosi. In the 1960s he collaborated with other glassworks for short periods, including Galliano Ferro. In 1991-92 he designed for the Vetreria de Majo. In his collections of glassware he always expressed the sense of humour that characterized his graphic work, but tempered by an extraordinary refinement, so that even his glass figurines never strayed into the realm of kitsch. In his blown glass he demonstrated a capacity of invention unrestricted by conventions and always backed up by an exceptional sense of colour.

Corrado Bonomi (1956)
Corrado Bonomi was born in Novara (Italy) in 1956. Like a good toy-maker, he constructs a universe of perfectly working toys in which robots, toy soldiers, model aeroplanes and remote-control cars are an independent microcosm created with all kinds of materials, including glass. The logic of this game is put forward as an alternative to the logic of reality. This conceptual path has as its aim the analysis of language: Bonomi respects the signifier but acts on the meaning, creating a surprising visual short circuit and constantly ridiculing the integrity and the supposed exactness of the art world. He has exhibited in numerous galleries in Italy and overseas, at the Museo d'Arte Su Logu S'Iscultura at Tortolì (Nuoro, Sardinia) in 1999 and at the Centro d'Arte Contemporanea of Bellinzona in 2001. He lives and works in Novara.

Louise Bourgeois (1911)
Louise Bourgeois was born in France in 1911. After studying in Paris, she moved to New York in 1938. At first she dedicated herself to painting and then mainly to sculpture. For a time she worked side by side with the Surrealists, though she avoided becoming a part of that or any other group. She has often highlighted how her art is born of lived emotion and experience rather than a specific artistic and cultural environment. Her drawings, sculptures, paintings and graphic art works are obsessively autobiographical and filled with memories of her infancy; they relentlessly show the isolation of women and the pain of existence. She has used many different materials in her installations, preferring marble, bronze, fabric and sometimes, though rarely, glass. Her many solo and group shows include an invitation to participate in *Magiciens de la Terre* at the Centre Georges Pompidou in Paris in 1986, the ninth edition of *Documenta* (Kassel) and at the Venice Biennale in 1991 (United States pavilion) and 1999. She lives and works in New York.

Philippe-Joseph Brocard (1831-1896)
An artist, craftsman and restorer, Philippe-Joseph Brocard ran the most important factory of enameled glassware in Paris from the 1860s onward. His early art glass was in the style of the Syrian glassware of the 13th and 14th centuries, such as the mosque lamps that he collected, inspired by Islamic, Indian and Renaissance models. He spent many years studying these objects and perfecting the technique of enameling. He obtained his first success at the International Exhibition held in Paris in 1867. While in his early works the entire surface was covered with Persian arabesques and other decorations of Islamic origin, he later simplified his style and adopted a more realistic representation of the plant world. Around 1880 he started to collaborate with his son Emile, in the firm Brocard et Fils. After Philippe-Joseph's death the glassworks continued to operate until around 1900, under the name Veuve Brocard et Emile Brocard.

Lucio Bubacco (1957)
Lucio Bubacco was born in Murano (Italy) in 1957 and in 1962 he started his apprenticeship as a self-taught lamp glass maker. He studied drawing and painting privately from 1980 to 1982 with the Venetian painter Alessandro Rossi. He quickly developed an extraordinary ability in the modelling of nudes in glass in dimensions that were unusual for the techniques used; he has no rivals in Italy and very few throughout the world in modelling the human figure using lamp technique. Parallel to this he has developed his own very personal style: Baroque and flamboyant, provocative and at the same time ironic. He enjoys experimentation and combining lamp technique with other glass making techniques such as blowing and casting. He has often lectured abroad especially in America, Australia and Japan and has exhibited in galleries and museums the world over.

Michele Burato (1957)
Michele Burato was born in Venice (Italy) in 1957 and

from 1980 to 1995 dealt in antique glass. In 1990 he began to experiment in the manufacture of *murrine* by melting glass rods and glass tesserae. He debuted with an exhibition at the Galleria Junck in 1998. Today he is considered one of the most interesting contemporary glass artists and some of his works are to be seen at the Corning Museum of Glass and Murano Museo Vetrario.

Erwin Walter Burger (1909)
Erwin Walter Burger was born in Geislingen (Germany) in 1909. He received his early training in engraving on glass from Jakob Wiedermann at the Würtenbergische Metallwarenfabrik (1923-27). He worked first as an engraver at Neustadt an der Waldnaab in Bavaria (1927-28), and then as a glasscutter with the firm Franz Wittwerk K.G. at Altheide-Bad near Breslau. After winning the competition staged by the Eugenio Binchi company of Milan for the creation of a service of cut crystal for the Italian royal family, he moved to Italy (1928). In 1930 he worked briefly with Cappellini & C. of Murano and Carlo Vezzosi's Vedar in Milan. From 1931 to 1945 he was head cutter and engraver at the firm Luigi Fontana & C. and produced pieces designed by Pietro Chiesa and Giò Ponti for the section of art objects, La Fontana Art, and carved large blocks of crystal for Giacomo Manzù. In 1945 he set up his own company, Erwin Walter Burger Cristalli d'Arte, as well as a school with five apprentices. From 1957 onward he collaborated with his son Willi. He ceased his teaching activity in 1960. After his retirement the workshop was run by his son Willi until 1982. However, he continued to execute very important commissions, although only sporadically. Burger's sculptural ability was such that he did not get lost in detail but achieved a formal synthesis in which the treatment of the surface, sometimes polished and sometimes left rough, was fundamental. The unfinished form was a recurrent characteristic of his sculptural works.

Maurizio Camerani (1951)
Maurizio Camerani was born in Ferrara (Italy) in 1951. His background was initially in sculpture, but in the 1980s he dedicated himself to video installation, creating videos with a strong narrative structure. In the last ten years his work has led him to produce sculptures with photovoltaic panels. His video sculptures, within the sphere of Conceptual art, play on the primordial spatial relationship between what is broadcast from the monitor and what exists in external space and between the title and the represented object. Camerani has participated in numerous international festivals including the Locarno festival, where in 1991 he received the Grand Prix de la Ville. Among his solo shows in Italian galleries and group shows to which he has been invited, mention must be made of *Arte elettronica. Metamorfosi e metafore* at the Palazzo dei Diamanti in Ferrara in 2001.

Chen Zhen (1955-2000)
Chen Zhen was born in 1955 in Shanghai (China) and died in Paris in 2000. After attending the School of Fine Arts in Shanghai, he studied at the Shanghai Drama Institute. He moved to Paris in 1986 to attend courses at the Ecole Nationale Supérieure des Beaux-Arts and Institut des Hautes Etudes en Arts Plastiques. His works are mainly large and complex installations that address the barriers between East and West, between traditional culture and contemporary culture, and between communist and capitalist politics in Asia. To create his complex structures, Chen Zhen utilized all types of materials without having any preferences. Throughout the 1990s, Chen Zhen exhibited his work in Asia, Africa, Europe and North America. He was invited to show at the first Biennale in Shanghai (1996), at the Biennale of Contemporary Art in Lyon (1997), at the second Biennale in Johannesburg (1997), and at the Venice Biennale in 1993 and 1999. He had many solo shows, including one at the National Maritime Museum in Stockholm, at the Art Museum in Tel Aviv in 1998 and at the ADDC-Espace Culturel François Mitterrand in Périgueux in 1999.

Dale Chihuly (1941)
Dale Chihuly was born in Tacoma (Washington, USA), in 1941; he graduated from the renowned Rhode Island School of Design, and subsequently studied at the University of Wisconsin under Harvey Littleton, a pioneer of American glass, and at the University of Washington. In 1968 he began a long period of working experience at the Venini glassworks Murano thanks to a Fulbright scholarship. In 1969 he began an important programme on glass at the Rhode Island School of Design and in 1971 he founded the Pilchuck Glass School in Seattle, joining the American Studio Glass Movement, which saw glass as a suitable material for art. He has been a great promoter of glass art, not only in the USA, and has encouraged the most daring experimentation. He has created many extremely fascinating collections over the years, the *Blanket Cylinders* of the 1970s, his first *Seaforms*, the *Macchias* and his *Venetians* in the first years of the 1980s. In 1995 he created great heavy chandeliers for installations called *Chihuly over Venice* in different parts of the world.

Piergiorgio Colombara (1948)
Piergiorgio Colombara was born in Genoa (Italy) in 1948. After his high school years, where he concentrated on art, he graduated in architecture in 1974. During the 1970s he worked principally as a painter on canvas, but in the 1980s he became a sculptor and installation artist. He created relatively large works using a wide range of materials, including metal, wax, mirror and glass. Today his work centres mainly on the contamination of language, paying particular attention to music and poetry. He has had many solo shows and participated in numerous group shows, the most recent being at the Paris Grand Palais (1992), at the Kunstverein in Hamburg (1992), at the *Skulptur Heute* in Hochefelden (1995), and at Palazzo Barolo in Turin in 2002. He was invited to participate in the 1993 Venice Biennale. He lives and works in Genoa.

Gunnar Cyrén (1931)
Born in 1931, Gunnar Cyrén studied metallurgy at the State School of Arts, Crafts and Design in Stockholm (Sweden). In 1959 he commenced his collaboration with Orrefors, to which he brought youthful enthusiasm and new ideas, with the creation of painted, cut and Graal glassware. In the 1960s the hot-worked glass objects he called Pop Age, with irregular shapes and brightly coloured horizontal stripes, were famous. His sculptural projects were very different, blocks of pure crystal cut in geometric forms.

Daum Frères, glassworks
The Daum Frères glassworks was founded at Nancy (France) in 1878 by Jean Daum, for the production of articles for daily use. In 1883 the jurist Jean-Louis-Auguste Daum took over the running of the company, while the artistic direction was entrusted in 1887 to the engineer and artist Jean-Antonin Daum. Stimulated by Gallé's success in 1889, the manufacturer shifted its emphasis to art glass from 1890 onward and attracted considerable attention at the Universal Exhibition of Paris in 1900. Important artists and decorators contributed to the designs: Jacques Gruber, Henry Bergé, Almaric Walter and Charles Schneider, in succession. In 1907 Jean Daum took over the management of the firm and in 1911 it headed in a new artistic direction, with the participation of Paul Daum and the influence of the artistic director Emile Wirth. In the 1920s and 1930s production was successfully adapted to the style of the time and the firm has continued its activity to the present day. While initially imitating Gallé's techniques in its art nouveau output, Daum Frères soon began to specialize in the use of powders on the outside or inside (*nuagé* effect). In the 1920s and 1930s it produced glassware of solid and geometrical structure.

Wim Delvoye (1965)
Wim Delvoye was born in Wervik (Belgium) in 1965. An exponent of the latest generation of art, the distinguishing feature of Delvoye's installations is the irony he uses to address quite weighty cultural themes. The artist appropriates well-known images that are commonly considered "artistic," such as Delft ceramics, Oriental rugs, or more generally the varied elements of domestic décor, and he decontextualizes them by putting them alongside objects they have no association with. His works, which are expressions of witticisms, are finely hand made under his direction. Delvoye often uses fragile materials such as glass, porcelain, and majolica, creating a dialogue about the preciousness of the applied arts. He has exhibited in many galleries and museums, most recently in 1991 at the Castello di Rivoli (Turin), in 1992 at *Documenta* (Kassel), in 1997 at the Middelheim Open Air Museum of Sculpture in Antwerp, in Belgium. He lives and works in Ghent (Belgium) and London.

Enrico Tommaso De Paris (1960)
Enrico Tommaso De Paris was born in Mel (Italy) in 1960. He debuted in 1990 in Turin artistic circles with figurative painting, and had his first solo show at the Galleria Carbone in Turin in 1991. At the beginning of his career he created canvasses having a comic-strip feel, indebted to the Pop Art of Lichtenstein. He then became a part of so-called Pittura Mediale and his works were filled with houses, skyscrapers, cities, and planets, building up a universe with a positive nature. In 1992 De Paris began to transcend the boundaries of the canvas and started working on installation paintings, which disassemble firstly into diptychs and then into polyptychs, and then into an increasingly higher number of panels. He then created sculptures and installation works that are real environments made up of fragments and objects *exiled* from his paintings. He has had many solo shows and participated in numerous group shows, including *Nebbia* at the Magazzini del Sale in Venice in 1995, and *Officina Italia* at the Galleria d'Arte Moderna in Bologna in 1997. He lives and works in Turin.

Alessandro Diaz de Santillana (1959)
Alessandro Diaz de Santillana was born in Paris (France) in 1959, he studied art history at Venice University. In 1981 he began his collaboration with Venini & Co. glassworks, where he curated exhibitions of historical Venini glass and new productions from 1981 to 1985. His designs of lamps and vases have been successful. From 1987 to 1992 he collaborated occasionally with Rosenthal and the EOS glassworks of Murano. After this he devoted his time exclusively to freelance activities exhibiting in private galleries and museums and taking part in important international exhibitions. His research has led him to create sculptures of increasingly greater impact where glass is the most important material and he

stresses both its material essence and its surface qualities while at the same time he has taken his distance from glass as pure craftsmanship. Between 1997 and 1999 he worked in the USA and collaborated as a Visiting Professor at the University of California in San Diego. Today he lives and works in Venice but his work has an international stature.

Laura Diaz de Santillana (1955)
Laura Diaz de Santillana was born in Venice (Italy) in 1955, she attended the School of Visual Arts in New York from 1975 to 1977. She has worked in graphics in New York and Milan and in 1977 she began to work for the family firm of Venini & Co. She began exhibiting as an artist in 1979 and from 1980 to 1985 she was co-artistic director of Venini. She then became artistic director from 1989 to 1993 of EOS. Since 1986 she has collaborated with Rosenthal (porcelain), with Ivan Baj, Salviati and Steuben. Since 1983 she has been a freelance artist and she creates unique art works in glass. She has always shown an extraordinary sensitivity for glass and has a deep knowledge of this material. Her artistic development has distanced her from the traditional techniques of working glass towards an essential language. While her first works have been characterized by intense polychromatism and complex decorative techniques such as *murrine*, filigree and *incalmo*, her most recent works tend towards transparent or lightly tinted glass and plastic sculptural forms.

Ludovico Diaz de Santillana (1931-1989)
Ludovico Diaz de Santillana was born in Rome (Italy) in 1931 and died in 1989. He graduated from the University of Architecture in Venice, where he was to teach, as Ignazio Gardella's assistant, up until 1968. Marrying Anna Venini in 1963, he took the place of his brother-in-law, following his death in 1959, at the administrative and artistic head of the Venini glassworks. He designed numerous models of blown glass, some of which had extraordinary success, and made a great contribution to the field of illumination, designing lamps and large lighting systems himself as well as commissioning them from well-known architects. He shepherded the company through the difficult period of the 1960s and 1970s, maintaining its leading position in the glass sector. In the 1960s he opened up the glassworks to young American artists interested in learning how to use the material, some of whom were later to become artists of international standing and important promoters of American Studio Glass. With partners from outside Venice, he founded VeArt with the aim of applying the design skills of Venini to a more industrial type of production, but in 1981, disappointed by the results, he withdrew from the project.

Marcel Duchamp (1887-1968)
Marcel Duchamp was born in Blainville-Crevon (France) in 1887 and died in Neuilly in 1968. He is known unequivocally as a precursor in the development of 20th-century art. Initially influenced by Cubist and Futurist painting, in 1913 he began experimenting new expressive tools that were to change the course of contemporary art. From that time, the artist began using objects from everyday life and placing them in a museum context, giving the so-called ready-made the dignity of a work of art. He was a scrupulous enthusiast of hermeneutical and alchemical science, and in 1913 he started to develop his major work, the *Large Glass*, which would keep him committed for the rest of his life, and in fact remained unfinished. In 1915 he moved to New York where he would live for the greater part of his life. In the mid-1920s he almost abandoned artistic life and dedicated himself almost exclusively to the game of chess and to the international promotion of the Surrealist movement. The list of his works is limitless: Robert Label wrote the artist's first monograph in 1955 and in 1966 the Tate Gallery in London dedicated a first great retrospective to him. Many others followed, including one at the Venetian Palazzo Grassi in 1993.

Chiara Dynys (1958)
Chiara Dynys was born in Mantua (Italy) in 1958. She began working in 1987 and in 1993 had her first solo show at the Galleria Monica De Cardenas in Milan. The work of her debut, in the early part of the 1990s, looks back to the abstract tradition, though the works resist asymmetry and irregularity, which are often barely perceptible. As her career developed, Dynys began to explore the *limen* between the languages of theatre, new technology, poetry and literature through video and installation work. The use of wax, plaster, silk, resins and natural pigments, glass, natural plastic materials, precious stones, fabrics and velvets reveals Dynys' proficiency in many techniques. She has exhibited in many public spaces and private galleries in Italy and overseas, including the Centre National d'Art Contemporain in Montreal (1994), the Centre Culturel Français in Milan in 1999, the ex-church of Santa Maria delle Croci in Ravenna in 2001 and at the Museo Cantonale d'Arte in Lugano in 2001. She lives and works in Milan.

Friedrich Egermann (1777-1864)
Friedrich Egermann was born a Slukov (Czech Republic) in 1777 and died in 1864. After learning the craft of painting on glass at Chøibská, he obtained a post as painter at the Meissen porcelain factory: in order to discover the secrets of the preparation of colours he passed himself off as a deaf-mute. Returning to Bohemia, he produced vases of antique form in his studio at Polevsko, using opaline glass as well as other colours. He established a reputation as an extraordinary painter on glass. However, his name is linked to the rediscovery of yellow staining with silver oxide, in 1816, and the discovery of the red staining with copper oxide in 1832. These techniques entailed covering the object made of glass with metal oxides: applied with a brush, they stained the outer layer of the glass after it was reheated in the furnace. Later he used these staining techniques to produce Lithyalin glass, which imitated the veining of stones. Some of his competitors, conscious of the importance of his technique of staining with copper oxide, managed to penetrate his studio and steal the secret, taking it to France. Egermann holds a special place in the history of Bohemian glass, a painter and technician endowed with great artistic sensibility, he opened up new horizons for the Bohemian industry.

Peter Fischer (1968)
Peter Fischer was born in 1968 in Aargovie (Switzerland). Self-taught, he is one of the most famous new generation Swiss artists. He creates true projection machines: objects that are not produced by modern technology but that are bizarre mechanisms pertaining to another time. As he works with projections, glass is present in all his works, always in the form of lenses, sometimes as fixed or moving screens, and at other times as mirrors. In addition to producing video installations, he has also worked on musical composition, and in 1993 he formed a rock band. He has participated in two editions of the *Videoform* Festival (1998 and 2000) at Clermont-Ferrand (France) and the Prix de l'art electronique in Aarau in 1999.

Lucio Fontana (1899-1968)
Lucio Fontana was born in Rosario (Argentina) in 1899 and died in 1968 at Comabbio (Italy). After working in his native country with his sculptor father, he moved to Italy to attend the Brera Academy in Milan. In the 1930s he entered into the sphere of the Lombardy abstract artists. In addition to painting he was also interested in cement sculpture and ceramics. He returned to Argentina during the Second World War and in 1946 signed the *Manifiesto Blanco*, a declaration of neo-Futurist poetics for an art appropriate to the times. In 1947 he returned to Milan and created the *ambienti*, designed to be "shapes, colours, and sounds through space", and the *concetti spaziali*, large canvases marked with ceramic and glass material, perforations and cuts. Creator of the first works using Wood light and neon, Fontana worked alongside the experiments of the Rationalist architects, participating in numerous editions of the Milan Triennale and the Venice Biennale. Fontana's works straddle the historic avant-garde and contemporary experimentation, and many exhibitions have been dedicated to him, such as the one at Palazzo delle Esposizioni in Rome in 1998 and in Milan on the occasion of the centenary of the artist's birth in 1999.

Piero Fornasetti (1913-1988)
Piero Fornasetti was born in Milan (Italy) in 1913 and died in 1988. He attended the courses of painting and sculpture at the Milan Brera Academy, while devoting himself in his own time to life drawing and the study of the great classical painters and architects. He then enrolled at the Scuola Superiore di Arte Applicata. He was also a great collector of the most disparate objects. Linked to the artists of the Novecento group, he made his debut as a painter, experimenting with a variety of media, including fresco, mosaic, enamel painting, the embossing of metals and the techniques of engraving. Interested above all in the print, he invented an original method that allowed him, after a special treatment with varnish, to print on any material. A man of many talents, he exhibited furniture, engravings, tapestries and lace at the 6th Milan Triennale in 1940; in the metal and glass section he showed the glassware he had designed for SALIR of Murano, engraved or painted in enamel. After the war he intensified his collaboration with Giò Ponti, begun in the 1930s, on fittings and furnishings for ships, hotels, bars and private homes. In 1954 he designed a series of Hunting Horn goblets for Venini. In the 1950s he reached the peak of his success and his decorated products were sold at his own store, Fornasetti of Milan, and exported all over the world. In 1991 the Victoria & Albert Museum dedicated an anthological exhibition to him. His works are now eagerly sought after by collectors.

Emile Gallé (1846-1904)
Emile Gallé was born in Nancy (France) in 1846 and died in 1904. The son of Charles Gallé, proprietor of a firm selling glass and pottery, he went to Weimar in 1865-66 to study design, botany and mineralogy at the Institute of Art and Architecture, travelling in Germany and Czechoslovakia. In 1866-67 he received practical training at a number of workshops in Alsace and in 1867 began to produce his own designs, first for glass and pottery and then for furniture and other objects. He made long stays in London and Paris. He took over the artistic direction of his father's firm in 1874 and the general management in 1877. Between 1885 and 1896 he collaborated constantly with the Burgum, Schwerer & Co. factory, which in those years made much of the Gallé glassware. From 1894 onward, most of the pro-

duction was shifted to the new firm in Nancy. In 1884 he started to achieve extraordinary success at international exhibitions, especially at the Universal Exhibitions of Paris in 1889 and 1900. In the era of Art Nouveau, it was Gallé who dictated style in France. When the Ecole de Nancy, a consortium of firms based in Lorraine, was founded in 1901, he was elected its president. Gallé only designed part of the large amount of glassware that was produced under his name, but it always bore the mark of his personal taste as he coordinated the entire output. The execution of the objects was carried out by specialists at the furnace and the workshops. But both they and the designers adhered perfectly to Gallé's formulation and out of the individual personalities was born a unitary style: the *genre Gallé*. With him the art of glass became a vehicle for feelings or ideas that often had their origin or their parallel in the Symbolist poetry of the time.

Omar Galliani (1950)
Omar Galliani was born in Montecchio (Italy) in 1950 and in 1977 he graduated in painting from the Accademia di Belle Arti in Bologna. Painter and sculptor, his art belongs to the citazionist current that observes the museum, the history of modern art (particularly Correggio and Parmigianino) and classical sculpture. His artistic work is based mainly on drawing, which represents the common denominator of his paintings and installations. He uses glass in a sporadic way. He had his first solo show in 1977 at the Galleria Studio G7 in Bologna. During the 1980s and 1990s he had many solo shows, including one at the Museo d'Arte Moderna in Modena (1992), one at the Modern Art Museum at San Jose in Costa Rica and one at the *Tour Fromage* in Aosta in 1987. He participated in the 16th San Paolo Biennale in Brazil, at the 12th Biennale in Paris, and at three editions of the Venice Biennale (1982, 1984, 1986). He currently teaches at the Academy of Fine Arts in Carrara. He lives and works in Montecchio.

Luciano Gaspari (1913)
Luciano Gaspari was born in Venice (Italy) in 1913 and attended the Accademia di Belle Arti in both Venice and Bologna. As a painter he has participated in important exhibitions since the 1932 Biennale and has been one of the principal exponents of Venetian Spatialism. He employed his very personal chromatic sensitivity and creative daring in glass design when he was artistic director of Salviati & C. from 1955 to 1968; he has also collaborated occasionally with this firm between 1981 and the early 1990s. His collections produced between 1991 and 1992 and for the *Aperto Vetro* exhibition in 1996 were created with the glass master Pino Signoretto of Murano.

Simon Gate (1883-1945)
Simon Gate was born in 1883 and died in 1945. Trained first at the Technical School in Stockholm (Sweden) and then at the Royal Academy of Art in the same city, he was the first artist to collaborate with Orrefors, becoming its director in 1916 and remaining there until the year of his death. A charismatic and energetic innovator, he investigated the possibilities of cased glass in collaboration with the craftsman Knut Bergkvist, whose skill made possible the development of artistic glassware. Experimenting together, they invented the Graal technique in 1916. He also did a great deal of work with engraved glass, then a neglected sector, in collaboration with the great engraver Gustav Abels. He established a reputation for Swedish glass at the international level, getting the company to participate in the most important exhibitions. Engraved glass soon came back into fashion and the demand for it increased, prompting an expansion of the workshops. His engraving was inspired by the Renaissance: parades of classical nudes ran around the walls, standing out sharply from the pure crystal. He was one of the most important figures in the glass of the 20th century.

Mieke Groot (1949)
Mieke Groot was born in 1949 in Alkmar (Netherlands) and attended the Gerrit Rietveld Academie in Amsterdam, where she graduated from the department of jewellery in 1974 and from the department of glass in 1976. Since 1976 she has managed a studio in Amsterdam with the glass artist Richard Meitner. She was a freelance designer for Royal Leerdam from 1978 to 1981. She taught from 1981 to 2000 at the Gerrit Rietveld Academie. Since 1993 she has been curator of the Glass Museum Alter Hof Herding, Ernsting Stiftung, Coesfeld-Lette, Germany. She has taught in many European schools of glass and is one of the most established artists in contemporary glass.

Ale Guzzetti (1953)
Ale Guzzetti was born in Tradate (Italy) in 1953. He studied at the Brera Academy in Milan, and at the same time studied electronic music (Milan Polytechnic and Padua University) and three-dimensional sculpture (European Institute of Design in Milan). In 1983 he began working on *sculture sonore*, objects in plastic assembled with electronic circuits that produce sounds and interact with the viewer. In the 1990s he made the *acquarelli elettronici* (synthetic images taken from musical tunes processed by a computer) and the *vetri parlanti* (glass sculpture that reworks sounds, reproduces images, and emits luminous signals). His works received an award at the Prix Ars Electronica in Linz (1991). Guzzetti was among the one hundred artists recommended by the Victoria & Albert Museum in London for the museum of the new millennium, and he has had many solo shows, including one at the Bevilacqua La Masa Foundation in Venice and the Mudima Foundation in Milan. He lives and works in Saronno (Varese).

Edward Hald (1883-1980)
Edward Hald was born in Stockholm (Sweden) in 1883 and died in 1980. Initially he studied business at Leipzig in Germany (1903-05), architecture at Dresden and painting, first at the Artistic Studio in Copenhagen and then at the School of the Artistic League of Stockholm. In the years 1908-09 he was a pupil of Matisse in Paris. A designer of porcelain for Rörstrand (1917-27) and Karls Krona (1924-43), he was above all the principal designer and experimenter at Orrefors, joining the firm in 1917 and remaining there until 1978. He held the post of director from 1933 to 1944. Hald brought a breath of freshness and extravagance to Orrefors, with a style that was less severe and more ironic than that of his colleagues and predecessors. He displayed an extraordinary pictorial sensibility with the Graal and the subsequent developments of the technique known as Fish Graal. He was one of the greatest figures in 20th-century glass.

Harrach, glassworks
The Harrach glassworks was founded at Nový Svět (Crimea) in 1630. In 1798 it was taken over by Count Harrach, who entrusted its management to Johann Pohl. The manufacturer produced splendid coloured glass, even managing to create a ruby red on gold. The quality of the glass was enhanced by the deep cutting and the thickness of the walls, modelled in the forms typical of Biedermeier glassware. After Pohl's death, in 1850, the firm expanded considerably and by the end of the century was second only to Lobmeyer. In 1887 it was taken over by Josef Riedel, who also produced luxury glassware that was exported to many parts of the world.

Josef Maria Hoffmann (1870-1956)
Josef Maria Hoffmann was born in Pirnitz (Moravia). He was regarded as one of the most important European artists of the 1920s and was rediscovered towards the end of the 20th century. He began his studies in architecture at the Höhere Staatsgewerbeschule of Brno in 1887 and went on to study at the Akademie der Bildenden Künste, Vienna, where his teachers included Otto Wagner and Carl von Hasenauer. After graduating in 1895 he accompanied Joseph Maria Olbrich on a journey to Italy where he expanded his artistic horizons by studying ancient artefacts. In 1897 he worked in Otto Wagner's studio in Vienna and contributed to the Viennese Secession. From 1899 to 1936 he taught architecture and design at the Kunstgewerbeschule in Vienna. He founded the Wiener Werkstätte in 1903 together with Koloman Moser, he was the artistic director and one of the most prolific designers of this cooperative laboratory. Many metal artworks by Hoffmann were architectonic in nature while others were based on grid patterns known as Hoffmannquadratl, which can also be found in his furniture design. He created objects in glass for the glassworks of J. & L. Lobmeyer and Loetz Witwe where the coloured or black layers are highlighted against the underlying layers. Moreover he had a highly successful architecture studio in Vienna. In 1907 he participated in the foundation of the Deutsche Werkbund and from 1912 to 1920 he was president of the Austrian Werkbund. His approach to architecture and design was strongly influenced by the British Arts & Crafts Movement and his terse and linear forms were to have a strong influence on the geometric language developed by the Modern Movement.

Mats Jonasson (1945)
Mats Jonasson was born in 1945. Demonstrating a particular talent for drawing, he was taken on at the age of fourteen, in 1959, as an engraver at the Målerås Glasbruk, an independent Swedish glassworks. Ten years later he moved to the Kosta glassworks, but returned to Målerås in 1975, becoming then its artistic director. He specialized in the engraving of animals in blocks of pure crystal. These were cast in an iron mold, carved with a sandblaster and finished by engraving and if necessary polishing. He designed and executed his works and his skills extended from extremely realistic engravings to stylizations in the modern manner. He had excellent collaborators.

Thorsten Kirchhoff (1960)
Thorsten Kirchhoff was born in Copenhagen (Denmark) in 1960. His work is marked by the transgression and corruption of various languages of contemporary culture, such as cinema, music, design and architecture. He accumulates magazine stills and pages, selecting images in order to disclose the illusory nature of the media and the distortions of the technological universe. He recently produced the musical CD *Wedding Bells*, and the short film *Una serata con il dottor Hoffmann* presented in November 2001 at the nineteenth edition of the Turin Film Festival. He has had solo shows in many Italian galleries and public museums, including the Galleria d'Arte Moderna of Bologna in 1999 and the British Academy in Rome (1997). He participated in the 1990 and 1993 editions of the Venice Biennale. He lives and works in Rome and Milan.

René Lalique (1860-1945)
René Lalique was born in Ay (France) in 1860 and died in 1945. At the age of sixteen he left school and became an apprentice with Louis Auroc, one of the best gold and silversmiths in Paris. During his apprenticeship he took courses at the Ecole des Arts Décoratifs. In 1878 he went to England, where he attended Sydenham College. Returning to Paris in 1880, he formed a partnership with an old family friend to produce jewelry designs for important Parisian stores. His first collection of jewelry was shown at the Paris International Exhibition of 1889. In 1900 another collection of jewelry proved a triumph at the Universal Exhibition. Attracted by glass as a sculptural material, from 1902 onward he created figurines and vases with high relief decorations, using the lost-wax technique. In 1908 he rented a glassworks at Combs-la-Ville, buying it the following year and using it for the production of *objets d'art* and other articles in glass. In 1913 he gave up making jewelry. In 1918 he founded La Verrerie d'Alsace René Lalique & Cie at Wingen-sur-Moder, for the production of glassware on an industrial scale. In the 1920s and 1930s he obtained worldwide recognition. He made constant use of the mold, but not at the expense of the quality of his products. He preferred opalescent glass but did make some pieces in extraordinarily brilliant colours. In 1930 his son Marc took over the management of the firm, but René remained its artistic director until his death. The firm is still in existence today.

Legras & Cie, glassworks
The glassworker August-Jean-Francois Legras acquired the Verreries et Cristalleries de Saint-Denis et des Quatre-Chemins in 1864, in order to produce his tableware and decorative objects. These were made of coloured glass, sometimes enameled or decorated in gold, or crystal. In 1894 Legras was granted a patent for the application of flowers or other decorative motifs on blown glass. In 1897 he took over the Vidié glassworks, going on to employ some 1400 people, including 150 decorators. An admirer of Gallé, Legras started to make Art Nouveau glassware with several engraved layers and finished in enamel. Later he used glass powders, in imitation of Daum, to create a clouded effect. Under the management of his son Charles, the company went on producing glassware with the technique of the double engraved layer.

Silvia Levenson (1957)
Silvia Levenson was born in Buenos Aires (Argentina) in 1957. She has been living in Italy since 1981. The artist's preferred theme is infancy considered not as a carefree time but as a period painfully connected to the events of her native country under a dictatorship and the memory of experiencing tragedy. In 1982 she participated in the *Kanazawa International Exhibition of Glass* in Japan, and in the late 1990s she made a mark on the international art scene with her *Fashion Glass* series, a collection of clothes, shoes, bags, underwear, hats and jewels all made in glass. Each item of clothing also contains nails, razor blades, knifes and other objects that can cause injuries. She has exhibited in many galleries and public museums such as the Museo Archeologico in Padua (2001), the Credito Valtellinese Foundation in Milan (2000), and the Glasmuseum of Ebeltoff in Denmark in 1993. She lives and works in Vigevano.

Stanislav Libenský (1921-2000) and Jaroslava Brychtová (1924)
Stanislav Libenský and Jaroslava Brychtová have always collaborated in the creation of marvellous works in glass. Libenský was born in Sesezeniche in the Czech Republic and Brychtová at Železný Brod. Libenský studied at the Specialization School for Glass at Novy Bor and subsequently at Železný Brod, then attending the School of Applied Arts in Prague and the Academy of Applied Arts in Prague. He taught at the Specialization School for Glass at Novy Bor and was artistic director from 1945 to 1954. From 1954 he began to collaborate with his wife Jaroslava Brychtová who had attended the Academy of Applied Arts and the Academy of Fine Arts in Prague. In 1984 they opened a studio at Železný Brod where they created sculptures of great impact and both artists were invited to teach in schools for glassmaking in Europe and America. They have been the leaders of an important school of Bohemian glass art, which has shown the value of glass as a plastic medium. They are the most important representatives of contemporary Bohemian art.

Johann Lötz Witwe, glassworks
Johann Lötz Witwe was a manufacturer of art glass based at Klostermühle in Bohemia. Founded in 1836 by Johann Baptiste Eisner, it was acquired in 1851 by Franz Gerstner and his wife Susanne, the widow of Johann Lötz, who took over its direction. The trademark Johann Lötz Witwe was registered in 1858. Alongside household glassware, it also produced refined luxury articles. In 1879 the enterprise was transferred to Susanne's uncle Maximilian Ritter von Spaun, who was able to attain international recognition in the art sector. *Phaenomen Glas*, made iridescent by a costly process, was a real success. After 1900 it established ties with the artists of the Viennese group headed by Josef Hoffman and Koloman Moser. In 1911 the firm went bankrupt. It resumed production in 1913 but went bankrupt again in 1939. It was to close definitively in 1947.

Giuseppe Maraniello (1945)
Giuseppe Maraniello was born in Naples (Italy) in 1945. His education took place in the same circles from which the Transavanguardia movement sprang. Following experiments with black and white photography, the artist returned to painting and concentrated on the spontaneous gesture of both primitive and children's art, and at the same time was inspired by votive Etruscan pottery and his son's preschool drawings. The work produced for the Aosta exhibition is Maraniello's first work in glass. The artist held his first solo show at the CAE of Beppe Morra in Naples in 1973. Throughout the 1980s and 1990s he had solo shows in Italian galleries and museums, including a show in 1993 at the Galleria Civica d'Arte Contemporanea in Trento and at the Villa delle Rose in Bologna. He participated in the Venice Biennale in 1990 and 1995. He teaches at the Accademia di Belle Arti in Milan. He lives and works in Milan.

Richard Marquis (1945)
Richard Marquis was born in Bumblebee (Arizona, USA) in 1945 and in 1964 attended Berkeley University of California and graduated with a Bachelor of Arts degree in 1969. After having attended a ceramics course held by Peter Voulkos and Ron Nagle based on a refusal of the traditional distinction between major and minor arts, he developed an interest in the working of glass and ceramics. He took part in the Funk Art movement. He quickly realized that glass was his ideal medium of expression and he has employed it with irony, ingenuity and imagination. In 1969 he was awarded a scholarship to study in Italy from the Fulbright studio and he moved to Venice where he worked at the Venini glassworks collaborating with glass master Checco Onagro. It was in this period that he developed his passion for the *murrina* technique with which Carlo Scarpa had created wonderful works for the same producers. He returned to the USA in 1970 and took his Master of Arts degree always at Berkeley University of California. After considerable experience in teaching and research he is considered one of the major artists of the American Glass Studio. *Murrina* technique remains Marquis's principal technique, which he combines with the most unexpected materials and objects. He lives and works in Seattle.

Napoleone Martinuzzi (1892-1977)
Born in Murano (Italy), Napoleone Martinuzzi attended the Accademia di Belle Arti in Venice. While still very young he joined the Cà Pesaro Secessionist group where he exhibited in 1908. He worked in Rome in 1910-11 and exhibited at the Rome Secession of 1914; from that moment on he worked intensely as a sculptor exhibiting at major artistic events. He was a favourite artist of Gabriele D'Annunzio for whom he designed a funeral monument and there are three of his sculptures and numerous glass works housed in D'Annunzio's residence the Vittoriale on lake Garda. From 1922 to 1931 he was the curator of the Museo Vetrario of Murano and in 1925 he became a partner and artistic director of Vetri Soffiati Muranesi Venini & Co. In his early years he designed transparent works in the style of those by Vittorio Zecchin. In 1928 Martinuzzi produced his first *pulegosi* (with translucent glass full of bubbles called *puleghe* for the most part in dark green), in well-modelled classic forms and in opaque glass and bright colours. For Venini he also created animals, glass fruit and cacti, some of these of abnormal dimensions and therefore in several glass parts supported by metal structures. These works, at the Venice Biennale of 1928 and 1930 and the Monza Triennale in 1930, revealed Martinuzzi as Murano's 20th-century artist. In 1932 together with the engineer Francesco Zecchin he opened the glassworks Zecchin Martinuzzi, which operated for only a few years and produced classic blown glass, opaque for the most part, modern sculptures of female figures and animals in both solid and blown glass, executed by Otello Nason and the very young Alfredo Barbini.

Richard Meitner (1949)
Richard Meitner was born in Philadelphia (Pennsylvania, USA) in 1949 and obtained a Bachelor of Arts degree at Berkeley University of California, studying under Marvin Liposfsky in 1972. From 1972 to 1975 he attended the Rijksakademie voor Beeldende Kunst in Amsterdam, and in 1975 he received a diploma at the Gerrit Rietveld Akademie of Amsterdam. From 1981 to 1989 he was a professor at the Gerrit Rietveld Akademie in Amsterdam. At his Amsterdam studio he has created and creates his works in glass and is one of the most interesting artists on the contemporary glass scene. He has always shown complete indifference to the rules of "beauty" and conventionality in glass, adapting this material to novel effect in his installations where it is combined with other materials or reused objects. These works are oneiric, sometimes disturbing with animals or objects from a Wunderkammer. He has used many techniques, without any restrictions, in the past including painting on glass but he has however shown a preference for lamp work with borosilicate glass, an extremely anonymous and aseptic material, and for this reason, all the more malleable.

Massimo Micheluzzi (1957)
Massimo Micheluzzi attended the faculty of Arts at Venice University (Italy) and undertook a career in antiques and became the dealer of a number of Venetian

glass artists. Having entered the world of glass in this way he embarked on design projects personally supervising the execution of his designs. He designs classic works in opaque glass and avant-garde pieces with deeply ground cuts that look like hard cut stones.

Ritsue Mishima (1962)
Ritsue Mishima was born in Kyoto (Japan) in 1962 and worked as a free lance stylist in Tokyo from 1982 to 1984 in the advertizing sector and for some interior design magazines. Since 1985 she has been working with decoration with floral installations. In 1989 she moved to Venice where she now lives and has her studio. She has been creating art works in glass in Murano since 1995 collaborating with glass masters Livio Serena and Andrea Zilio. Her extremely delicate works in glass indirectly recall organic forms though the pure transparent crystal, at times brilliant and at times opaque, because of grinding, gives them an almost abstract dimension. Her works have been shown in Venice, Milan, London and Tokyo.

Igor Mitoraj (1944)
Igor Mitoraj was born of Polish parentage in 1944 at Oederan in Germany and studied at the Art School and the Academy of the Arts in Krakow (Poland). In Poland he participated in numerous group shows, and had his first solo show at the Krzysztofory Gallery in Krakow. In 1968 he moved to Paris in order to continue his studies. In the early part of the 1970s he spent a year in Mexico and on his return to Paris dedicated himself exclusively to sculpture. He travelled frequently to Greece to study Hellenistic sculpture. In the 1980s his work changed direction and he turned to a neoclassic and classic art; he began to use marble, bronze, cast-iron, travertine stone and fibreglass, and he also created mosaic works. In 1983 he opened a studio in Pietrasanta in Italy. In 1986 he was invited to the Venice Biennale. In 1989 a show at the Academy of Art in New York confirmed his international success. A solo show at the Museo Archeologico in Florence in 1999 reaffirmed his talent. He lives in France and Italy.

Aldo Mondino (1938)
Aldo Mondino was born in Turin (Italy) in 1938. In 1959 he moved to Paris to attend courses at the Ecole du Louvre. He exhibited for the first time at the Galerie Bellechasse in Paris in 1960, inspired by the Surrealists. His series of paintings having writing with the letters in the form of figurines and his *Tavole anatomiche*, with depictions of the human body on a chequered background, date from the 1960s. In 1969 the *Porco Dio* work was confiscated and Mondino was fined for blasphemy. In 1972 he returned to Paris and his work started to become conceptual. He participated in the Venice Biennale in 1976. The linguistic paradoxes of the titles of these works play an important role. Mondino uses all possible materials, from chocolate to glass, fish and metals, and all techniques, from painting to sculpture and installation. In 1984 he became interested in Oriental cultures and travelled from Morocco to Turkey. He participated in the 1993 Venice Biennale. In 2000 he travelled to India for the first time, and held a solo show at the Galleria Civica d'Arte Moderna in Trento. He lives and works in Monferrato.

Eva Moosbrugger (1957)
Eva Moosbrugger was born in Stuttgart (Germany) in 1957, she lived in Dornbirn (Austria) and Zurich (Switzerland). As an artist she is largely self-taught though she attended some academic courses and private lessons with various artists. She has worked in the fields of painting, photography and engraving. Since 1984 she has worked in three-dimensional art with wood, iron, concrete and stone (since 1989) and from 1985 has included ceramics and media mix works. From 1995 she has privileged glass as her expressive medium and she began exhibiting glass works in 1997. Her glass works are executed in Murano with the collaboration of a glass master from the island while the finishing is carried out in her studio in Dornbirn where she lives and works.

Carlo Moretti (1934)
Carlo Moretti was born in Murano (Italy) in 1934 into a family with a long tradition of glassmaking. In 1958 he and his brother Giovanni founded the Vetreria Carlo Moretti s.r.l. for the production of blown glass. Initially the production was based on coloured and often cased glass, but in the 1970s the emphasis shifted to colourless crystal tableware of modern and essential design, although with links to the Murano tradition. Over the last decade decorative and sometimes brightly coloured blown glass has assumed an ever greater importance in the company's catalogue. With few exceptions the models are designed by Carlo Moretti himself. Since 1996, he has shown numbered sculptural works at prestigious international exhibitions. Carlo Moretti is one of the best-known designers in the glass sector.

Richard Neumann (1969)
Richard Neumann was born in Brisbane (Queensland, Australia) in 1969. He studied at the Canberra Institute of Technology and graduated with a Bachelor of Built Environment degree (Major in Industrial Design), from the Queensland University of Technology in 1997. In 2001 he took a Bachelor of Visual Art degree (Major in Glass) at the Canberra School of Art, The Australian National University. Since 1998 he has been a freelance glass artist taking part in exhibitions and creating works on commission.

Anne Nilsson (1953)
Anne Nilsson was born in 1953. She studied ceramics and design at Dickinson College in Pennsylvania and glass and ceramics at the Swedish State School of Arts, Crafts and Design in Stockholm. She worked for several years as a designer at Höganäs Ceramics. She began to work for Orrefors in 1982.

Kerttu Nurminen (1943)
Kerttu Nurminen was born in 1943 in Lathi (Finland). She attended the ceramics course at the Institute of Industrial Art in Helsinki. A student of Kaj Franck, she has been a designer since 1972 at Hackman Designor Oy Ab at the Nuutajärvi glassworks. In 1996 she was awarded the Kaj Franck Prize for Design, at the Design Forum in Helsinki. She is one of Finland's most refined designers and has created both pressed glass utility objects and extremely refined works. Her activity also includes the creation at the Nuutajärvi glassworks of limited series of *Pro Arte* objects and also unique works similar to paintings, often figurative, in multi-layered glass subsequently sand blasted, wheel engraved or acid etched; these are often the inspiration for works in the *Pro Arte* collections. Her experimentation is carried out at the glass works in Nuutajärvi where she lives.

Yoichi Ohira (1946)
Yoichi Ohira was born in Tokyo (Japan) in 1946. He experimented briefly with glass making in Japan but because he sought techniques more in keeping with his sensibility he moved to Italy in 1973. After a diploma in sculpture at the Accademia di Belle Arti in Venice and participation in a number of exhibitions with sculptures in iron and sheet-glass, he began to experiment with glass making at the Fucina degli Angeli. He began his collaboration as a designer at the Vetreria De Majo in 1987 and created collections of blown glass of extreme formal and technical refinement. Since 1992 he has been a freelance glass artist and produces glass works at a furnace in Murano collaborating with the glass master Livio Serena. His first works for De Majo and as an independent artist were in transparent glass and were based on formal elegance and a play of superimposed colours and decorative intertwining. After 1996 he preferred opaque glass, *murrina*-like textures in polychrome compositions with tesserae or canes in clear glass that exalt the essence of the material. His works are the perfect fusion of Oriental and Venetian culture: refined colour combinations and forms from the Orient, the techniques of working hot glass and cold finish from Venice combined with his particular sensitivity for glass. He enjoys experimenting in the furnace following the execution of his works down to the smallest detail. He is one of the best-known artists working with glass on the international scene.

Luca Pancrazzi (1961)
Luca Pancrazzi was born in Figline Valdarno (Florence, Italy) in 1961. After studying at the Accademia di Belle Arti in Florence, he dedicated himself mainly to painting. His works, which tend to be monochrome, are built up of layers of colour and replicate photographs of urban spaces and "non places" (Augè) that the artist himself takes and selects. Pancrazzi is known principally through his paintings, but the Tuscan artist also creates light boxes, video installations and sculptures in glass and crystal. He has worked with Sol LeWitt and Alighiero Boetti. Between 1986 and 2001 he held many solo shows in Italian and overseas galleries and public spaces, including the most recent at the Museo Marino Marini in Florence, the Galeria Marta Cervera in Madrid and the Spazio Base in Florence, all held in 2000, and at the Galleria Mazzoli in Modena in 2001. Pancrazzi participated in the 1997 Venice Biennale. Since 1994 he has been living and working in Milan.

Franz Pelzel (1900-1974)
Franz Pelzel was born in 1900 in Sudeti (Bohemia). He studied Glass making at the Haida High School graduating with a diploma as "master engraver of art glass." First he collaborated with the firm Oertel & Co. in Haida, and then with Lobmeyer in Vienna; finally he went to Florence to work with the designer Guido Balsamo Stella. In 1925 his "bottega d'arte" moved to the Giudecca island in Venice where Pelzel continued his activity as an engraver until 1927, the year in which he began his long association with SALIR of Murano, at first together with Balsamo Stella, and later becoming the founder of a number of glass wheel engraving schools. He was a master engraver and executed exceptional works for important artists and designers such as Carlo Scarpa, Giò Ponti and Ettore Sottsass. He also created many works of his own design and works by his son Pietro. He took part in all the major national and international expositions and won many awards. His activity in Murano was interrupted by the war in 1942 but he returned in 1949 after a brief period in Bavaria. An exquisite engraver he was admired for the plastic quality of his work and he continued working until 1967. His works can be found in the most important museums and in private collections all over the world.

Pietro Pelzel (1937)
Pietro Pelzel, son of the Bohemian master engraver Franz Pelzel, was born in Murano (Italy) in 1937. He graduated in architecture at IUAV (supervisor Franco Albini) in 1964. His first contact with Murano glass was in 1952 at the SALIR decoration workshop founded by his father with whom he was soon to become a close collaborator. He took part in the Biennali, Triennali and other important international exhibitions. From 1959 to 1964 he collaborated as a designer with the Vetreria Vistosi and from 1968 to 1971 with the Vetreria La Murrina; then with Vetrelco in Treviso and Vecris in San Giovanni Valdarno. His projects range from vases and tableware to lighting, he also creates unique works and applied artworks. At the same time he designs works in other fields such as porcelain and wood also taking care of the graphic, publicity and advertising sides of his projects. Until 1999 he also ran a studio as an architect developing projects in both town planning and construction. Now having ceased to practice he has again taken up design and operates on the island of Murano. He collaborates as a consultant in the rebirth of the local glass-making schools.

Gaetano Pesce (1939)
Gaetano Pesce was born in La Spezia (Italy) in 1939 and graduated in architecture and industrial design at Venice University in 1967. Between 1959 and 1967 he worked as an artist and independent cinema director in Padua. From 1962 to 1967 he also worked in Padua as a designer and from 1968 in Venice too, he designed projects for C&B Italia, Cassina, Venini and Bracciodiferro that were innovative both in the materials used and production methods. In 1973 he formulated a theory whereby architecture and design ought to be a representation of reality and a document of their time. In his search for freedom he explored the concept of performance design. In 1972-73 he carried out his first experiments in "diversified series". In 1983 he moved to New York for an intense period of lecturing combined with numerous projects in both architecture and design. Being an innovative anti-conformist he was against the uniformity proposed by the Modern Movement and he conceived architecture and design as multidisciplinary activities that should give the artist limitless expressive freedom.

Jaume Plensa (1955)
Jaume Plensa was born in Barcelona (Spain) in 1955. He studied at the Fine Arts High School of Sant Jordi and learnt sculpture technique by working in a machine workshop. In 1983 he began to work iron and bronze in anthropomorphic shapes. More recently he has combined these organic shapes with inanimate objects such as containers, doors, and shapes that are more generically architectonic. In recent years he has also been working with alabaster, laser and glass, using the materials to their optimum potential. Though Barcelona is the artist's native home, he has also lived in Berlin, Brussels, England (invited by the Henry Moore Foundation) and France (Atelier Alexander Calder). He has had solo shows in numerous galleries and museums, such as the Städtische Kunsthalle in Mannheim (1997), the Palais Liechtenstein in Vienna (1999) and the Museo Reina Sofia in Madrid (2000). He lives and works in Barcelona.

Flavio Poli (1900-1984)
Flavio Poli was born in Chioggia (Italy) in 1900 and died in 1984. He attended the Istituto d'Arte in Venice. He worked as a designer of ceramics in Venice and Murano. In 1929 began to work with glass for Libero Vitali's IVAM (Industrie Vetri Artistici Murano). Later he collaborated with the Compagnia di Venezia e Murano, the glassworks of Mario and Lino Nason and the engraver Gino Francesconi. In 1934 he assumed the post of artistic director of Barovier Seguso & Ferro (later Seguso Vetri d'Arte), eventually becoming a partner in the firm. With the craftsman Archimede Seguso, he started to produce works of an essentially sculptural character that were of undisputed importance for the artistic development of Murano glass. With the series *Harmonious Dissonances*, objects of asymmetrical shape but soft and harmonious in their modelling, made of green glass corroded on the outer surface, Poli became a leading exponent of the Novecento style. He also designed avant-garde lighting systems. He received numerous prizes, including the Compasso d'Oro in 1954 for his *sommersi* or "sunk" glassware, characterized by the way that their essential forms and the colours came together to create "a perfect unity." In 1957 the Milan Triennale put on a major exhibition of his works. He left Seguso Vetri d'Arte in 1963 and in 1964 was given the task of organizing a sector of art glass at the Società Veneziana di Conterie e Cristallerie, giving up the post in 1966. Through his research into the expressive possibilities of glass, Flavio Poli established a reputation as one of the finest designers in Europe.

Giò Pomodoro (1930)
Giò Pomodoro was born in 1930 in Orciano (Pesaro, Italy). In the mid 1950s he moved to Milan where, together with his brother Arnaldo, he was part of the Movimento Nucleare and experimented a gestural style of avant-garde art. During this period his preferred materials were silver and bronze, revealing his training as a goldsmith. He was invited to exhibit at the Venice Biennale in 1956 and 1958 and had his first solo show at the Galleria del Naviglio in Milan. He participated in the second and third edition of *Documenta* in Kassel (1959, 1964). In the mid 1970s he became passionate about using stone and marble, creating large-scale works and deepening his understanding of the spatial and tensile aspects of materials. He has created works for public spaces in various cities, such as Monza, Padua and Florence, and has participated in numerous editions of the Venice Biennale (in addition to 1956, in 1962, 1978, 1984, and 1988). In 1995 he exhibited at the Yorkshire Sculpture Park, in 1996 at the Arms Hall of Palazzo Vecchio in Florence and in 1998 at the Centro Saint-Benin in Aosta. He lives and works in Milan.

Man Ray (1890-1976)
Man Ray (Man Emmanuel Radenski) was born in Philadelphia (Pennsylvania, USA) in 1890 and died in Paris in 1976. After studying architecture and industrial design he dedicated himself to painting. The *Armory Show* in New York (1913) showed him the different innovatory currents in European painting. He became fascinated with Cézanne, Cubism and Marcel Duchamp; he met Duchamp by mixing with the artists who gathered around the photographer Alfred Stieglitz. Man Ray experimented new techniques (airbrush painting, ready-mades) and became the main exponent of American Dadaism. In 1921 he began travelling frequently to Paris, where he actively participated in the Dada movement by working on *rayographes*, photographs without apparatus obtained by resting objects directly onto light sensitive emulsion. He quickly acquired fame and created short films with surrealists he became involved with in the 1930s. He spent a long time in Hollywood (1940-1950) and collaborated with H. Richter on the film *Dreams That Money Can Buy*. Innumerable publications and exhibitions, such as the 1988 Milan show *Tutto Man Ray*, have described his life and work.

Antonio Riello (1958)
Antonio Riello was born in 1958 in Marostica (Italy). He studied chemistry and architecture. His work is a study of youth culture and the collective imagination; it is part of the "playful-conceptual" tendency crossing contemporary Italian art that spans from Piero Manzoni to Wim Delvoye. The tools used to reveal contradictions and clichés are maliciousness, black humour, irony and paradox. In his manipulation of everyday objects, Riello also uses glass, though not in a continuous way and without specific study into the material and its potential. He was Visiting Professor at the University of Derby (Great Britain) and at the Muthesius Hochschule in Kiel (Germany). At the Brera Academy (Milan) he worked in multimedia and has created one of the first art works in Italy in video-game form (1997). Recently he has been creating web art projects. He lives and works in Marostica and Milan.

Maria Grazia Rosin (1958)
Maria Grazia Rosin was born in Cortina d'Ampezzo (Italy) in 1958 and attended the Art Institute there; she graduated in painting under Emilio Vedova at the Accademia di Belle Arti in Venice in 1983 and also attended the faculty of architecture. She devoted herself to painting, a strongly chromatic figurative-type of painting and also worked in design, advertizing graphics and illustration. She soon opted for work with a strong three-dimensional effect though always characterized by colour. In 1992 she became involved in *Progetto Vetro* an exhibition organized by the Fondazione Bevilacqua La Masa: young artists who were working with glass for the first time. She found this path very congenial to her talents. She has developed two different currents in her work, one is very ironic seeking its irony in daily life as in *Detergens* and in her *Glasses with Pills*, and the other is based on a distortion of natural forms, for example *Organicosmici*, *Venussiani*, *Folpi*. She creates animal and vegetable forms, played down by the use of brilliant surfaces and primary colours. Her works reflect her lively and creative personality.

Rosanna Rossi (1937)
Rosanna Rossi was born in 1937 in Cagliari (Italy). From 1968 to 1983 she taught specialized courses in an art high school, and from 1984 to 1990 she was a teacher at the European Design Institute. Her work, which is of a conceptual nature, cannot be placed within a school or movement but moves freely from addressing formal problems such as form and colour relationships to reflecting on the major themes of contemporary society. Rossi has worked with various materials, including steel, iron, fabric, rods and glass. She has been a part of numerous group shows (*Trash*, Palazzo delle Albere in Trento, 1997) and has had many solo shows, including one at the Museo Su logu de s'iscultura in Tortolì (Nuoro) in 1997. She lives and works in Cagliari.

Silvano Rubino (1952)
Silvano Rubino was born in Venice (Italy) in 1952. After art high school, he attended the Accademia di Belle Arti. He had his first important solo show in 1975 at the Meeting and Research Centre in Bruxelles. Throughout his career he has experimented a number of expressive mediums, such as installation, photography, video and video installation, creating unsettling and disturbing images. He has produced many works in glass that speak about the glass tradition in his native city. Rubino has

also worked as a costume and set designer. Between 1990 and 1996 he spent long periods in Curitiba in Brazil. He has exhibited in many Italian and overseas spaces, including the Gabriela Misral Gallery in Santiago de Chile in 2000 on the invitation of the Minister for Education, and the Galleria Lipanje Puntin in Trieste in 1998. He lives and works in Venice.

Markku Salo (1954)
Markku Salo was born in Nokia (Finland) in 1954. He attended the Kankaanpää Art School and the industrial design courses at the University of Industrial Art in Helsinki from 1974 to 1979. In 1979 he became director of the design department for Salora electronic productions. From 1982 to1983 he was a part time lecturer at the University of Industrial Art in Helsinki. From 1983 to 1991 he was a designer at Hackman Designor Oy Ab at the Nuutajärvi glass works. Since 1997 he has been an independent designer for Hackman Designor Oy Ab at the Iittala glass works. He lives and works in Nuutajärvi where he has his studio. At the outset of his career in glass he designed mostly serial pieces, which gave him the opportunity of understanding the potential of glass. His later activity in this sphere has developed in three different directions: designed utility glass, limited series collections *Pro Arte* (Nuutajärvi and Iittala) and his unique art pieces. He draws inspiration from antiquity and nature but is also attracted by the use of industrial materials. He is one of the most interesting and many-sided personalities of Scandinavian glass.

Salviati & C., glassworks
In 1859 the lawyer Antonio Salviati of Vicenza (Italy) founded the Salviati laboratory of mosaic art. In 1866 he decided to venture into the manufacture and sale of blown glass, but within a few months of the opening of this company he formed a company with some English investors and in 1872 the resulting company became The Venice and Murano Glass and Mosaic Company Limited (Salviati & C.). The company, of which Antonio Salviati was artistic director, had a mosaic and decoration workshop in Venice and a furnace for glass blowing and mosaic paste tesserae on the island of Murano. The best glass masters and decorators of the time were employed; among these were Antonio Seguso, Giovanni Barovier and later Giuseppe Barovier. The company produced very refined works; copies of ancient Venetian glass in every style and some partially lost techniques were recovered. They met with success at the Universal Expositions of Paris in 1867, 1878 and 1889, Vienna in 1873 and at Italian expositions. The technique for enamel decoration was also revived and in 1878 the ancient Roman *murrina* technique was also rediscovered thanks to the efforts of glass technician Vincenzo Moretti; so were early Christian glass gold leaf grafito and cameo technique. Salviati was the firm that contributed most to Murano glass in the second half of the 19th century. In 1877 Antonio Salviati left the company and it was taken over by the Barovier family.

Salviati dott. Antonio, glassworks
Antonio Salviati (1816-1890), after being liquidated from the Venice Company in Murano (Italy), founded the new glassworks Salviati dott. Antonio in 1877 with the collaboration of Giovanni, Giuseppe, Benvenuto and Benedetto Barovier, among the best glass masters of the island, and glass technician Giovanni Camozzo. Production was not very different from the previous company but with time it began to make a name in the production of a "modern" style characterized by strong chromatic contrasts and forms derived from the renaissance but enriched by decidedly 19th century elements, such as serpents, dragons, storks and flowers, etc. With these models, but also with pieces from the archaeological repertoire, he was present at the Universal Exposition of Paris in 1878. In 1884 Salviati left the glassworks to the Barovier family and Camozzo, and kept the management of the Venice sales outlets; by reserving exclusive rights on the production the Baroviers agreed to maintain the name Salviati. After Antonio Salviati's death these relations were less exclusive and the Baroviers began to use the name Artisti Barovier.

Timo Sarpaneva (1926)
Born in 1926, this many-sided Finnish designer has created some of the most important glass artworks of the 20th century and is a promoter of Finnish glass on an international level. He was born in Helsinki and studied in the Graphics faculty of the Central School of Industrial Design in Helsinki from 1941 to 1948. In 1950 he collaborated with the Karhula-Iittala glass works and debuted with extraordinary sculpture-like vases including Kajakki and delicately coloured glass plates. His works won him the Grand Prix at the Milan Triennale in 1954 and 1957 and numerous awards in Finland and abroad including the International Design Award in 1963. In the mid 1950s he launched the I-Glass line: a mass-produced but refined series for daily use available in different colours. He has held a teaching post at the University of Applied Arts in Helsinki and following this has received awards and prizes. His work in glass has always been connected with Iittala, but since 1988 he has also collaborated with the Venini glassworks of Murano, and consequently, since he wished to create unique artworks in glass, with glass master Pino Signoretto.

Carlo Scarpa (1906-1978)
Born in Venice (Italy), Carlo Scarpa graduated from the Accademia di Belle Arti of Venice in 1925. His activity as a teacher began at the Scuola Superiore di Architettura in Venice. In 1927 he took on the directorship of the M.V.M. Cappellini & C. glass factory, in 1932 he began to collaborate occasionally with the Venini & C. glassworks and became the artistic director in 1934. Alongside his work in the glass factory he also worked on the installation of exhibitions in galleries and museums, after the war his activity in this field increased further. From 1947 he was artistic director of Venini: in 1940 the Venice Biennale devoted a room to new works designed by Scarpa – *vetri battuti, velati, granulari, tessuti*. After the war Scarpa devoted almost all his time to architecture. He returned to glass in 1961 with Venini at the Turin exposition creating an exceptional waterfall chandelier composed of polyhedrons; and in 1968 he collaborated with Mario De Luigi on a stained glass window for the Montreal exposition. His most noteworthy installation projects for museums include Palazzo Abatellis in Palermo, some rooms of the Galleria degli Uffizi in Florence, the Gipsoteca Canoviana in Possagno, the Fondazione Querini Stampalia and Museo Correr in Venice. Only rarely did he design objects for mass production, but he frequently designed unique pieces. In 1972 he was appointed director of IUAV. In 1978 he was given an honorary degree in Venice and he died the same year in Sendai (Japan).

Marina Sent (1963) and Susanna Sent (1955)
Marina Sent was born in Venice (Italy) in 1963; after attending the faculty of Industrial Chemistry in Venice she began to work in the factory owned by her father Renzo Sent. Susanna Sent was born in Venice in 1955. After graduating in architecture at IUAV, she joined her father's company Sent Guglielmo Snc, reorganizing its production structure. The two sisters have set up a firm specialized in necklaces and jewelry in glass based on the traditional techniques of Murano but employing the best of contemporary design. Their works are to be found in galleries and museum shops. They also produce exceptional pieces and at times unique pieces for special events and fashion shows.

Medhat Shafik (1956)
Medhat Shafik was born in Egypt in 1956. A well-known actor and dubber, he moved to Italy in 1976 to attend the Accademia di Belle Arti in Milan, where he graduated in painting and set design. His work blends the charm and colour of Oriental art with the compositional techniques of western avant-garde art. A first acknowledgement of his talent came in 1995 at the Venice Biennale, where he exhibited in the Egyptian pavilion and won the Nations Award. Throughout the years, Medhat Shafik has extolled the clear signs of his Egyptian identity, producing a very unique artistic body of work. In addition to shows in Italian and overseas galleries, Medhat Shafik was invited to two editions of the International Art Biennale of Cairo in 1998 and 2001. In 2001 the Galleria Civica d'Arte Moderna in Spoleto dedicated a solo show at the Palazzo Racani Arroni. The artist lives and works in Italy.

Anna Skibska (1960)
Anna Skibska was born in Kluczbork (Poland) in 1960 and studied at Painting Department and the Ceramics and Glass Department of the Wroclaw Art Academy (under Eugeniusz Get Stankiewicz). She graduated in 1984 in painting, glass design and graphic arts. Here she also taught from 1985 to 1996. She then taught in Seattle, where she lives and works and also in Japan. Initially she devoted herself to stained-glass and it was only after moving to Seattle in 1994 that she found the glass technique that was suited to her sensitivity: the lamp technique which she has developed in a totally personal and autonomous manner. The artist heats clear or slightly coloured canes on the flame and delicately draws them out to become very thin threads of glass, which are reheated and soldered one onto the other forming a three-dimensional net. The artist has had students who have developed this technique autonomously.

Sandy Skoglund (1946)
Sandy Skoglund was born in Quincy (Massachusetts, USA) in 1946. After her studies she moved to France, first to Aix-en-Provence and then to Paris to study at the Sorbonne and the Ecole du Louvre. She then returned to her native country to study and obtain a Masters in Fine Arts. She began to teach art history in 1973, first at Hartford University in Connecticut and then at the Rutgers University (New Jersey), where she continues to teach. Sculptor, photographer and film director, Skoglund's special skill is her ability to combine elements of fantasy with elements of reality. In this way she assembles post-atomic images of life that are both surreal and full of loneliness. She has had many solo shows in Italian and overseas museums, such as the Dayton Art Institute in Dayton, Ohio (2002), the American Craft Museum of New York (2000), the Columbia Museum of Art (1998), the Hunting Museum of Art, Virginia (1995) and Fundación La Caixa in Barcelona (1992). She lives and works in New York.

Ettore Sottsass (1917)
Ettore Sottsass was born in Innsbruck (Austria) in 1917. He graduated in architecture from the Turin polytech-

nic. In 1947 he opened a studio in Milan named The Studio where he worked on architecture and design. In 1957 he went to the United States where he worked for George Nelson for a short period. On his return to Italy the same year he was appointed artistic director of Poltronova and became involved in the furniture and lamp design. In 1958 he began to work for Olivetti and created a number of celebrated projects for them, among these were Lexicon 90, and he won the Compasso d'Oro prize for the computer Elea 9003. After a journey to India he designed ceramics inspired by transcendentalism and Oriental forms. In 1968 he was awarded an honorary degree at the Royal College of Art in London. He was an important exponent of the Radical Design movement and in 1973 he contributed to the foundation of Global Tools. The Design Centre of Berlin organized a retrospective exposition of his works in 1976, which was then seen in Venice, Paris, Barcelona, Jerusalem and Sydney. In 1981 he founded the Memphis Group, which lasted until 1985; it included young, recently graduated designers and defending anti-design it proposed furniture and decorative objects based on geometry and colour contrasts. The Sottsass Associati studio has created many architectural projects on an international level. Apart from architecture he has always enjoyed creating furnishing accessories and jewels. He was a major exponent of Postmodernism in the 1980s. His work in glass has involved collaborations with SALIR, Toso Vetri d'Arte and Venini.

Daniel Spoerri (1930)
Daniel Spoerri was born in Galati (Romania) in 1930. He fled to Switzerland in 1941 as a victim of Nazi persecution. An eclectic, after many jobs and travels throughout Europe Spoerri began to work as a ballet dancer, an assistant film director, artist and restaurateur. During a brief trip to Paris he met Yves Klein and began his first work, *Pourquoi pas un Tapies?*, a piece of a wall hung on a wall. In 1960 he worked on his *tableaux-piège* (gadget paintings) where objects placed casually on a canvas were pasted there, and the whole then hung on the wall. In 1960 he signed the Nouveaux Réalistes' manifesto. In 1962 he came into contact with Fluxus. In 1970 he created *Eat Art*, an artwork made of edible material. Between 1983 and 1989 he taught at the Academy in Munich. In 1990 the Centre Georges Pompidou gave him an extensive retrospective. Since 1992 he has been living and working in Seggiano, in the Grosseto district.

Mauro Staccioli (1937)
Mauro Staccioli was born in Volterra (Italy) in 1937. His artistic career has developed alongside his intellectual activism. In 1968 Staccioli began concentrating on sculpture marked by straightforward forms and using simple materials such as iron, cement and *pietra serena*. He has created large installations with a minimalist flavour, such as those for the 37th and 38th editions of the Venice Biennale, following the theory that "creating sculpture means existing in a place." In the 1990s Staccioli shifted to a more unusual design concept expressed in large-scale steel solids suspended in space, sunken in the earth, hanging on a wall or laid delicately on stairs. At the end of the 1980s he travelled to California and South Korea. His solo shows have included one at the Museum of Contemporary Arts in La Jolla (San Diego) in 1987, at the Museo d'Arte Contemporanea in Bolzano in 1995 and at the Museo Su logu de s'iscultura at Tortolì (Nuoro) in 1995. In recent years, the clean sharp lines of his works have been softened by curves. He lives and works in Milan.

Marialuisa Tadei (1964)
Marialuisa Tadei was born in Rimini (Italy) in 1964. After obtaining a diploma from the Accademia di Belle Arti in Bologna and graduating from DAMS, Tadei undertook a Masters at the Domus Academy in Milan and obtained a post-degree diploma at Goldsmiths College at London University. Although she has been working for a few years only, she has made her mark as a sculptor among the new generations in the Italian art scene. As she herself has said: "I think night time is the most creative time. Perhaps because when we sleep we are more relaxed, and when the mind is less vigilant, the subconscious can flow more freely." The artist has had solo shows at the Museum und Galerie im Prediger, Schwäbisch Gmünd in Germany (2002) and at Santa Maria delle Croci, Ravenna (2001). She lives in Rimini, Milan and London.

Lino Tagliapietra (1934)
Lino Tagliapietra was born in Murano (Italy) in 1934 and joined Archimede Seguso's glassworks as a *garzon* (apprentice) in 1945; this early experience had a lasting effect on his taste. He moved to the Galliano Ferro glassworks in 1956 and soon became a glass master. After a short period at the Venini glassworks (1966-67) he became *primo maestro* at La Murrina where he created his first designs. Between 1976 and 1989 he was *primo maestro* and artistic director at the Effetre International glassworks, where he had the opportunity of experimenting interesting new techniques and models. Around 1989 he collaborated for a short period with the EOS glassworks. From 1989 he began his personal activity as an independent glass master which guaranteed him the total creative freedom that enabled him to reach international fame. From 1979 he began teaching in the USA and all over the world. He has won numerous international prizes and is the most noted artist from Murano today. His technique in making traditional Venetian glass is very refined and he has developed completely new effects, boldly seeking new polychrome textures with daring forms and unusual dimensions. His example is followed in Murano and all over the world.

Toso, glassworks
In 1854 the brothers Angelo, Carlo, Giovanni, Gregorio, Ferdinando and Liberale Toso, sons of Pietro Toso, founded the Fratelli Toso glassworks for the production of common glass, the production of artistic glass was soon added to their activities with traditional models and particularly chandeliers. The firm was composed of family members in all the important positions without any dominating personality. The family characteristic of the company continued into the 20th century. In the 19th century they produced mostly blown glass in the renaissance and baroque styles, always executed in superb style, but inspiration was also taken from archaeological pieces. Around 1900 they produced goblets, decorative pieces, floral chandeliers, later they devoted a large part of their production to *murrine*. Their production followed the various styles of the successive decades, but in 1936 when Ermanno Toso joined the company, production was modernized and the company's style became more pronounced.

Antonio Trotta (1938)
Antonio Trotta was born in Stio Cilento (Salerno, Italy), and lived in Argentina between 1948 and 1968. When he returned to Italy, he settled in Milan and began creating sculptures having a simple structure and a minimalist feel. International recognition came with the Venice Biennale in 1968; in the Argentine pavilion the artist created a spatial environment inspired by the work of Fontana. Throughout his working life the artist has explored the qualities of many materials, including marble, bronze, crystal, glass, and mirrors, perfecting the technique of sculpture and attaining very refined levels of illusionism. In the mid 1970s he turned to Conceptualism, using video and photography also. His solo shows have included one at the PAC in Milan in 1990, one at the Galleria d'Arte Contemporanea in San Marino in 1998 and at the Torre Viscontea in Lecco in 1999. In addition to the 1968 Venice Biennale he participated in the 1976, 1978 and 1990 editions. The artist lives and works in Milan and Pietrasanta.

Bertil Vallien (1938)
Bertil Vallien was born in Stockholm (Sweden) in 1938 and studied art and industrial design at the National School of Art, Crafts and Design in Stockholm from 1956 to 1961. From 1961 to 1963 he studied on a scholarship in the USA and Mexico. He was in charge of the glass programme of the National School of Art, Crafts and Design in Stockholm from 1967 to 1984. Since 1974 he has lectured in art schools all over the world. On his return from America, Bertil Vallien signed a contract with the Åfors glass works of the Kosta Boda group whereby he worked for six months in their factory and had the other six months of the year to devote to his artistic output. Therefore he designed functional glass pieces and experimented on unique pieces and blown glass decorated by sand blasting. He created mould-blown vases and bottles of sculpture-like form, which were mostly unique pieces. He has been working now for some time in this double role of designer and freelance artist. During the 1960s he experimented within Åfors on new techniques and the modification of existing techniques which have led to the creation of the so-called *Artists Collection*, where each piece though being part of a series still had individual characteristics. Also during the 1960s he experimented with glass blowing in sand moulds, first in the USA and then at Åfors, unique pieces that were subsequently engraved by sand blasting. It was only in the 1980s that he used sand moulds for melting solid glass, which, from that moment on, gave his work a decisive sculptural imprint. He is the best-known contemporary Swedish glass artist and is the leader of an international school.

Giorgio Vigna (1955)
Giorgio Vigna was born in Verona (Italy) in 1955. After completing his studies in 1975 he worked as a costume designer, stage designer and director in theatre. From 1982 he designed and created jewels for opera, film and theatre. Between 1984 and 1986 he experimented with engraving techniques at the Laboratorio della Calcografia Nazionale in Rome, and at the same time he created jewels and body sculpture. From 1989 to 1996 he has conceived a series of special collections of jewels for stylists in Europe and the USA. In 1997 he began to collaborate with Venini creating vases and jewels in glass for the collection *Stilla, Fonte, Sasso*. He has taught at the European Design Institute in Milan, at the Domus Academy of Milano, and at the Wetterhoff Polytechnic, Finland, where he has organized a workshop on glass jewelry. In 1992 an exhibition devoted to his work was held at the Museo di Arte Contemporanea Luigi Pecci, in Prato, Florence. He exhibits in galleries and museums. His love for different materials is wide ranged; he likes to explore the potentials of traditional techniques and is a tireless researcher. At present he is working on an amusing and provoking project on objects that adorn the body.

Wilhelm Wagenfeld (1900-1990)
Wilhelm Wagenfeld was born in 1990 in Bremen (Germany) where he was an apprentice silversmith and attended the Kunstgewerbeschule. He studied in Hainau, and then took a preparatory course at the Bauhaus in Weimar, specializing in the metals section and was a co-designer of the famous *Bauhaus Lamp* that was then mass-produced. In 1927 he began to work as an independent designer in industrial design and created some objects for domestic usage. The following year he became director of the metals laboratory of Bauhochschule. Always in connection with Bauhaus he refused the theoretic doctrine of the school considering it to be too theoretical, but still agreed that functionality was an essential requisite for good design. From 1929 he worked as an independent designer for Schott & Gen glassworks in Jena. In 1931 he was appointed professor at the Staatliche Kunsthochschule in Berlin and in 1935 he became artistic director at Vereinigte Lausitzer Glaswerke in Weisswasser. Here he created ideal objects for industrial production. The most famous model was the *Kubus* collection. He also designed ceramics. Having refused to join the Nazi party he was sent to fight on the Russian front. In the post-war years he wrote for specialized magazines, he was professor of industrial design at the Hochschule für Bildende Künste in Berlin, and he designed cutlery and lamps. He opened the Wagenfeld laboratory of industrial design in 1954. Wagenfeld's teachings underlined the moral, social and political obligations of the designer and had a great influence on the following generation of German designers.

Sunny Wang (1972)
Sunny Wang was born in Yun-Lin (Taiwan) in 1972. She attended the School of Commercial Design in Taiwan. She began working with glass at a workshop in Taiwan with Swedish artist Bertil Vallien. After further experience of different glass making techniques, in particular with Australian Stephen Procter, she attended the Australian National University, Canberra School of Art Glass. Sunny Wang is now considered one of the most interesting young artists of the Canberra school.

Tapio Wirkkala (1915-1985)
Tapio Wirkkala was the poet of Finnish glass and lived in Finland and Lapland drawing his inspiration from the natural environment. He was born in Hanko (Finland) and studied at the Central School for Industrial Design in Helsinki, in the department of decorative sculpture from 1933 to 1936. In 1946 he became a designer for Iittala and remained in contact with this company until his death. It was in this period that he created the *Kantarelli* vases, fluid blown-glass forms emphasized by engraved lines, the first in a long series inspired by nature. He also worked with silver and met with great success at the Milan Triennale of 1951, 1954 and 1960 winning the Grand Prix. He opened his studio in 1966. His works were in many different materials like glass, wood and porcelain on an industrial scale and also creating unique pieces or limited series of handmade pieces. If functionality, ennobled by absolutely original forms, prevails in some of his works, he also enjoyed devoting his time to personally creating unique pieces or prototypes created for limited numbers. The Nordic natural environment inspired some of his greatest works in glass and wood, but when he collaborated with the Venini glassworks of Murano he showed how he could understand the Venetian techniques and the soft colours of the lagoon. Though he had many pupils his style cannot be imitated.

Andrea Zilio (1966)
Andrea Zilio was born in Venice (Italy) in 1966 but came very late to working in glass, his early experience being in furniture restoration. He joined the Anfora glassworks and studied under the glass masters Giulio Ferro and Luigi Buratto from whom he learned the traditional glass-making techniques. While being an extraordinarily fine master of antique style pieces, over the last years he has also designed and produced his own works giving a modern interpretation to the techniques of the past. He has taken part in international exhibitions and has now also started teaching.

Gilberto Zorio (1944)
Gilberto Zorio was born in 1944 in Andorno Micca (Vercelli, Italy). He attended the Accademia di Belle Arti in Turin (painting and sculpture) and exhibited for the first time in 1967 at the Galleria Sperone in Turin. He was a part of the Arte Povera group, and participated in all their group shows. His first works looked at language. Following this he became interested in phenomena relating to consumption and the emission of energy, and studied electricity originating from chemical and alchemical processes. In his complex sculptures Zorio has often used fragile materials such as terracotta and Pyrex glass, tending to precariously suspend and balance elements (for example, alembics). The first important shows of his works were held at the Kunstmuseum in Lucerne (1976) and at the Stedelijk Museum in Amsterdam (1979). In 1992, the Centro d'Arte Contemporanea Luigi Pecci in Prato gave him a retrospective, followed by a show at the Musée d'Art Moderne et Contemporain in Nice. The artist lives and works in Turin.

Bibliography

Acciaio Arte Architettura, 2001 = M. Cescon, "Vibrazioni di luce in sospensione," in *Acciaio Arte Architettura*, no. 8, 2001.

Adriani, 1955 = A. Adriani, "Segnalazioni alessandrine," in *Archeologia Classica*, VII, 1955, pp. 124-38.

Alberici, 1976 = C. Alberici, "Vetri e vetrate," in *Grandi collezioni di arte decorativa nel Castello Sforzesco*, Milan 1976.

Almagro, 1952 = M. Almagro, *Las inscripciones Ampuritanas Griegas, Ibéricas y Latinas*, Monografias Amporitanas II, Barcelona 1952.

Alvar ja Aino Aalto, 1988 = Var. Authors, *Alvar ja Aino Aalto lasin muotoilijoina*, exhibition cat., Iittala Glass Museum, 1988.

Angelini, Artioli, Bellintani, Diella, Polla, 2002 = I. Angelini, G. Artioli, P. Bellintani, V. Diella, A. Polla, "Progetto 'I materiali vetrosi nella protostoria dell'Italia del Nord'. Un primo bilancio," in *2° Congresso Nazionale A.I.Ar.* (Bologna, 29 January - 1 February 2002), abstract, vol. 34.

Angelini, Artioli, Bellintani, Diella, Polla, 2002b = I. Angelini, G. Artioli, P. Bellintani, V. Diella, A. Polla, "Chemical analysis of Bronze Age glasses from Frattesina di Rovigo, Northern Italy," in *Journal of Archaeological Science*, 2002.

Antico Polesine = M. De Min, R. Peretto (eds.), *L'antico Polesine. Testimonianze archeologiche e paleoambientali*, cat. of the exhibitions at Adria and Rovigo, Padua 1986.

Aperto Vetro, 1996 = A. Dorigato, D. Klein (eds.), *Venezia Aperto Vetro, International New Glass*, exhibition cat., Venice, Murano (13 September - 10 November 1996), Arsenale, Venice 1996.

Aperto Vetro, 1998 = Var. Authors, *Venezia Aperto Vetro, International New Glass*, exhibition cat., Venice, Murano (16 October 1998 - 16 January 1999), Electa, Milan 1998.

Aperto Vetro, 2000 = M. Romanelli (ed.), *Venezia Aperto Vetro 2000, Il vetro progettato, Architetti e designer a confronto con il vetro quotidiano*, exhibition cat., Museo Correr, Venice (15 October 2000 - 14 January 2001), Electa, Milan 2000.

Arezzo, 1988 = *Gioielli e ornamenti dagli Egizi all'Alto Medioevo*, exhibition cat., Arezzo 1988.

Art du verre à Murano (L'), 1995 = Var. Authors, *L'art du verre à Murano au XXème siècle*, exhibition cat., Passage de Retz, Paris (17 May - 15 June 1995), Grafiche Veneziane, Venice 1995.

Arti a Vienna (Le), 1984 = Var. Authors, *Le Arti a Vienna, dalla Secessione alla caduta dell'Impero Asburgico*, exhibition cat., Palazzo Grassi, Venice (20 May - 16 September 1984), La Biennale di Venezia - Mazzotta, Milan 1984.

Artisti di Venini (Gli), 1996 = A. Bettagno (ed.), *Gli artisti di Venini - Per una storia del vetro d'arte veneziano*, exhibition cat., Fondazione Giorgio Cini, Isola di San Giorgio Maggiore, Venice (24 April - 7 July 1996), Electa, Milan 1996.

Arveiller-Dulong, Arveiller, 1985 = V. Arveiller-Dulong, J. Arveiller, *Le verre d'époque romaine au Musée archéologique de Strasbourg*, Paris 1985.

Arveiller-Dulong, 1996 = V. Arveiller-Dulong, *Les verres antiques*, Musée départemental de l'Oise-Beauvois, Paris 1996.

Arwas, 1987 = V. Arwas, *Glass Art Nouveau and Art Deco*, Academy Editions, London 1987.

Atlante, 1981 = Var. Authors, *Atlante delle forme ceramiche, I: Ceramica fine romana nel bacino del Mediterraneo*, supplement to the *Enciclopedia dell'arte antica, classica e orientale*, Rome 1981.

Auth, 1975 = S. H. Auth, "Ancient Glass from excavations at Salona held from 1968-71," in Christopher Clairmonts, *Excavations at Salona*, Noyes Press 1975, pp. 145-80.

Autriche, Suède et Finlande, 1995 = Var. Authors, *Autriche, Suède et Finlande, les nouvelles frontières du verre européen*, exhibition cat., Musée National d'Histoire et d'Art, Luxembourg (14 October - 26 November 1995), Museum voor Sierkunst, Ghent (15 March - 5 May 1996), Skira, Milan 1995.

Barberi, 1988 = S. Barberi, *Il corpus delle vetrate valdostane: aspetti e problemi*, report to the conference: *I laboratori vetrari lombardi sotto il dominio dei Visconti e degli Sforza*, Milan 1988 (unpublished).

Barkóczi, 1988 = L. Barkóczi, *Pannonische Glasfunde in Ungarn*, Budapest 1988.

Barocelli, 1920 = P. Barocelli, "Aosta. Sepolcreto romano," in *Notizie degli Scavi di Antichità*, fascs. 4, 5 and 6, 1920, pp. 97-8.

Barocelli, 1921 = P. Barocelli, "Notizie di scavi d'Antichità. Aosta. Sepolcreto di età romana," in *Bollettino Società Piemontese di Archeologia e Belle Arti*, 1921, p. 76.

Barocellli, 1923 = P. Barocelli, "L'âge préromain dans la Vallée d'Aoste," in *Augusta Praetoria*, 3-4, pp. 41-8 and 5-7, pp. 89-98.

Barocelli, 1926 = P. Barocelli, "Sepolcri d'età romana scoperti in Piemonte," in *Bollettino Società Piemontese di Archeologia e Belle Arti*, 1926, pp. 91-4.

Barocelli, 1948 = P. Barocelli, *Forme Italiane. Regio XI Transpadana*, vol. I, *Augusta Praetoria*, Rome 1948.

Barovier Mentasti, 1978 = R. Barovier Mentasti (ed.), *Vetri di Murano dell'800*, exhibition cat., Museo Vetrario, Murano (8 July - October 1978), Alfieri Edizioni d'Arte, Venice 1978.

Barovier Mentasti, 1982 = R. Barovier Mentasti, *Il Vetro Veneziano, dal Medioevo al Novecento*, Electa, Milan 1982.

Barovier Mentasti, 1992 = R. Barovier Mentasti, *Vetro Veneziano 1890-1990*, Arsenale, Venice 1992.

Barovier Mentasti, 1994 = R. Barovier Mentasti (ed.), *Vetri veneziani del '900, La collezione della Cassa di Risparmio di Venezia, Biennali 1930-1970*, Marsilio, Venice 1994.

Barovier, 1997 = M. Barovier, *Carlo Scarpa - I vetri di un architetto*, exhibition cat., Palazzo Martinengo, Brescia (15 November 1997 - 15 February 1998), Skira, Milan 1997.

Battuto, 2002 = *Battuto 2002*, exhibition cat., Glas Museet, Ebeltost 2002.

Baume, 1978 = P. la Baume, *Glas der Antiken Welt, 1, Wissenschaftliche Kataloge des Römisch-Germanischen Museums*, Cologne 1978.

Bayer, Waller, 1988 = P. Bayer, M. Waller, *The Art of René Lalique*, London 1988.

Bellintani, 1997 = P. Bellintani, "Frattesina: l'ambra e la produzione vitrea nel contesto delle relazioni transalpine," in Endrizzi, L. Marzatico (eds.), *Ori delle Alpi*, exhibition cat., Trent 1997, pp. 117-29.

Berger, 1960 = L. Berger, *Römische Gläser aus Vindonissa*, Basel 1960 (reprint 1980).

Berlin, 1976 = *Antike Gläser*, exhibition cat., Berlin 1976.

Berndt, 2001 = L. Berndt, "Seguendo la linea giusta: Monica Guggisberg e Philip Baldwin," in *Vetro*, IV, no. 10, January-March, 2001.

Berti, 1993 = F. Berti, "Vetri incisi," in *Ravenna e il porto di Classe - Venti anni di ricerche archeologiche tra Ravenna e Classe*, UPB, Bologna 1993, pp. 191-4.

Bertil Vallien, 1990 = G. Lindqvist, *Bertil Vallien*, Carlsson Bokförlag, Stockholm 1990.

Biaggio Simona, 1991 = S. Biaggio Simona, *I vetri romani provenienti dalle terre dell'attuale Cantone Ticino*, I-II, Locarno 1991.

Bietti Sestieri, 1981 = A. M. Bietti Sestieri, "Lo scavo dell'abitato protostorico di Frattesina di Fratta Polesine (Rovigo). I. La sequenza stratigrafica del quadrato U6," in *Bollettino Paleontologico Italiano*, 1975-80, 1981, pp. 221 *et sqq.*

Boesen, 1960 = G. Boesen, *Venetianske Glas På Rosenborg*, 1960.

Bohemian Glass, 1991 = Var. Authors, *Bohemian Glass, Tradition and Present*, Crystalex, Nový Bor 1991.

Bolla, 2001 = M. Bolla, "Vetri romani," in P. Marini, M. Bolla, D. Modonesi (eds.), *Collezioni restituite ai Musei di Verona*, exhibition cat., Verona 2001, Milan, pp. 32-5.

Bologna, 1959 = R. Pincelli, C. Volpe, G. Gualandi (eds.), *Iridescenze e colori di vetri antichi*, exhibition cat., Bologna 1959.

Bologna, 1964 = *Arte e civiltà romana nell'Italia settentrionale dalla Repubblica alla Tetrarchia*, exhibition cat., Bologna 1964.

Bologna, 1976 = *Pelagio Palagi artista e collezionista*, exhibition cat., Bologna 1976.

Bologna, 1999 = G. Meconcelli Notarianni, D. Ferrari (eds.), *In visita alla mostra... Vetri antichi. Arte e tecnica*, exhibition cat., Bologna 1999.

Bonomi, 1986 = S. Bonomi, "Note su alcuni vetri romani del Basso Polesine," in *Aquileia Nostra*, LVII, 1986, cc. 437-52.

Bonomi, 1996 = S. Bonomi, *Vetri antichi del Museo Archeologico Nazionale di Adria*, in "Corpus delle collezioni archeologiche del vetro nel Veneto," 2, Venice 1996.

Borger, 1977 = H. Borger, *Das Römisch-Germanische Museum in Köln*, Munich 1977.

Bossaglia, 1993 = R. Bossaglia, *I vetri di Fulvio Bianconi*, Umberto Allemandi, Turin 1993.

Brandt *et al.*, 1972 = E. Brandt, A. Krug, W. Gercke, E. Schmidt, *Antike Gemmen in Deutschen Sammlungen. Band I: Staatliche Munzsammlung München -Teil 3: Gemmen und Glaspasten der römischen Kaiserzeit sowie Nachträge*, Munich 1972.

Brecciaroli Taborelli, 1986 = L. Brecciaroli Taborelli, "Tombe del periodo medio-imperiale a Susa (Segusio)," in *Quaderni della Soprintendenza Archeologica del Piemonte*, 5, 1986, pp. 45-66.

Brecciaroli Taborelli, 2000 = L. Brecciaroli Taborelli, with the collaboration of M.C. Preacco Ancona and S.

Salines, *Catalogo delle deposizioni* in *Alle origini di Biella. La necropoli romana*, edited by L. Brecciaroli Taborelli, pp. 155-334, Turin 2000.

Brilliance of Swedish Glass (The), 1996 = Var. Authors, *The Brilliance of Swedish Glass, 1918-1939, An Alliance of Art and Industry*, exhibition cat., Bard Graduate Center for Studies in the Decorative Arts (21 November 1996 - 2 March 1997), Yale University Press, New Haven-London 1996.

Brizio, 1958 = A. M. Brizio, "Le vetrate della Cattedrale e della Collegiata di Sant'Orso di Aosta," in *La Valle d'Aosta*, Proceedings of the XXXI Congresso Storico Subalpino (Aosta 1956), I, Turin 1958, pp. 366-79.

Brunod, 1975 = E. Brunod, *La Cattedrale di Aosta*, Aosta 1975.

Brunod, 1981 = E. Brunod, *Arte sacra in Valle d'Aosta. Diocesi e Comune di Aosta*, Aosta 1981.

Brunod, 1995 = E. Brunod, *Arte sacra in Valle d'Aosta. Alta Valle e valli laterali*, Aosta 1995.

Brunod, Garino, 1996 = E. Brunod, L. Garino, *La Cattedrale di Aosta*, 2, Aosta 1996.

Brusin, 1929 = G. B. Brusin, *Aquileia. Guida storica e artistica*, Udine 1929.

Bühler, 1973 = H. P. Bühler, *Antike Gefässe aus Edelsteinen*, Mainz 1973.

Buljević, 1994 = Z. Buljević, *Kasnoanticko staklo, Salona Christiana*, Artes minores Salonae Christianae, Split 1994, pp. 258-64.

Buora, 1998 = M. Buora, "Le necropoli dell'Istria e della Dalmazia: tra romanizzazione e sopravvivenza di tradizioni locali," in *Trasparenze imperiali. Vetri romani dalla Croazia*, exhibition cat., Milan 1998, pp. 57-61.

Byzance, 1992 = *Byzance. L'art byzantin dans les collections publiques françaises*, exhibition cat., Musée du Louvre, Paris 1992.

Caimi, 1874 = A. Caimi, "Il Museo Patrio di archeologia," in *Archivio Storico Lombardo, Bollettino della Consulta Archeologica del Museo Storico-artistico di Milano*, 1874, pp. 3-10.

Calvi, 1968 = M. C. Calvi, *I vetri romani del Museo di Aquileia*, Aquileia 1968.

Calvi, 1974-75 = M. C. Calvi, "La barchetta vitrea del Museo di Treviso," in *Aquileia Nostra*, XLV-XLVI, 1974-75, cc. 479-86.

Caramella, De Giuli, 1993 = P. Caramella, A. De Giuli, *Archeologia dell'Alto Novarese*, 1993.

Carazzetti, Biaggio Simona, 1988 = R. Carazzetti, S. Biaggio Simona (eds.), *Vetri romani del Canton Ticino*, exhibition cat., Locarno 1988.

Carboni, Whitehouse, 2001 = S. Carboni, D. Whiteouse, with essays by R. H. Brill and W. Gudenrath, *Glass of the Sultans*, exhibition cat., Corning (New York), May-September 2001, New York, October 2001 - January 2002, Athens, February-May 2002.

Carlo Moretti, 1998 = *Carlo Moretti*, catalogue of the firm, 1998.

Carreras Rossell, 1992 = T. Carreras Rossell, "La colección de ungüentarios dobles del Museo Arqueológico de Barcelona," in *Boletín Asociación española de amigos de la arqueología*, 32, 1992, pp. 65-72.

Castelnuovo, 1954 = E. Castelnuovo, "Vitraux de France al Musée des Arts Décoratifs," in *Paragone*, 51, 1954, pp. 38-47.

Castelnuovo, 1958 = E. Castelnuovo, "Vetrate italiane," in *Paragone*, 103, 1958.

Castelnuovo, 1961 = E. Castelnuovo, "Varietà di componenti culturali," in *Tutt'Italia. Piemonte, Valle d'Aosta*, II, Florence-Novara 1961, pp. 629-35.

Catalogo Blu, n.d. = *Catalogo Blu*, catalogue of models, Venini, Murano n.d.

Catalogo Compagnia di Venezia e Murano, n.d. = *Catalogo di disegni della Compagnia di Venezia e Murano*, catalogue, n.d.

Catalogo Fratelli Toso, n.d. = *Catalogo Fratelli Toso*, catalogue, n.d.

Catalogo Salviati & C., n.d. = *Salviati & C.*, catalogue, n.d.

Cermanović-Kuzmanović, 1976 = A. Cermanović-Kuzmanović, "Pregled i razvitak rimskog stakla u Crnoj Gori," in *Arheološki vestnik*, 25, Ljubljana 1976.

Ceselin, 1996 = F. Ceselin, "Vetri romani provenienti dal parmense e da Velleia," in *Diadora*, 18, Zadar 1996.

Charleston, 1984 = R. J. Charleston, *English Glass and the Glass Used in England, c. 400 - 1940*, London 1984.

Cinzano Glass Collection, 1974 = *Cinzano Glass Collection*, catalogue of the collection, Amilcare Pizzi, Milan 1974.

Coarelli, 1963 = F. Coarelli, "Su alcuni vetri dipinti scoperti nella Germania indipendente e sul commercio alessandrino in Occidente nei primi due secoli dell'Impero," in *Archeologia Classica*, XV, 1, 1963, pp. 61-85.

Colivicchi, 1999 = F. Colivicchi, "Il commercio dei vetri ellenistici in Adriatico: la Daunia e il Piceno," in *Atti del 1° Convegno Multidisciplinare "Il vetro in Italia meridionale ed insulare"* (6 Naples - 8 March 1998), Naples 1999, pp. 109-18.

Collezioni Napoli, 1986 = *Le collezioni del Museo Nazionale di Napoli*, I, 1, Rome-Milan 1986.

Colliard, 1979 = L. Colliard, *La Vieille Aoste*, I-II, Aosta 1979.

Colori di Murano (I), 1999 = Var. Authors, *I Colori di Murano nell'800*, Arsenale, Venice 1999.

Colori e trasparenze, 2001 = Var. Authors, *Vetri Veneziani dal Rinascimento all'Ottocento. Colori e trasparenze*, Electa, Naples 2001.

Constable Maxwell, 1979 = *The Constable Maxwell Collection of Ancient Glass*, Sotheby Parker Burnet Sale Catalogue, 4-5 June, London 1979.

Conti, 1983 = R. Conti, *Il Tesoro. Guida alla conoscenza del Tesoro del Duomo di Monza*, Monza 1983.

Conti, 1990 = R. Conti, "Ampolle di Terrasanta," in G. Morello (ed.), *Splendori di Bisanzio. Testimonianze e riflessioni d'arte e cultura bizantina nelle chiese d'Italia*, exhibition cat., Ravenna 1990, Milan 1990, pp. 137-9.

Conti, 1990b = R. Conti, "Ampolline in vetro della Basilica di San Giovanni Battista, Monza," in G.C. Menis (ed.), *I Longobardi*, exhibition cat., Codroipo, Villa Manin di Passariano - Cividale del Friuli 1990, Milan 1990, p. 352.

Conti, 1998 = R. Conti, "Ampolline di Terrasanta," in G. Sena Chiesa (ed.), *Tesori della Postumia. Archeologia e storia intorno a una grande strada romana alle radici dell'Europa*, exhibition cat., Cremona 1998, Milan 1998, p. 653.

Conti, 1999 = R. Conti, "Due ampolline per gli oli santi dei martiri," in M. d'Onofrio (ed.), *Romei e giubilei. Il pellegrinaggio medievale a San Pietro (350-1350)*, exhibition cat., Rome 1999, Milan 1999, p. 349.

Crew, 1988 = H. Crew, "La tombe gallo-romaine de Saintes. Nouvel examen du matériel," in *Anthologie National*, 20, 1988, pp. 35-61.

Curina, 1993 = R. Curina, "Vetri," in *Ravenna e il porto di Classe. Venti anni di ricerche archeologiche tra Ravenna e Classe*, UPB, Bologna 1993, pp. 166-70.

Czechoslovakian Glass, 1980 = Var. Authors, *Czechoslovakian Glass, 1350-1980*, exhibition cat., Corning Museum of Glass, New York (2 May - 1 November 1981), Dover Publications, New York 1981.

Czurda-Ruth, 1979 = B. Czurda-Ruth, *Die römischen Gläser vom Magdalensberg*, Klagenfurt 1979.

Dall'Osso, 1915 = I. Dall'Osso, *Guida illustrata del Museo Nazionale di Ancona*, Ancona 1915.

Damevski, 1976 = V. Damevski, "Pregled tipova staklenog posuda iz italskih, galskih, mediteranskih i porajnskih radionica na području Hrvatske," in *Arheološki vestnik*, 25, Ljubljana 1976, pp. 62-87.

Darder, 1988 = M. Darder, *Noms d'aurigues i de gladiadors en dos peces de vidre d'Empúries, Espacio, Tiempo y Forma*, series II, Historia Antigua I, 1988.

Davidson, 1952 = G. R. Davidson, *The Minor Objects, Corinth XII*, Princeton 1952.

Davidson Weinberg, 1962 = G. Davidson Weinberg, "An Inlaid Glass Plate in Athens," in *Journal of Glass Studies*, 4, 1962, pp. 29-36.

Davidson Weinberg, 1973 = G. Davidson Weinberg, "Notes on Glass from Upper Galilee," in *Journal of Glass Studies*, 15, 1973, pp. 35-51.

De Bersa, 1913 = *Guida del museo di S. Donato in Zara*, archeological section edited by G. De Bersa, I.R. Austrian Archeological Institute, Vienna 1913.

Deboni, 1996 = F. Deboni, *Murano '900*, Bocca, Milan 1996.

De Carolis, 1997 = E. De Carolis, "La pittura popolare," in *Pompei. Picta Fragmenta*, Turin 1997, pp. 55-60.

Dell'Acqua, Silva, 2002 = F. Dell'Acqua, R. Silva (eds.), *Il colore nel Medioevo. Arte simbolo tecnica*, Lucca 2002.

De Maine, 1983 = M. R. De Maine, "Ancient Glass Distribution in Illyricum," in *Journal of Glass Studies*, 25, 1983, pp. 79-86.

De Marinis, 1986 = R. De Marinis, "Le necropoli" in *Gli Etruschi a nord del Po*, exhibition cat., I, Mantua 1986, pp. 288-99.

De Marinis, 1986b = R. De Marinis, "L'età gallica in Lombardia (IV-I sec. a.C.): risultati delle ultime ricerche e problemi aperti," in *La Lombardia tra protostoria e romanità. Atti del 2° Convegno archeologico regionale*, Como 1986, pp. 93-152.

De Tommaso, 1986 = G. De Tommaso, "Ipotesi sulla produzione di vasellame vitreo in Italia tra il III e il IV secolo," in *Opus*, V, 1986, pp. 111-25.

De Tommaso, 1990 = G. De Tommaso, *Ampullae vitreae. Contenitori in vetro di unguenti e sostanze aromatiche dell'Italia romana (I sec. a.C. - III sec. d.C.)*, Rome 1990.

De Tommaso, 1999 = G. De Tommaso, "Gli strumenti del gioco," in B. Massabò (ed.), *Magiche trasparenze, i vetri dell'antica Albingaunum*, Milan 1999, pp. 142-4.

Dolino, 2001 = E. Dolino, "Le vetrate," in B. Orlandoni, E. Rossetti Brezzi (eds.), *Sant'Orso di Aosta. Il complesso monumentale*, Aosta 2001, pp. 205-18.

Donati, 1987 = P. Donati, "Ascona. La necropoli romana," in *Quaderni d'informazione*, 12, Bellinzona 1987.

Doppelfeld, 1966 = O. Doppelfeld, *Römisches und fränkisches Glas in Köln*, Cologne 1966.

Dorigato, 1983 = A. Dorigato, *Il vetro a tavola ieri e oggi*, exhibition cat., Museo Vetrario, Murano (July 1983), 1983.

Dorigato, 1989 = A. Dorigato (ed.), *Ercole Barovier 1889 - 1974, vetraio muranese*, exhibition cat., Museo Correr, Venice (October-November 1989), Marsilio, Venice 1989.

Drahotová, 2000 = O. Drahotová, "Bohemian Glass Development Until 1945," in *Glass Style*, III, no. 2, 2000.

Ducati, 1929 = P. Ducati, "Vetri dorati romani nel Museo Civico di Bologna," in *Rivista dell'Istituto di Archeologia e Storia dell'Arte*, I, 1929, pp. 232-48.

Dusembery, 1971 = E. B. Dusembery, "Ancient Glass in the Collections of Wheaton College," in *Journal of Glass Studies*, XIII, Corning (New York) 1971, pp. 9-33.

Eisen, 1927 = G. A. Eisen, *Glass, Its Origin, History, Chronology, Technique and Classification to the Sixteenth Century*, New York 1927.

European Glass, 1994 = Var. Authors, *European Glass in Use*, exhibition cat., Finnish Glass Museum, Riihimäki 1994.

Eva Moosbrugger, 1999 = Var. Authors, *Eva Moosbrugger Sculpture in Glass*, Hämmerle Druck Quintessence, Hohenems 1999.

Evison, 1983 = E. I. Evison, *Bichrome Glass Vessels of the Seventh and Eighth Centuries*, Studien zur Sachsenforschung 3, 1983, pp. 7-21.

Fabre, Mayer, Rodà, 2002 = G. Fabre, M. Mayer, I. Rodà, *Inscriptions romaines de Catalogne* V. *Supplementum* I-IV *et instrumentum*, 2002.

Facchini, 1995 = G. M. Facchini, *Vetri in Angera romana - Scavi nell'abitato 1980-1985*, edited by Sena Chiesa and Lavizzari Pedrazzini, Rome 1995, II, pp. 217-24.

Facchini, 1995b = G. M. Facchini, "Studio di una forma vitrea di età romana: la merkurflasche (forma Isings 84)," in *Postumia*, VI, no. 6, 1995, pp. 150-73.

Facchini, 1998 = G. M. Facchini, "Vetri romani della prima e media età imperiale," in L. Mercando (ed.), *Archeologia in Piemonte. L'età romana*, Turin 1998, pp. 265-70.

Facchini, 1999 = G. M. Facchini, *Vetri antichi del Museo archeologico al Teatro Romano di Verona e di altre collezioni Veronesi*, in *Corpus delle collezioni archeologiche del vetro nel Veneto*, 5, Venice 1999.

Fadić, 1986 = I. Fadić, *Antićko staklo Argyruntuma*, Zadar 1986, pp. 1-56.

Fadić, 1988 = I. Fadić, "Antićko staklo Asserije iz Arheološkog muzeja u Splitu, Benkovaški kraj kroz vjekove," in *Zbornik*, 2, Benkovac 1988, pp. 27-70.

Fadić, 1989 = I. Fadić, *Antićko staklo Argyruntuma*, Zadar 1989, pp. 1-44.

Fadić, 1998 = I. Fadić, "Invenzione, produzione e tecniche antiche di lavorazione del vetro," in *Trasparenze imperiali. Vetri romani dalla Croazia*, exhibition cat., Milan 1998, pp. 75-92.

Felice, 1931 = C. A. Felice, "I vetri alla Triennale di Monza," in *Dedalo*, XI, 1931.

Fiell, 2001 = C. Fiell, P. Fiell, *Design del XX secolo*, Taschen, Cologne 2001.

Filippi, 1987 = F. Filippi, "Un recupero di materiali archeologici a contesto funerario a Cavour (To) Forum Vibii Caburnum," in *Quaderni della Soprintendenza Archeologica del Piemonte*, 6, 1987, pp. 159-90.

Filippi, 1997 = F. Filippi, "La documentazione archeologica suburbana," in *Alba Pompeia*, Alba 1997, pp. 258-93.

Finnish Glass, 1993 = Var. Authors, *Nuutajärvi 200 Years of Finnish Glass*, Oy Hackman Ab, Tampere 1993.

Finnish Post-war Glass, 1996 = J. Dawson, *Finnish Post-war Glass: 1945-1996*, University of Sunderland, School of Arts, Design and Communications, Sunderland 1996.

Finocchi, 1959 = S. Finocchi, "Scavi e scoperte nel territorio di Aosta," in *Cisalpina*, 1959, pp. 103-15.

Finocchi, 1959b = S. Finocchi, "Note di protostoria valdostana," in *Relazioni e comunicazioni presentate al XXXI Congresso Storico Subalpino*, vol. I, 1959, pp. 53-61.

Fitzwilliam Museum, 1978 = J. D. Bourriau, J. E. A. Liversidge, R. V. Nicholls, "The Ancient World," in *Glass at the Fitzwilliam Museum*, Cambridge 1978.

Fleming, 1999 = S. Fleming, *Roman Glass. Reflections on Cultural Change*, Philadelphia 1999.

Fogolari, Scarfì, 1970 = G. Fogolari, B. M. Scarfì, *Adria antica*, Venice 1970.

Follmann-Schulz, 1992 = B. Follmann-Schulz, *Die römischen Gläser im Rheinischen Landesmuseum Bonn*, Bonn 1992.

Forlati, Mariacher, 1963 = B. Forlati, G. Mariacher, "I vetri antichi del Museo di Zara depositati al Correr," in *Bollettino dei Musei Civici Veneziani*, VIII, 1, 1963, pp. 8-20.

Fortuna Canivet, 1969 = M. T. Fortuna Canivet, "I vetri di Cornus conservati al Museo di Cagliari," in *Journal of Glass Studies*, 11, 1969, pp. 19-26.

Foy, 1977-80 = D. Foy, "Notes sur quelques découvertes de verres dans le Sud-Est de La France," in *Bulletin de l'Association Internationale pour l'Histoire du Verre*, 8, Liège 1977-80, pp. 211-17.

Frantz, 1989 = S. K. Frantz, *Contemporary Glass, A World Survey from the Corning Museum of Glass*, Harry N. Abrams, Inc., New York 1989.

Frazer, 1989 = M. Frazer, "Oreficerie altomedievali," in R. Conti (ed.), *Il Duomo di Monza. I Tesori*, Milan 1989, pp. 15-48.

Fremersdorf, 1933 = F. Fremersdorf, *Der römische Gutshof in Köln-Müngersdorf*, Römisch-Germanische Forschungen 6, Berlin-Leipzig 1933.

Fremersdorf, 1937 = F. Fremersdorf, *Inschriften auf Römischen Kleingerät aus Köln*, Bericht der Römisch-Germanischen Kommission, 27, 1937, pp. 32-50.

Fremersdorf, 1939 = F. Fremersdorf, *Römische Gläser aus Köln. Museum und Öffentlichkeit*, Heft 7, Cologne 1928, 2. Auflage, Cologne 1939.

Fremersdorf, 1939b = F. Fremersdorf, "Erzeugnisse Kölner Manufakturen in den Funden von Kastell Saalburg und Zugmantel," in *Saalburg-Jahrbuch*, 9, 1939, pp. 6-22, pls. 5-18.

Fremersdorf, 1955 = F. Fremersdorf, "Aus der Tätigkeit des Römisch-Germanischen Museums Köln," in *Kölner Jahrbuch für Vor- und Frühgeschichte*, 1, 1955, pp. 117-23.

Fremersdorf, 1958 = F. Fremersdorf, *Römisches Buntglas in Köln*. Die Denkmäler des römischen Cologne 3, Cologne 1958.

Fremersdorf, 1958b = F. Fremersdorf, *Das naturfarbene sogenannte blaugrüne Glas in Köln*, Die Denkmäler des römischen Cologne 4, Cologne 1958.

Fremersdorf, 1959 = F. Fremersdorf, "Römische Gläser mit Fadenauflage," in *Cologne. Schlangenfadengläser und Verwandtes*, Die Denkmäler des römischen Cologne 5, Cologne 1959.

Fremersdorf, 1961 = F. Fremersdorf, *Römisches geformtes Glas in Köln*, Die Denkmäler des römischen Cologne 6, Cologne 1961.

Fremersdorf, 1962 = F. Fremersdorf, *Die römischen Gläser mit aufgelegten Gocce*, Die Denkmäler des römischen Cologne 7, Cologne 1962.

Fremersdorf, 1965-66 = F. Fremersdorf, "Die Anfänge der römischen Glashütten Kölns," in *Kölner Jahrbuch für Vor- und Frühgeschichte*, 8, 1965-66.

Fremersdorf, Polóny Fremersdorf, 1984 = F. Fremersdorf, E. Polóny Fremersdorf, *Die farblosen Gläser der Frühzeiten Köln, II und III Jahrhundert*, Die Denkmäler des römischen Cologne 4, Cologne 1984.

Friedhoff, 1989 = U. Friedhoff, "Beigaben aus Glas in Köpergräbern des Späten 3. und des 4. Jahrhunderts: Ein Indiz für den Sozialen Status des Bestatteten?" in *Kölner Jahrbuch für Vor- und Frühgeschichte*, 22, Berlin 1989, pp. 37-48.

Froehner, 1879 = W. Froehner, *La Verrerie antique: Description de la collection Charvet*, Le Pecq, J. Charvet, Château 1879.

Froehner, 1903 = W. Froehner, *La Verrerie antique. Collection Jules Gréau*, Paris 1903.

Frontini, 1986 = P. Frontini, "Vasetti e perle di vetro policromo," in *Gli Etruschi a nord del Po*, exhibition cat., I, Mantua 1986, pp. 236-7.

Frova, 1971 = A. Frova, "Vetri romani con marchi," in *Journal of Glass Studies*, 13, Corning (New York) 1971, pp. 38-44.

Fusion, 1999 = Var. Authors, *Fusion, Giovani designer nella tradizione del vetro muranese*, exhibition cat., Openspace, Milan (16 April - 9 May 1999), Commune of Milan, Milan 1999.

Gabrielli, 1958 = N. Gabrielli, "L'arte nella Valle d'Aosta," in *La Valle d'Aosta*, Proceedings of the XXXI Congresso Storico Subalpino (Aosta 1956), I, Turin 1958, pp. 393-421.

Gabucci, 1997 = A. Gabucci, "Vetri: la mensa, la dispensa, gli unguenti e i giochi," in F. Filippi (ed.), *Alba Pompeia*, 1997, pp. 465-83.

Gabucci, 2000 = A. Gabucci, "Alcune considerazioni sui balsamari e il vasellame in vetro," in Brecciaroli Taborelli (ed.), *Alle origini di Biella. La necropoli romana*, Turin 2000, pp. 93-104.

Gaetano Pesce, 1992 = Var. Authors, *Gaetano Pesce, Cinq techniques pour le verre/Experience au CIRVA*, exhibition cat., Chapelle, Centre de La Vieille Charité, Marseilles (3 October 1992 - 17 January 1993), Musées de Marseilles, Marseilles 1992.

Gallo, 1967 = R. Gallo, *Il Tesoro di San Marco e la sua storia*, Florence 1967.

Gasparri, 1975 = C. Gasparri, "A proposito di un recente studio sui vasi antichi in pietra dura," in *Archeologia Classica*, XXVII, 2, 1975, pp. 350-77.

Gasparri, 1979 = C. Gasparri, "Vasi antichi in pietra dura a Firenze e a Roma," in *Prospettiva*, 19, 1979, pp. 4-13.

Gebhard, 1989 = R. Gebhard, "Le verre à Manching: données nouvelles et apport des analyses," in *Le verre préromain*, 1989, p. 99.

Glass from the Ancient, 1957 = *Glass from the Ancient World. The Ray Winfield Smith Collection. A special exhibition. 1957*, Corning Museum of Glass, Corning (New York) 1957.

Glass Objects = *Venini - Glass Objects 1994-1995*, sales catalogue, Venini Spa, Murano, Venice.

Glass Sunny Wang, 2001 = Var. Authors, *Please Touch: Chinese Character-Drawing in Glass Sunny Wang*, exhibition cat., Drill Hall Gallery, Canberra 2001.

Global Art Glass, 1999 = Var. Authors, *Global Art Glass Triennial*, exhibition cat., Borgholms Slott, Sweden (19 June - 29 August 1999), Ölandstryckarna AB, Borgholm.

Goethert-Polaschek, 1977 = K. Goethert-Polaschek, *Katalog der römischen Gläser der Rheinischen Landesmuseums Trier*, Mainz 1977.

Goldstein, 1979 = S. M. Goldstein, *Pre-Roman and Early Roman Glass in the Corning Museum of Glass*, Corning (New York) 1979.

Gorini, Parise Labadessa, Saccocci, 1991 = G. Gorini, R. Parise Labadessa, A. Saccocci, *A testa o croce. Immagini d'arte nelle monete e nelle medaglie del Rinascimento. Esempi dalle collezioni del Museo Bottacin*, Padua 1991.

Grabar, 1984 = A. Grabar, "Calici bizantini e patene bizantine-medievali," in *Il Tesoro di San Marco*, work directed by H. R. Hahnloser, II, 1984.

Grandi vetri (I), 1998 = Var. Authors, *I grandi vetri - Sculture e disegni*, exhibition cat., Loggia del Palazzo della Ragione, Biblioteca Angelo Mai, Bergamo (8 March - 13 April 1998), Mazzotta, Milan 1998.

Grose, 1983 = D. F. Grose, "The Formation of the Roman Glass Industry," in *Archaeology*, 36, 4, 1983, pp. 38-45.

Grose, 1984 = D. F. Grose, "Glass Forming Methods in Classical Antiquity: Some Considerations," in *Journal of Glass Studies*, 26, 1984, pp. 25-34.

Grose, 1989 = D. F. Grose, *Early Ancient Glass: Core Formed, Rod-Formed, and Cast Vessels and Objects from the Late Bronze Age to the Early Roman Empire, 1600 B.C. to A.D. 50*, The Toledo Museum of Art, 1989.
Gudiol Ricart, 1941 = J. Gudiol Ricart, *Els vidres Catalans. Monumenta Cataloniae* III, Barcelona 1941.

Haberey, 1942 = W. Haberey, *Spätantike Gläser aus Gräbern von Mayen*, BJb 147, 1942, pp. 249-284, pls. 28-40.
Hackin, 1939 = J. Hackin, *Nouvelles recherches archéologiques à Bégram*, Mémoires de la Délégation Archéologique Française en Afghanistan 9, Paris 1939.
Hackin, 1954 = J. Hackin, *Nouvelles recherches archéologiques à Bégram, ancienne Kâpîci (1939-1940)*, Mémoires de la Délégation Archéologique Française en Afghanistan 11, Paris 1954.
Haevernick, 1960 = E. Haevernick, *Die Glas-Armringe und Ringperlen der Mittel- und Spätaltenzeit auf dem Europäischen Festland*, Bonn 1960.
Haevernick, Pfeffer, 1958 = E. Haevernick, W. Van Pfeffer, "Zarterippenschalen," in *Saalbyb*, 17, 1958, pp. 76-91.
Hagen, 1906 = J. Hagen, "Ausgewählte römische Gräber aus Köln," in *Bonner Jahrbücher des Rheinischen Landesmuseums in Bonn*, 114/115, 1906, pp. 379-434.
Harden, 1935 = D. B. Harden, "Romano-Syrian Glasses with Mould-Blown Inscriptions," in *Journal of Roman Studies*, XXV, 1935, pp. 163-86.
Harden, 1936 = D. B. Harden, "Roman Glass from Karanis Found by the University of Michigan Archeological Expedition in Egypt 1924-1929," in *University of Michigan Studies, Humanistic Series*, 41, Ann Arbor 1936.
Harden, 1944-45 = D. B. Harden, *Two Tomb Groups of First Century Date from Yahmour, Syria, and a Supplement to the List of Romano-Syrian Glasses with Mould-blown Inscriptions*, Syria 24, 1944-45, 81-95, 291-92.
Harden, 1956 = D. B. Harden, "Glass and Glazes," in C. Singer *et al.*, *A History of Technology*, 2, Oxford 1956, pp. 311-46.
Harden, 1956b = D. B. Harden, "Glass Vessels in Britain AD 400 - 1100," in *Dark Age Britain*, London 1956.
Harden, 1968 = D. B. Harden, "The Canosa Group of Hellenistic Glasses in the British Museum," in *Journal of Glass Studies*, 10, 1968, pp. 21-47.
Harden, 1981 = D. B. Harden, *Catalogue of Greek and Roman Glass in the British Museum, Vol. 1. Core and Rod-Formed Vessels and Pendants and Mycenean Cast Objects*, London 1981.
Harden, 1988 = D. B. Harden, *Vetri dei Cesari*, exhibition cat., Cologne-Corning-London, Milan 1988.
Harden, Price, 1971 = D. B. Harden, A. J. Price, *The Glass*, edited by B. Cunliffe, in *Excavations at Fishbourne 1961-1969, II, The Finds*, Reports of the Research Committee of the Society of Antiquaries 27, London 1971, pp. 317-68.
Harden, Toynbee, 1959 = D. B. Harden, J. M. C. Toynbee, "The Rothschild Lycurgus Cup," in *Archaeologia*, 97, 1959, pp. 179-212, pls. 59-75.
Haupt, 1976 = D. Haupt, "Blauer Glaskrater aus Bonn," in T. E. Haevernick, A. V. Saldern (eds.), *Scritti in onore di W. Haberey*, Mainz 1976, pp. 51-57, Farbtaf. A, pls. 14-17.
Hayes, 1975 = J. W. Hayes, *Roman and Pre-Roman Glass in the Royal Ontario Museum*, Toronto 1975.
Heikamp, 1986 = D. Heikamp, *Studien zur Mediceischen Glaskunst*, L. S. Olschki, Florence 1986.
Henderson, Towle, Bellintani, Gambacurta, 2001 = J. Henderson, A. Towle, P. Bellintani, G. Gambacurta, "Frattesina and Beyond Part I: Preliminary Report of Scientific Analyses of Early Glass from the Veneto," in *Padusa*, XXXVII, 2001.
Hilschenz, 1973 = H. Hilschenz, *Das Glas des Jugendstils, Katalog der Sammlung Hentrich im Kunstmuseum, Düsseldorf*, Prestel-Verlag, Munich 1973.
Hilschenz-Mlynek, Ricke, 1985 = H. Hilschenz-Mlynek, H. Ricke, *Glas, Historismus, Jugendstil, Art Déco*, Prestel-Verlag, Munich 1985.
Homo Faber, 1999 = A. Ciarallo, E. De Carolis (eds.), *Homo Faber. Natura, scienza e tecnica nell'antica Pompei*, exhibition cat., Milan 1999.
Hot glass, Cold glass, 2001 = Var. Authors, *Hot glass, Cold Glass, Monica Guggisberg & Philip Baldwin - Glass Artists - Switzerland*, exhibition cat., Eretz Israel Museum, Tel Aviv (winter 2001), Tel Aviv 2001.

Ibrahim, Scranton, Brill, 1976 = L. Ibrahim, R. Scranton, R. Brill, *Kenchreal, Eastern Port of Corinth, II, The Panels of Opus Sectile in Glass*, Leiden 1976.
Isings, 1957 = C. Isings, *Roman Glass from Dated Finds*, Groningen-Djakarta 1957.
Isings, 1971 = C. Isings, *Roman Glass in Limburg*, 9, Groningen-Djakarta 1971.
Israeli *et al.*, 2001 = Y. Israeli *et al.*, *Ancient Glass in the Israel Museum*, Israel Museum, Jerusalem 2001.
Italienisches Glas, 1996 = H. Ricke, E. Schmitt, *Italienisches Glas, Murano-Mailand 1930-1970*, exhibition cat., Kunstmuseum Düsseldorf im Ehrenhof, Glasmuseum Hentrich (10 November 1996 - 26 January 1997), Prestel-Verlag, Munich 1996.

Kaene, 1990 = G. Kaenel, "Recherches sur la période de la Tène en Suisse occidentale. Analyse des sépoltures," in *Cahiers d'Archéologie romande*, 50, Lausanne 1990.
Kaenel, Peyer, 1986 = G. Kaenel, S. Peyer, *L'âge du Fer - Le Valais avant l'histoire*, Sion 1986.
Kangas, 2000 = M. Kangas, "A New Paradigm," in *Glass*, no. 80, autumn 2000.
Kirigin, 1984 = B. Kirigin, "Roman Glass Bowls from the Archaeological Museum at Split," in *Vjesnik za arheologiju I historiju dalmatinsku*, 77, Split 1984, pp. 121-31.
Kisa, 1908 = A. Kisa, *Das Glas im Altertum*, I-III, Leipzig 1908.
Klausen Nottmeyer, 1995 = B. Klausen Nottmeyer, *Eulogien - Transport und Weitergabe von Segenskraft*, Proceedings of the XII International Congress of Christian Archeology (Bonn, 1991), 2, Vatican-Münster, 1995, pp. 922-7, pls. 125-27.
Klesse, Saldern, 1978 = B. Klesse, A. von Saldern, *500 Jahre Glaskunst*, Sammlung Bieman, Zurich 1978.
Kocsis, 1991 = L. Kocsis, "A Glass Bowl with Engraved Ornament from the Mithraeum in the Legionary Fort at Aquincum (Budapest)," in *Journal of Glass Studies*, 33, 1991, pp. 29-31.
Kolesnik, 1996 = O. O. Kolesnik, "Antićne sklo z Ol'vij u zbirtzi Natzional'nogo muzeju istorij Ukrajni," in *Mir Ol'vii. Tesisy dokladov meždunarodnoj konferentzii, posvjaśćennoj 90-letiju professora L.M. Slavina*, Kiev 1996, p. 134.
Kraskovská, 1981 = L. Kraskovská, "Roman Glass. Vessels from Slovakia," in *Journal of Glass Studies*, 23, 1981, pp. 11-17.
Kunina, 1997 = N. Kunina, *Ancient Glass in the Hermitage collection*, The State Hermitage Arts Publisher, 1997.

Lalique Glass, 1981 = René Lalique et Cie, *Lalique Glass, The Complete Illustrated Catalogue for 1932*, Dover Publications, Mineola (NY) 1981.
Lalique, 1988 = M. C. Lalique (ed.), *Lalique*, Editions Edipop S.A., Geneva 1988.
Lamboglia, 1943 = N. Lamboglia, "Recensione a Ch. Simonett Tessiner Graberfelder," Basel 1941, in *Riv. St. Liguri*, IX, 1943, pp. 163-94.
Lancel, 1967 = S. Lancel, *Verrerie antique de Tipasa*, Paris 1967.
Lanmon, Whitehouse, 1993 = D. P. Lanmon, D. B. Whitehouse, *The Robert Lehman Collection*, The Metropolitan Museum of Art, New York, in association with Princeton University Press, Princeton, Lausanne 1993.
Laura de Santillana, 2001 = A. Dorigato (ed.), *Laura de Santillana Works*, exhibition cat., Museo Correr (31 March - 26 April 2001), Barry Friedman Ltd., New York (8 May - 28 June 2001), Silvana Editoriale, Cinisello Balsamo, Milan 2001.
Laurent, 1868 = P. Laurent, "Découvertes d'antiquités préhistoriques dans la ville d'Aoste," in *Bull. de l'Académie de Saint Anselme*, VI, Aosta 1868, pp. 9-14.
Lembke, 1994 = K. Lembke, *Das Iseum Campense in Rom. Studie über den Isis Kult unter Domitian.* Archäologie und Geschichte, 3, Heidelberg 1994.
Libenský - Brychtová, 2000 = Var. Authors, *Stanislav Libenský, Jaroslava Brychtová, Karolinum 2000*, exhibition cat., Karolinum, Prague, 2000, Tiskárna Didot, spol. s.r.o., Brno 2000.
Libenský - Brychtová, 2002 = Var. Authors, *Libenský - Brychtová, Retrospektiva*, exhibition cat., Prague 2002.
Liefkes, 1997 = R. Liefkes (ed.), *Glass*, V&A Publications, London 1997.
Lierke, 1999 = R. Lierke, *Antike Glastöpferei. Ein vergessenes Kapitel der Glasgeschichte*, Mainz 1999.
Lissia, 1994 = D. Lissia, "Catalogo della Collezione dei vetri del Museo di Asti," in Var. Authors, *Museo Archeologico di Asti: La collezione dei Vetri*, Asti 1994, pp. 88-146.
Lissia, 2000 = D. Lissia, *La collezione dei vetri romani del Museo "G.A. Sanna" di Sassari*, Piedimonte Matese 2000.
Lith, 1988 = S. M. E. von Lith, "Late Roman and early Merovingian Glass from a Settlement site at Maastricht (Dutch South Limburg)," in *Journal of Glass Studies*, 30, 1988, pp. 62-77.
Lith, Randsborg, 1985 = S. M. E. von Lith, K. Randsborg, *Roman Glass in the West: A Social Study*, ROB 1985, pp. 413-82.
London, 1979 = *Catalogue of the Constable Maxwell Collection of Ancient Glass Including a Late Roman Glass Diatretum or Cage-Cup Which Will Be Sold by Auction by Sotheby Parke Bernet and Co., London. Day of Sale, 4th June 1979, 5th June 1979*, London 1979.
London, 1987 = *Sotheby's London. Ancient Glass. Day of Sale Friday 20th November 1987*, London 1987.
Lucerne, 1981 = *3000 Jahre Glaskunst von der Antike bis zum Jugendstil* exhibition cat., Lucerne 1981.

Maaskant-Kleibrink, 1978 = M. Maaskant-Kleibrink, *Catalogue of the Engraved Gems in the Royal Coin Cabinet, The Hague*, The Hague 1978.
Maccabruni, 1983 = C. Maccabruni, *I vetri romani dei Musei civici di Pavia, Lettura di una collezione*, Pavia 1983.
Maccabruni, 1999 = C. Maccabruni, "I vetri di Albenga nella Liguria romana," in B. Massabò (ed.), *Magiche trasparenze. I vetri dell'antica Albingaunum*, Milan 1999, pp. 157-66.
Maestri vetrai creatori, 1995 = R. Barovier Mentasti (ed.), *Maestri vetrai creatori di Murano del '900*, exhibition cat., Palazzo Bellini, Comacchio (17 June - 24 September 1995), Electa, Milan 1995.
Maestri vetrai creatori, 1998 = "Maestri vetrai creatori, Alfredo Barbini," in *Vetro anno 1*, no. 0, June 1998.
Maioli, 1994 = M. G. Maioli, "Cristalli di rocca dal Padovano," in *Studi di Archeologia della X Regio in ricordo di Michele Tombolani*, Rome 1994, pp. 365-71.
Maiuri, 1932 = A. Maiuri, *La casa del Menandro*, Rome 1932.
Mandruzzato, 1997 = L. Mandruzzato, *Importazione e*

produzione di vetro soffiato a stampo nella Regio decima, postgraduate thesis at Trieste University, 1997.

Marcello, 1956 = J. Marcello, *La via Annia alle porte di Altino*, Venice 1956.

Marchini, 1972 = G. Marchini, *Antiquari e collezioni archeologiche dell'Ottocento veronese*, Verona 1972.

Marcilhac, 1989 = F. Marcilhac, *René Lalique*, Les éditions de l'amateur, Paris 1989.

Marconi, 1932 = M. Marconi, "Vetri romani nel museo di Zara," in *Bollettino d'arte*, 26/3, 1932, pp. 33-41.

Mariacher, 1960 = G. Mariacher, *Il vetro soffiato da Roma antica a Venezia*, Milan 1960.

Mariacher, Tamaro Forlati, 1963 = G. Mariacher, B. Tamaro Forlati, "I vetri antichi del Museo di Zara depositati al Correr," in *Bollettino dei Musei Civici Veneziani*, I, Venice 1963, pp. 3-15.

Mariacher, 1966 = G. Mariacher, "Vetri del Museo di Zara restaurati," in *Bollettino dei Musei Civici Veneziani*, XI, 4, 1966, pp. 17-32.

Mariacher, 1983 = G. Mariacher, "Vetri," in *Museo Poldi Pezzoli. Ceramiche - Vetri, Mobili e Arredi*, Milan 1983.

Mariotti, 1988 = V. Mariotti, "Tre corredi dalla necropoli tardo antica di Corso Magenta a Brescia," in *Vetro e Vetri. Preziose iridescenze*, exhibition cat. (Milan Museo Archeologico, 1 November 1998 - 18 April 1999), Milan 1988, pp. 105-10.

Martini, 1990 = Var. Authors, *Bellezza e seduzione nella Roma imperiale*, exhibition cat., Rome 1990.

Marucchi, 1933 = O. Marucchi, *Manuale di archeologia Cristiana*, Rome 1933.

Maslennikov, 1997 = A. A. Maslennikov, *Semejnye sklepy sel'skogo poselenija pozneanticnogo Bospora*, Moscow 1997, pp. 15, 80.

Maslennikov, 2000 = A. A. Maslennikov, "Gruntovye nekropoli sel'skich poselekij Karalarskogo poberež'ja pervich vekov nascej ery," in *Drevnosti Bospora*, no. 3, Moscow 2000, pp. 144-78.

Massimo Micheluzzi, 2000 = *Massimo Micheluzzi, Vetri*, catalogue, texts by R. Barovier Mentasti and L. Berndt, 2000.

Masterpieces, 1968 = D. B. Harden *et al.*, *Masterpieces of Glass*, London 1968.

Meconcelli Notarianni, 1979 = G. Meconcelli Notarianni, *Vetri antichi nelle collezioni del Museo Civico Archeologico di Bologna*, Bologna 1979.

Menninger, 1996 = M. Menninger, *Untersuchungen zu den Gläser und Gipsabgüsse aus dem Fund von Begram (Afghanistan), Würzburg Forschungen zur Altertumskunde*, Würzburg 1996.

Mercando, 1976 = L. Mercando, "L'ellenismo nel Piceno," in *Hellenismus in Mittelitalien. Kolloquium im Göttingen vom 5. bis 9. Juni 1974*, proceedings edited by P. Zanker, Göttingen 1976, vol. I, pp. 161-72.

Merten, 1935 = H. Merten, *Deutsches Glas. Zweitausend Jahre Glasveredelung*, exhibition cat., Darmstadt 1935.

Mieke Groot, 1999 = *Mieke Groot*, exhibition cat., Glas Museum Alter Hof Herding, Coesseld-Lette, 1999.

Migliaccio, 1999 = P. Migliaccio (ed.), *Vetri in tavola, i vetri di Murano per la tavola nell'800*, Arsenale, Venice 1999.

Milano capitale, 1990 = *Milano capitale dell'impero romano 286-402*, exhibition cat., Milan 1990.

Milano meets Canberra, 2001 = *Milano meets Canberra*, exhibition cat., La Scaletta di Vetro, Milan (2 April - 5 May 2001), Milan 2001.

Mille anni, 1982 = Var. Authors, *Mille anni di arte del vetro a Venezia*, Albrizzi, Venice 1982.

Millenium meum, 1999 = Var. Authors, *Timo Sarpaneva, millenium meum*, exhibition cat., Finnish National Opera (18 October 1999 - 29 February 2000), Libtris, Helsinki 1999.

Mirabella Roberti, Tamassia, 1964 = M. Mirabella Roberti, A. M. Tamassia, *Mostra dei vetri romani in Lombardia*, exhibition cat., Milan 1964.

Mirti *et al.*, 1993 = P. Mirti, A. Casoli, L. Appolonia, "Scientific analysis of Roman glass from Augusta Praetoria," in *Archaeometry*, 35, 2, 1993, pp. 225-40.

Miti, Sarni Opes, 2000 = Var. Authors, *Nuova indagine archeologica in località Murecine*, Naples 2000.

Moderne Zeiten, 1998 = U. Laurén, *Moderne Zeiten - Finnisches Glas 1929-1999*, exhibition cat., Karisto Oy, Hämeenlinna 1998.

Mollo Mezzena, 1981 = R. Mollo Mezzena, "Augusta Praetoria e il suo territorio," in *Archeologia in Valle d'Aosta*, Aosta 1981, pp. 63-138.

Mollo Mezzena, 1982 = R. Mollo Mezzena, "Augusta Praetoria. Aggiornamento sulle conoscenze archeologiche della città e del suo territorio," in *Atti del Congresso sul Bimillenario della città di Aosta (Aosta 1975)*, Bordighera 1982, pp. 205-315.

Mollo Mezzena, 1982b = R. Mollo Mezzena, "Il complesso cimiteriale fuori Porta Decumana ad Aosta," in *Atti del V Congresso nazionale di Archeologia Cristiana (Torino, Valle di Susa, Cuneo, Valle d'Aosta, 1979)*, Rome 1982, I, pp. 319-33.

Mollo Mezzena, 1987 = R. Mollo Mezzena, "Primi elementi per lo studio della pietra ollare in Valle d'Aosta," in *La pietra ollare dalla preistoria all'età moderna*, Proceedings of the Conference (Como 1982), Como 1987, pp. 59-114.

Mollo Mezzena, 1992 = R. Mollo Mezzena, "Augusta Praetoria tardoantica. Viabilità e territorio," in *Felix Temporis Reparatio*, Proceedings of the Conference "Milan Capitale dell'Impero Romano" (Milan, 8-11 March 1990), Milan 1992, pp. 273-320.

Mollo Mezzena, 1994 = R. Mollo Mezzena, "Il celtismo in Valle d'Aosta: documentazione archeologica e aspetti culturali," in *Numismatica e Archeologia del Celtismo Padano*, Proceedings of the International Conference (Saint Vincent, 8-9 September 1989), Aosta 1994, pp. 143-192.

Mollo Mezzena, 1995 = R. Mollo Mezzena, "Ritrovamento archeologico a Saint Christophe. Contributo alla conoscenza del territorio in età romana," in *Società e Cultura della Valle d'Aosta tra ottocento e novecento*, Pierre Louis Vescoz, Aosta 1995, pp. 111-27.

Mollo Mezzena, 1997 = R. Mollo Mezzena, "Dal Bronzo Antico all'Alto Medioevo," in L. Endrizzi and F. Marzatico (eds.), *Oro delle Alpi*, exhibition cat., Castello del Buonconsiglio, Trent 1997, pp. 353-69.

Morey, 1959 = C. R. Morey, *The Gold-Glass Collection of the Vatican Library (with additional catalogues of other gold-glass collections)*, Vatican City 1959.

Mori, 1996 = G. Mori, *La Collezione dei Vetri Artistici, Civiche Raccolte d'Arte Applicata - Castello Sforzesco*, Milan 1996.

Morin-Jean, 1922-23 = J. Morin-Jean, *La Verrerie en Gaule sous l'Empire romain*, Paris 1922-23.

Mottola Molfino, 1972 = A. Mottola Molfino, "Mobili, tappeti, tessuti, arazzi, porcellane, vetri," in *Museo Poldi Pezzoli*, Milan 1972.

Museo di Cagliari, 1994 = *I vetri romani del Museo Archeologico Nazionale di Cagliari*, edited by D. Stiaffini and G. Borghetti, Oristano 1994.

Napoleone Martinuzzi, 1992 = M. Barovier (ed.), *Napoleone Martinuzzi, Vetraio del Novecento*, Il Cardo Editore, Venice 1992.

Negro Ponzi Mancini, 1988 = M. M. Negro Ponzi Mancini, "Un vetro policromo romano della necropoli di Testona," in *Quaderni della Soprintendenza Archeologica del Piemonte*, no. 8, 1988, pp. 65-84.

New Look (The), 1991 = L. Jackson, *The New Look, Design in the Fifties*, exhibition cat., Manchester City Art Galleries (13 October 1991 - January 1992), Glasgow Art Gallery and Museum (31 January - 5 April 1992), Thames and Hudson, London 1991.

Niessen, 1911 = S. Loeschke, H. Willers, *Beschreibung römischer Altertümer gesammelt von C. A. Niessen*, 2 vols., Cologne 1911.

Oldknow, 1997 = T. Oldknow, *Richard Marquis: Objects*, Seattle 1997.

Oliver, 1967 = A. Oliver, "Late Hellenistic Glass in the Metropolitan Museum," in *Journal of Glass Studies*, 9, 1967, pp. 13-33.

Oliver, 1984 = A. Oliver, "Early Roman Faceted Glass," in *Journal of Glass Studies*, 26, 1984, pp. 35-8.

Oliver, 2001 = A. Oliver, "A Glass Opus Sectile Panel from Corinth," in *Hesperia*, 70, 2001, pp. 349-63.

Omodeo, 1970 = A. Omodeo, *Bottiglie e bicchieri nel costume italiano*, Görlich, Milan 1970.

Orlandoni, 1996 = B. Orlandoni, *Architettura in Valle d'Aosta. Il Quattrocento*, Ivrea 1996.

Orrefors Gallery '90 = *Orrefors Gallery '90*, sales catalogue, 1990.

Ortalli, 1989 = J. Ortalli, "I monumenti romani," in *Storia illustrata di Rimini*, 4, Milan 1989.

Ortalli, 1998 = J. Ortalli, "Riti, usi e corredi funerari nelle sepolture romane della prima età imperiale in Emilia Romagna (valle del Po)," in *Bestattungssitte und kulturelle Identität* (Xanten 1995), edited by P. Fasold, T. Fischer, H. Von Hesberg, M. Witteyer, *Xantener Berichte*, 7, Xanten 1998, pp. 49-86.

Ortalli, 2000 = J. Ortalli, "Rimini: la domus 'del Chirurgo,'" in M. Marini Calvani (ed.), *Aemilia: La cultura romana in Emilia Romagna dal III secolo a.C. all'età costantiniana*, Venice 2000, pp. 513-26.

Paffgen, 1989 = B. von Paffgen, "Glasbeigaben in Römischen Gräbern bei St.Severin in Köln," in *Kölner Jahrbuch für Vor- und Frühgeschichte*, 22, Berlin 1989, pp. 17-23.

Painter, 1988 = K. Painter, "Navicella," in *Vetro dei Cesari*, exhibition cat., 1988.

Painter, Whitehouse, 1990 = K. Painter, D. Whitehouse, "Early Roman Cameo Glasses," in *Journal of Glass Studies*, 32, 1990, pp. 138-65.

Pannuti, 1983 = U. Pannuti, *Museo Archeologico Nazionale di Napoli. Catalogo della Collezione Glittica*, I, Rome 1983.

Paolucci, 1997 = F. Paolucci, *I vetri incisi dall'Italia settentrionale e dalla Rezia nel periodo medio e tardo imperiale*, Florence 1997.

Paolucci, 1999 = F. Paolucci, "Il vasellame da mensa e da dispensa," in B. Massabò (ed.), *Magiche trasparenze. I vetri dell'antica Albingaunum*, Milan 1999, pp. 55-110.

Pasini, 1886 = A. Pasini, *Il tesoro di San Marco a Venezia*, Venice 1886.

Paškvalin, 1976 = V. Paškvalin, "Antićko staklo s područja Bosne i Hercegovine," in *Arheološki vestnik*, 25, Ljubljana 1976, pp. 109-39.

Pazaurek, von Philippovich, 1976 = G. E. Pazaurek, E. von Philippovich, *Gläser der Empire- und Biedermeierzeit*, Klinkhardt & Biermann, Braunschweig 1976.

Périn, 1972 = P. Périn, "Deux verreries exceptionnelles provenant de la nécropole mérovingienne de Mézières," in *Journal of Glass Studies*, 14, 1972, pp. 67-76.

Petru, 1976 = S. Petru, "Rimsko steklo Slovenije," in *Arheološki vestnik*, 25, Ljubljana 1976.

Phönix Aus Sand Und Asche, 1988 = E. Baumgartner, I. Krueger, *Phönix Aus Sand Und Asche, Glas des Mittelalters*, exhibition cat., Rheinisches Landesmuseum, Bonn (3 May - 24 July 1988), Historisches Museum (26 August - 28 November 1988), Klinkhardt & Biermann, Munich 1988.

Pinder-Wilson, Ezzy, 1976 = R. H. Pinder-Wilson, W. Ezzy, "Glass," in D. Jones, G. Michell, *The Arts of Islam*, exhibition cat., Hayward Gallery, London 1976, pp. 131-44.

Pirina, 1999 = C. Pirina, *Due pannelli della Cattedrale di Aosta: S. Stefano e La Madonna dei garofani*, report deposited in the Archivio Soprintendenza per i Beni e le Attività Culturali della Valle d'Aosta (unpublished), 1999.

Pirzio Biroli Stefanelli, 1984 = L. Pirzio Biroli Stefanelli, "Vasa diatreta: frammenti da Roma," in *Bollettino della Commissione Archeologica Comunale di Roma*, 89, 1, 1984, pp. 35-40.

Pirzio Biroli Stefanelli, 1988 = L. Pirzio Biroli Stefanelli in *Vetri dei Cesari*, exhibition cat., Milan 1988.

Pirzio Biroli Stefanelli, 1989 = L. Pirzio Biroli Stefanelli, "Vetri dei Cesari: breve nota sulla collezione dell'Antiquarium Comunale," in *Bollettino dei Musei Comunali di Roma*, 3 n.s., 1989, pp. 31-41.

Platz-Horster, 1976 = G. Platz-Horster, *Antike Gläser*, exhibition cat., Antikenmuseum Berlin, Staatliche Museen Preußischer Kulturbesitz, Berlin 1976.

Please Touch, 2001 = Var. Authors, *Please Touch: Chinese Character-Drawing in Glass Sunny Wang*, exhibition cat., Drill Hall Gallery, Canberra 2001.

Plesnicar-Gec, 1972 = L. Plesnicar-Gec, "Severno Emonsko Grobisce. Katalogi," in *Monografie 8*, Ljubljana 1972.

Poldi Pezzoli Ceramiche-Vetri, 1983 = Var. Authors, *Musei e Gallerie di Milano, Museo Poldi Pezzoli Ceramiche-Vetri, Mobili e Arredi*, Electa, Milan 1983.

Poppelreuter, 1906 = E. Poppelreuter, "Die römischen Gräber Kölns," in *Bonner Jahrbücher des Rheinischen Landesmuseums in Bonn*, 114/115, 1906, pp. 344-78.

Poppelreuter, 1911 = E. Poppelreuter in *Wallraf-Richartz-Museum der Stadt Köln 1861-1911*, Cologne 1911.

Price, 1987 = J. Price, "Glass vessel production in Southern Iberia in the First and Second Centuries A.D.: a survey of the archeological evidence, in *Journal of Glass Studies*, 29, 1987, pp. 30-9.

Price, 1991 = J. Price, "Decorated Mould-Blown Glass Tablewares in the First Century AD," in *Roman Glass: Two Centuries of Art and Invention*, exhibition cat., London 1991, pp. 56-75.

Primaire 9.9.99 = Var. Authors, *Emmanuel Babled Primaire 9.9.99, Ou microcosme*, exhibition cat., Galerie Clara Scremini, Paris (9 September 1999), Nava Web, Milan 1999.

Prosdocimi, 1981 = A. Prosdocimi, "I monumenti romani di Padova," in *Padova antica. Da comunità paleoveneta a città romano-cristiana*, Trieste 1981, pp. 251-81.

Puklina, 1997 = O. Puklina, "Skljana posudnika z kolektzij V.P. Grin'kivskogo," in *Povidomlennja na muzejnu aukovo-praktinanu konferentziju za pidsumkami roboti 1996*, Kiev 1997, pp. 62-5.

Puklina, 2001 = O. Puklina, "Novye postuplenija antićnogo stekla iz ćastnoj kollektzii v sobraii Natzional'nogo muzeja istorii Ukrainy," in *175 let Kerćenskomu muzeju drevnostej. Materialy meždunardodnoj konferentzij*, Kerch 2001, pp. 138-9.

Quattrocchi Pisano, 1977 = G. Quattrocchi Pisano, "Un gruppo di vasetti in vetro policromo," in *Notizie dal Chiostro del Monastero Maggiore. Rassegna di studi del Civico Museo Archeologico e del Civico Gabinetto Numismatico di Milano*, XIX-XX, pp. 69-73, 1977.

Raeck, 1992 = W. Raeck, *Modernisierte Mythen. Zum Umgang der Spätantike mit klassischen Bildthemen*, Stuttgart 1992.

Rasmussen, 1996 = K. E. Rasmussen, "A venator in Bologna. A new interpretation of a gold-glass image," in *Mitteilungen zur christlichen Archäologie*, 2, 1996, pp. 71-2.

Ravagnan, 1994 = G. L. Ravagnan, *Vetri antichi del Museo Vetrario di Murano. Collezioni dello Stato*, Venice 1994.

Redaelli, 2000 = A. Redaelli, "Anna Skibska, La sostenibile leggerezza del vetro," in *Arte*, December, 2000.

Richard Meitner, 2001 = *Richard Meitner*, monograph, 2001.

Ricke, 1980 = H. Ricke, *Ausgewählte Werke*, Kunstmuseum, Düsseldorf 1980.

Ricke, 1995 = H. Ricke, *Glaskunst, Reflex der Jahrunderte*, Prestel-Verlag, Munich-New York 1995.

Ricke, 2000 = H. Ricke, *Zugriff Glaskünstlerinnen heute*, exhibition cat., Glastec 2000 and Kunstmuseum, Düsseldorf 2000.

Roffia, 1981 = E. Roffia, "Viadana (Mantova), Museo Civico; Milano, Civico Museo Archeologico; Luni di Ortonovo (La Spezia), Museo Archeologico Nazionale," in *Bulletin de l'Association Internationale pour l'histoire du Verre*, 9, 1981-83, pp. 48-9, 53-7, 114-15, 214-15.

Roffia, 1993 = E. Roffia, *I vetri antichi delle Civiche Raccolte Archeologiche di Milano*, Milan 1993.

Roffia, 1995 = E. Roffia, "Il Tesoro del Duomo di Monza: precisazioni sulla cronologia dei vetri," in G. Cavalieri Manasse and E. Roffia (eds.), *Splendida civitas nostra. Studi archeologici in onore di Antonio Frova*, Rome 1995, pp. 443-52.

Roffia, 1998 = E. Roffia, "I vetri romani della collezione Personeni," in *Vetro e vetri*, exhibition cat., 1998, pp. 149-64.

Roffia, 2000 = E. Roffia, *Vetri antichi dall'Oriente. La collezione Personeni e i piatti da Cafarnao*, exhibition cat. (Sondrio, 1 December 2000 - 5 January 2001), Verona 2000.

Römer am Rhein, 1967 = *Römer am Rhein*, Römisch-Germanisches Museum Cologne, exhibition cat., Cologne 1967.

Ross, 1962 = M. C. Ross, *Catalogue of the Byzantine and Early Medieval Antiquities in the Dumbarton Oaks Collection*, Washington 1962.

Rütti, 1988 = B. Rütti, "Beiträge zum römischen Oberwinterthur, Die Gläser", in *Vitudurum 4, Berichte der Zürcher Denkmalpflege*, Monographien, 5, Zurich 1988.

Rütti, 1991 = B. Rütti, *Die römischen Gläser aus Augst und Kaiseraugst*, I-II, Augst 1991.

Saldern, 1964 = A. Saldern, "Ancient Glass in Split," in *Journal of Glass Studies*, 6, 1964, pp. 42-46.

Saldern, 1968 = A. Saldern, *Alte Gläser*, Kunstmuseum, Düsseldorf 1968.

Saldern, 1974 = *Kataloge des Kunstmuseums Düsseldorf*, Kunstmuseum, Düsseldorf 1974.

Saldern, 1980 = A. Saldern, *Glass 500 BC to AD 1900*, The Hans Cohn Collection, Mainz 1980.

Saldern *et al.*, 1974 = A. Saldern *et al.*, *Gläser der Antike, Sammlung Erwin Oppenländer*, Mainz am Rhein 1974.

Šaranović-Svetek, 1986 = V. Šaranović-Svetek, *Antićko Staklou jugoslovenskom delu provincije Donje Panonije*, Monografije, 7, Novi Sad 1986.

Sarpellon, 1989 = G. Sarpellon, *Salviati, il suo vetro e i suoi uomini 1859-1987*, Venice 1989.

Scarfì, Tombolani, 1985 = B. M. Scarfì, M. Tombolani, *Altino preromana e romana*, Musile di Piave 1985.

Scatozza, 1999 = L. A. Scatozza, "Pompei. Alcuni contesti degli scavi del XX secolo," in *Il Vetro in Italia Meridionale e Insulare*, Proceedings of the First Multidisciplinary Conference, edited by C. Piccioli and F. Sogliano, Naples, 5-6-7 March 1998, Naples 1999, pp. 93-107.

Scatozza Horicht, 1986 = L. A. Scatozza Horicht, *I vetri romani di Ercolano*, Rome 1986.

Secret of Murano (The), 1997 = Var. Authors, *The Secret of Murano*, exhibition cat., Museum Het Palais, The Hague (13 September - 7 December 1997), Marsilio, Venice 1997.

Sena Chiesa, 1966 = G. Sena Chiesa, *Gemme del Museo Nazionale di Aquileia*, Padua 1966.

Sena Chiesa, 1979 = G. Sena Chiesa, "Scavi dell'Università degli Studi di Milano nella Necropoli romana di Angera," in *Acme*, XXXII, 1979, pp. 37-79.

Sennequier, 1994 = G. Sennequier, "Roman Glass found in Upper Normandy," in *Journal of Glass Studies*, 36, 1994, pp. 56-66.

Sennequier *et al.*, 1998 = G. Sennequier *et al.*, *Les verres romains à scènes de spectacles trouvés en France*, Rouen 1998.

Sensi, 1992 = L. Sensi, "Il Mundus muliebris," in S. Settis (ed.), *Civiltà dei Romani. Il rito e la vita privata*, Rome 1992, pp. 176-86.

Silice e fuoco, 1992 = Var. Authors, *L'arte del vetro, silice e fuoco: vetri del XIX e XX secolo*, Marsilio, Venice 1992.

Sorokina, 1971 = N. P. Sorokina, "O stekljannych sosudach s kapljami sinego stekla iz Pricernomor'ja", in *SA*, 1971, no. 4, pp. 85-100.

Sorokina, 1978 = N. P. Sorokina, *Antićnoe steklo v sobranii Odesskogo archeologićeskogo muzeja*, Archeologićeskie issledovanija Severo-Zapadnogo Pricernomor'ja, Kiev 1978.

Stern, 1995 = E. M. Stern, *The Toledo Museum of Art. Roman Mold-blown Glass. The first through sixth centuries*, Rome 1995.

Stern, 2001 = E.M. Stern, *Roman, Byzantine, and Early Medieval Glass, 10 BCE-700 CE*, Ernesto Wolf Collection, 2001.

Stern, Schlick Nolte, 1994 = E. M. Stern, B. Schlick Nolte, *Early Glass of the Ancient World. 1600 B.C. - A. D. 50*, Ernesto Wolf Collection, Stuttgart 1994.

Sternini, 1990 = M. Sternini, *La Verrerie Romaine du Musée Archeologique de Nîmes, 1ère partie*, Cahiers des Musées et Monuments de Nîmes, 8, Nîmes 1990.

Sternini, 1999 = M. Sternini, "Il vetro romano: processo produttivo e tecniche di lavorazione," in B. Massabò (ed.), *Magiche trasparenze. I vetri dell'antica Albingaunum*, exhibition cat., Milan 1999, pp. 45-54.

Stevenson, 1988 = J. Stevenson, "Glass Lamps from San Vincenzo al Volturno, Molise," in *Papers of the British School at Rome*, 56, 1988, pp. 198-209.

Stiaffini, 1985 = D. Stiaffini, "Contributo ad una prima sistemazione tipologica dei materiali vitrei altomedievali," in *Archeologia Medievale*, 12, 1985, pp. 667-88.

Stiaffini, Borghetti, 1994 = D. Stiaffini, G. Borghetti, *I vetri romani del Museo Archeologico Nazionale di Cagliari*, Oristano 1994.

Storia del vetro, 1984 = D. Klein, W. Lloyd, *The History of Glass*, Orbis Publishing, London 1984 (Italian edition edited by A. Dorigato, *Storia del vetro*, Istituto Geografico De Agostini, Novara 1984).

Strano ma vetro, 2000 = A. Dorigato (ed.), *Strano ma vetro, Maria Grazia Rosin*, exhibition cat., Museo Correr, Venice (2 September - 8 October 2000), Silvana Editoriale, Cinisello Balsamo, Milan 2000.

Šubic, 1976 = Z. Šubic, "Tipološki in kronološki pregled rimskega stekla v Poetovioni," in *Arheološki vestnik*, 25, Ljubljana 1976, pp. 39-62.

Sunkowski, 1956 = R. Sunkowski, *Antike Gläser in Carnuntum und Wien*, Vienna 1956.

Svenskt Glas, n.d. = Var. Authors, *Svenskt Glas under Fem Sekler*, Kulturspridaren Förlag, Växjö, n.d.

Taborelli, 1982 = L. Taborelli, "Vasi di vetro con bollo monetale. Note sulla produzione e il commercio degli unguenti aromatici nella prima età imperiale," in *Opus*, I, 2, 1982, pp. 315-40.

Taborelli, 1983 = L. Taborelli, "Nuovi esemplari di bolli già noti su contenitori vitrei dell'area centro-italica (Regg. IV, V, VI)," in *Picus*, III, 1983, pp. 23-69.

Taborelli, 1992 = L. Taborelli, "Sulle 'ampullae vitreae'. Spunti per l'approfondimento della loro problematica nell'ottica del rapporto tra contenitore e contenuto," in *Archeologia Classica*, XLIV, 1992, pp. 309-28.

Taborelli, 1999 = L. Taborelli, "In Liguria i riflessi di un mondo," in B. Massabò (ed.), *Magiche trasparenze. I vetri dell'antica Albingaunum* (Genoa, 17 December 1999-15 March 2000), Milan 1999, pp. 35-43.

Taborelli, 1999b = L. Taborelli, "Unguentari di vetro delle necropoli marchigiane: tipi di medie e grandi dimensioni, tra II e III secolo d.C.," in *Picus*, XIX, 1999, pp 267-98.

Tait, 1979 = H. Tait, *The Golden Age of Venetian Glass*, British Museum Publications, London 1979.

Tait, 1991= H. Tait (ed.), *Cinquemila anni di vetro*, Silvana Editoriale, Milan 1991.

Talbot Rice, 1966 = D. Talbot Rice (ed.), "Opere d'arte paleocristiane e altomedievali," in L. Vitali, *Il Tesoro del Duomo di Monza*, Milan 1966.

Tamaro Forlati, Mariacher, 1963 = B. Tamaro Forlati, G. Mariacher, "I vetri antichi del Museo di Zara depositati al Correr," in *Bollettino dei Musei Civici Veneziani*, VIII, 1, 1963, pp. 3-15.

Tamassia, 1967 = A. M. Tamassia, "Note di protostoria mantovana: Rivalta e la valle del Mincio", in *Studi Etruschi* XXXV, 1967.

Tapio Wirkkala, eye..., 2000 = Var. Authors, *Tapio Wirkkala, eye, hand, thought*, exhibition cat., Museum of Art and Design, Helsinki (25 August 2000 - 14 January 2001), WS Bookwell Oy, Porvoo 2000.

Tassinari, 1993 = S. Tassinari, *Il vasellame bronzeo di Pompei*, vols. I-II, Rome 1993.

Tirelli, 1994 = M. Tirelli, *Vetri romani di Altino restaurati grazie al Banco Ambrosiano Veneto*, Padua 1994.

Tirelli, 1995 = M. Tirelli, *L'archeologia invita: il Museo Nazionale e gli scavi di Altino*, Padua 1995.

Tirelli, 2000 = M. Tirelli, "Gruppo di tre vasi in vetro," in *Restituzioni 2000*, exhibition cat., Vicenza-Milan 2000-01.

Toesca, 1911 = P. Toesca, *Aosta. Catalogo delle cose d'arte e di antichità d'Italia*, Rome 1911.

Tognon, 2001 = P. Tognon, "Richard Marquis e gli oggetti del desiderio," in *Vetro*, IV, no. 13, October-December, 2001.

Toniolo, 2000 = A. Toniolo, *Vetri antichi del Museo Archeologico Nazionale di Este*, Venice 2000.

Tosi, 2001 = A. Tosi, "Vetro in movimento, La sensualità narrativa di Lucio Bubacco," in *Vetro*, IV, no. 11, April-June, 2001.

Toso Fei, 2000 = A. Toso Fei, "Labirinti di luce, Anna Skibska, attraversando il confine con un filo," in *Vetro*, III, no. 9, October-December, 2000.

Toth, 1969 = E. H. Toth, *Kora-Bizanci uyegpohar egy Szabadszallasi maganyos sirbol. Early Byzantine glass cup in a solitary grave at Szabadszallas*, Keeskemét 1969.

Trasparenze imperiali, 1998 = *Trasparenze imperiali. Vetri romani dalla Croazia*, exhibition cat., Milan 1998.

Triennale, 1954 = *Decima Triennale di Milano*, exhibition cat., SAME, Milan 1954.

Trois millénaires, 1958 = *Trois millénaires d'art verrier à travers les collections publiques et privées de la Belgique*, exhibition cat., Musée Curtius, Liège 1958.

True Color, 2000 = *Michele Burato, True Color*, catalogue, 2000.

UDV 1974 = *The UDV Glass Collection - ex Cinzano Glass Collection*, London 1974.

Uglietti, 1991 = M. C. Uglietti, "Vetri d'epoca romana nel Piemonte orientale", in *Helvetia Archeologica*, 87-88, 1991, pp. 125-132.

Van den Bossche, 2002 = W. Van den Bossche, *Antique Glass Bottles*, Antique Collector's Club (UK), 2002.

Var. Authors, 2001 = *Natzional'nij muzej istorij Ukrajni*, Kiev 2001.

Venezianisches Glas der Veste Coburg, 1994 = A. E. Theuerkauff-Liederwald, *Venezianisches Glas der Veste Coburg*, Luca Verlag, Lingen 1994.

Venini Diaz de Santillana, 2000 = A. Venini Diaz de Santillana, *Venini, Catalogo ragionato 1921-1986*, Skira, Milan 2000.

Verrerie Européenne des Années 50 (La), 1988 = Var. Authors, *La Verrerie Européenne des Années 50*, exhibition cat., Centre de la Vieille Charité, Marseilles (31 March - 12 June 1988), Michel Aveline Editeur, Marseilles 1988.

Verres de Bohême, 1989 = Var. Authors, *Verres de Bohême 1400-1989, Chefs d'œuvre des musées de Tchecoslavaquie*, exhibition cat., Musée des Arts Décoratifs, Paris (17 October 1989 - 28 January 1990), Musée des Art Décoratifs, Flammarion, Paris 1989.

Vescoz, 1909 = P. L. Vescoz, "Urne funéraire découverte aux environs d'Aoste du côté de Saint-Christophe," in *Bulletin de la Sociéte de la Flore valdotaine*, 5, 1909, pp. 40-1.

Vessberg, 1952 = O. Vessberg, *Roman Glass in Cyprus*, *Opuscula Archaeologica*, VII, 1952, pp. 109-65.

Vetri dei Cesari, 1988 = D. B. Harden (ed.), *Vetri dei Cesari*, exhibition cat. (Rome, November 1988 - January 1989), Milan 1988.

Vetri di Fulvio Bianconi, 1993 = R. Bossaglia, *I vetri di Fulvio Bianconi*, Umberto Allemandi, Turin 1993.

Vetri europei dell'Ottocento, 1980 = Var. Authors, *Vetri europei dell'Ottocento*, exhibition cat., Museo Vetraio, Murano (July-September 1980), Electa, Milan 1980.

Vetri Murano oggi, 1981 = Var. Authors, *Vetri Murano oggi*, Electa, Milan 1981.

Vetri nelle collezioni bresciane, 1987 = Var. Authors, *Vetri nelle civiche collezioni bresciane*, exhibition cat., Santa Maria in Solario (June-October 1987), Società Editrice Vannini, Brescia 1987.

Vetri veneziani, 1998 = A. Dorigato (ed.), *Vetri veneziani, Ohira, collezione Pasta Vitrea*, exhibition cat., Museo Correr, Venice (13 March - 30 April 1998), Arsenale, Venice 1998.

Vetro a Milano (Il), 1998 = Var. Authors, *Tra Creatività e progettazione. Il Vetro italiano a Milano 1906-1968*, Electa, Milan 1998.

Vetro alle Biennali (Il), 1995 = Var. Authors, *Il vetro di Murano alle Biennali 1895-1972*, Leonardo Arte, Milan 1995.

Vetro e vetri, 1998 = *Vetro e vetri. Preziose iridescenze*, exhibition cat. (Milan 1998-99), Milan 1998.

Viale, 1939 = V. Viale, *Gotico e Rinascimento in Piemonte*, exhibition cat., Turin 1939.

Viale, Viale Ferrero, 1967 = V. Viale, M. Viale Ferrero, *Aosta romana e medievale*, Turin 1967.

Vicquéry, 1997 = D. Vicquéry, "Il restauro della vetrata della chiesa parrocchiale di Avise," in *Nouvelles d'Avise*, no. 125, July-August 1997.

Whitehouse, 1997 = D. Whitehouse, *Roman Glass in the Corning Museum of Glass*, vol. I, Corning (New York) 1997.

Whitehouse, 2001 = D. Whitehouse, *Roman Glass in the Corning Museum of Glass*, vol. II, Corning (New York) 2001.

Wichert, 1999 = G. Wichert, "Anna Skibska," in *Neues Glas*, no. 2, 1999.

Williams, 1982 = C. K. Williams, II, "Corinth, 1981: East of the Theater," in *Hesperia*, 51, 1982, pp. 115-44.

Wirges, 1969 = J. Wirges, *Untersuchungen über die Zweckbestimmung von römischen Gläsern im Kölner Raum*, Cologne 1969.

Wunderkammer siciliana, 2001 = Var. Authors, *Wunderkammer siciliana*, Electa, Milan 2001.

Yacoub, 1971-72 = M. Yacoub, "Les Verres Romains des Musées de Sfax, de Sousse et du Bardo," in *Association Internationale pour l'Histoire du Verre*, 6, Liège 1971-72.

Zampieri, 1997 = G. Zampieri, *"Gioielli" del Museo Archeologico di Padova: vetri, bronzi, metalli preziosi, ambre e gemme* (Quaderni del Pedrocchi. Il collezionismo), Padua 1997.

Zanchi Roppo, 1969 = F. Zanchi Roppo, *Vetri paleocristiani a figure d'oro conservati in Italia*, Bologna 1969.

Zanda *et al.*, 1994 = E. Zanda, M. C. Preacco Ancona, M. Soma, "Nuclei di necropoli di Forum Fulvi ed Hasta," in *Quaderni della Soprintendenza Archeologica del Piemonte*, 12, 1994, pp. 127-92.

Techniques and materials

Barnes V. E., "Tektite Research 1936-1990," in *Meteorics*, 25, 1990, pp. 149-59.

De Lotto E., *Dallo smeraldo di Nerone agli occhiali del Cadore*, Nuovi Sentieri, Belluno 1956.

Doria G. (ed.), *La lente: storia scienza e curiosità attraverso la collezione F. Rathschuler*, exhibition cat., Museo civico di storia naturale, ECIG, Genoa 1988.

Dorigato A., *L'arte del vetro Murano*, EBS, Verona 2002.

Dri P., *Serendippo, come nasce una scoperta: la fortuna nella scienza*, Editori Riuniti, Rome 1994.

Franceschini F., *Trattato generale di tecnologia vetraria*, Hoepli 1955.

Gruppo di lavoro Assovetro, Enea, Stazione Sperimentale del Vetro, *Gruppo di lavoro per la valorizzazione del rottame di vetro*, published by the study group.

Locardi B., "Proiezione a plasma di vetri bioattivi su impianti protesici," in *Smalto Porcellanato*, no. 1, 1997, pp. 35-9.

Moldi Ravenna C. (ed.), *I colori della luce*, Marsilio, Venice 1996.

Newton R., Davison S., *Conservation of Glass*, Butterworth & Heinemann, Oxford 1997.

Ravaglioli A., Krajewsky A., *Bioceramica e corpo umano*, Faenza 1984.

Scarincini G., Toninato B., Locardi T., *Vetri - Quaderni di chimica applicata*, edited by E. Mariani, Casa Editrice Ambrosiana, 1983.

Sternini M., "Il vetro romano: processo produttivo e tecniche di lavorazione," in B. Massabò (ed.), *Magiche trasparenze. I vetri dell'antica Albingaunum*, exhibition cat., Milan 1999, pp. 45-54.

Van den Bossche W., *Antique Glass Bottles*, Antique Collector's Club (UK), 2002.

li già noti su contenitori vitrei dell'area centro-italica (Regg. IV, V, VI)," in *Picus*, III, 1983, pp. 23-69.
Taborelli, 1992 = L. Taborelli, "Sulle 'ampullae vitreae'. Spunti per l'approfondimento della loro problematica nell'ottica del rapporto tra contenitore e contenuto," in *Archeologia Classica*, XLIV, 1992, pp. 309-28.
Taborelli, 1999 = L. Taborelli, "In Liguria i riflessi di un mondo," in B. Massabò (ed.), *Magiche trasparenze. I vetri dell'antica Albingaunum* (Genoa, 17 December 1999-15 March 2000), Milan 1999, pp. 35-43.
Taborelli, 1999b = L. Taborelli, "Unguentari di vetro delle necropoli marchigiane: tipi di medie e grandi dimensioni, tra II e III secolo d.C.," in *Picus*, XIX, 1999, pp 267-98.
Tait, 1979 = H. Tait, *The Golden Age of Venetian Glass*, British Museum Publications, London 1979.
Tait, 1991= H. Tait (ed.), *Cinquemila anni di vetro*, Silvana Editoriale, Milan 1991.
Talbot Rice, 1966 = D. Talbot Rice (ed.), "Opere d'arte paleocristiane e altomedievali," in L. Vitali, *Il Tesoro del Duomo di Monza*, Milan 1966.
Tamaro Forlati, Mariacher, 1963 = B. Tamaro Forlati, G. Mariacher, "I vetri antichi del Museo di Zara depositati al Correr," in *Bollettino dei Musei Civici Veneziani*, VIII, 1, 1963, pp. 3-15.
Tamassia, 1967 = A. M. Tamassia, "Note di protostoria mantovana: Rivalta e la valle del Mincio", in *Studi Etruschi* XXXV, 1967.
Tapio Wirkkala, eye..., 2000 = Var. Authors, *Tapio Wirkkala, eye, hand, thought*, exhibition cat., Museum of Art and Design, Helsinki (25 August 2000 - 14 January 2001), WS Bookwell Oy, Porvoo 2000.
Tassinari, 1993 = S. Tassinari, *Il vasellame bronzeo di Pompei*, vols. I-II, Rome 1993.
Tirelli, 1994 = M. Tirelli, *Vetri romani di Altino restaurati grazie al Banco Ambrosiano Veneto*, Padua 1994.
Tirelli, 1995 = M. Tirelli, *L'archeologia invita: il Museo Nazionale e gli scavi di Altino*, Padua 1995.
Tirelli, 2000 = M. Tirelli, "Gruppo di tre vasi in vetro," in *Restituzioni 2000*, exhibition cat., Vicenza-Milan 2000-01.
Toesca, 1911 = P. Toesca, *Aosta. Catalogo delle cose d'arte e di antichità d'Italia*, Rome 1911.
Tognon, 2001 = P. Tognon, "Richard Marquis e gli oggetti del desiderio," in *Vetro*, IV, no. 13, October-December, 2001.
Toniolo, 2000 = A. Toniolo, *Vetri antichi del Museo Archeologico Nazionale di Este*, Venice 2000.
Tosi, 2001 = A. Tosi, "Vetro in movimento, La sensualità narrativa di Lucio Bubacco," in *Vetro*, IV, no. 11, April-June, 2001.
Toso Fei, 2000 = A. Toso Fei, "Labirinti di luce, Anna Skibska, attraversando il confine con un filo," in *Vetro*, III, no. 9, October-December, 2000.
Toth, 1969 = E. H. Toth, *Kora-Bizanci uyegpohar egy Szabadszallasi maganyos sirbol. Early Byzantine glass cup in a solitary grave at Szabadszallas*, Keeskemét 1969.
Trasparenze imperiali, 1998 = *Trasparenze imperiali. Vetri romani dalla Croazia*, exhibition cat., Milan 1998.
Triennale, 1954 = *Decima Triennale di Milano*, exhibition cat., SAME, Milan 1954.
Trois millénaires, 1958 = *Trois millénaires d'art verrier à travers les collections publiques et privées de la Belgique*, exhibition cat., Musée Curtius, Liège 1958.
True Color, 2000 = *Michele Burato, True Color*, catalogue, 2000.

UDV 1974 = *The UDV Glass Collection - ex Cinzano Glass Collection*, London 1974.
Uglietti, 1991 = M. C. Uglietti, "Vetri d'epoca romana nel Piemonte orientale", in *Helvetia Archeologica*, 87-88, 1991, pp. 125-132.
Van den Bossche, 2002 = W. Van den Bossche, *Antique Glass Bottles*, Antique Collector's Club (UK), 2002.
Var. Authors, 2001 = *Natzional'nij muzej istorij Ukrajni*, Kiev 2001.
Venezianisches Glas der Veste Coburg, 1994 = A. E. Theuerkauff-Liederwald, *Venezianisches Glas der Veste Coburg*, Luca Verlag, Lingen 1994.
Venini Diaz de Santillana, 2000 = A. Venini Diaz de Santillana, *Venini, Catalogo ragionato 1921-1986*, Skira, Milan 2000.
Verrerie Européenne des Années 50 (La), 1988 = Var. Authors, *La Verrerie Européenne des Années 50*, exhibition cat., Centre de la Vieille Charité, Marseilles (31 March - 12 June 1988), Michel Aveline Editeur, Marseilles 1988.
Verres de Bohême, 1989 = Var. Authors, *Verres de Bohême 1400-1989, Chefs d'œuvre des musées de Tchecoslavaquie*, exhibition cat., Musée des Arts Décoratifs, Paris (17 October 1989 - 28 January 1990), Musée des Art Décoratifs, Flammarion, Paris 1989.
Vescoz, 1909 = P. L. Vescoz, "Urne funéraire découverte aux environs d'Aoste du côté de Saint-Christophe," in *Bulletin de la Sociéte de la Flore valdotaine*, 5, 1909, pp. 40-1.
Vessberg, 1952 = O. Vessberg, *Roman Glass in Cyprus*, *Opuscula Archaeologica*, VII, 1952, pp. 109-65.
Vetri dei Cesari, 1988 = D. B. Harden (ed.), *Vetri dei Cesari*, exhibition cat. (Rome, November 1988 - January 1989), Milan 1988.
Vetri di Fulvio Bianconi, 1993 = R. Bossaglia, *I vetri di Fulvio Bianconi,* Umberto Allemandi, Turin 1993.
Vetri europei dell'Ottocento, 1980 = Var. Authors, *Vetri europei dell'Ottocento*, exhibition cat., Museo Vetraio, Murano (July-September 1980), Electa, Milan 1980.
Vetri Murano oggi, 1981 = Var. Authors, *Vetri Murano oggi*, Electa, Milan 1981.
Vetri nelle collezioni bresciane, 1987 = Var. Authors, *Vetri nelle civiche collezioni bresciane*, exhibition cat., Santa Maria in Solario (June-October 1987), Società Editrice Vannini, Brescia 1987.
Vetri veneziani, 1998 = A. Dorigato (ed.), *Vetri veneziani, Ohira, collezione Pasta Vitrea*, exhibition cat., Museo Correr, Venice (13 March - 30 April 1998), Arsenale, Venice 1998.
Vetro a Milano (Il), 1998 = Var. Authors, *Tra Creatività e progettazione. Il Vetro italiano a Milano 1906-1968*, Electa, Milan 1998.
Vetro alle Biennali (Il), 1995 = Var. Authors, *Il vetro di Murano alle Biennali 1895-1972*, Leonardo Arte, Milan 1995.
Vetro e vetri, 1998 = *Vetro e vetri. Preziose iridescenze*, exhibition cat. (Milan 1998-99), Milan 1998.
Viale, 1939 = V. Viale, *Gotico e Rinascimento in Piemonte*, exhibition cat., Turin 1939.
Viale, Viale Ferrero, 1967 = V. Viale, M. Viale Ferrero, *Aosta romana e medievale*, Turin 1967.
Vicquéry, 1997 = D. Vicquéry, "Il restauro della vetrata della chiesa parrocchiale di Avise," in *Nouvelles d'Avise*, no. 125, July-August 1997.

Whitehouse, 1997 = D. Whitehouse, *Roman Glass in the Corning Museum of Glass*, vol. I, Corning (New York) 1997.
Whitehouse, 2001 = D. Whitehouse, *Roman Glass in the Corning Museum of Glass*, vol. II, Corning (New York) 2001.
Wichert, 1999 = G. Wichert, "Anna Skibska," in *Neues Glas*, no. 2, 1999.
Williams, 1982 = C. K. Williams, II, "Corinth, 1981: East of the Theater," in *Hesperia*, 51, 1982, pp. 115-44.
Wirges, 1969 = J. Wirges, *Untersuchungen über die Zweckbestimmung von römischen Gläsern im Kölner Raum*, Cologne 1969.
Wunderkammer siciliana, 2001 = Var. Authors, *Wunderkammer siciliana*, Electa, Milan 2001.

Yacoub, 1971-72 = M. Yacoub, "Les Verres Romains des Musées de Sfax, de Sousse et du Bardo," in *Association Internationale pour l'Histoire du Verre*, 6, Liège 1971-72.

Zampieri, 1997 = G. Zampieri, *"Gioielli" del Museo Archeologico di Padova: vetri, bronzi, metalli preziosi, ambre e gemme* (Quaderni del Pedrocchi. Il collezionismo), Padua 1997.
Zanchi Roppo, 1969 = F. Zanchi Roppo, *Vetri paleocristiani a figure d'oro conservati in Italia*, Bologna 1969.
Zanda *et al.*, 1994 = E. Zanda, M. C. Preacco Ancona, M. Soma, "Nuclei di necropoli di Forum Fulvi ed Hasta," in *Quaderni della Soprintendenza Archeologica del Piemonte*, 12, 1994, pp. 127-92.

Techniques and materials

Barnes V. E., "Tektite Research 1936-1990," in *Meteorics*, 25, 1990, pp. 149-59.
De Lotto E., *Dallo smeraldo di Nerone agli occhiali del Cadore*, Nuovi Sentieri, Belluno 1956.
Doria G. (ed.), *La lente: storia scienza e curiosità attraverso la collezione F. Rathschuler*, exhibition cat., Museo civico di storia naturale, ECIG, Genoa 1988.
Dorigato A., *L'arte del vetro Murano*, EBS, Verona 2002.
Dri P., *Serendippo, come nasce una scoperta: la fortuna nella scienza*, Editori Riuniti, Rome 1994.
Franceschini F., *Trattato generale di tecnologia vetraria*, Hoepli 1955.
Gruppo di lavoro Assovetro, Enea, Stazione Sperimentale del Vetro, *Gruppo di lavoro per la valorizzazione del rottame di vetro,* published by the study group.
Locardi B., "Proiezione a plasma di vetri bioattivi su impianti protesici," in *Smalto Porcellanato*, no. 1, 1997, pp. 35-9.
Moldi Ravenna C. (ed.), *I colori della luce*, Marsilio, Venice 1996.
Newton R., Davison S., *Conservation of Glass*, Butterworth & Heinemann, Oxford 1997.
Ravaglioli A., Krajewsky A., *Bioceramica e corpo umano*, Faenza 1984.
Scarincini G., Toninato B., Locardi T., *Vetri - Quaderni di chimica applicata*, edited by E. Mariani, Casa Editrice Ambrosiana, 1983.
Sternini M., "Il vetro romano: processo produttivo e tecniche di lavorazione," in B. Massabò (ed.), *Magiche trasparenze. I vetri dell'antica Albingaunum*, exhibition cat., Milan 1999, pp. 45-54.
Van den Bossche W., *Antique Glass Bottles*, Antique Collector's Club (UK), 2002.

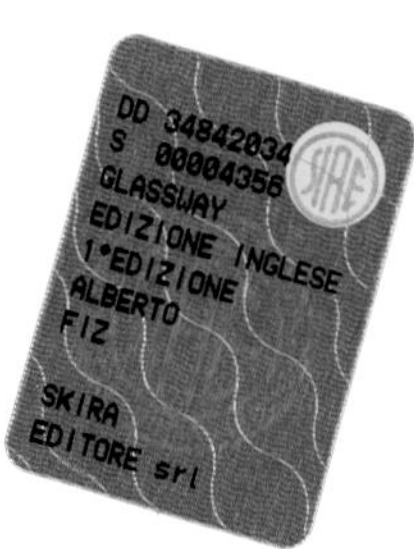
DD 34842034
S 00004356
GLASSWAY
EDIZIONE INGLESE
1°EDIZIONE
ALBERTO
FIZ
SKIRA
EDITORE srl
SIAE